MUD FLAT

Nankhari Pt.

INDIA — WEST COAST

BOMBAY
HARBOUR

Chiefly from Surveys by
COMMANDER L. S. DAWSON R.N.
assisted by the
Surveying Officers of the I.G.S. Investigator
1881-2

The Port of Bombay and Eastern portion of the Harbour
by Officers of the Royal Indian Marine under the direction of
COMMANDER E.H. DAUGLISH, R.I.M. 1920-21
with additions from Surveys by the Chief Engineer Bombay Port Trust 1924-5
and corrections from Surveys by the Royal Indian Marine, 1929-33

Kalaba Observatory — Lat. 18°53'46" N.Long.72°48'47" E.

All Bearings are Tree, thus 126° etc; and are given from Seaward
Underlined figures on the dry banks express the heights in feet above the datum of soundings
All other heights are expressed in feet above High Water Springs
For abbreviations see Admiralty Chart 50 B
SOUNDINGS IN FEET
reduced approximately 11 feet below the level of Indian Spring Low Water.

MUMBAI
A CITY THROUGH OBJECTS

101 Stories from the Dr. Bhau Daji Lad Museum

MUMBAI
A CITY THROUGH OBJECTS

101 Stories from the Dr. Bhau Daji Lad Museum

Edited by
TASNEEM ZAKARIA MEHTA

With entries co-authored by
Ruta Waghmare-Baptista
Ishrat Hakim
Ruchika Jain
Himanshu Kadam
Laharee Mitra
Alisha Sadikot
Puja Vaish

DR. BHAU DAJI LAD
MUMBAI CITY MUSEUM

An Institution of the Municipal Corporation of Greater Mumbai
Supported by the Jamnalal Bajaj Foundation

HARPER DESIGN
An Imprint of HarperCollins Publishers

First published in hardback in India by Harper Design 2022
An imprint of HarperCollins *Publishers*
4th Floor, Tower A, Building No. 10, Phase II, DLF Cyber City,
Gurugram, Haryana – 122002
www.harpercollins.co.in

in association with
Dr. Bhau Daji Lad Museum
Veer Mata Jijabai Bhosale Udyan
91/A, Dr. Babasaheb Ambedkar Road, Byculla (E), Mumbai 400027, India
www.bdlmuseum.org
Facebook, Instagram and Twitter: @BDLMuseum

2 4 6 8 10 9 7 5 3 1

Front and back cover and inside photographs: Anil Rane

Design by Ruchita Madhok and Kahani Designworks • www.kahanidesignworks.com

The city's name was changed from Bombay to Mumbai in 1995. The name Bombay is used in the book in a historical context. All proper names and spellings of people and places referred to in this book are used in a historical context.

Typeset in Tiempos Text by 9/13

Printed and bound at Thomson Press (India) Ltd
f in ⊙ ✔ HarperCollinsIN

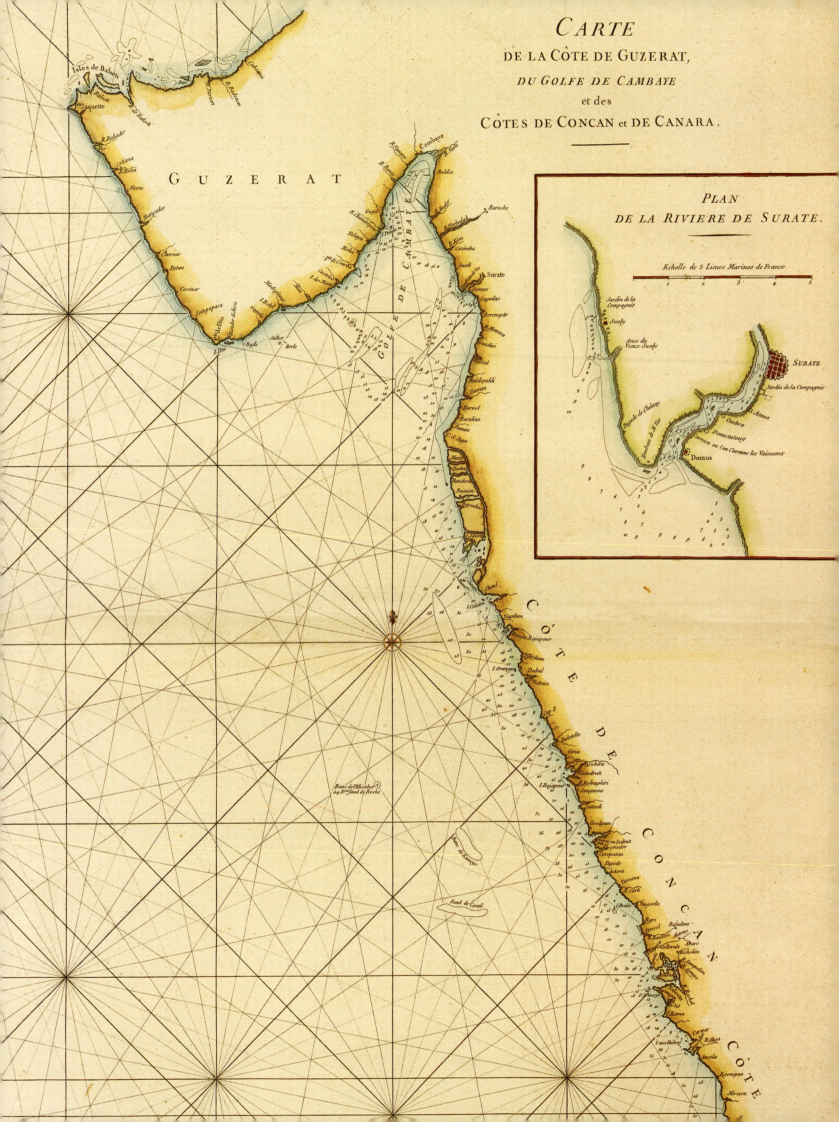

CARTE
DE LA CÔTE DE GUZERAT,
DU GOLFE DE CAMBAYE
et des
CÔTES DE CONCAN et de CANARA.

PLAN
DE LA RIVIERE DE SURATE.

Echelle de 5 Lieues Marines de France

GUZERAT

GOLFE DE CAMBAYE

CÔTE DE CONCAN

CÔTE

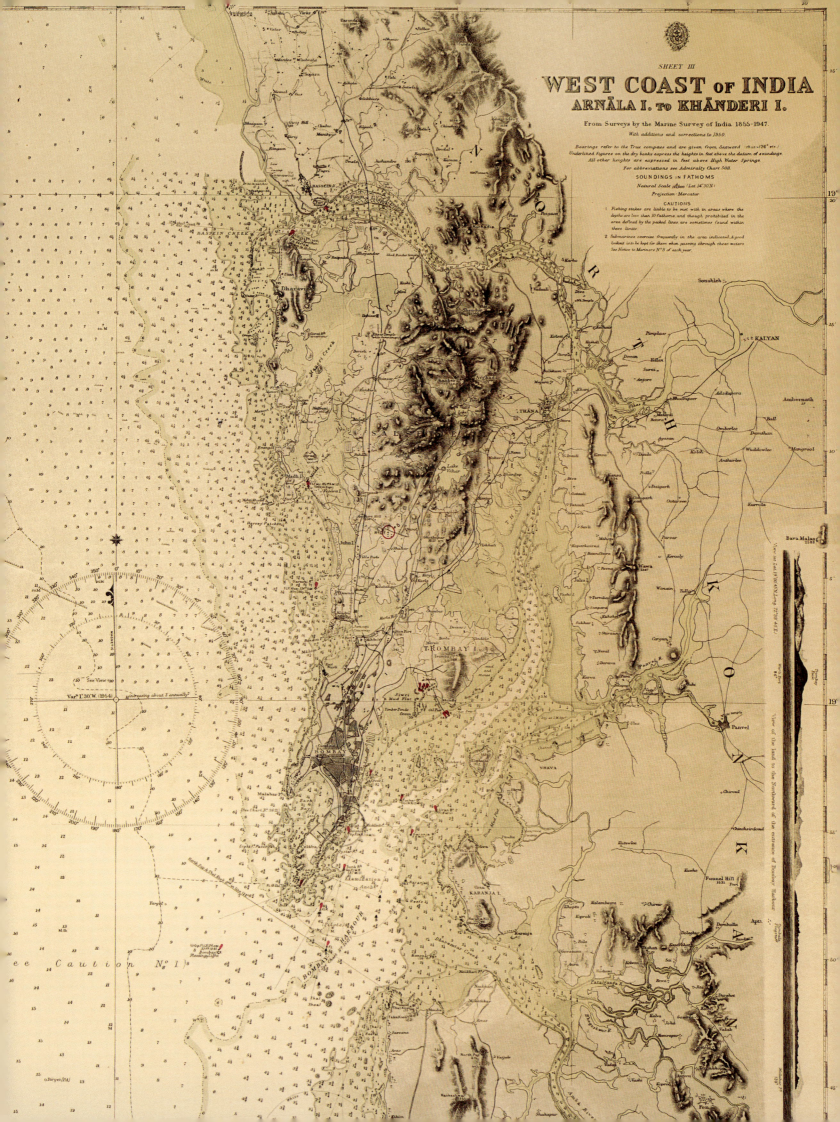

SHEET III

WEST COAST of INDIA
ARNĀLA I. TO KHĀNDERI I.

From Surveys by the Marine Survey of India. 1855-1947.

With additions and corrections to 1950.

Bearings refer to the True compass and are given from Seaward thus 176° *etc.*
Underlined figures on the dry banks express the heights in feet above the datum of soundings.
All other heights are expressed in feet above High Water Springs.

For abbreviations see Admiralty Chart 5011.

SOUNDINGS IN FATHOMS

Natural Scale 1/150,000 (Lat. 14°30'N.)

Projection - Mercator

CAUTIONS

1. Fishing stakes are liable to be met with in areas where the
depth are less than 10 fathoms and though prohibited in the
area defined by the pecked lines are sometimes found within
these limits.

2. Submarine exercises frequently in the area indicated. A good
lookout is to be kept for them when passing through these waters.
See Notice to Mariners N°8 of each year.

Contents

CHIEF SECRETARY'S FOREWORD   6

PATRON'S FOREWORD   7

PREFACE   10

INTRODUCTION   12

1 • **BOMBAY/MUMBAI: THE MAKING OF A CITY**   **20**

2 • **NATURAL HISTORY: DOCUMENTING THE EXOTIC**   **96**

3 • **INDUSTRIAL ARTS: A NEW TASTE FOR DESIGN**   **120**

4 • **PEOPLE OF INDIA: INTERROGATING IDENTITY**   **200**

5 • **RAJA RAVI VARMA: THE INFLUENCE OF A MASTER**   **244**

6 • **CLASSICAL ARTS: COMMODIFYING CULTURE**   **266**

7 • **EARLY MODERN PAINTING: A NEW PERSPECTIVE**   **314**

8 • **CONTEMPORARY ART: THE ARTIST IN FOCUS**   **334**

ACKNOWLEDGEMENTS   357

CONTRIBUTORS   360

ARTIST BIOGRAPHIES   361

BIBLIOGRAPHY   362

NOTES   372

Sitaram Kunte
Chief Secretary

Chief Secretary's Foreword

On August 15, 2021, India commenced the celebrations for seventy-five years of independence. This is a significant moment in our history and many books will be written, reflecting on our achievements as a nation. *Mumbai: A City through Objects*, I am sure, will be among the most important of these books. Mumbai is India's premier city and it has been so since the 1850s when trade and industry were first concentrated here. However, Mumbai is not only the financial and business capital of the county, it has been the cultural capital as well. The city has a rich archaeological heritage, and it has pioneered architectural and artistic development, as well as nurtured the film and entertainment industry. From textiles and fashion to food and festivals, Mumbai is famous for the many communities who have migrated from across the country to the city, bringing with them their traditions and their culture. All these aspects of the city have been captured in this book which is a must-read for anyone who wants to understand Mumbai better.

The Dr. Bhau Daji Lad Museum, the erstwhile Victoria and Albert Museum, is unique among museums in India as it captures the complex history of the city in a variety of expressions. Established in 1857 with an encyclopaedic mission, it was in a dilapidated state post-Independence as it was considered a colonial relic. In 2003, INTACH Mumbai, headed by Tasneem Mehta approached the Municipal Corporation of Greater Mumbai (MCGM) to restore and revitalise the Museum. The Jamnalal Bajaj Foundation agreed to donate half the funds needed for the project and the MCGM contributed rest. A tripartite agreement was signed for fifteen years from the complete restoration and revitalisation of the Museum and a public-private partnership was initiated through a trust for the management of the Museum. This was the first such partnership for cultural management in the country and the restoration received UNESCO's Award of Excellence for Cultural Conservation, the highest honour in the field.

At the time, I was the Additional Municipal Commissioner in the MCGM and I oversaw the restoration on behalf of the Corporation and worked with Ms Mehta and her team to ensure that the project met its stated objectives. In April 2012, I became Municipal Commissioner of Mumbai and Co-Chairman of the Dr. Bhau Daji Lad Museum Trust, which has the Mayor as Chairman and eminent citizens of Mumbai, experts as well as leaders of the MCGM as trustees. A friendly and cooperative spirit of public-private partnership has fostered the achievements of the Museum. In 2014, under my leadership, the Museum presented a proposal for a major expansion plan to make it one of the most significant museums in the country, showcasing not only the history of the city but also its impact on the development of the country.

The achievements of the Museum leadership and the team are most commendable and have been recognised through several awards and felicitations. I wish the Museum all the best and I am confident it will continue to contribute immensely to the development of this great city.

SITARAM KUNTE   **14 September 2021**
Chief Secretary, Government of Maharashtra

Patron's Foreword

In 2002, when I first walked into the Dr. Bhau Daji Lad Museum to review a proposal from Tasneem Mehta to support the project for its restoration and revitalisation, I was not familiar with the world of museums and conservation. Now, almost twenty years later, having closely observed the development of the institution, I am proud of its achievements and pleased that we, in the Bajaj group, took a leap of faith to support it. This book is testimony to the passion that has driven the project from the beginning and reflects the Museum's constant attention to detail and the commitment to excellence.

Mumbai has nurtured the business and commercial community for many centuries and has a remarkable history as this book shows us. The city was built with the philanthropy of the leading businessmen of the nineteenth and twentieth centuries and the Jamnalal Bajaj Foundation is happy to continue that tradition and contribute to the renewal of this historic city as well as support endeavours to develop its future. Gandhiji called Jamnalal Bajaj, my grandfather, his fifth son for his unswerving commitment to the principles of truth, justice, equality and empowerment of the nation. The Foundation embodies that commitment through its philanthropic efforts.

Developing an institution is similar to growing a business. It involves nurturing human potential in the field, managing your assets judiciously and ensuring that your customers are satisfied with the product that you serve them. Unlike a business, however, a museum is a not-for-profit public institution and is therefore even more challenging, in some ways, to manage. Many different constituencies have to be considered in the decision-making process. Rebuilding and sustaining such public institutions is very important, for they shape the thinking of future generations. What is gratifying in this two-decade-long journey is this coming together of Government agencies and private resources and expert management. I must compliment the Government of Maharashtra and the Municipal Corporation of Greater Mumbai for showing the wisdom to opt for this public-private mode of revitalising public institutions. And the result is there for all to see.

India has several extraordinary museums but most have not achieved their full potential. The Dr. Bhau Daji Lad Museum has received many awards but it has the capability to fly much higher with the right support.

This project is Ms Tasneem Mehta's doing all the way. I must thank and compliment her for her vision and unflagging zeal, as also those of her team. My brother Niraj and his wife, Minal, too have played an active role in the management of the Dr. Bhau Daji Lad Museum Trust, which was the first public-private partnership in the field of culture. The Trust, under the leadership of the Municipal Corporation of Greater Mumbai, has created a remarkable institution that has set a benchmark for museums in India. This book, I am sure, will set another benchmark.

I wish the Museum all success in its future endeavours.

RAHUL BAJAJ
Chairman, Jamnalal Bajaj Foundation
Chairman Emeritus, Bajaj Auto

14 September 2021

*Interior view of the Museum with the marble sculpture of
Prince Albert flanked by the Muses of Art and Science,
surrounded by displays from the natural history and
zoological collections; glass negative,
c. 1910 to 1920, V&A Museum, Bombay, 24.5 x 30 cm.
Accessioned: 1910–20.*

Preface

MUMBAI has captured the imagination of many distinguished writers, poets, scholars and artists since it evolved from a group of sleepy islands into the roaring metropolis it is today. No institution of the city presents this journey better than the Dr. Bhau Daji Lad Museum. The collection is small but unique, and bears testimony to the city's constant renewal. It gives voice to the vision and dynamic energy of the many people who have laboured for, supported, or contributed in some way to the city's making. The variety of objects in the Museum is a record of these ambitions and dreams, and the traumas and upheavals the city has experienced on its extraordinary journey of transformation.

The idea of reading the history of the city through the objects in the Museum was inspired by former director of the British Museum Neil MacGregor's remarkable book, *A History of the World in 100 Objects*. But we differ in that we have tried to tell the story of not only the city, but also the Museum, through the objects, albeit from a post-colonial perspective. The two stories interweave, inflecting each object with a particularity, and inscribing the past into the present. As you turn the pages, people, periods and practices that have defined the city's sociocultural character, as well the evolution of the Museum over 165 years, come alive. India celebrates its 75th year of independence from colonial rule on August 15, 2022, and the Museum will celebrate its 150th year since the building was established and the idea of the Museum was given physical form on May 2, 1872. The book is a reminder of the promise of these momentous dates.

Museums in India were a British import, a modern construct created to house collections of antiquities and anything that was rare and unusual in nature and to educate 'native taste' by showcasing beautiful crafts or 'economic products'. The earliest museums were established when the East India Company controlled vast swathes of the country and mercantile objectives dominated. These museums were not only repositories for the study of objects, but also places where merchants could examine samples of products or 'specimens' for export and trade. From the 1860s, when Bombay developed as an important port and trading centre, the interests of the city and those of the scholar jostled with each other in the development of the Museum's collection.

Not all the objects in the book speak directly to Mumbai's evolution though they establish its protean character. There are some objects whose journey reflects the city's importance as a trading centre. These objects speak about tastes, manners and customs in Bombay, in other parts of India, and occasionally, in Europe and the world. They inform us about the many cross-cultural influences that are a distinctive facet of the city's cosmopolitan outlook. Other objects demonstrate the importance of certain communities or craft practices that flourished in the city as it expanded. Many objects reflect changing tastes and customs due to colonial intervention. For much of the late nineteenth and early twentieth centuries, Bombay was the main entrepôt to India, and materials and goods both entered the country and left for other destinations from here, creating new synergies in production and taste with consequences that would ripple through the rest of the country. Objects collected just prior to Independence suggest a desire to unshackle the colonial presence in the city and Indianise the institution. Each object too has its own story to tell about its maker and its making. Exemplary artists and great traditions nurtured and shaped these outcomes.

The contemporary collection, created over fifteen years, brings the story into the present by reappraising the city and the institution's history. It attempts to decolonise this fraught colonial archive through artist interventions that challenge our assumptions. The broad art historical sweep, ranging from the mid-eighteenth century to current art practice, captures the Early Modern movement in the city and, to a limited extent, the Modern Art movement as well, though there are significant gaps. The most important lacuna is that there is no representation of the important post-Independence painters from the Sir J.J. School of Art. The Museum unfortunately does not include works by the important Progressive Artists' Group, formed in Bombay in 1947, which defined Modernism in India by challenging colonial conventions and the revivalist modern school of Bengal.

Museum objects are time machines. They allow us a peek into a civilisation long past or bring us face to face with today's issues, in a sense harking the future. Like architectural treasures, objects are record keepers that reveal their mysteries as you get more deeply engaged. The book unravels the enigma of a forgotten museum and is a mosaic of 101* stories for both the serious scholar and the passing friend. It has auxiliary vignettes highlighted in blue boxes embedded in most of the stories to amplify the main text. The narrative unpacks the colonial legacy to enable new readings of the city, the Museum and the objects. It generally follows a chronological path and for ease of understanding, objects are grouped in traditional typologies, though their timelines and display in the Museum overlap. Each chapter speaks through a cohort of objects about a particular thematic development during a period in the life of both the city and the Museum. Original names and spellings of people and places have been used to maintain historical integrity.

As you read the many object stories, you begin to glean Mumbai's evolution from a small group of marshy islands—that the Greek polymath and geographer Ptolemy called Heptanesia—into the dynamic powerhouse it is today. You begin to understand the many layers of the city's history as the Museum shifted focus over 165 years, from being an institution dedicated to economic products and natural history, the decorative arts, documenting the people of India and the city's history to the comprehensive cultural campus it is today. In the early years after Independence, it started collecting more traditional objects representative of what was considered a distinctly 'Indian' identity. In the 1990s, it began a collection of paintings by pre-Independence artists of the Sir J.J. School of Art, many of whom have since acquired substantial fame. The Museum Trust has acquired an important collection of contemporary art of the past fifteen years that responds to the history of the city and the institution and represents the finest talent of this period in the country.

We hope the experience of the book will encourage you to visit the Museum again and again to discover the many more stories waiting to be shared, and that it will enable you to relish and remember this great, constantly churning city. This is not a comprehensive history but a sociocultural reckoning, making the 101 stories a rich archive of historical intention and contemporary interpretation.

In India the additional 1 in 101 is considered auspicious and lucky.

TASNEEM ZAKARIA MEHTA
Managing Trustee and Honorary Director

Introduction

THE Dr. Bhau Daji Lad Museum, Mumbai, the erstwhile Victoria and Albert Museum, Bombay, is unique among museums in India. Established in 1857, it represents the emergence of an Early Modern aesthetic movement that would redefine Indian art and architecture. As museums proliferated in the country in the latter half of the nineteenth century, while India was still under British rule, a new aesthetic pedagogy emerged that would lead to the development of a public visual culture of collecting and displaying, which would eventually permeate palaces, homes and offices across the land. The collection in the Museum, one of the earliest to be established in pre-Independence India, represents the radical shift in the artistic production of the traditional arts and crafts to serve new aesthetic, social, political and economic goals. Unlike the museums established earlier in the other two major Presidencies of Calcutta and Madras, the Bombay Museum was a product of the modernising and mercantile intentions that define the character of the city even today, rather than the esoteric scholarly objectives that preoccupied the early English antiquarians in India. As Bombay developed and prospered, it played an increasingly important role in the evolution of a modern and distinctive urban cultural ethos reflected in the Museum's collections.

The initial impetus for the establishment of the Museum was the Great Exhibition of 1851. Prince Albert, whose statue dominates the central hall of the Museum, conceived of what was then considered the 'Greatest Show on Earth'—the Crystal Palace Exhibition—officially titled the 'Great Exhibition of the Works of Industry of all Nations'. Intended to stimulate trade and create an appetite for new products, the exhibition was an outstanding success. Samples of the best Indian craftsmanship as well as specimens of rare plants and stuffed animals were collected from across the country and sent to London. More than six million people visited the show over a period of six months. The success of the Great Exhibition spawned a cult of expositions that were hosted by competing European states, the United States of America and Australia, creating a new phenomenon of world fairs that persists to this day. In 1855, preparations for the Exposition Universelle in Paris, the French counterpart of the Crystal Palace Exhibition, generated much excitement in India. Many mofussil towns and principalities contributed to the selection of objects sent to the exhibition. The duplicates of selected artefacts that were retained in Bombay became the inspiration for the idea of establishing a 'Central Museum of Natural History, Economy, Geology, Industry and Arts' in the city which eventually became the Victoria and Albert Museum.[1]

Lord Elphinstone, the Governor of Bombay, set up a committee to establish the new museum for the edification of the native population and to promote trade between India and the world. In September 1855, a resolution was passed constituting the new museum and George Buist, a man of considerable energy and talent, was appointed its first curator. Buist was the editor of the *Bombay Times* and was most enthusiastic about setting up a museum.[2] Members of the Museum committee had visited the Great Exhibition of 1851 as well as European museums and felt that Bombay must have a museum to advance its reputation as a noteworthy town.[3]

In the late 1840s and early 1850s, Bombay was a small, pretty town with yellow and white houses and clean streets, surrounded by massive Fort walls to protect it from marauders and enemies.[4] It was cradled by hills that were dense with coconut groves and palm trees which were visible from a distance to the many ships that

sailed into its deep natural harbour. The bazaars were humming with activity as the East India Company that ruled the town promoted a policy of free trade and laissez-faire. The Bombay Chamber of Commerce had been established in 1836 to encourage private enterprise, and the first bank in the city, the Bombay Bank, was set up in 1840.[5] The first steamship set sail from Bombay in 1830, carrying passengers and cargo for Aden, from where travellers went overland to Alexandria and embarked on another steamer headed for Europe. By the late 1840s, London was only a thirty-day journey from Bombay.[6] In 1853, the first passenger train ran from Bori Bunder, where the erstwhile Victoria Terminus, now Chhatrapati Shivaji Maharaj Terminus, stands, to Thane, carrying 400 passengers in fourteen carriages. The railways and steam power forever altered the rural idyll that was the Bombay of previous centuries. The climactic decade, however, followed in the 1860s when the Fort walls were brought down and the city embarked on an unprecedented expansion that launched Bombay's transformation into one the most important cities of the Empire. The cotton boom of the early 1860s and the opening of the Suez Canal in 1869 created immense wealth and development. The swampy marshland of the early 1800s became the 'City of Gold' and Urbs Prima in Indis, the 'First City in India'.[7]

On March 24, 1857, shortly before the Uprising, now called the First War of Independence, a small nucleus collection that constituted the earliest form of the Museum officially opened to the public at the Town Barracks. It had been briefly inaugurated during the visit of the Governor General of India and later the first Viceroy, Lord Canning, in February 1856, and was opened for a week to the eager public who probably had never seen a Museum before.[8] Some 13,000 people visited during that first week, fascinated by the strange exhibits which consisted of stuffed birds, a pair of water tortoises in a small aquarium at the entrance, different types of seeds and grains in glass jars, materials for building, unusual dried plants, a broken Chinese pillar (that is still on the Museum grounds), and other 'specimens' of natural history and artistic production that had been hurriedly put together for Lord Canning's visit.[9] This first iteration of the Museum, however, had a short life as several public buildings, including the Museum, were sequestered for the incoming defence forces when the Uprising broke out in May 1857. The infant Museum was hurriedly moved out and several exhibits were damaged in the haste. Today, very few objects remain from that earliest beginning.

In the same year, the Sir J.J. School of Art, which had an umbilical link with the Museum, was established with a generous donation from Sir Jamsetjee Jeejeebhoy, who was determined that Indian craftsmen should be able to compete with the best across the world. George Buist was appointed the School's first director, and several of the Museum's later curators also served as superintendents and principals.[10] Like the Museum, which was established to help improve trade and taste by educating merchants and craftsmen alike, the School of Art was to provide the means to skill artisans and teach them to produce beautiful objects for trade. Originally, the Museum and the School were conceptualised as sister institutions that would sit side by side on the Esplanade (see pp. 68-69), a vast swathe of land that abutted the sea, and where Mumbai's neo-Gothic ensemble of buildings stands today as sentinels of the city's earliest ambitions. The Museum was intended as a showcase for the best practices of the School and as a forum to educate the population through visual displays of the best available craftsmanship. However, the Fort, which was the nucleus of the town, had become congested. Meanwhile, Byculla, where the governor's house was located, had developed into a more salubrious and exclusive suburb. The original plan was abandoned and it was decided that the Museum would be situated next to the Botanical Gardens in Byculla. The School would become one of the most important art education institutions in the country, helping define the curricula of all the other art schools, as it was the only institution empowered to conduct teacher training exams.[11] The facades of Bombay's important institutional buildings were carved and embellished by students of the School. Several of the Museum's important exhibits were purchased from the School, which was a site of extensive artistic experimentation. The umbilical relationship between the two institutions continued till Independence in 1947 and defined the cultural and artistic production in the city.

The year 1857 also heralded the establishment, in London, of the South Kensington Museum, which later became the second Victoria and Albert Museum in 1899. The museum was governed by similar objectives as its namesake in India. Like most cultural institutions of the period, both museums were under the jurisdiction of the Department of Science and Art in London, that was supervised by the fastidious Henry Cole, architect of the Great Exhibition. Their primary goal was to encourage trade and help audiences cultivate a taste for the best in design, craftsmanship and artistic production. The two museums also sought to address the long-felt need to stem the degradation of craftsmanship due to industrialisation. Both museums showcased the finest examples of handmade objects and set an example for artisans to accomplish the highest standards in the execution of their work. Sir George Birdwood (see pp. 56–57), an eminent scholar and the first curator of the V&A Museum, Bombay, would go on to become the first curator of the Indian section of the V&A, London.

The year 1857 was momentous for many reasons but the Uprising was the most significant and had a cataclysmic effect on India. The city experienced no serious conflict because Charles Forjett, the commissioner of police, managed to foil the plans of the Bombay Sepoys, who had conspired to mutiny.[12] Buist, however, was devastated by the Uprising and became very critical of Indians, writing openly against them in the *Bombay Times*. He had earlier resigned from the Museum, disillusioned with its progress. The Indian proprietors of the *Bombay Times* were unhappy with this change of attitude and prevailed on him to quit the publication and he left the city for Allahabad.[13] George Birdwood was given charge as curator of the Botanical Gardens and the Bombay Museum, which was moved in 1858 to the Town Hall.

Soon after the Queen's proclamation on the steps of the Town Hall on November 1, 1858, taking over the governance of India from the East India Company, a group of public-spirited citizens decided that the first important public institution to be built in Bombay would be the Museum, with the natural history and botanical gardens attached to it. A meeting was called in the Town Hall to raise funds for the new museum building, which would house the nascent collection and would be dedicated to Queen Victoria.[14] Juggannath Sunkersett (see pp. 58–59), one of the prominent merchant princes of Bombay, chaired the meeting, which was attended by city patrons from different communities, including Hindus, Muslims, Christians and Parsis, highlighting the cosmopolitan character of the city. Sunkersett drew attention to the importance of their mission,

> I will not dwell on the immense importance to Bombay of the institution we are about to establish ... Others, no doubt, will fully dilate on their benefits in aiding the development of the raw products of this colossal and almost unknown empire, in stimulating and improving its slow and crude manufactures, in supplying resorts of healthy recreation to the densely crowded inhabitants of Bombay, in ornamenting the town, in inciting amongst the masses habits of observation and taste for rational pleasures, in subserving, in fact, for the millions, the purposes of a most influential, educational and reformatory institution ... The Museum must start on its higher career as a College of Inquiry.[15]

Dr Bhau Daji Lad and Dr George Birdwood, the two secretaries of the Museum committee, were charged with raising funds to establish the building and enlarge the collection with the best specimens of 'Indian manufactures', 'with the special object of aiding the economic progress of this country.'[16]

The construction of the Museum building took fourteen years and was bedevilled by a lack of funds. The Palladian architecture with High Victorian interiors is not only unique in the city but unrivalled in the country. When the Museum committee decided to construct a grand building for the Museum, there were few institutional buildings in Bombay apart from the Town Hall, now home to the Asiatic Society. The grand Renaissance Revival style chosen for the Museum building reflected the European perception that the Classical period represented the acme of human achievement in the arts, in architecture and in statecraft. The building is one of the most important historical artefacts of the city. Though the Victoria and Albert Museum was the third museum to be established in India, it was the first colonial building to be built for the specific purpose of housing a museum.

The 150-year-old Museum building was conceived to dazzle visitors. During the efforts to raise funds by public subscription, it was presented as a 'Hall of Wonder' as most of Bombay's citizens had never seen a formal museum. The original design for the building was conceived by George Birdwood, whose concept included all the basic features of the building visible today: 'a long hall', 'Doric pillars', galleries on either side of the building, and large windows for light and ventilation. Capt. Wilkins, the PWD engineer who worked with Birdwood on the design, envisioned a building to rival the best in the world. The design was sent to London for approval and was considered too expensive (the colonial government was always reluctant to pay for urban projects unless absolutely required). It was later modified for the new location on the Mount Estate in Byculla by another British PWD engineer, William Tracey, who died before the plans could be implemented. Scott McClelland & Co. architects completed the design with further modifications, though they retained most of Birdwood's specifications.[17]

Having one of the few Palladian facades in Mumbai, the Museum boasts exterior column capitals made of terracotta, a first for the city's buildings. The interior is a rare example of High Victorian design in India. Not a surface has been left without embellishment, and the intricate craftsmanship on display is a testimony to the artistic skills of native craftsmen. Intricate patterns are stencilled on the ceiling and beautiful wood carvings adorn the teak doors and blind ventilator windows. Elaborate gilt stucco work frames the windows of the upper floor, creating an impression of palatial magnificence. The grand cast-iron palisades, staircase railings and arched supports, as well as the Corinthian capitals and columns which are the defining features of the building, were imported from England. The richly coloured details, the intricate wood carving, the Minton-tiled floors, the delicately etched glass windows and the extensive gold gilding make it a unique example of nineteenth-century architecture in the country.

The V&A Museum, Bombay, was conceived as an encyclopaedic institution to showcase the best examples of both traditional and contemporary artistic production. Its collection included rare and interesting objects bequeathed by maharajas who were keen to showcase the crafts of their states, as well as archaeological finds from the Bombay Presidency that extended from Sindh to northern Karnataka. A large group of Gandhara sculptures was sent to the Museum by Henry Hardy Cole, son of Henry Cole, who became Curator of Ancient Monuments for India in 1880. Ten important Assyrian slabs from the excavation undertaken by Sir Henry Layard, similar to those in the British Museum, were bequeathed to the Museum by Lord Falkland, the Governor of Bombay (see p. 268). Many of Bombay's rich merchants donated important artefacts and occasionally, departing British officers or their wives made a bequest. The Museum was an unusual institutional experiment in shaping the sensibilities of a population that was deeply conservative and suspicious of the motives of their apparent benefactors. By 1877, however, when Queen Victoria was declared Empress of India, the educated elite were co-opted into this 'progressive' education mission of which the Museum was an important part.

The economic function of the Museum, was central to its development and it came to be known as an 'Economic Products' Museum, which was a euphemism for the beautiful objects produced especially for a European clientele and the Indian elite. These, along with raw materials that could be traded, were displayed for potential buyers who could order the same from workshops and 'factories' set up by the School of Art or from craftsmen and dealers directly.[18] In the early days, the Museum had a strong focus on natural history as the British sought to understand and document the people, the archaeology, the flora, fauna and resources of the colony. As an archive of the period, the collection is unique in its focus on the life and culture as well as the economy of the nineteenth and early twentieth centuries of the Bombay Presidency. Its organisation was strongly influenced by the overarching tropes of science and scientific taxonomies that defined the Victorian age, when science was considered as endowing merit and usefulness to artistic practice.

With the city's growth, the sociopolitical contexts altered as did the curatorial mission of the Museum. It evolved from a 'Cabinet of Curiosities' and an 'Economic Products' Museum', into a 'City Museum' in the early twentieth century. As the nodal museum, it helped other such institutions develop by contributing collections and 'specimens'.[19] In 1975, the name was changed to Dr. Bhau Daji Lad Museum, after the man who had worked tirelessly for its establishment. However, its distance from the town centre and lack of funds remained a perennial problem. When the Prince

Municipal Corporators in the Corporation Hall; glass negative, c. early twentieth century, Bombay; 16.5 x 12 cm. Accessioned: early twentieth century.
Indians representing various communities in Bombay are seen seated around the table in the Assembly Hall of the erstwhile Bombay Municipal Corporation (BMC), constructed in 1893. The busts of the British Governors of Bombay seen in the backdrop were moved to the Museum in 1948-49 after Independence.

of Wales Museum (now the Chhatrapati Shivaji Maharaj Vastu Sangrahalaya) was established in 1922, many of the V&A Bombay's archaeological collections, especially its prized Gandhara and Assyrian artefacts, were shifted to the new premises and it became increasingly marginalised. After Independence it was considered a colonial relic and was rendered obsolete. Deprived of funds and interest, it slowly deteriorated into dilapidation and utter disrepair.

In 2003, INTACH (Indian National Trust for Art and Cultural Heritage) and the Jamnalal Bajaj Foundation signed an agreement with the Municipal Corporation of Greater Mumbai, which owns the Museum, to restore and revitalise it. The Bhau Daji Lad Museum Trust took over the management of the Museum for a period of fifteen years from its complete restoration. The Trust chair is the mayor of Mumbai and the municipal commissioner is the co-chair, with seventeen trustees representing both the civic body and cultural expertise. The restoration, which took five years, won UNESCO's 2005 Asia-Pacific Award of Excellence, the highest honour for cultural conservation in the region. Not only were the building and its surroundings refurbished, but more than 3,000 objects were conserved and restored. The Museum display was retrofitted, re-curated and redesigned, restoring its historical character.

The Museum reopened in 2008 with an extensive exhibition and education programme committed to promoting traditional and contemporary art, design, craftsmanship and culture. Mumbai has gone through a manifold metamorphosis as it evolved from an industrial town dedicated to textile production into a financial, technological and entertainment hub. Notwithstanding these changes, the city's early industrial history and its working-class ethos, documented by the Museum, continues to define its character and form. From the beginning of the project in 2003, the trustees have felt that the Museum must reflect the city's multi-cultural history through its outreach programmes and by evolving into a many-faceted institution that responds to Mumbai's complex society. An ambitious expansion plan, spanning 2 acres of land that abuts the north side of the Museum, drew over 100 international and national submissions, and eight world-renowned architectural firms were selected to submit a proposal and make a presentation. The extraordinary American architect Steven Holl won the competition to transform the institution into a city campus. An eminent jury commended his design for its innovation, architectural qualities and inclusion of local craft practices.

A series of provocative exhibitions, eighty-five in all from 2008 to 2019, have been presented, giving a platform to India's young and established contemporary artists, photographers and designers. These exhibitions have changed the paradigm of museum curation in India. Several international shows in partnership with international museums, like the V&A, London; the Dresden Museum, Germany; the Guggenheim Museum, New York; the British Library and Iniva, London; and the Duomo Museum, Florence, have brought exciting ideas and cultural practices to Mumbai. The Museum has collaborated with consulates and international cultural centres, not-for-profit institutions and foundations, cultural theorists and curators, educators and specialists, to bring a vast variety of programming to the city. It gives free access to organisations dedicated to promoting Indian craftsmanship and has worked with master craftsmen and contemporary artists to encourage and showcase their practice.

An intensive education and outreach programme has been initiated to build and diversify the Museum's audiences. A rich selection of programmes—including film, music and art history courses and lectures on many different aspects of contemporary culture—focus on providing stimulating, participatory experiences that respond to different age, interest and language groups, and recognise a diversity of backgrounds. A partnership with Google Arts and Culture has enabled a strong digital footprint. The Museum has received many awards for its pioneering role and today, is acknowledged as a leader among museums in India. • TZM

View of the Kamalnayan Bajaj Mumbai Gallery, Dr. Bhau Daji Lad Museum, Mumbai.

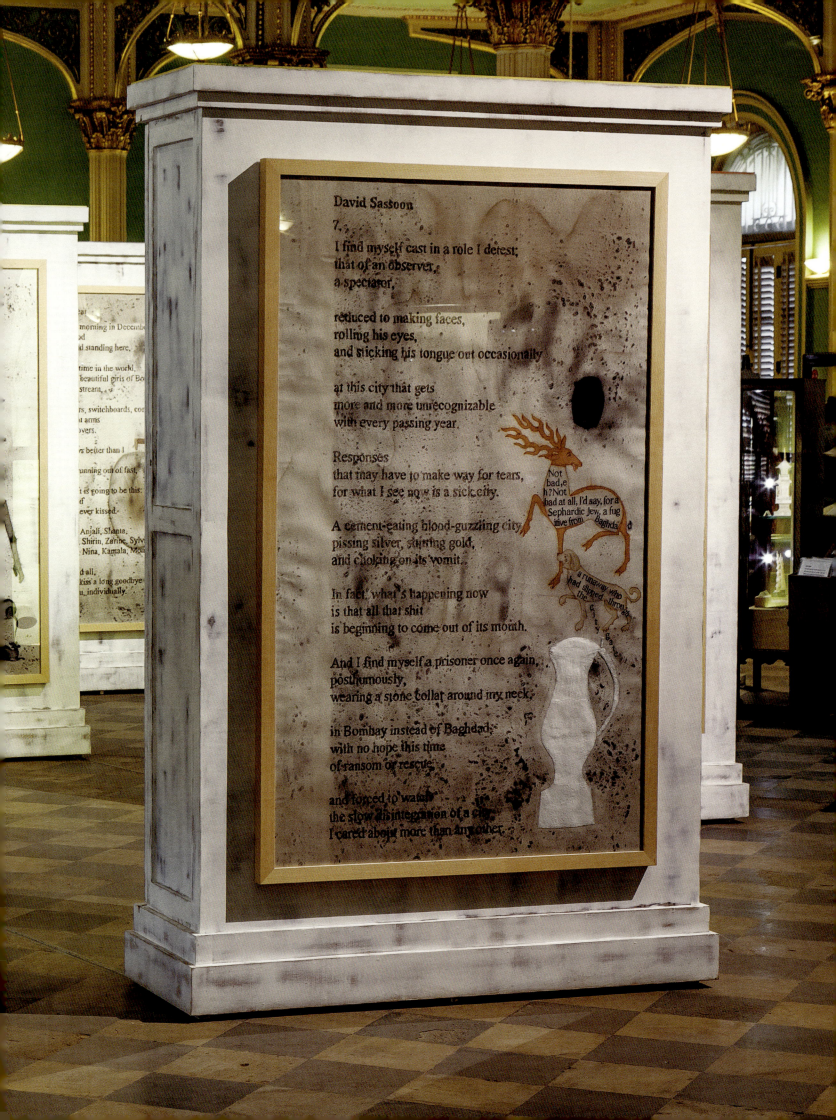

BOMBAY/MUMBAI
The Making of a City

'*This mysterious impression of unfathomable Beauty emanates like an exhalation from Bombay itself in spite of all architectural lapses, of commercial adulation, of the sacrifice of Civic glory on the altars of a pitiful opportunism. The most fevered efforts of Reinforced Concrete, of gaudy brick, and mortar have not and cannot destroy the Beauty of Bombay. Seas, and Skies; Palms and Mountains, Beaches, Islands, and Lagoons combining together for one gesture of immutable defiance have frustrated the Philistines.*'

— Gladstone Solomon[1]

DESPITE the lapse of almost 100 years since Solomon, who was the principal of the Sir J.J. School of Art, declared his love for Bombay in such an unabashed tone, the words could have been spoken yesterday. Undoubtedly, significant architectural aberrations have occurred and the rude reorganisation of the city's urban form with utter disregard for its historical layers is a painful loss that deprives the city of its unique tangible and intangible cultural legacy. But there are still many pockets that hold memories of Mumbai's compelling and extraordinary cosmopolitan history.

The Dr. Bhau Daji Lad Museum is one such space. Though the collection of historical material that details the evolution of the city's cultural ethos, its architectural form and artistic diversity is not comprehensive, it is extensive. The city shaped and determined the form and character of the Museum. And equally the Museum was involved in defining the social, cultural and economic landscape of the city through its displays and purchases, its participation in several national and international exhibitions, representing the city (see pp. 102-03, 126-27), and showcasing the economic products of both the city and the country. The emphasis, however, to represent the city through displays that showcased its modernisation, progress and the development of its urban form started in the early twentieth century and is unique to the Museum.

Cecil Burns, curator of the Museum (1903–18), decided to showcase the tremendous urban and demographic development of the much-admired colonial city. He observed that the 'natives' who visited the Museum in great numbers were especially interested in the dioramas and models as well as the photographs and prints on display, which were considered the 'popular' (i.e. not erudite) part of the collection. But a shrewd political intention was also coded into these displays as they were a demonstration of progress under the British Raj and showcased the colonial efforts to modernise and industrialise the city. Much of the material about the city in the Museum's collection therefore documents Bombay's earliest development and its changing urban form in the eighteenth, nineteenth and early

David Sassoon – 7 (poem by Arun Kolatkar), Atul Dodiya; watercolour, charcoal, soft pastel and marble dust on paper, 2014; 182.8 x 114.3 cm. Exhibition: *7000 Museums: A Project for the Republic of India*; Industrial Arts Gallery, 2014-2015.
Atul Dodiya assembled an encyclopaedic vision of potentialities in vitrines that mimicked the Museum's display cases. In an inspired binary juxtaposition, the 'Bombay' poems of Arun Kolatkar are painted on the reverse of the vitrines, inscribing a sharp edge into the informal playfulness of their formal display. Like the poet who takes on the persona of the legendary David Sassoon, whose statue graces the central atrium of the Museum, the artist calls out the city, built as it is on loss and hope.

twentieth centuries through dioramas and models, photographs, maps, prints, rare books and paintings. The focus, of course, especially of the rare photographic collection, was the grand colonial city with its neo-Gothic ensemble of buildings that today is a World Heritage precinct, as well as the palatial houses of the early East India Company officials.

But Bombay was much more than the formal city of rich merchants, canny financiers, and smug colonial officials. It was the informal city that developed on the margins and in the interstices of the planned city that gave life and character to Bombay, as it does even today. However, there is little documentation of the 'native' or indigenous city at the Museum. The temples fascinated the Europeans and Burns collected photographs of these, including the rock-cut cave temples in Bombay at Mahakali and Jogeshwari, and at Elephanta (see pp. 30-31). In the latter part of the nineteenth century, there were few 'cities' in India and urban growth was concentrated in the Presidency towns. Migration to Bombay grew exponentially with the advent of the railways, the expansion of the port, the establishment of many craft and artisan ateliers, the development of the textile mills, and due to famines in adjacent rural areas. The lure of riches as well as the city's reputation for tolerance and its many forms of glamorous entertainment attracted both the well-heeled and the impoverished.[2]

Industrialisation changed lifestyles in unprecedented ways, and like other great cities of the world that were being built and repurposed in the latter half of the nineteenth century, Bombay too experienced a radical change in keeping with its newfound status as a major trading centre of the Empire. With the British Crown taking over the governance of the country after the Uprising of 1857, colonial attitudes—that were earlier cooperative and based on mercantile imperatives—changed and new hierarchies emerged that altered the demographic composition of Bombay. Development and education led to the creation of new professions in medicine, engineering, the law and administration services, besides merchants, moneylenders and bankers. The production of a multitude of necessities and luxuries by small traders and artisans ensured that there was never a want for employment in the city.

The development of Bombay was a collaborative venture between the British and the city's merchant elite, who funded most of the city's significant building projects, but competing business interests and rigid social distinctions exacerbated existing tensions between indigenous communities and between Europeans and Indians.[3] The expansion of the city reflected this bias—the southern 'white' town was open, with large green spaces and palatial bungalows, whereas the northern end beyond the Civil Lines was congested, with dank, ramshackle dwellings and the reek of open sewers resulting in constant epidemics.[4]

In the early 1860s, when the Museum building was being planned at the site of the new Botanical Gardens established by the Agri Horticultural Society at Byculla, the location was considered a salubrious, green suburb of Bombay. The Fort in South Bombay had become congested and Byculla and its adjacent areas had developed as an affluent outpost with grand houses that had large gardens. Some of the Museum's important neighbours included San Souci, the resplendent residence of David Sassoon; the governor's house, which was located in neighbouring Parel; the Byculla Club (see p. 77), the only place of its kind for Europeans till 1898; as well as the Race Course, where Bombay's gentry gathered to frolic on weekends.

There had been much debate as to where the Museum should be located. Originally, it was to sit beside the Sir J.J. School of Art on the Esplanade, as the two institutions were considered interdependent. However, George Birdwood, Secretary and Curator of the Museum Trust, argued forcefully to ensure that the Museum came up at the Mount Estate in Byculla, next to the Botanical Gardens. One of his many reasons was that if the Museum was located at the far end of the Esplanade, next to the School, it would attract the 'native' hordes from Dhobi Talao on the

Esplanade's northern edge, and this would deter the elite and the merchant classes from visiting.[5] He stated confidently that with time, the Byculla area would become the central affluent node of the city and the Museum was sure to attract the 'right' clientele as it developed. Climate and commerce were to prove him wrong at the time, though perhaps prescient, as today the area is indeed the heart of the city with much gentrification taking place.

By the 1880s, the cotton boom and the frenzied industrial expansion had changed Byculla from an upper-class suburb into a densely packed working-class precinct with drainage problems that arose from the rapid reclamation to connect the seven islands. In 1883, Lady Fergusson, the wife of Governor James Fergusson, died of cholera in the governor's residence at Parel, creating much concern regarding the unhealthy atmosphere of the area and prompting many of the elite to move out.[6] Malabar Hill, meanwhile, had transformed into the city's most gracious neighbourhood. Prosperous Parsis, rich Marwari bankers and British officials built spacious bungalows with large gardens that offered beguiling views of the city and the sea. The governor's residence moved to Malabar Point and soon, the Byculla Club also closed. In 1890, the erstwhile governor's residence was handed over to the Plague Research Laboratory (see p. 82) and is now the Haffkine Institute for Training, Research and Testing. Today, in the Byculla area where the Museum is located, amidst the densely populated chawls, the decaying mills and the overwhelming shiny new towers, one can catch an occasional glimpse of Sassoon's grand residence (now converted into a hospital), a school and a police station built for a different era, a railway station, a cinema hall and other such landmarks struggling to keep intact their architectural integrity.

The 'native' town that grew rapidly northwards in the latter half of the nineteenth century was the antithesis of South Bombay and Malabar Hill in urban form. Some of these ethnic enclaves housed the artisans and craftsmen who produced many of the objects in the Museum. A large number of the petty traders who set up shop to service the growing needs of the city came from different parts of the country, bringing their traditions with them, and lived in these ethnic

Photograph of the Museum staff at Curator Cecil Burns' retirement; glass negative, 1918, at the erstwhile V&A Museum, Bombay; 16.5 x 12 cm. Accessioned: 1918. Seated in the centre (L-R): D. A. Pai, Assistant Curator (1903 to 1930), Ernest Fern, Curator (1918 to 1930) and Cecil Burns, Curator (1903 to 1918).

neighbourhoods. The 'native villages' expanded upon the reclaimed lands which were earlier marshy swamps separating the seven islands. Each of these had a distinctive character that reflected the cultural practices of the particular residential community. Some of the better-known urban villages include Khotachiwadi and Matharpakadi, where East Indian Christians, who had been converted by the Portuguese, settled.[7] In other areas, like Bhuleshwar, Girgaum and Bhendi Bazaar (see pp. 70-71) some of the earlier urban form is extant even today, though it is rapidly being eroded. These villages comprised many different types of spatial agglomerations and informal accretions as the city's population grew. The Gujaratis from Kutch and Saurashtra were the most populous group and formed the backbone of the city's trade and commerce.[8] They set up shop at Bhuleshwar, Kalbadevi Road, and Zaveri Bazaar, the city's jewellery and gold market (see pp. 70-71).

Native merchant houses comprised an interesting hybrid architectural form incorporating the basic features of a large Indian courtyard house, that reflected the typical architecture of their region. Built by local contractors and artisans, these often sported a mélange of styles that announced an aspirational, hybrid modernity. Scalloped arches supported by Corinthian columns, and fenestration with lintels and pediments designed in a European style and embellished with animals and floral motifs or apsaras (celestial nymphs) were not uncommon.[9] Indigenous housing complexes built for particular communities, known as *wadas* for Hindus, *baghs* for Parsis, and *mohallas* for Muslims, incorporated religious sites, usually including water tanks for ritual purification, markets, *dharamshalas* (pilgrim rest houses) and community halls besides the residences. These were closely integrated spatial enclaves, knit together by intricate streets that served the needs of the community. It was common for *wadas*, especially of the Gujarati and Rajasthani communities, to be decorated with paintings of deities and religious symbols. In contrast to the colonial city, which stood tall and stately and looked outwards, the 'native' villages were intimate and looked inwards, especially protecting their women who were usually in *purdah* (veiled).[10] Many of these villages included the famous Bombay *chawls* or working-class housing to accommodate the increasing influx of labour (see pp. 84-85).

Bombay's social character reflected this twin city approach with the latest European trends in fashion, art, photography and theatre permeating the conservative layers of the native city.[11] The well-known Bombay artist M.V. Dhurandhar (see p. 211, pp. 318-19) painted his women in the typical nine-yard saree worn by the local women, but they were always in stylish Western blouses. Dr Bhau Daji Lad (see pp. 54-55) was known for his interest in theatre, ancient Indian art and photography, and he actively promoted an intercultural understanding between the British and the local population. Theatre particularly provided an important space for cultural interface. K.N. Kabraji the editor of *Rast Goftar*, the Gujarati newspaper, records, 'A well-known Marathi company gave a series of performances before delighted audiences under the auspices of the late Dr Bhau Dajee. A special performance of King Gopichand was given at Government House, Parel before Lord Elphinstone, who had invited the elite of the European and native communities to witness it.'[12] Raja Raja Varma, the painter Ravi Varma's brother, who kept a detailed diary of their long stays in Bombay, writes about elegant soirees in the evenings accompanied by music and dance performances. By the latter part of the nineteenth century many foreign communities also resided in Bombay. They came to trade and many writers of the period record the hum of different languages in the bazaars which included Armenians, Greeks, Chinese, Arabs and Jews among others.[13] James Maclean in his Guide to Bombay notes, '... the people, as a rule, live good-humouredly enough together, and mingle freely with one another in the streets ...'[14]

It is this integrative cultural ethos that is reflected in the collections of the Museum and in the architecture of the city. Like many of the buildings, most of the objects express an emerging modernity with different stylistic influences apparent in their rendition. Though these hybrid styles were criticised by British ideologues like Birdwood, who were concerned with purity and authenticity, the new repertoire of forms and designs represents a robust and eclectic negotiation with a variety of visually expressive idioms. This modern urban context would shape the sensibilities not only of the master craftsmen but also the artists of the Bombay School of Art.

Bombay, in the 1930s, had become synonymous with the notion of Indian modernity, both in terms of artistic and industrial development. It was a thriving city, with all the modern facilities that at the time defined urban culture—wide roads, street lighting, modern transport infrastructure, elegant apartment buildings, a proper drainage system, plenty of green spaces and the benefit of beautiful beaches and afternoon sea breezes. Gladstone Solomon was not only the principal of the Sir J.J. School of Art but also curator of the newly established Prince of Wales Museum and he did much to promote an artistic turn in the city (see pp. 315-317). The British Government, along with the city's merchant elite, had established several educational and civic institutions in a parade of grand neo-Gothic buildings flanking the Esplanade,[15] which reflected a sense of civic pride peculiar to Bombay among Indian cities. It included the University (1857), the High Court (1862), the Telegraph Office (1869), and the Central Post Office (1913). There were movie theatres like the elegant Art-Deco Eros (1938) (see pp. 90-91) and Regal (1933); the Royal Opera House (1911); play houses such as the Art Deco Excelsior, (1909) that presented the latest theatre from England, and the famous Gaiety Theatre (1879) now the Capitol Cinema; department stores like the Army and Navy Stores (established 1891); a variety of shops and bazaars; and a public tram system that made the different parts of the city easily accessible (see pp. 72-73). Further north stood the magnificent, High Gothic, Victoria Terminus, now a World Heritage site, that connected the city to many parts of the country.

Bombay's history represents not only architectural and artistic innovation but also the advent of cultural modernity on the subcontinent. It was an experiment in urban development, which was itself a new art form in the mid-nineteenth and early twentieth century. The plague, which had devastated the city in the late nineteenth and early twentieth century, had given rise to several new urban development schemes that changed the city's landscape. Housing proposals like Cuffe Parade, and the notorious Back Bay reclamation scheme that created Marine Drive (see p. 92), encouraged a speculative real estate market with the Government offering attractive sops to builders. This ensured an ever-expanding perimeter of the city. The Bombay Improvement Trust (see pp. 80-81) made efforts to rehabilitate and redevelop some of the congested native villages but these often met with resistance as the colonial government was rarely sensitive to the cultural constraints of the indigenous communities and considered their requests as impeding urban progress.[16] Much of the city's famed Art Deco buildings were built in response to health and housing imperatives and subsequent apartment living brought with it a change of lifestyle and a modern urbane outlook (see pp. 90–92).[17]

Though the British governed the city, it was Indian philanthropy that built and gave it shape and substance. It was determined and visionary men like Dr Bhau Daji Lad, Juggannath Sunkersett (see pp. 58-59) and Jamsetjee Jeejeebhoy (see pp. 62-63) who shaped the city and the lives of the many who came with little but a sense of hope to seek sustenance and succour, as they do even today. Dr Bhau Daji Lad and his close associate, Dr George Birdwood (see pp. 56-57), were the two men who determined the paradigm of a museum in Bombay. The architectural and cultural form emulated the latest trends in London and Europe, albeit with a nod to Indian design elements, as much of the city was designed by the British with the help of Indian architects and engineers. However, within the vernacular heart of the city, the foreign and the Indian blended more vigorously to create a hybrid modernity that was peculiar to Bombay. By the 1940s, Bombay was considered one of the most beautiful and advanced cities in Asia. • TZM

1 MUMBADEVI

MUMBAI derives its name from its patron goddess, Mumbadevi. Her origins are shrouded in myth, mystery and the story of Mumbai's fishing communities, its colonial past and commercial beginnings. The statue of the goddess in brass was the first object commissioned in 2009, after the restoration and reopening of the Museum. It was made by National Awardee M.V. Lakshmanan in the traditional casting method. The iconography and representation honour her local character and the inclusive tradition, which welcomes all communities located in Mumbai.

The Mumbadevi temple is one of the two oldest in Mumbai; the other is the Walkeshwar temple. The Koli community, the original inhabitants of Mumbai, worshipped

the goddess Mumba. A record from the twelfth century titled *Bimbakyan* mentions the existence of the temple and worship of the goddess.[1] The exact time period of the establishment of the original temple, however, cannot be ascertained. Historians suggest that Mumbadevi may belong to a tradition of 'earth mothers' dating back to the Indus Valley civilisation.[2]

Legends abound regarding the origins of Mumbadevi. One claims that a Koli fisherman named Munga first built a temple to worship the deity, and called it 'Mungachi Amba'. Another belief, mentioned in the *Mumbadevi Mahatmya* (a religious text on the goddess), states that the temple commemorates the victory of the goddess over the demon Mumbaraka who harassed the inhabitants of Mumbai.[3]

From her origins as an earth goddess worshipped by the Kolis, Mumbadevi has been transformed into a *nagaradevata*, the city's reigning female deity. Worship rituals changed as the city evolved and waves of migration brought communities to Bombay from across the country. Each community venerated the goddess in their tradition, and these inclusive practices are reflected in the diverse patterns of worship evident even today. Several shrines to other deities—Ganesha, Maruti, Mahadeva, Indrayani, Murlidhara, Jagannatha, Narsoba and Balaji—have been added to the main Mumbadevi temple at Kalbadevi, near Zaveri Bazaar.

The original temple was located at Phansi Talao near the Esplanade. It was demolished in 1766 to make way for the Victoria Terminus railway station. The temple was rebuilt on its present site by a notable Marathi goldsmith named Pandu (or Pandurang), whose family also took care of its management. The tank of Mumbadevi was a later construction, added in 1830.

The architecture of the temple amalgamates traditional Hindu spire construction with European neoclassical pilasters and cornices that were the fashion at the time in the city. Temple pujaris or priests are chosen from all over India.

The local character of Mumbadevi is reflected in her iconography and adornment. The *Mumbadevi Mahatmya* notes that she is armed with weapons like a bow, an arrow, a mace, a sword and a spear that indicate her role as protector of the city. She also has a benign face, and wears a pearl necklace, earrings, armlets and bangles. She wears the traditional Maharashtrian saree, a paisley-shaped *nath* (nose ring) and a *kirti mukut* (crown).

During Navratri, the vehicle which the Goddess Mumba rides changes every day of the week, as does her manifestation. She is celebrated as Annapurna, Durga, Laxmi, Saraswati, Kali and Bahuchara Mata, each avatar denoting a different aspect of the goddess, on different days of the week. • PV

Opposite:
Mumbadevi; brass, 2009, Mumbai; 109 x 72 x 64 cm.
Accessioned: 2009.
Mumbadevi, seated on a lion, with eight arms bearing iconography symbolising valour, wisdom, compassion, and victory: *sudarshan-chakra* (disc), sword, mace, spear, trident, bow, *chowri* (fly whisk) and *kamandal* (water pot).
•
Below:
Mumbadevi; stone, pigment, Mumbadevi Temple, Mumbai.

LORD GANESHA

Lord Ganesha or Ganapati, one of the most popular deities across India, is known by as many as 108 names. The elephant-headed god is the son of Lord Shiva and Goddess Parvati, and the brother of Kartikeya, the god of war. Ganesha is the benevolent god of intellectual and artistic pursuits, and prosperity, and the remover of obstacles. In Maharashtra, he is worshipped before commencing any important project or journey with the chant '*Ganapati Bappa, Morya!*' (Lord Ganesha, come and bless us!).

Ganesh Chaturthi, the first day of Ganeshotsav, is the biggest and most important event in Mumbai's calendar of festivities. Ganeshotsav begins in the month of Bhadrapa (August/September) in the Hindu calendar and lasts for ten days, marking Lord Ganesha's arrival from his abode in the Himalayas. The idol is venerated and treated like a guest visiting the city; *pandals* (temporary structures) are set up on the streets, in neighbourhoods as well as in homes. Special meals and *modaks* (sweet dumplings made with rice flour, jaggery and coconut) are made to welcome the Lord and distributed amongst family members. There is much rejoicing and celebration in the community with visits to friends' and relatives' homes and a joyous atmosphere pervades the city. On the tenth day, worshippers bid farewell to Lord Ganesha by immersing him in the Arabian Sea, or the nearest water body, with a chant requesting the Lord to return the next year.

Under the Peshwa rule (late eighteenth to early nineteenth century), Ganeshotsav was publicly celebrated in Poona as well as in private homes. Later, in order to curb dissent and resistance to colonial rule, the British Government banned large-scale public gatherings of Indians and the festival began to be celebrated in private. By the late nineteenth century, there was growing unrest among Indians against the British. Bal Gangadhar Tilak, one of the leaders of the Indian Nationalist movement, advocated the revival of mass public celebrations of Ganeshotsav and Chhatrapati Shivaji Maharaj Jayanti as he was aware that the British would be wary of banning religious activities in such a charged atmosphere. These public celebrations provided cover for political leaders to rally people to the cause of *Swaraj* (self-rule). In 1894, Tilak inaugurated a Sarvajanik Ganapati (Ganapati festival open to the general public) at Keshavji Naik Chawl, Girgaum. In Bombay, as well as in Poona, Tilak and his associates distributed pamphlets with the message of unity at the festivals. Theatrical performances inspired by Indian mythology conveyed similar messages of unity during the festival as propaganda for *Swaraj* and the eventual overthrow of the foreign power.[1]

The festival continues to have mass appeal in the city, cutting across class, caste and religious boundaries, encouraging people to come together in the spirit of unity. In 1934, the vendors and mill workers in the Lalbaug-Parel area of Mumbai, very close to the Museum, set up a Ganapati pandal as their *navas* (prayer, wish) for a new marketplace to replace the one shut down by the Municipality in 1932 was fulfilled. The tradition of Lalbaugcha Raja (The King of Lalbaug) continues and is celebrated on a grand commercial scale with over a million visitors. The immersion ceremony for the Lalbaug Ganapati lasts for two days as the idol, approximately 18–20 feet in height, is carried from Lalbaug to the Girgaum *chowpatty* (seafront), accompanied by a frenzy of dancers, musicians and young volunteers playing the *dhol-tasha* (double-sided drums).

Earlier, both the large and small idols were made of *shadu* or clay by hereditary sculptors. Over the last few decades, plaster of Paris and fibreglass have replaced clay, though the Lalbaugcha Raja is still made traditionally by the Kambli family, many of whom have been trained at the Sir J.J. School of Art, and hold the copyright for their specific style of Ganapati sculpture. Except during the 1896 plague and the 2020 pandemic, the Ganapati festival continues to be celebrated with great fervour in the city. • RWB

Opposite:
Ganesha; rosewood, early nineteenth to mid-twentieth century, Mysore; 33.6 x 12.5 x 24.4 cm. Accessioned: 1959, purchased from the Khadi Village Industries, Bombay.
Executed in the south Indian carving style, the idol depicts a four-armed Ganesha holding a mace (denoting strength); a knotted noose (for divine knowledge and concentration); one hand holding half a tusk, raised in blessing (symbolising freedom from negativity); and the other holding a sweet (for prosperity). His *vahana* (vehicle), a rat, is carved on both sides of the pedestal, and a *kirtimukha*, an essential element of temple iconography in south India, is carved into the top of the arch over Ganesha's head.

2 THE ELEPHANTA ELEPHANT

THE lucrative overseas trade and maritime activity from the ports of Kalyan, Panvel and Thana on the western coast close to Bombay from c. 1000 BCE, made the island of Elephanta, or Gharapuri, an important site in the bay of Bombay. The island is famous for its rock-cut cave complex with towering sculptures depicting mythological episodes from the life of Lord Shiva. The cave complex is tentatively dated to the fifth to seventh century CE and was designated as a UNESCO World Heritage site in 1987. Pulakeshin II, the Chalukyan king who commissioned a significant portion of the caves, noted that the island of 'Puri'—interpreted by several noted art historians to be 'Gharapuri'—was the 'Fortune of the Western Seas'.[1] In December 1875, a special banquet was hosted in honour of the

Below:
Elephant; stone, c. sixth century CE, Elephanta Island, Bombay; 213.3 x 426.7 x 244.8 cm.

•

Opposite:
On the Island of Elephanta, William Daniell; engraving, c. 1835, London; 14.5 x 10 cm. Accessioned: 2021.

Prince of Wales, Albert Edward, inside the caves, which were illuminated with a thousand lamps.[2]

The Portuguese arrived on the island in the sixteenth century and named it 'Elefante' or 'Elephanta' after the stone sculpture of the elephant that once stood about 228.6 metres to the right of the Rajabunder, or the king's landing site, on the island. Elephants have traditionally been associated with kingship in India. The other two landing sites were Morabunder, for the Mauryan vassals of the reigning Chalukyas, and Shethbunder, which was reserved for merchants and the public. The British acquired the islands of Elephanta, Karanja and Salsette from the Portuguese in 1774.

Many European travellers to India wrote about the caves in the eighteenth and nineteenth centuries. It was observed that the sculpture of the elephant had gradually begun sinking into the ground. In 1863, the British attempted to move the elephant to England but the chains of the crane broke.[3] In 1864, when the conservation of the caves was entrusted to the Public Works Department, an engineer proposed breaking down the elephant's fragments into road metal. When George Birdwood, the curator of the erstwhile Victoria and Albert Museum, Bombay, heard about this, he enlisted the help of William Edward Frere, Director of the Kew Gardens, London, to stop such desecration, and transferred the pieces to the Victoria Gardens. This action earned the ire of some influential colonial administrators, but Birdwood put up a strong defence. He did not restore the figure of the elephant, but instead 'put earth between the more broken and corroded stones and planted flowering plants sacred to Lord Shiva'.[4]

It was under the curatorship of Cecil Burns, also the principal of the Sir J.J. School of Art, Bombay, that the reconstruction of the stone elephant took place. In 1914, it was re-erected by P.R. Cadell, the Municipal Commissioner of Bombay.[5] The stone sculpture of the elephant is among the oldest artefacts in Mumbai and the Museum. • RWB

3 HEPTANESIA RELIEF MAP

ONE of the most important preoccupations of the European powers who had territorial ambitions in India was the detailed surveying and mapping of the land. Mapping was intimately related to the colonial project of governance and was a necessary political expedient to ensure domination. It was required to demarcate borders, to assess taxes and collect tributes, as well as to secure defence positions. The Museum has an important collection of maps of Bombay, which were acquired by curator Cecil Burns during his tenure (1903–18) to create a record of the city's history and rapid transformation.

Among these is a set of relief maps titled *Heptanesia* and *Island of Bombay, 1700–1800*—the first depicts Bombay before the British took over the city from the Portuguese and the second after. The second map also shows the land fill that

took place from 1700 to 1800. 'Heptanesia' is the name given to the seven islands that comprised Bombay as recorded in the Greek mathematician Ptolemy's *Geographia*, written in the second century CE.

The *Geographia* was an attempt to accurately map the world for the Roman Empire. It mentions 'Heptanesia' or 'a cluster of seven islands', located approximately where the city of Mumbai is today.[1] King George V and Queen Mary visited the Old Bombay Exhibition that took place at the Esplanade, on December 4, 1911, where replicas of the *Heptanesia* set were shown. The exhibition committee presented the royal couple with a miniature silver replica of the set.[2]

The relief map *Heptanesia* presents the earliest configuration of the Bombay islands and depicts the territory

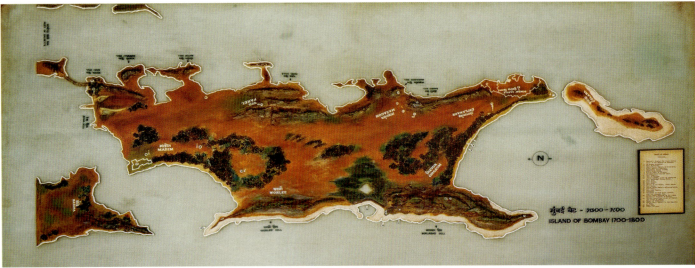

handed over by the king of Portugal to the British Crown in 1662 as part of the dowry for the Portuguese princess Catherine of Braganza, given in marriage to Charles II of England. The map shows a large part of the central area of Bombay as a shallow swamp. Several local sites are marked on the map, including temples like the *Temple of Mahalanamee* (Mahalaxmi, below). Many of Bombay's place names owe their origins to local tree groves, such as a 'clump of *Bhendees*' marked on the map, or *Thespesia populnea*, which is now Bhendi Bazaar, and a 'Tamarind Dell', now Chinchpokli.[3] The Portuguese churches at Mahim and Dadar, and the Franciscan church next to the Museum, Nossa Senhora de Gloria, built in 1632 is also marked, as are the British forts in Sion (c. 1669–77), Worli (c. 1675) and Mahim (c. 1684–85).

Juxtaposed alongside *Heptanesia* is the *Relief map of Bombay 1700–1800*, dated to 1914. Designed as a companion piece for *Heptanesia*, it was identical in scale and visual treatment, and intended to dramatise the new land mass created by the British during the eighteenth century. The British had realised the importance of Bombay's port but its swampy malarial character made settlement very difficult and it was known as a 'charnel house in which two monsoons were the age of a man'.[4] Landfill not only eliminated the swamps but also created the possibility of building a new town. Many of the hills recorded on the earlier Heptanesia map no longer exist as they were demolished to fill in the swamps. The homes of important British administrators with exotic names such as Belvedere and Vaucluse are marked and appear to be on Malabar Hill, an area that was dense forest and where the British frequently hunted. Mark House, so called as it was painted white for ships sailing into the harbour to assess their bearings, is also marked. Other landmarks reflect the multi-faith character of the city as the location for last rites are labelled for Christians, 'Mohammedans', Hindus and Parsis. The two relief maps were intended to demonstrate how much land was created from the sea and the swamp by the British and to show the significant progress that had been made in making Bombay into an important port city. • TZM

Temple of Mahalanamee (Mahalaxmi), established in 1782–85; lithograph, 1852, London: Richard Bentley; 22 x 14 cm.
Accessioned: 2021. Marked on the earlier map.
•

Opposite:
Heptanesia before 1600s (above) and **Island of Bombay, 1700– 1800** (below); plaster of Paris and pigment on fibreglass, 1913–14, made at the erstwhile V&A Museum, Bombay; 93 x 192.5 cm each.

4 FRYER'S MAP

FRYER'S Map, 1672, is one of the earliest maps of Bombay. It shows the island of Bombay and its surrounding harbour, with shallow reefs, settlements, vegetation along the coast, hills and fishing stakes, soon after it was acquired by the British. Dr John Fryer (1650–1733) was among the few scientifically trained servants of the English East India Company at the time, and his book, *A New Account of India and Persia, in Eight Letters being Nine Years' Travels*— describing his travels and experiences aboard the ship *Unity* from 1672 to 1681—was published after he returned to England in 1698. The book was described as: 'Original observations and first-hand reports on the state of the sciences in India and Persia in the late seventeenth century give a glimpse— through western eyes—of the situation there during an important period in the development of modern science.'[1] An enterprising and observant traveller, Fryer arrived in Bombay, then called Bombaim, on December 9, 1673, after stopping at Madras (Chennai), Carwar (Karwar), Surat and Goa, before moving on to Persia.

Fryer's Map of Bombay served as an illustration to the chapter titled 'Bombaim', which describes the colony, the natives and their customs and manners. The Museum's facsimile appears to be a tracing of the original, with a few omissions, additions and corrections. Fryer probably referred to an earlier map as his first map of the region appears strangely accurate and precise. The Portuguese, who preceded the British in Bombay, were experts in making maps. Portuguese sailing maps, known as *roteiros*, provided sailing and navigation information such as charts, data of winds, currents, landmarks, etc., and had been available in English translation since 1598. They were a must for every seafaring East Indiaman, as the British ships were called. The Museum's map differs from the original in the style of writing (the norm of an elongated 'ʃ' being replaced by the more modern 's') and the omission of certain landmarks.

Several important sites are indicated on the Museum's map. Canora Island (Kanheri), where the earliest rock-cut Buddhist caves are located; Fryer's description of the caves alludes to the assumptions made by the Portuguese at the time that King Alexander cut out the Kanheri structures from a solid rock. Basein (Bassein) City, a former fortified stronghold of the Portuguese, is marked on the original map with a church and on the facsimile as a plain structure without a cross. Also marked are Bandura (Bandra) with the nearby 'Aogoda' or 'Agoada' i.e. a place with fresh water, which was a strategic outpost of the Portuguese armies that managed the trade route in northern Bombay; Salset (Salsette) or *shashti* meaning sixty-six villages which were home to the original inhabitants of Bombay such as the Kolis (fishermen), Kunbis (farmers),

and East Indians, among others; and Trombay, now the site of India's first nuclear reactor, set up in 1985. On the Bombay Island are marked: Mayem (Mahim); Worlee (Worli); Sciam (Sion); Salt Pond, where the salt pans still exist; the Great Inlet or the Great Breach from where sea gushed in at high tide; and Mendham's Point, the only English cemetery till 1765, now the site of the Regal Theatre. Some of the other islands marked are: Butcher Island (Jawahar Dweep), now used to store crude oil by the Bombay Port Trust; Elephanta; Henry-Kenry (Underi-Khanderi), now called Jaidurg and Kanhoji Angre islands respectively. The latter is named after the famous Maratha admiral who fought the Siddis and the European powers.

Fryer describes the physical and social characteristics in great detail, estimating the island's population as 60,000 in 1673, and the island's circumference as 20 miles.[2] He notes that the name Bombaim suggests 'Boon Bay' as the islands served as a granary for the Portuguese, supplying plenty of rice and corn to feed their 'armadas'. Describing the town of low, thatched houses, he says, 'in which confusedly live the English, Portuguese, Topazees, Gentues, Moors, Cooly Christians, most Fishermen.'[3]

Fryer's account of his nine-year voyage provides an insight into the 'Moral, Natural, and Artificial Estate of Those Countries: Namely, Of their Government, Religion, Laws, Customs. Of the Soil, Climates, Seasons, Health, Diseases. Of the Animals, Vegetables, Minerals, Jewels. Of their Housing, Clothing, Manufactures, Trades, Commodities. And of the Coins, Weights, and Measures, used in the Principal Places of Trade in those Parts'.[4]

In the seventeenth century, a large number of physicians and surgeons were employed by the East India Company to provide medical assistance to soldiers and officials of the company. Fryer sailed with a fleet of ten ships commissioned as men-of-war since the British were in open conflict with the Dutch at the time. He served as a surgeon in Surat and Bombay and was required to carry out statistical inquiries, and is credited as the first person to record the curative powers of citrus fruit on scurvy. After eight years in the east, he returned to England in August 1682.

James Douglas, in his 1893 book *Bombay and Western India*, points out that the Mahim woods and the fishing stakes in the harbour were at that time precisely where they were on Fryer's map, showing that not much had changed in the intervening 200 years![5] • **AS**

Fryer's Map of Bombay, 1672; facsimile, watercolour and ink on paper, 1909–12, made at the erstwhile V&A Museum, Bombay; 35.5 x 25 cm.

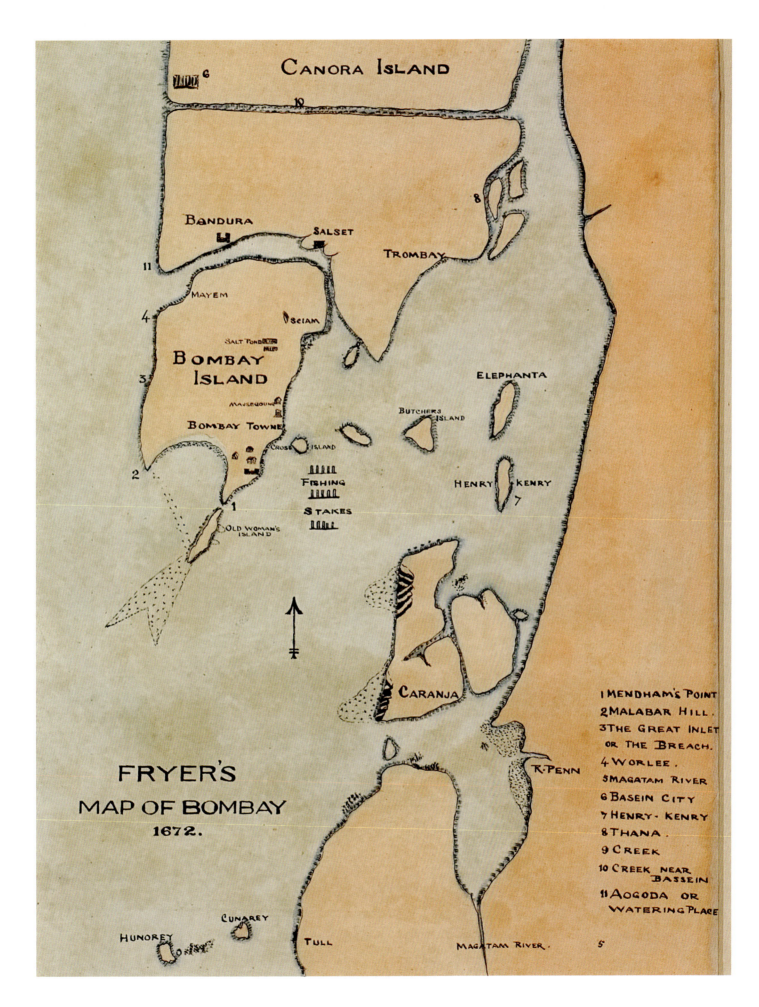

CANORA ISLAND

BANDURA

SALSET

TROMBAY

8

11

MAYEM

4

SCIAM

SALT POND

BOMBAY
ISLAND

3

ELEPHANTA

MASSEGOUM

BUTCHERS
ISLAND

BOMBAY TOWNE

CROSS ISLAND

2

FISHING

HENRY KENRY

7

1

STAKES

OLD WOMAN'S
ISLAND

CARANJA

R. PENN

FRYER'S
MAP OF BOMBAY
1672.

1 MENDHAM'S POINT
2 MALABAR HILL.
3 THE GREAT INLET
OR THE BREACH.
4 WORLEE.
5 MAGATAM RIVER
6 BASEIN CITY
7 HENRY - KENRY
8 THANA.
9 CREEK
10 CREEK NEAR
BASSEIN
11 AOGODA OR
WATERING PLACE

CUNAREY

HUNOREY

TULL

MAGATAM RIVER.

5

5 BOMBAY CASTLE

BOMBAY CASTLE was the East India Company's first government house built in Bombay in the late 1660s, and the first of the many grand structures that signify the city's early history, though little of it remains today. The English settlement developed with the Castle as its nucleus, on land adjoining the harbour. A fortification wall was built around the settlement, which was completed and guarded by 1715. In the Museum model, the walls of the Bombay fort are missing, which implies that this is an early view of the Castle, from the late seventeenth century.

The model is replicated from a print of the Bombay Castle in Phillipus Baldaeus' publication, *A true and exact description of the most celebrated East-India coasts of Malabar and Coromandel as also of the isle of Ceylon,* published in Dutch in 1672 and in English in 1703. Baldaeus was a minister with the Dutch East India Company, officially the United East India Company (VOC or Vereenigde Oostindische Compagnie). Both the Dutch and the English editions are in the Museum's collection and are among the oldest books on the history of Bombay. The print is titled *The English Fort of Bombay Towards the Water Side*. The model in the Museum collection is a close but not an exact copy. In the image, a prominent English flag is seen.

Below:
Bombay Castle; plaster of Paris, pigments, wood, metal, 1932–33, made at the erstwhile V&A Museum, Bombay; 34.5 x 54 cm. Accessioned: 2021.

•

Opposite, above:
Northwest View of the Fort of Bombay; William Westall, aquatint, c. 1826, London; 37 x 29.5 cm. Accessioned: 2021.

•

Opposite, below:
The English Fort of Bombay (interior and exterior views); Phillipus Baldaeus, reissued by A. and J. Churchill, engraving, 1747–52, London; 37.5 x 31.5 cm. Accessioned: 2021.

The English Fort of Bombay

The English Fort of Bombay.
towards y water side.

The most striking feature of Bombay's physical appearance at the time were its many thousand coconut, brab and date palms.[1] The earliest records refer to the Castle being in the possession of the famous Portuguese botanist, antiquarian and physician Garcia da Orta. In 1534, Bassein was signed over to the Portuguese by the sultan of Gujarat. The king of Portugal granted da Orta the island of Bombaim around 1563. His double-storeyed Manor House or Quinta stood just behind the present Town Hall. The area was shaded with trees, a natural laboratory for da Orta's work as a botanist. His garden delighted many visitors to the city in the sixteenth century.[2]

The Portuguese Manor House gradually gave way to the British Castle. The English got possession of the island in 1661, when Catherine of Braganza married Charles II of England, bringing the island as her dowry. After prolonged disputes, the British finally succeeded in taking over all the islands in 1665, when the 'Treaty of Surrender and Delivery' was signed in the then largest existing structure, the Manor House, which at the time belonged to Senhora de Miranda or Donna Ignes de Miranda. She was the widow of Don Rodrigo de Monsanto, and was addressed as the 'Lady of the Island'. The British chose to fortify it and renamed it Bombay Castle.

Three years later, the Crown handed over the islands to the British East India Company 'at a farm rent of ten pounds payable on September 30 in each year', thus assuring Bombay's future as a trading centre. As an incentive to future settlers, a clause in the royal charter stated that 'all persons born in Bombay were to be accounted natural subjects of England.'[3] One of the few surviving remnants of the Portuguese period is a sundial. It is 10 feet high and embellished with gargoyles, and with carved heads of men, monsters and animals intermingled with leaves towering high above the dial. The marking of the hours is still distinctly visible. This is the oldest sculptured artefact in Bombay belonging to the period of Portuguese occupation.

A brab or *tadgolla* tree located at Bombay Castle was used as a landmark by ships entering the harbour. The Brab Tree Bastion (in the Bombay Castle) was named after the 70- to 80-foot tall *tadgolla* trees that could be seen from the harbour.[4] Gerald Aungier (1640–77), whom many consider the man who transformed Bombay into an important town, was the first British resident in the Castle. From then on, it served as the government house for the first twenty governors of Bombay.

Attacks on Surat by the Marathas and continuing dissension with the Mughal governor led Aungier to shift the Company's trading headquarters from Surat to Bombay. Predicting that 'it is a city which by God's assistance is intended to be built', Aungier laid out a town plan in the vicinity of Bombay Castle, established a mint, built a small hospital, opened a printing press and imported English ladies to marry the early British settlers in Bombay. He improved the fortifications and recommended the creation of a walled town. This suggestion of an enclosed town, however, was only implemented some decades later during the governorship of Charles Boone. To expand trade in Bombay, Aungier encouraged mercantile communities to migrate to the islands. He guaranteed them religious freedom and also permitted them to build residential complexes within the fort walls.

Within a few years of the East India Company takeover of Bombay, a bustling trading town grew around the Castle. Threatened by pirates, the Dutch and the Portuguese, as well as the growing Maratha power in the neighbourhood, the East India Company authorities encircled this scraggly group of dwellings within a wall in 1665. This came to be known as the 'Fort'.

In the early eighteenth century, the Castle was described as a neat, regular fortification that was well governed, gunned and manned. Like all castles, this one was fitted with dungeons, dark vault-like spaces just high enough for a man to stand upright in, and with no openings except the entrance. By 1710, the Castle was provided with a strong magazine, quarters for soldiers and two tanks large enough to provide water supply for 1,000 people for twenty months. The arrival of Governor Charles Boone in 1715 gave further impetus to the growth of the settlement. By the following year, Boone had expanded and erected the Bombay Fort by executing Aungier's proposed plan of a walled town, with bastions extending from the hillock of Dongri to Mendham's Point. Six gates regulated traffic in and out of the structure, and the Castle stood between two of the three seaward gates. He enlarged the old dockyard in the Fort, established a marine force and encouraged construction of several buildings, including St. Thomas' Cathedral.

Through the eighteenth century the town of Bombay suffered from rampant organised crimes including looting and arson at dockyards, warehouses and shops. Nights were particularly unsafe. A Bhandari militia, recruited from the land-owning community of toddy-tappers, was charged with patrolling within and outside the Fort limits. They assembled near the Church Gate for their daily briefing in the presence of a British officer.[5] By 1811, the Bombay police was formalised and this lowered the crime rate and enabled the town to trade and prosper. When the Fort walls came down in 1862-63, the governor's residence moved to Byculla and the Castle became a storehouse for the British army's arsenal. Post Indian independence, the Bombay Castle was renamed Indian Naval Service (INS) *Angre*, after the Maratha naval chief Kanhoji Angre who had challenged the British during the governorship of Charles Boone. • AS

GROSE'S PLAN
OF
BOMBAY
1750.

REFERENCES.

A THE FORT.   11 BURING GROUND
1 FLAG STAFF   NEAR MENDHAMS
                   BASTION, 12 THE APPOLLO GAT
2 THE TANK BASTION 13 CHURCH GATE
3 THE GOVERNOR'S   14 THE CHURCH
      HOUSE   15 THE BAZAR GAT
4 THE BUNDER OR   16 THE FOUNDRY &
COMPANY'S WARE HOUSES SMITHS SHOPS.
5 THE BUNDER PIER 17 MANDEVIE OR CUS
6 THE HOUSE OF THE   TOM HOUSE
  SUPERINTENDENT OF
  THE MARINE & MARINE 18 THE TANK HOUSE
      STORE HOUSE 19 THE MINT
7 THE HOSPITAL &
  DOCTOR'S HOUSE 21 LOW WATER-MA
8 THE MARINE YARD 21 LOW WATER-MA
9 THE DOCKS.   22 THE BAY
10 ROYAL BASTION 23 BARRACKS.

VILLE DE BOMBAY.

FRENCH PLAN
OF
BOMBAY FORT
1758.

Top: *Grose's Plan of Bombay, 1750*; facsimile, watercolour and ink on paper, 1909–18, made at the erstwhile V&A Museum, Bombay; 25 x 35.5 cm.

Above: *French Plan of Bombay Fort, 1758*; facsimile, watercolour and ink on paper, 1909–12, made at the erstwhile V&A Museum, Bombay; 25 x 35.5 cm.

GROSE'S PLAN OF BOMBAY

The Bombay Castle, the East India Company's first government house in Bombay, is the subject of this detailed map. It shows the fortified town on the island of Bombay, which was developed around the Bombay Castle in the late seventeenth century. The walls of the Fort, completed in 1715, are illustrated, as are important landmarks and streets. The plan is restricted to the main fortified town, even though there was already significant building activity and life beyond the walls by the mid-eighteenth century.

John Henry Grose was a writer and covenanted employee of the East India Company. He came to Bombay in 1750 on one of the East Indiamen and published his account *A Voyage to the East Indies* in two parts in 1772. The plan is invaluable, for every street within the walls is laid down and accompanied by a scale in feet. It is based on a similar map published in the *Gazetteer of the Bombay City and Island* (Volume 1), 1909. • **AS**

6 CHHATRAPATI SHIVAJI MAHARAJ'S ESCAPE

THE Marathas presented the biggest challenge to British domination especially in western, central and southern India. Chhatrapati Shivaji Maharaj (r. 1674–80) was the founder of the Maratha kingdom in the seventeenth century in the Deccan region. He engaged in numerous battles and signed treaties with the Mughal Empire, the Adil Shahi and Qutub Shahi states, as well as the British and other European powers to benefit his domains. He captured and constructed fortresses and formed a strong army to expand the Maratha kingdom and strengthen his rule. The epicentre of his activities was the present-day Pune and Konkan regions.

The seventeenth century witnessed a struggle between the Marathas and the Bijapur rulers for mastery over the Konkan littoral. Chhatrapati Shivaji Maharaj's naval commander, Kanhoji Angre, succeeded in occupying and fortifying Khanderi, a desolate small island at the tip of the Bombay harbour in 1679.[1] Following the death of Chhatrapati Shivaji Maharaj in 1680, his son Sambhaji Raje continued his father's legacy of consolidating the Deccan Empire. As Mughal power waned a vacuum arose that the Marathas attempted to fill through diplomatic endeavours as well as military tactics. The East India Company's Bombay factory, which was in the middle of Maratha territory, had no option but to maintain peaceful and cordial relations with the Marathas to carry out its business unhindered.

Chhatrapati Shivaji Maharaj not only threatened the British but also engaged in a protracted guerrilla war with the Mughal Emperor Aurangzeb who was determined to expand the Mughal Empire and subdue the Deccan. However, Shivaji Maharaj proved to be invincible in the Deccan. It was only after many encounters and through a ruse that he was finally captured and imprisoned by the Mughals. His escape is one the Marathas' most famous legends, which has been depicted in a diorama in the Museum collection. Chhatrapati Shivaji Maharaj is shown in captivity with his son Sambhaji Raje, his close confidant Hiroji Farzand (a minister in his court) and Raja Ram Singh, the son of Mirza Raja Jai Singh, the commander of the Mughal army. The scene is set in the Mughal fort at Agra, where Chhatrapati Shivaji Maharaj and his son were imprisoned on the orders of the Mughal Emperor Aurangzeb.

Legend has it that Mirza Raja Jai Singh and Emperor Aurangzeb invited Chhatrapati Shivaji Maharaj to Agra in 1666.[2] Mirza Raja Jai Singh assured him security and treatment in accord with his royal status. Chhatrapati Shivaji Maharaj suspected the Emperor's intentions but accepted the invitation. Both Chhatrapati and his son Sambhaji Raje were taken hostage and imprisoned at Agra Fort for many months. As can be observed in the diorama, Chhatrapati Shivaji Maharaj was allocated quarters in the royal wing and given treatment befitting his exalted status. While under imprisonment, he gathered intelligence on the movements of his enemies by befriending the Mughal Emperor's subordinates. He feigned illness and after his 'recovery', expressed a desire to pay his respects to and thank the family's patron goddess Sri Bhavani by distributing sweets and money, as was the tradition. Raja Ram Singh agreed and sweets were prepared in vast quantities to be distributed to his doctors and attendants as well as all the people of the fort and the nearby villages. Every day two enormous baskets of sweets were carried out of his chambers. The guards checked the baskets for the first few days but soon let the attendants pass unchecked. Seizing the opportunity, Chhatrapati Shivaji and Sambhaji Raje escaped, hiding in the baskets. Two of the Maharaj's courtiers dressed in their clothes lest the guards and attendants realise that they had escaped. Ram Singh is believed to have aided in Shivaji's escape in order to restore his father's honour, who had pledged the Maratha chief's safety. He was held accountable and, for his complicity, was stripped of his rank and banished from the court. The diorama captures the strategic moment of the planning for Chhatrapati Shivaji Maharaj's daring escape.

Sirdar Bagwe, who created the piece, was a well-known architect and sculptor who had made several dioramas for the Museum. The inspiration for this scene was a painting titled *Imprisonment at Agra* by Archibald Herman Muller, which was commissioned in 1930 by Balasaheb Pant Pratinidhi, the ruler of Aundh (Satara), an important state in the Deccan and the Bombay Presidency. Balasaheb published several illustrated books with paintings on the life of Chhatrapati Shivaji Maharaj. He commissioned several distinguished artists, including S.L. Haldankar, K.R. Ketkar, N.R. Sardesai, Rao Bahadur M.V. Dhurandhar, M.R. Chaphalkar, A.H. Muller, to create these artworks. He himself painted some vignettes.

This is one of the most famous stories of Chhatrapati Shivaji Maharaj's life and Sirdar Bagwe has enhanced the impression of glory and victory by painting the whole diorama in gold. Shivaji Maharaj is revered in Maharashtra and occupies a prominent position in modern India's history as a symbol of resistance to oppression. His example motivated people during the resistance to British rule in the nineteenth and early twentieth centuries. • HK

Opposite:
Chhatrapati Shivaji Maharaj's Imprisonment at Agra, Sirdar S.L. Bagwe; clay and plaster of Paris, 1934, Bombay; 148 x 230 x 85 cm. Accessioned: 1934-35.
•
Right:
Imprisonment at Agra, A.H. Muller; print, *Chhatrapati Shivaji Maharaj Album II*, Shrimant Balasaheb Pant Pratinidhi, 1930, Satara: R.K. Kirloskar; 29 x 22.5 cm. Accessioned: 1930–50.

7 PESHWA MAP

IN the latter half of the eighteenth century, as Mughal power waned, the British and Marathas vied for power on the western coast of India. Maps were an important instrument of martial strategy, and the British were adept at map-making. However, this Maratha map, which has a unique perspective and informality, reveals that map-making was yet a nascent art for the Marathas. It was probably made before the outbreak of the First Anglo-Maratha War (1775–82) and dates to the Maratha ascendency in the 1770s, after the Third Battle of Panipat (1761), which was a turning point in Maratha history.

The map shows Bombay and the surrounding areas, including Panvel, Kalyan and Dharavi. The upper half of the map is occupied by the landmass, with Bombay Fort placed slightly off-centre. The lower half shows the Arabian Sea. The map possesses no legend. The most striking feature is the delicate delineation of the boats and fish. The forts and landmass, on the other hand, appear to be hastily drawn. The names of locations are written in Marathi, in the Devanagari script; however, the cartouche is in English. It has no inscription apart from the English one, which could have been a later addition.

While the purpose of the map is not known, it would be fair to hypothesise that it was intended as a study of the landforms and waterways surrounding the British fort at Bombay in preparation for an attack. The map shows a definite influence of British cartography, as by then they had extensively mapped out Bombay and the rest of India. This map is on a smaller scale, as was the convention when creating maps of large areas. It is not drawn to scale and leaves out identifying features and landmarks, except the Maratha bastions.

The prominent use of boats and fish in the waterways surrounding the islands were conventions employed in Maratha map-making.[1] The fish indicate tidal limits, and those depicted show the map-maker's familiarity with the types found in the region. The single- and double-mast crafts, beautifully drawn with unfurled sails, indicate routes employed by them. The larger of the crafts appears to be flying a forked orange flag, the standard of the Marathas. They reveal an understanding of the sailing crafts then seen in the harbour. Their proportion, relative to the map and the land, were a matter of taste, and depended largely on the space available to the maker.

The Maratha bastions are depicted as massive buildings on top of the hills, all flying the Maratha standard. This map identifies five centres: (from top left) Gadi Kalyan (Kalyan Fort) marked in red; Belapur Sarkar (Belapur Fort) situated next to Panvel creek; Karnala Sarkar located near the Bandar Panvel (Panvel Harbour); Kille Devgad Sarkar (Deogarh Fort) situated at the bottom towards the sea; and an unidentified one. These points are located strategically at the mouths of the waterways or on headlands. The map-maker also identified a few forts using the accepted convention of a square with circles at the corners: (from top left) Parshik on the mainland and Sashti (possibly Thana fort) which was the capital of Salsette; and Yeshwant Gad (fort) on Salsette Island. On the Bombay Island, Mahim and Mumbai Ingrez Fort (English Bombay Fort) are marked; 'Kos' written in the centre of the two signifies the distance from a certain point. The small landmass in the harbour, marked Ingrez, is possibly the island of Elephanta, which was conquered by the Marathas in 1738 and came into the possession of the British in 1774. According to the convention for forts and royal palaces, they were depicted in variable sizes and in different colours based on their importance. In identifying different areas in Bombay, the map also pointed out the various authorities ruling at the time, and their strongholds in forts strategically located around Bombay.

The water, which is painted with a blue wash, is lacking the customary basket-weave pattern that the Maratha map-makers were fond of.[2] The waterways, while not being accurate for navigational purposes, are in correct sequence and, with the tidal information, could have also served as a trade or fishing map.

Most early maps were entirely pictorial; text was later used to indicate ownership and distance. In the absence of any guiding principles, the map-maker would arrange the pictorial elements according to his understanding. Like most Hindu maps from western India and the Maratha maps of the time, this one too is oriented with east on top as it was made facing the sun.[3]

In keeping with tradition, the map is painted using a wash technique on paper, with natural pigments derived from vegetable dyes—ochre, blue, yellow-grey, brownish-red and red. This map is a facsimile of the original, specially prepared for the Museum in 1909–12. The original map is in a private collection. • AS

Map of Bombay and District Prepared for the Peshwa by the Peshwa's Agent in Bombay, About 1770; facsimile, watercolour and ink on paper, 1909-12, made at the erstwhile V&A Museum, Bombay; 25 x 35.5 cm.
The Peshwa referred to in the map is Madhavrao I (1745–72). Most of the important Maratha strongholds of the area are indicated on the map: (from left to right) Ghod Bandar, Dharavi (island), Praant Sashti (District Thane), Parsik, Bandar Colaba, Gadi Kalyan, Sashti (fort), Yeshwant Gad (fort), Chowky Vandre Sarkar (Bandra), Mahim, Ingrez (probably Elephanta Island), Belapur Sarkar, Mumbai Ingrez (Bombay Fort), Bandar Panvel, Karnala Sarkar, Bandar Aavade and Kille Devgad Sarkar.

MAP OF BOMBAY AND DISTRICT PREPARED
FOR THE PESHWA BY THE PESHWA'S AGENT
IN BOMBAY ABOUT 1770.

8 BOATS IN BOMBAY HARBOUR

MUMBAI's deep water harbour, crowded with boats and ships of all sizes and shapes, holds a singular place in the history of the city and defines its identity. Numerous early travellers have written about the dramatic beauty of the harbour as well as its strategic position for trade and naval security. An engraving titled *Fishing Boats in the Monsoon, Northern Part of Bombay Harbour* by William Clarkson Stanfield, reproduced in the book *Scenery, Costumes and Architecture, Chiefly on the Western Side of India* by Captain Robert Grindlay, captures the harbour's picturesque beauty that transfixed the imagination of visitors. It depicts the approaching monsoon from a point on Malabar Hill, near the Parsi Tower of Silence. The hills and the fort in the distance, along with the fishermen at sea, pulling in nets, evoke a Turner-esque landscape.

The large boat with open sails on the right, riding the crest of a wave, bears a resemblance to the model of a boat in the

Museum's impressive collection of sea crafts. This is possibly a *machwa*, a common fishing boat native to the western coast of India, from Kathiawar down to Ratnagiri. These boats were built at Sewri, Bassein and Uran. The term *machwa* is colloquially used to describe a variety of boats, therefore, records of *machwa* are inconsistent. Boats classified in this type varied in size and functionality, and were used both for fishing as well as for trade.[1] *Machwas* were used by the Kolis, the original inhabitants of the island, and later were adapted by other communities for various purposes.

The geographical location and accessibility of Bombay's harbour by land and sea boosted trade and commerce. Under the Portuguese occupation in the early sixteenth century, trading in Bombay was limited to few commodities like dried fish, salt and coconuts with neighbouring coastal towns. In the next century, with the

Fishing Boats in the Monsoon, Northern Part of Bombay Harbour; coloured aquatint, 1844, London; 39.3 x 29.2 cm. Accessioned: 2013. Reproduced from a hand-coloured engraving by William Clarkson Stanfield for Stanfield. R. Grindlay, *Scenery Costumes and Architecture, Chiefly on the Western Side of India*. London: Smith, Elter, & Co., 1826–30.

Left:
Kotia; wood, cloth and thread, late nineteenth to early twentieth century, Bombay; 86.2 x 60.8 x 28.3 cm. Accessioned: 1908–09.

•

Top:
Boats in Bombay Harbour Display; wood, cloth and thread, late nineteenth to early twentieth century, Bombay. On view at the Kamalnayan Bajaj Gallery, Dr. Bhau Daji Lad Museum.

•

Above:
Kotia (detail of the parrot-shaped bow).

Top, left:
Battil; wood, cloth and thread, late nineteenth
to early twentieth century, Bombay; 74 x 66.4
x 17 cm. Accessioned: 1908-09.

•

Top, right:
Machwa; wood, cloth and thread, late
nineteenth to early twentieth century,
Bombay; 81 x 117 x 20.5 cm. Accessioned:
1908-09.

•

Left:
Boats in the Bombay Harbour; wood, cloth
and thread, late nineteenth to early twentieth
century, Bombay. Accessioned: 1908-09.

•

Opposite:
View of the Bombay Harbour; glass negative,
late nineteenth to early twentieth century,
Bombay; 25.4 x 30 cm. Accessioned:
1903–20.

advent of the British, foreign trade greatly increased. Local merchants traded in various articles, from salt to betelnut, rice, ivory, lead, sword blades and other European goods.[2] Describing the port facilities of the city, Gerald Aungier, the second Governor of Bombay (from 1669 to 1677) declared, 'The great bay or port is certainly the fairest, largest and securest in all these parts of India, where a hundred sail of tall ships may ride all the year safe with good anchorage'.[3] By the late eighteenth century, Bombay received, among others, imports of pearls, silk, dates and fruits from the Persian Gulf; coffee, gold and medicinal material from Arabia; tea, sugar and porcelain from China; and ivory and enslaved people from Africa. Exports included cotton, precious metal, pepper and Surat textiles. Bombay also traded by sea with other parts of the country, sending grain, vegetables, poultry and fish.

Bombay played a significant role as a shipbuilding centre from 1735 until the launch of steamships in the next century. Renowned Parsi master shipbuilder Lowji Nusserwanji Wadia of Surat is credited for this development. Under the East India Company and Lowji Wadia's charge, the first dry dock, Government Dockyard, was constructed in 1748. The port was further extended in 1875, with the construction of the first wet dock, built by David Sassoon & Co. In the years that followed, Bombay opened more dry and wet ports of increased dimensions and berthing facilities.

In peak seasons, it is recorded that sailing vessels of nearly every kind docked at the harbour, including *baggalas* from the Persian Gulf, *kotias* from Kutch and Sind, and *battelas* from the Konkan.[4] The harbour in the nineteenth and early twentieth centuries hosted a number of different types of boats, models of which are in the Museum's collection. These include crafts like the *machwa*, tony and jolly boats, which were primarily used to fish, but also carried cargo and passengers from Bombay to Salsette, Thane and the mainland. There are larger models of ships that could withstand harsh weather and were used for long-distance travel.[5] A prime example of this is the *kotia*. The *kotia*, although smaller than its Arabian variants (*baggala*, *gunjo* or *dhow*), was well equipped to travel long distances and was ideal for trade. The *kotia* can be distinguished from the Arabian variants by its parrot-head design at the bow.

The *battil* boat is another interesting Indian variant of the Arab *sambuk*. Similar to the *kotia*, it is a craft that was used primarily by native traders who journeyed to the Persian Gulf, Aden, Yemen and even as far as Zanzibar in Africa.[6] These models were acquired by the Museum in the early twentieth century. A large showcase was fitted with the boats and included miniature clay models of passengers of various nationalities, seaman and fishermen and a diorama with large waves, that created the impression of being at sea. It was created by students of the Sir J.J. School of Art under the guidance of curator Cecil Burns, to enliven the display.[7] • **LM**

9 THOMAS DICKINSON'S MAP

IN the early nineteenth century, the East India Company was consolidating its commercial interests and governing systems in the Bombay Presidency. Land revenue was the major source of income and this necessitated the demarcation of land holdings. The early maps of Bombay were drawn from the perspective of the harbour and limited to the Fort walls. After a devastating fire in February 1803, over 400 buildings needed to be rebuilt and property titles had to be established through a cadastral survey.[1]

Without any cultivable land for agrarian purposes, the toddy trees were targeted for taxes and excise duties by the Bombay Government. The Revenue Survey began in 1811 to ascertain the number of coconut, brab, date and betel nut trees, their quality and uses, and names of the proprietors. The same year, an increase in taxes on oarts (coconut/brab groves) and distilled toddy led to riots by the Bhandari community who owned the oarts or were employed to tap *tadi-madi* (*tadi* is alcohol tapped from a brab tree, and *madi* is made from distilled coconut water).[2] The headmen appointed by the Government to oversee the revenue collection and yield were from the community and were threatened with expulsion from their caste if they didn't join the riots to prevent surveys of the plots. The issue was complex as property transfers were a root cause of corruption, and often the English Sheriff was involved, thus making it difficult for the Government to curb the riots. The situation was resolved by discontinuing the practice of paying the village headmen and making the Excise Inspector responsible for collecting taxes, increasing the Government's control.

In 1812, Captain Thomas Dickinson, a Company engineer, took over the survey.[3] A map was made to extend the survey operations in Bombay and define the boundaries of the East India Company's holdings as well as private properties. This detailed map defined the cartographic representation of Bombay for over a century.[4] Land measurements, soil types, and trees were recorded and revenue was assessed for each holding. Inadequate or outdated ownership documents and multiple forms of tenure often caused delays. In 1821, Lt. Tate, who took over the survey from Captain Dickinson, recruited Indians to assist him with the primary documentation.

Completed in August 1827, the survey detailed maps of the Fort, the old and new Town of Bombay, Colaba, Malabar Hill, Cumballa Hill and Mazgaon. The maps were drawn on a scale of 40':1' or 100':1' depending on the use of land for agricultural purposes, oarts, rice fields, salt pans, garden plots or buildings. The rules for the assessment and collection of land revenue passed in 1827 formed the basis of the Bombay City Land Revenue Act of 1876, last amended in 1960. • RWB

LIMITS OF THE TOWN OF BOMBAY

In an effort to demarcate the extent of the town, in 1794, Governor George Dick directed the Civil Architect Lt. John Cunliffe to set up stone markers announcing the boundary limits of the town of Bombay. In 1926, the Museum acquired two stone markers of the 'Limits of the Town of Bombay' that were found at Bhendi Bazaar in 1876. They were located at the Memonwada Road–Parel Road Junction in Bhendi Bazaar.

In 1813, the Government tried to reduce the limits of the town up to the walls of the Fort, but eventually it was extended from Back Bay to Parel Road.[1] By 1864, the limits of Bombay were further redefined to include 'the island of Bombay and Colaba and Old Woman's Island'. The Municipal Corporation was established in 1865 and ten wards were created. Mandvi, Umarkhadi and the surrounding areas were designated as the 'Old Town', while Bhuleshwar and the area up to Byculla was known as the 'New Town'.[2] • RWB

Limits of the Town of Bombay; stone, c. 1784, Bombay; 65 x 32.9 x 31.5 cm. Accessioned: 1926.

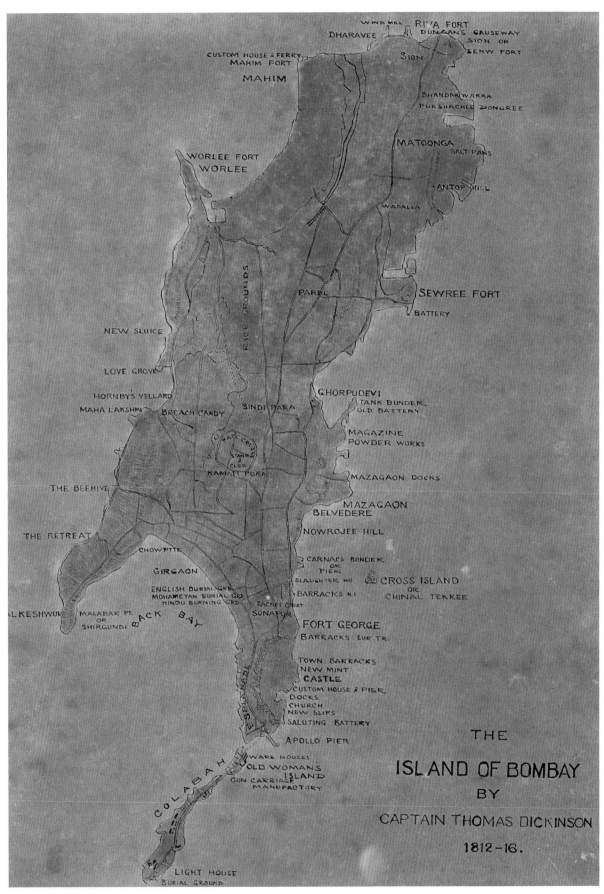

The Island of Bombay by Captain Thomas Dickinson, 1812-16; facsimile, watercolour and ink on paper, 1909–12, made at the erstwhile V&A Museum, Bombay; 35.5 x 25 cm.
Based on 'The Island of Bombay reduced from the original survey undertaken by order of the Government by Captain Thomas Dickinson in the years 1812-16', drawn by J.B. Jervis.

Queen Victoria (1819-1901), unknown sculptor; marble, early twentieth century, made at the Sir J.J. School of Art, Bombay; 75.5 x 46.5 x 46 cm. Accessioned: 1948-49.

•

Opposite, left:
Queen Victoria; glass negative, early twentieth century, Bombay; 30 x 25.4 cm. Accessioned: 1903–20.

•

Opposite, right:
Queen Victoria, Matthew Noble; marble, 1869, London; 273 x 166 x 183.9 cm. Accessioned: 1965.

STATUES serve as more than memorials to a person; they demonstrate how political regimes validate their rule in the public domain. The British Crown symbolically manifested its might and supremacy in its colonies through an active programme of architectural embellishment, of which sculpture and statuary were an integral part. These were commissioned to mark important events, and as sites of celebration. The transfer of power to the British Crown in 1858 and the Queen's Declaration symbolised a new era for educated Indians who viewed this as an opportunity for economic prosperity and social change.[1] Several statues commemorating Queen Victoria were erected for public display around India. The statue on the Museum's east lawn, possibly one of the first statues of the monarch, was earlier placed strategically on the busy Esplanade Road so it was almost impossible to miss.

The bust of Queen Victoria in the central atrium of the Museum, behind Prince Albert and facing the grand staircase, was originally housed in the Bombay Corporation Hall and was moved to the Museum in 1948-49 along with eight other busts from the Hall, including those of Sir Frank Souter, Sir Charles Ollivant and Dr Thomas Blaney. It was created at the Sir J.J. School of Art. The sculpture has no inscriptions on it, so the date and the sculptor are unknown. Museum records do not indicate who made it or even who donated it to the Corporation. However, in *The Story of Sir J.J. School of Art*, there is a mention in a photograph of the artist A.X. Trindade, who seems to be inspecting a beautiful bust of the Queen Empress.[2]

In 1947, after Independence, there were widespread revolts in the country against symbols of the British Empire. The Bombay Municipal Corporation passed a resolution in November 1947 to remove the busts of British officers from the Corporation Hall.[3] In 1966, the Museum rejected a proposal by Kilachand Devchand to donate a bust of the Prime Minister of England in 1880, William Ewart Gladstone. The letter from the curator declining the offer stated that eight statues from the Corporation Hall had already been moved to the Museum 'because of the rising tide of nationalism in India at the time.'

The letter also references the damage to the statues of colonial officers and figures in Bombay, which were damaged on August 12, 1965, during the Samyukta Maharashtra movement. A number of these statues were removed from their original locations and shifted to the Museum's east lawn, adjacent to the Museum building. These include the statues of the former British Governor-Generals of India, Lord Wellesley and Lord Cornwallis. The large sculpture of Queen Victoria, commissioned by Khanderao II Gaekwad, the Maharaja of Baroda, and sculpted by British sculptor

Matthew Noble in 1869, that was once situated at the junction of Esplanade (Mahatma Gandhi Road) and Mayo Road (Karmaveer Bhaurao Patil Marg), was also moved to the Museum garden. Originally, the statue was intended to sit on a terrace abutting the Museum as a complement to the statue of Prince Albert within the building. It was enclosed by an ornate marble canopy and stood on a pedestal. The Queen was portrayed in regal clothes, sitting on a throne and holding the crown jewels in her hands.

The statue, as it now stands, carries few traces of the crown jewels, and the Queen's face bears marks of the damage from 1965. The canopy and the pedestal of the sculpture were separated. The canopy was acquired by Vijaypat Singhania, the chairman emeritus of the Raymond Group and former Sheriff of Mumbai, for his garden. At the time of writing, it is displayed outside the Raymond showroom at Breach Candy.

In 1896, there had been an isolated attempt to disfigure the statue. It was found tarred, with a pair of sandals tied around its neck. A year later, on the day of Queen Victoria's Diamond Jubilee, brothers Damodar Chapekar and Balkrishna Chapekar were arrested on the charge of murdering two British officers. They also confessed tarring the statue. Both these acts of rebellion were against the British administration's treatment of Indians by Col. Rand, who headed the Plague Committee during the Bombay epidemic.

The statue was informally unveiled for Queen Victoria's Diamond Jubilee celebrations (after the tarring incident), and locals gathered around it with garlands, flags and banners to celebrate her reign. Conversely, it was also the monument that was most severely damaged post-Independence. • LM

Prince Albert (1819–61),
Matthew Noble; marble,
1864, London; 225 x 97 cm.
Accessioned: 1872.

11 PRINCE ALBERT

THE monumental marble sculpture of Prince Albert, consort of Queen Victoria, in the atrium of the Museum is the first artefact the visitor encounters. It is the only statue of Prince Albert in India. It was commissioned by David Sassoon and made by the eminent sculptor Matthew Noble in 1864 for the then princely sum of £3,000. It took five years to complete, after which it was displayed in the North Hall of the South Kensington Museum, London, until 1870.[1] It was unveiled at the V&A Museum, Bombay, by Governor Seymour Fitzgerald in 1872, when the Museum opened to the public. The sculpture consists of three parts. The Prince, draped in the robes of the Order of Garter, stands on a marble pedestal with his left hand on his chest, holding the insignia of the Star of George; in his right hand is a scroll. The pedestal is flanked at the plinth by two female figures, the Muse of Science and the Muse of Art, to emphasise his commitment to these fields and his impact on Indian society and the museum movement around the world.

Prince Albert was keenly interested in the industrial fairs which were hosted across England to showcase the ingenuity of British art and design. This interest evolved into the idea of the Great Exhibition of 1851 in London, which was his brainchild, and was organised by the Royal Society of Arts, Manufactures and Commerce. The exhibition was intended to position England as the world's leader in art and industry. With over 6 million visitors over five months, the profits generated from the Great Exhibition were used to purchase a site in South Kensington for the establishment of a museum, that was opened in 1857 and eventually became the Victoria and Albert Museum, London, in 1909. The objects from the 1851 exhibition became the nucleus collection of the South Kensington Museum, inspiring a movement for the establishment of encyclopaedic museums across the world.[2]

Queen Victoria and Prince Albert, unlike earlier British monarchs, were very involved in public affairs and conscious of their public image. The many exhibitions and grand openings ensured that they were continuously in the public eye. In addition to commissioned painted portraits, the advent of photography and the mass consumption of newspapers facilitated the distribution of images of the royal family. From state visits to commissioned photographs, the couple were well-recognised figures in the popular culture of Britain and its colonies. The marriage of Prince Albert and Queen Victoria and the birth of their first two children were widely celebrated with speeches, durbars and fireworks across all the Presidencies. Similarly, the news of the Prince's untimely death elicited a strong reaction from Indian citizens. Local governments paid profuse tributes, including establishing commemorative monuments, portraits and this statue from public conscription.

When it was first planned, the Museum was to be named after the Queen only. Deeply grieved by her husband's death, she wrote to Lord Elphinstone asking that Prince Albert's name be included as he was the architect of the new museum movement in India. On January 30, 1862, a Museum committee meeting was held at the Town Hall to convey condolences to Queen Victoria. The committee raised funds for the establishment of the Museum and changed the name as proposed by the president of the committee, Juggannath Sunkersett. Over Rs 60,000 was donated for the cause and the Museum was thereafter known as the Victoria and Albert Museum, Bombay.[3] In 1975, it was renamed the Dr. Bhau Daji Lad Museum.

The front of the pedestal, on which the statue stands (see p. 12), bears the following text painted in gold in English and Hebrew:

Albert
Prince Consort
Dear to Science, dear to Art
Dear to thy land and ours, a Prince indeed
Dedicated by David Sassoon
1864

The same is painted on the back in four Indian languages: Hindi, Marathi, Urdu and Gujarati. The dedication is from Alfred Tennyson's collection of poems, *Idylls of the King*. Tennyson was a close friend of the royal family and wrote this poem shortly after the unexpected death of Prince Albert in 1861.

The words 'dear to thy land and ours' highlight Albert's significant contribution to building Britain's relationship with the rest of the world. In 1849, at the formative meeting of the Great Exhibition of 1851, Prince Albert was ardently in favour of opening the exhibition to other countries, going on to say that British industry may benefit from 'placing it in fair competition with other Nations'.[4] His status as a member of the English and the German royal families ensured the participation of several European countries.

One of his earliest interests in Indian culture involved his patronage, in the 1830s, of Sanskrit scholars, who aimed to study the common root between Sanskrit and European languages.[5] His greatest impact on India, however, was a result of his engagement with the study of arts and science, best demonstrated by the organisation of the Great Exhibition in 1851 and its profound effect on museums across the world. The two female figures on either side of the statue of Prince Albert are the personification of this amalgamation of science and art. • LM

12 DR BHAU DAJI LAD

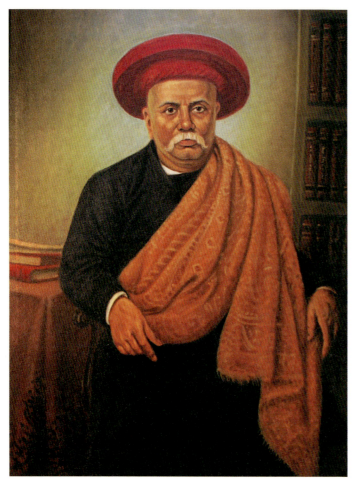

Dr Bhau Daji Lad, P.D. Parasnis; oil on canvas, 1972, Bombay; 113.1 x 97.4 cm. Accessioned: 1975. Gifted to the Museum by Shatabdi Samaroha Samiti (a committee formed to commemorate Dr Bhau Daji Lad's centenary).

•

Opposite:
The Travellers, Hurrichand Chintamon; engraving, Vincent Brooks Day & Son, c. 1870, London, *Journal of Travels in India*, Ardaseer Framjee Moos, Byculla: Education Society Press, 1871; 22.8 x 13.9 cm. Accessioned: 2013.
The original photograph was taken for the *Archaeological Survey of India Collections: India Office Series (Volume 42)*, and displayed at the 1867 Paris Exhibition. Figures identified as (standees, from left to right) Prof. Edward Rehatsek, Rustomjee Fackerjee, Mancherjee Merwanji Nalliarwala, Ardaseer Framjee Moos, and (seated, from left to right) Dr Bhau Daji Lad, K.R. Cama, Cursetjee Nuserwanjee Cama.

Dr BHAU DAJI Lad is an important figure in the cultural and medical annals of Mumbai. A polymath who contributed to research in several fields, including museums and theatre, and a champion of the Indian voice at the Imperial Parliament, his legacy is reflected in the city's premier institutions.

Born in 1822 in Mandrem, Goa, Ramakrishna Vitthal Lad (also known as Parsekar, his ancestral village) moved to Bombay as a young boy, with his brother, to pursue higher education. A bright student, Bhau Daji excelled in academics and taught science and chemistry at Elphinstone College from 1843 to 1845. When Grant Medical College was established in 1845, he enrolled in the first batch of students to study allopathy. He graduated as a doctor in 1851 and began his independent medical practice soon after. It is believed that he found an early cure for leprosy. His study of medicine took him across the country to understand plants and their medicinal properties. He was an amateur botanist and his garden at home was known for the different specimens he acquired and planted along with his brother, Narayan Daji.

His role in establishing the Victoria and Albert Museum, Bombay, was seminal. In 1855, an English daily mentioned: 'To [Dr Bhau Daji's] exertions Bombay will owe the Economic Museum and Zoological Gardens, and the various galleries of science and art now in process of organisation.'[1] On December 15, 1858, the prominent citizens of Bombay met to discuss the establishment of the Victoria Museum and Gardens. The meeting was chaired by Juggannath Sunkersett. Dr Bhau Daji, who was Secretary along with George Birdwood of the Museum committee, made an impassioned speech urging the citizens present to aid the construction of a 'temple of science containing the wonders of ages, of Literature, Science and Art—a Museum, with Natural History and Pleasure Gardens'.[2] He made great efforts to build the collection and donated an expensive specimen of incense to the Museum.

He was elected as a member of the managing committee of the Bombay branch of the Royal Asiatic Society until 1859, serving as the Society's vice-president from 1865 to 1873. Keen on researching India's archaeological history, Dr Bhau Daji set out to collect epigraphical inscriptions across India. He was well versed in Sanskrit and an authority on Indology and deciphered ancient inscriptions, including those at Girnar in 1861 and the famous Elephanta and Ajanta-Ellora caves in 1863. He accompanied William Simpson and the Duke of Edinburgh as a scholarly guide when they visited the Elephanta caves in 1861 and 1870 respectively. His collection of archaeological relics, ancient texts and manuscripts was bequeathed to the Royal Asiatic Society of Bombay upon his death in 1874.[3]

Dr Bhau Daji Lad was the first Indian Sheriff of Bombay, appointed for two successive terms in 1868 and 1869 during the governorship of Sir Seymour Fitzgerald. He was also the leader of the Bombay branch of the East India Association, established by Dadabhai Naoroji in 1869. He defended civic rights while criticising the decisions of the Municipal Commissioner, Arthur Crawford.

A champion of education, Dr Bhau Daji became the first Indian president of the Students' Literary and Scientific Society in 1863, a position he held until 1873. The Society established girls' schools in Bombay and highlighted the need for social reform. In *Kesari*, published on January 22, 1901, Bal Gangadhar Tilak cited Dr Bhau Daji Lad as one of the leaders who inspired Madhavrao Ranade, one of the founding members of the Indian National Congress.

Dr Bhau Daji was an important patron of Marathi theatre and is credited with translating the famous Marathi play *Raja Gopichand* into Hindi. It was the first Hindi drama to be staged in Bombay in 1853 at the Grant Road Theatre.[4] Bhau Daji,

along with his brother Narayan Daji, was also among the first Indian members of the Indian Photographic Society, which was founded at the Town Hall in October 1854. As graduates in medicine and chemistry from Grant Medical College, their skills were well suited to the early photographic processes. Among the photos showcased at the Society's second exhibition in February 1856, over 200 were taken by Narayan Daji.[5]

Dr Bhau Daji lost his fortune in the stock market crash that followed the end of the American Civil War in 1865. He had to keep his medical clinic shut for a while. However, he continued helping patients afflicted with leprosy. Dr Bhau Daji Lad fell unconscious on the morning of January 14, 1873, during his regular medical rounds and suffered a paralytic stroke. He passed away on May 29, 1874.

On the occasion of his death centenary in 1975, the Victoria and Albert Museum was renamed Dr. Bhau Daji Lad Museum to recognise and honour his contribution to the city of Bombay and the key role he played in the establishment of the Museum. • RWB

13 GEORGE BIRDWOOD

Sir George C.M. Birdwood; glass negative, late nineteenth to early twentieth century, Bombay; 10.2 x 8 cm. Accessioned: 1903–20.

•

Opposite:
Botanical Gardens (Veermata Jijabai Bhosale Udyan); glass negative, late nineteenth to early twentieth century, Bombay, 25.4 x 30 cm. Accessioned: 1903–20.

SIR George Christopher Molesworth Birdwood was appointed the Secretary and Curator of the Museum from 1858 to 1868. He was one of the most eminent figures on the international cultural stage in the mid- to late nineteenth century. He was friendly with John Ruskin, William Morris and Owen Jones, and helped shape the general view of Indian art and aesthetics that prevailed for well over a century. Lord Curzon acknowledged that it was Birdwood who had advised him to set up the Archaeological Survey of India. Birdwood was also commissioner of several Indian exhibits at international exhibitions. After he returned to England from India, he was appointed curator of the India Museum and was responsible for organising the Indian exhibits at the South Kensington Museum, which later became the Victoria and Albert Museum, London.

Sir George Birdwood was born in Belgaum, in present-day Karnataka, India, and completed his medical training from England, before joining the Bombay Medical Service in 1855. He was posted in a number of places, including Belgaum and Solapur, before he settled in Bombay.[1] Birdwood's connection with the Museum predated his appointment as curator. In 1855, when a Museum committee was originally formed with Dr George Buist as the curator, the putative Museum was known as the Government Central and Economic Museum. In an advertisement requesting donations for the Museum's collection, Buist and other members of the Museum committee wrote that 'The Museum is proposed to be at once Educational and Economical; it is intended to contain as large a variety of Specimens of objects, Animal, Vegetable, and Mineral, as can be procured, not from India alone, but from any part of the world.' In response to this, Birdwood donated a significant collection of natural products from the different places where he had been posted.[2] This included 'specimens of grains, legumes and a vast variety of seeds', 'a large collection of dried plants in perfect preservation' and '100 specimens of birds stuffed and well prepared'. On receiving the collections, Buist was not only impressed by their wealth but also the measures Birdwood had taken to preserve and catalogue them before sending them to the committee. When Birdwood joined the Museum committee in 1858, he invested a great deal of his time looking for new donations that would fit the collection.

Birdwood wrote an important book regarding the classification of arts and crafts of India titled *Industrial Arts of India*. It is a catalogue of craft practices, tracing their history, production and markets. It was one of the first attempts to record crafts across India. His introduction elucidates his romantic illusion about the ordinary Indian craftsman and his disenchantment with Western industrialisation. Birdwood

echoes the opinions of designer William Morris and art historian John Ruskin, the main protagonists of the Arts and Crafts Movement in Britain. The movement marked a shift away from the dependency on mechanical production to a revival of creative hand-manufacturing processes.

The book changed the outlook towards the Indian crafts industry and Birdwood's extensive research established his authority as a scholar of Indian affairs. It highlighted important aspects of Indian craft, their occurrence within 'particular cultural circumstances of India', the value of 'hand production' and their significance to the 'definition of Indian culture'.[3]

However, Birdwood, like most of his compatriots, was prejudiced regarding the intellectual abilities of Indians to achieve the refinement required to produce great works of the fine arts, especially painting and sculpture. An infamous remark made by Birdwood in 1910 at a meeting of the Royal Society of the Arts on arts education in India illustrates this innate prejudice. He stated, 'I have up to the present,

and through an experience of seventy-eight years, found no examples [of fine art] in India; and, judging from my experience, I should say that India had never prized art for art itself sake alone.'[4]

This criticism may seem contradictory to Birdwood's efforts to promote and document the arts and crafts of India. However, Birdwood's catalogue viewed crafts as economic goods, and he was attempting to provide a cultural context for their potential manufacture and sale. He noted further that Indian art could not be termed as 'fine art', although it may be 'good enough symbolical art, and illustrative art, and even decorative art'.[5]

Nonetheless, despite his prejudices, Birdwood's painstaking documentation of the industrial arts of India and his efforts to record detailed botanical information about India in another book, as well as the several articles he wrote on similar subjects, attest not only to his great scholarship but also to his great love of India. • LM

14 JUGGANNATH SUNKERSETT

Juggannath Sunkersett; print reproduced from a glass negative, early twentieth century, Bombay; 113.1 x 97.4 cm. Accessioned: early twentieth century.

•

Above:
Cash box; ivory on wood, late nineteenth century, Bombay, 6.9 x 15.4 x 10.7 cm. Accessioned: 1872–1915.

JUGGANNATH Sunkersett (1803–65) was one of the city's most illustrious citizens, who contributed to education, political and social reform, and civic affairs. He belonged to a family of rich traders. Gunbow Street (Rustom Sindhwa Marg) was named after his ancestor Babulshet Ganbashet, who migrated from Konkan to Bombay in the mid-eighteenth century. The family had settled in Bombay for over three generations. Juggannath's sagacity, honesty and forthrightness impressed a succession of British governors, who consulted him on many delicate issues relating to governance. Popularly known as Nana, he was involved in setting up the Bombay Native School and Book Society that was instrumental in producing the first set of textbooks for schools. This organisation later became the Elphinstone Institute. He was also appointed the Executive Trustee of the Board of Education. The first girls' school in the city started out of his home. He patronised almost all the Bombay institutions of his time, and his charities in the field of education were legendary. He was the first president of the Bombay Association from 1852 to 1857. During 1862–65, he was a member of the Bombay Legislative Council, which had been set up as an advisory body by the British administration. Sunkersett's contribution in the movement to abolish *sati* (immolation of the widow) was also exemplary.[1]

The Indian Railway Association was formed in 1845 under the leadership of both Sunkersett and Jamsetjee Jeejeebhoy. The Great Indian Peninsula Railways was incorporated with the Railway Association in 1849, with Sunkersett and Jeejeebhoy as the only two Indians among the ten directors. In 1991, India Post commemorated Sunkersett's role in the establishment of the Indian Railways by issuing a special postage stamp bearing his name and portrait, along with an image of the Victoria Terminus (now the Chhatrapati Shivaji Maharaj Terminus).

Sunkersett played a key role in establishing the Museum. Along with Dr George Buist, Sunkersett was a member of the exhibition committee which was constituted to assemble a collection for the 1851 Crystal Palace Exhibition. George Birdwood, who had been appointed as the curator of the Museum, requested Sunkersett in 1858 for object donations, and the latter generously responded by presenting a set of boxes of Bombay inlay work to the Museum (see pp. 137–39).

Sunkersett chaired the meeting held in the Town Hall on December 15, 1858, to establish the Museum.[2] In his address, he highlighted the importance of such an institute, stating the 'benefits in aiding the development of the raw products of this colossal and almost as yet unknown empire, in stimulating and improving its slow and curious manufactures, in supplying resorts of healthy recreation to the densely crowded inhabitants of Bombay, in ornamenting the town, inciting amongst the

Sugarcane Processing (detail); half-baked terracotta, pigments, and mixed media, 1931-32, made at the erstwhile V&A Museum, Bombay, 57 x 217 x 104 cm.

masses habits of observation and taste for rational pleasures, in sub-serving, in fact, for the million, the purposes of a most influential, educational, and reformatory institution'.

To promote a scientific approach to agricultural education, the Agri-Horticultural Society was established with Sunkersett's active support and cooperation. A variety of seeds were brought from different regions and practical research was conducted on a large farm in Sewree, set up specifically for educational purposes. This research was then presented to the people, and literature on better agricultural practices was distributed to the farmers. To set a concrete example, Sunkersett created a small farm in the compound of his bungalow in Tardeo at Nana Chowk. Sunkersett's biographer Chodankar has claimed that the experience Sunkersett acquired while running the Agri-Horticultural Society inspired him to contribute towards the creation of the Victoria Gardens.

In those days, sugarcane was not cultivated in India and sugar was imported from Mauritius. Sunkersett called for sugarcane seeds and planted them in his farm. Many farmers from different parts of the country visited his farm to learn more about the new crop and the process of growing it. The Museum has two dioramas about sugarcane farming that explain the processes involved (see above).

Juggannath Sunkersett represents an extraordinary group of citizens in the mid-nineteenth century who came together to build Bombay's major civic institutions which even today stand proud. To recognise his remarkable contribution to the city, a life-size marble statue was sculpted by Matthew Noble, of England, that was insured and dispatched to Bombay from London. The statue was proposed in 1864, and was originally intended to be placed at the Museum but was eventually placed in the Town Hall, now the Asiatic Society of Mumbai.[3] • TZM

15 DAVID SASSOON

David Sassoon, Thomas Woolner; marble, 1865, London;
81 x 54.5 x 43.5 cm. Accessioned: 1872.
•

Opposite:
Interior view of the ceiling; Dr. Bhau Daji Lad Museum, Mumbai.

DAVID Sassoon (1792–1864) was a Jewish merchant and philanthropist, whose white marble bust stands in the Museum's central atrium near Prince Albert's statue. Sassoon moved to Bombay from Baghdad in 1832, attracted by the religious tolerance and trading opportunities provided by the city that was under the British East India Company at the time. He arrived in Bombay with little except his strong business skills and his desire to succeed, and soon became one of the most successful merchants in the city and a major landowner. By the end of the 1850s, the popular refrain about Sassoon claimed, 'Silver and gold, silks, gums and spices, opium and cotton, wool and wheat—whatever moves over sea or land feels the hand or bears the mark of Sassoon and Co.'[1]

Sassoon contributed generously to the Museum building and gifted the land for the Victoria Gardens and the Museum to the Agri-Horticultural Society of Western India. The Museum recognised this contribution by including 120 six-pointed stars to embellish its ceiling. The six-pointed Star of David is considered an important religious symbol for the Jewish community, as 120 is a sacred number in Judaism. Sassoon also donated funds for the construction of the clock tower at the entrance to the Museum, which was completed in 1865.

A Baghdadi Jew, David Sassoon and his sons had established a trade monopoly in parts of Central Asia through the Himalayan passes, which were unexplored by European travellers. Within a decade of their arrival in the city, they developed a strong business relationship with China, which rewarded them with great wealth.[2] Father of fourteen children, David Sassoon sent his sons to different trade centres to expand the business. In 1850, Elias, his most enterprising son, opened a branch in Shanghai, which soon became the second largest centre of their business empire. Besides branches in Shanghai, Canton and Hong Kong, there were agencies in Japan, in Yokohoma, Nagasaki and other cities, managed by other members of the family.[3] By 1854, David Sassoon was reputed to be a multi-millionaire.

In 1858, the eldest son, Sassoon David Sassoon, was called back from China and sent to represent the firm in London. The interruption in the supply of American cotton-yarn led to the search for alternative sources and this soon brought an enormous expansion in trade. Sassoon took advantage of this opportunity and London became the main centre of the firm's operations. Branches were also established in Liverpool and Manchester. With increasing profits, David Sassoon made large charitable donations in India, Baghdad and Palestine, establishing schools, libraries, synagogues, burial grounds and religious charities. He also funded the Sassoon Dock in Colaba. This was the first wet dock in Bombay, and is an important city landmark.

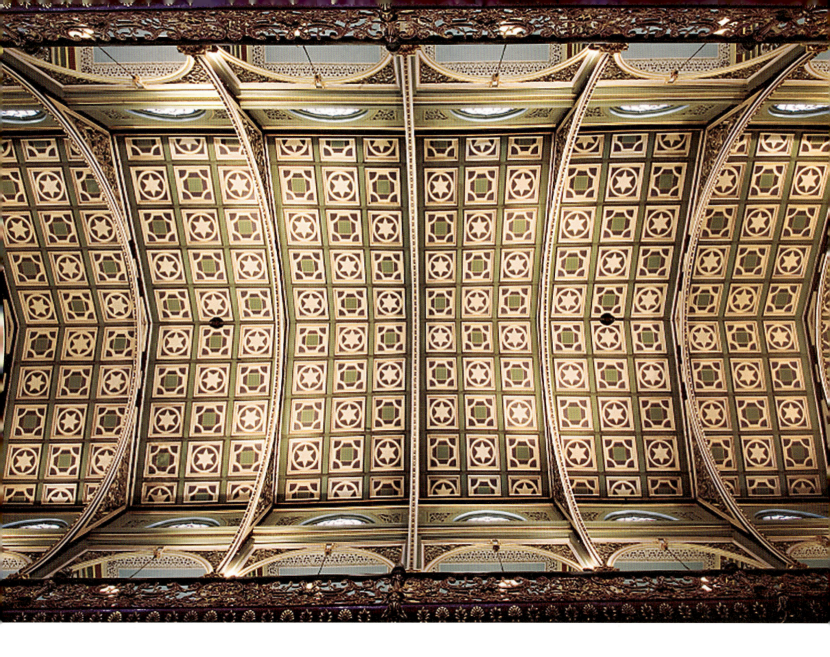

Following David Sassoon's death in 1864, Sir Bartle Frere, the Governor of Bombay, suggested that a statue be erected to commemorate his services to the city. He appointed his sculptor friend, Thomas Woolner, to undertake this assignment. The response to Frere's suggestion was so great that he decided not to limit the donors to those living in India.[4] Contributions, therefore, came from the Jewish communities in Persia and China, from the Rothschilds, Montagues and Mocattas in England, and the mill workers in Lancashire. The bust at the Museum is a study for the statue which is now at the Sassoon Library, Mumbai.

The Sassoon family continued supporting all the family charities. To commemorate the Prince of Wales' visit to Bombay in 1876, Albert Sassoon, the eldest son of David Sassoon, presented a splendid bronze statue of the prince astride his black horse. This statue, a city landmark locally known as Kala Ghoda, originally stood in front of the Town Hall in Fort. It was later moved to the square facing the David Sassoon Library and has now been moved to the Veer Mata Jijabai Bhosale Udyan, Byculla, while the plinth is in the Museum's collection. The plinth depicts the Prince of Wales landing at the Bombay docks and his reception by the Viceroy of India, Lord Northbrook, and prominent citizens of Bombay, on one side. The opposite side shows young women presenting flowers to the Prince on the Esplanade. In the mid-twentieth century, the Sassoon family decided to move to Shanghai, announcing it as their future headquarters. • **TZM**

16 JAMSETJEE JEEJEEBHOY

Sir Jamsetjee Jeejeebhoy; print reproduced from a glass negative, early twentieth century, Bombay;
113.1 x 97.4 cm. Accessioned: early twentieth century.
•
Opposite:
Technical School; half-baked terracotta, paper pulp, mixed media and pigments, 1957, M.S. Bhagwat & Co., Bombay; 217 x 104 x 57 cm. Accessioned: 1957.

JAMSETJEE Jeejeebhoy (1783–1859) was a leading merchant, philanthropist and influential citizen of Bombay during the mid-nineteenth century. Jeejeebhoy's remarkable contribution to the city has impacted generations and he stands out as an exemplar even today. His father was a textile merchant from Olpad, Gujarat, who migrated to Bombay in the 1770s. Jeejeebhoy's parents died in 1799, leaving the sixteen-year-old under the guardianship of his father-in-law and business partner, Framjee Nasserwanjee Batliwala.[1] Jeejeebhoy made his first voyage to China at the age of sixteen, with little formal education, to trade in cotton and opium.[2]

From his humble origins in Bombay to becoming a renowned merchant prince, Jeejeebhoy achieved success because of his integrity and business acumen. He was able to exploit novel business opportunities by forming alliances with other Indians and ultimately partnered with the British as well. Jeejeebhoy emerged as the principal Indian merchant who was successful in both the cotton and the opium trades, especially with China. In 1814, Jeejeebhoy purchased his first ship, *Good Success*, and gradually added six more and chartered others when the volume of trade increased. He built up a huge business empire, trading in ports as far afield as Canton in China.[3]

Jeejeebhoy was a leader of the Parsi community and a pioneer in the formation of a public civic culture in Bombay's colonial milieu. He cultivated friendships with the British and exemplified the collaborative relationship that formed between leading Indian businessmen and the British in Bombay. His extensive circle of friends and his helpful demeanour shaped his image as a great philanthropist and eminent citizen involved in promoting Indians and nurturing education and social reform.

He was part of the committee to select objects that were sent from the Bombay Presidency to the Great Exhibition of 1851, which made a huge impression on him.[4] Jeejeebhoy was keen that Indian 'economic products', as crafts were then called, should be able to compete successfully across the world. In 1853, he proposed that the Government of Bombay establish a school for the improvement of arts and manufactures, which he would endow. This became the famous Sir J.J. School of Arts. Having spent his early life in penury, Jeejeebhoy understood the challenges the Indian craftsmen faced. His solution was to build an art school that would introduce new technologies and offer instruction in painting, drawing and design, ornamental pottery, metal and wood carving and turning. He presented a generous donation of Rs 1,00,000 to the School, which started in 1857.

British India witnessed a change in the character of public charity after the Crown took over from the East India

Company, as the British encouraged new forms of Western-style contributions to educational institutions, hospitals and patriotic funds. Jeejeebhoy donated Rs 5,000 to the Patriotic Fund in 1855 to help wounded soldiers and the widows of those who had died in the Russo-Turkish War. Whether it was the famine in Ireland (1822), the floods in France (1856) or the fires which ravaged both Bombay (1803) and Surat (1837), he donated generously. He contributed to build a hospital known as the Sir J.J. Hospital, as well as Grant Medical College, Elphinstone College and many Parsi educational institutions. In 1849, a subscription of Rs 1,50,000 was raised by his friends and admirers. Jeejeebhoy added Rs 4,40,000 and established a trust that would be known as the Sir Jamsetjee Jeejeebhoy Parsee Benevolent Institution. The funds received were used for translating texts from European and Asiatic languages, ancient and modern, into Gujarati to make 'useful' knowledge accessible to the poorest of Parsis. By 1864, the trust administered twenty-one schools.[5] Jeejeebhoy also donated a sum of Rs 1,150 to the fundraising committee to build the Victoria and Albert Museum, Bombay, now the Dr. Bhau Daji Lad Museum. The next generation continued the family tradition of promoting science, civic development and philanthropy.

Jeejeebhoy enjoyed the good life and was known to throw lavish dinner parties where both Europeans and elite Indians mingled. The artist Henry Moses, who met him at one of his dinner parties, gives a first-hand account of the style and grandeur of Jeejeebhoy's house. It was replete with statuary, flower vases, musical clocks, elegant chandeliers, and exotic items from China, as well as furniture from across Europe.[6] Jeejeebhoy's house was one of the first to be lit by gas lamps between the 1830s and 1840s.

A knighthood was conferred upon him in June 1842 in recognition of his many acts of charity and public spiritedness, making him the first Indian to receive such an honour. On May 24, 1857, Queen Victoria conferred the first Indian baronetcy on him. He was one of the pioneers of a strong civic culture in Bombay, which marks the city even today. • TZM

17 STREET SCENE OF OLD BOMBAY
by EDUARD HILDEBRANDT

UNTIL the eighteenth century, European contact with India was limited to trade and military conquests. The Western imagination was taken up by early travellers' tales of the exotic excesses of the 'Orient'. From the late eighteenth century onwards, as the British Empire expanded, connections were strengthened and established. This engagement with other regions inspired a quest for empirical and scientific knowledge of these places, spurring travel and the documentation of experiences about new lands and peoples. Landscape painting became one of the means through which the experience of the world was documented and shaped. Many official voyages included painters on board in order to make comprehensive records with visual representations to accompany written accounts. The portrayal of local landscapes during this period reflected the economic objectives of the British Empire.

The paintings were printed as chromolithographs in folios and books that were eagerly sought after by the

Street Scene of Old Bombay, Eduard Hildebrandt; chromolithograph, late nineteenth century, Bombay; 23.5 x 32.5 cm. Accessioned: 1900-18.

elite as they offered insights into distant lands. Landscape painting employed the picturesque in which cities, streets and landscapes were executed and presented as aestheticised versions of reality. Some of these works are in the Museum's collection and bear witness to the painterly archive of the time.

Eduard Hildebrandt (1818–68) was a German landscape painter of repute who travelled widely to different places around the world. He was the official painter to the Royal Court of the Prussian king, Friedrich Wilhelm IV, who funded Hildebrandt's extensive travels. In 1862–64, Hildebrandt went on a 'Reise um die Erde' (Journey around the World), from Trieste through the Suez to India, and on to China, Japan, the Pacific and back via California and Central America. The travel studies he created in German during the trip were published by the Berliner Montagspost and subsequently compiled into a book.[1] Receiving much praise, his watercolours were exhibited in London (1866) and at the Crystal Palace Exhibition (1868). Hildebrandt died in 1868 in Berlin.

The chromolithograph in the Museum's collection is created from a watercolour sketch of this trip. The work depicts an elite residential quarter of mid-nineteenth-century Bombay, as suggested by the broad street, wooden verandas and elaborate facades of the houses. In the painting, Hildebrandt depicts the scene in a picturesque manner by distancing himself from the street. He focuses on detailing the sky, trees and the architecture, whereas people are indicated in sketchy, barely identifiable forms, avoiding the disorder of the street in a picturesque tradition. • PV

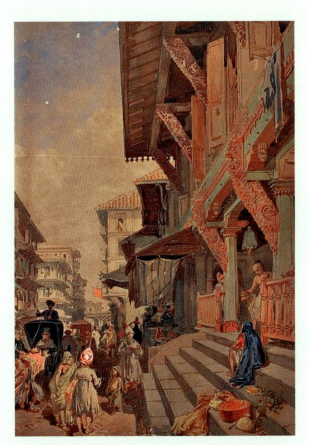

A Street in Bombay, William Simpson, chromolithograph J.W. Kaye, *India: Ancient and Modern with Descriptive Literature* (Vol. 2), 1867, London: Day & Son; 60 x 42.4 cm. Accessioned: 1900-18.

A STREET IN BOMBAY
by WILLIAM SIMPSON

William Simpson was a British artist who travelled extensively in India. He had fought in the Afghan War and in the Crimea. His first visit to India was from 1859 to 1862 to sketch places that were related to the Uprising of 1857. After the Uprising, in 1858, when the governance of India was transferred to the Crown from the East India Company, Simpson became a part of Lord Canning's (the first Viceroy of India) court.

The print of Simpson's painting titled 'A Street in Bombay' in the Museum's collection was produced by Day & Son, well-known lithographers in London. It was part of the volume, *India: Ancient and Modern*, published in 1867. The volume has detailed descriptions by John William Kaye accompanying Simpson's chromolithographs. The artwork depicts the bustling street from Horniman Circle to Bazaargate in the Fort area. Kaye mentions that the street is identifiable through its local character and architecture as well as the elaborate carving on the wooden pillars, beams and brackets of the house. The beams are coloured in contrasting red and green, a feature common in Gujarati houses of the time. The people in the picture have been painted with a keen sense of detail especially their dress and head-wear. As Kaye suggests, the scene shows 'Parsees' and 'Hindoos', identifiable by their turbans and attire. • PV

PHOTOGRAPHY was first practised in India in 1839, a few months after Louis Daguerre announced his invention of the daguerreotype in France. Soon after, portrait studios and photographic societies were established in Bombay, Calcutta and Madras, and photography gained widespread popularity facilitated by the Government. George Buist, editor of the *Bombay Times* and the first curator of the Museum, reported that the 'Government here and at home had shown the utmost anxiety to promote the Art of Photography'.[1] The first meeting of the Photographic Society of Bombay took place in the rooms of the Geographical Society, in the Town Hall on October 3, 1854, chaired by Captain Harry Barr with Lord Elphinstone, the Governor of Bombay, as patron.[2] Dr Bhau Daji Lad was one of the three Indians among the thirteen founding members. The membership grew rapidly and by the next year, there were more than 250 members. Many photographers would display their prints at the Bombay Society meetings. Narayan Daji, Dr Bhau Daji Lad's brother, was among the early photographers who displayed his work alongside officially supported photographers such as Captain Thomas Biggs.[3] Dr Bhau Daji himself was an accomplished amateur photographer. In 1855, Elphinstone Institute in Bombay started photography classes which became very popular.

Photography was thought to have a certain 'fidelity' or truthfulness that was better suited to documentation than pre-photography images such as paintings. Reverend Joseph Mullens, a British missionary, declared the desirability of a 'more complete and systematic' photographic endeavour to document the 'perfect specimen of all the minute varieties of Oriental Life, of Oriental Scenery, Oriental nations and Oriental manners'.[4] Before photography, the truthfulness of the image relied on the ability of the artist. Many lithograph volumes had written justifications emphasising the likeness to reality of the images.

A telling account in the Photographic Society's journal questioned the reliability of pre-photographic means to reproduce Indian antiquities, including those done in oil paintings, as it could not be ascertained whether the details

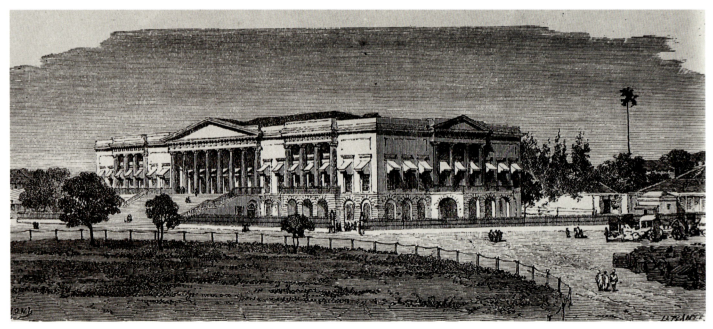

The Town Hall, Fort; glass negative, nineteenth century, Bombay; 25.4 x 30 cm. Accessioned: 1903–20.

were true to life or influenced by artistic licence. The journal further praised Captain Biggs' project to obtain photographic facsimiles of the western Indian caves.

With the coming of photography, painting and other mediums of documentation referenced the photograph, rather than create from life, in order to maintain the 'truthfulness' of the subject being represented. The advent of photography in India coincided with the establishment of the Museum, and in the years that followed, many of the folios with drawings and paintings that were collected for the Museum reflect this reference to photography. By the beginning of the twentieth century, photographs of India were also used on postcards to produce millions of collotypes and halftones that were exchanged around the world. Postcards became the first mass-transfusion of colour images and a popular tool to disseminate information.

The effort to collect photographs and glass negatives for the Museum was initiated by Cecil Burns, curator between 1903 and 1918. Burns started a collection of the pictorial records of the city of Bombay, which included maps, prints, books and photographs. This effort was aimed at stimulating the interest of the citizens of Bombay in the city's history as well as to encourage people with photographic records to assist in making the collection.

In 1911, six copies of the views of old Bombay were taken from prints collected by the late Justice L.H. Bayley, judge of the High Court, Bombay. The photographs were acquired through his son Vernon F. Bayley, of Vernon & Co., a photography and publishing company based in Bombay. Cecil Burns also sought permission from the Byculla Club's committee to copy photographs from their album of views of the city.[5] In order to form a comprehensive series of the old views of the city, he made further enquiries from other sources to collect photographs, drawings and prints. Photographs of old buildings were also collected, to be exhibited in a special room in the Museum dedicated to representing the city's history.

The glass negatives form an image archive of the city from the nineteenth to the early twentieth century, and give an insight into the socio-economic, civic and architectural developments of the time. The collection includes views of the Haffkine Institute (formerly the Governor's residence), the Oriental Bank, J.J. Hospital and Grant Medical College, the temporary structure of the Gateway of India as well as the Town Hall (now the Asiatic Society building), which was completed in the early 1820s in the neoclassical style. It housed the civic offices, where many important meetings regarding city planning were held, including the first meetings for the proposal of the Museum. • PV

King's Square; glass negative, late nineteenth to early twentieth century, Bombay; 25.4 x 30 cm. Accessioned: 1903–20.
Showing the headquarters of the Municipal Corporation of Greater Mumbai and the Chhatrapati Shivaji Maharaj Terminus c. 1900.

Elphinstone College and David Sassoon Library, Bombay; coloured postcard, late nineteenth to early twentieth century, Bombay; 10 x 15 cm. Accessioned: 2018. Gifted to the Museum by Omar Khan.

Elphinstone College, completed in 1888, was designed by James Trubshaw in the Gothic revival style and built under the supervision of Khan Bahadur Muncherjee Murzban, an eminent Parsi civic engineer. Prior to 1887, the Chemical and Physical Laboratories of Elphinstone College were located in the Museum. Next to it is the David Sassoon Library, built in 1870 and designed by architects J. Campbell and G.E. Gosling for Scott McClelland and Company in the Venetian Gothic style. Located on Rampart Row (K. Dubash Marg), these institutions are part of the popular Kala Ghoda Art District.

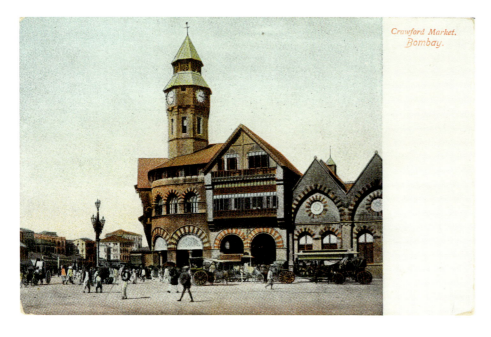

Crawford Market, Bombay; coloured postcard, late nineteenth to early twentieth century, Bombay; 10 x 15 cm. Accessioned: 2018. Gifted to the Museum by Omar Khan.

Crawford Market, the most renowned market in the city, was designed by British architect William Emerson. It reflects an early attempt to integrate Indian design forms with Victorian Gothic architecture. Completed in 1869, it was gifted to the city by Cowasji Jehangir and was originally named after Arthur Crawford, the city's first Municipal Commissioner. In the 1990s, the Market was renamed to honour Mahatma Jyotirao Phule, the Indian social reformer from Maharashtra. It houses the 'Kipling Fountain', designed by William Emerson in the Greek Revival and Neo-Gothic style of architecture. The carvings on the fountain depicting Indian river goddesses and birds were executed by John Lockwood Kipling when he was the principal at the Sir J.J. School of Art.

Royal Alfred Sailor's Home, Bombay; coloured postcard, late nineteenth to early twentieth century, Bombay; 10 x 15 cm. Accessioned: 2018. Gifted to the Museum by Omar Khan. Royal Alfred Sailor's Home was completed in 1876, and designed by British architect Frederick William Stevens in the Gothic Revival style. The historic structure was built at the height of maritime trade in Bombay, with the aim of providing accommodation for up to seventy-eight seamen. The Maharaja of Baroda, Khanderao II Gaekwad, contributed Rs 2,00,000 towards the construction of the building. After 1928, it served as the Legislative Assembly and Council Hall of Bombay and eventually became the headquarters for Maharashtra Police in 1982.

Royal Alfred Sailor's Home, Bombay.

View of Bombay; coloured postcard, late nineteenth to early twentieth century, Bombay; 10 x 15 cm. Accessioned: 2018. Gifted to the Museum by Omar Khan. Watson's Hotel in the foreground overlooks the harbour and the Esplanade. Named after its owner, John Watson, it is the oldest surviving cast-iron structure in India. The building was constructed in 1867–69 by the architect Rowland Mason Ordish, who also worked on the Crystal Palace in Hyde Park, London. The building's cast-and wrought-iron structures were prefabricated in England. On July 7, 1896, the hotel screened the first movie shown in India, made by the Lumiere Brothers, at a special theatre in its lobby. The event marked the advent of cinema in India. Considered one of the city's finest hotels, it had a strict European-only policy in its early years. The hotel's popularity declined with the establishment of the Taj Mahal Palace Hotel in 1903.

View of Bombay.

Moombadevi Road, Bombay;
coloured postcard, late nineteenth to early twentieth century, Bombay; 10 x 15 cm. Accessioned: 2018. Gifted to the Museum by Omar Khan.

Mumbadevi Road, named after the famous Mumbadevi temple, is located in Bhuleshwar, home to several old temples and shrines. The temple was relocated here in the eighteenth century and is visited by hundreds of worshippers and tourists daily. The route leading to the temple is lined with shops selling garlands, coconuts, rosaries and flowers. The densely populated street is located towards the end of Zaveri Bazaar, the jewellery market. At one end it is flanked by copper, steel and clothing markets. The temple complex included a tank built in 1830, used by worshippers for ritual cleansing, that was filled in the 1950s by the Municipal Corporation to create a recreational ground. In 1874, one of the first horse-drawn tramway services in Bombay began from Mumbadevi to Bazaar Gate and Elphinstone Circle.

Native Quarter, Null Bazaar, Bombay; coloured postcard, late nineteenth to early twentieth century, Bombay; 10 x 15 cm. Accessioned: 2018. Gifted to the Museum by Omar Khan.

Null Bazaar, located within the 'native' town in colonial Bombay, opened in 1867. The street was originally named after James Claudius Erskine, the first Director of Public Instruction. However, the area was popularly known as 'Null' (from the Hindi word 'nal' or pipe) as drainage pipes were installed to replace the open drains that once ran through this neighbourhood. The area is also known for its 'Gol Deval' or Shiva temple. The Sidis (an Indo-African community) lived here during the nineteenth and early twentieth centuries. The buildings were two to four storeys tall, with shops on the ground floor and dwellings on the upper floors. There were also pottery merchants, silk weavers, dyers and printers, and *kinkhab* (brocade) artists, as well as general markets further down the lane.

The Jumma Musjid, Bombay; coloured postcard, late nineteenth to early twentieth century, Bombay; 10 x 15 cm. Accessioned: 2018. Gifted to the Museum by Omar Khan. The Jumma Masjid (mosque) is a well-known landmark in Kalbadevi—a neighbourhood thriving with bazaars and residential pockets of Hindu and Muslim communities. The mosque's construction began in 1775 and was completed in 1802. The mosque was erected over a water reservoir, which accounts for the inscription 'Jahaz-i-Akhirat' or 'the ship of the world to come' on its chronogram. It underwent numerous expansions and renovations. Muhammad Ali Rogay, a highly regarded Muslim philanthropist in Bombay, funded the construction of an upper storey in 1837. During this period, the streets leading to the Jumma Masjid housed shops selling spices, jewellery, brocade and foreign delicacies.

Hindu Temple (Monkey Temple), Kalbadevi Road, Bombay; coloured postcard, late nineteenth to early twentieth century, Bombay; 10 x 15 cm. Accessioned: 2018. Gifted to the Museum by Omar Khan.

There are numerous temples in and around the Kalbadevi area, named after the shrine of Kalikadevi. The Monkey temple or Dwarkadhish temple houses the idol of Lord Krishna. Sunderdas, son of the textile baron Thakur Mulji Jetha, built the temple in 1875 in the style of the *havelis* (mansions) of Gujarat and Rajasthan from where many mercantile communities migrated to Bombay. The facade is ornamented with carved images of sages, milkmaids and monkeys (inspired by Lord Hanuman, a devotee of Lord Rama). In the late nineteenth century, Kalbadevi was the centre for the cotton and metal trade outside the Fort and had European-style retail shops for the elite. By the 1930s, it was the site of protests against imported British goods and known for its 'Swadeshi Market' that promoted Indian craftsmanship.

HINDU TEMPLE, (MONKEY TEMPLE,) KALBADEVI ROAD, BOMBAY.

19 B.E.S.T. TRAM

TRAFFIC first became a phenomenon in Bombay in the early twentieth century, when technological advances brought in motorised transport. Before the use of motor cars, two-wheeled bullock carts, horse-drawn carriages and palanquins were the popular modes of transport for Europeans as well as Indians. These early means operated alongside modern motorised vehicles.

The development of transport in Bombay is closely linked to the city's cotton export. During the American Civil War, cotton export from Bombay increased phenomenally, necessitating the development of infrastructure. The plan for a mass public transport system in the city was set in motion through a proposal in 1865 by an American company for a licence to set up horse-drawn tramways. Due to the economic depression that ensued after the American Civil War ended, however, the project did not materialise.

Some years later, in 1873, the Bombay Tramway Company Limited was set up, emulating the system established in London in 1870. The first trams in Bombay were drawn by one or two horses and the first tramway service began from Colaba and Bori Bunder to Pydhonie on May 9, 1874. The fare on the Colaba-Pydhonie route was three annas, whereas the Bori Bunder-Pydhonie route charged half an anna. From 1899, the fare was brought down to one anna for any distance.[1] The tram connected Grant Road, Pydhonie, Girgaum, Byculla Bridge and Sassoon Dock. When the service started, the Company had a stable of about 900 horses. Over time, with the development of industry, and as the city grew, horse-drawn tram cars no longer sufficed and were discontinued on August 1, 1905, and the Bombay Tramway Company was bought by the city's Municipality for Rs 98,50,000.[2] The Municipality set up the Bombay Electric Supply and Tramways (BEST) Company the same year. The first electric tram was started between the Municipal Office and Crawford Market on May 7, 1907.

Bombay was the first city in India to have double-decker trams in India, which were introduced by the BEST in September 1920 to manage the growing numbers using the service. But as the city expanded, the service was unable to accommodate the demand; the last tram ran on March 31, 1964. The city bid an emotional farewell to the service with people lining the route as the crowded tram left at 10 p.m. from Bori Bunder for Dadar, which is known as Dadar Tram Terminus (Dadar T.T.) even today.

To address the growing need for public transport in the city, motor buses were introduced in 1926. It was decided that a fleet of twenty-four buses would ply from July 15, 1926, from Afghan Church to Crawford Market, Dadar Tram Terminus to King's Circle, and Opera Tram Terminus to Lalbaug. Existing modes of transport such as horse-drawn carriages and taxis opposed the move as they viewed buses as competition. They pleaded with the police commissioner to intervene and stop the service. However, the commissioner declined to do so, explaining that the city required both services. The bus service was a big success. By the end of 1926, 600,000 passengers were recorded by BEST with the number growing exponentially, increasing to six times by the next year. Between 1928 and 1930, each bus also had a postbox for letters.

Double-decker buses were introduced in 1937 to address the growing number of commuters. Initially, buses were able to comfortably accommodate all the passengers. But with World War II, tyres and petrol were in short supply, restricting the use of private cars. This led to public transport being affected, with overcrowding in the buses.

A few days before Independence, on August 7, 1947, the Municipal Corporation acquired the operation of tramways and distribution of electricity in the city of Bombay as well as the bus service and the 'Bombay Electric Supply and Tramways Company' was renamed 'Bombay Electric Supply and Transport'. • PV

Opposite, above:
Double-Decker Tram Car (Route 5); glass negative, early to mid-twentieth century, Bombay; 25.4 x 30 cm. Accessioned: 1930–50.
•
Opposite, below:
B.E.S.T Bus from Flora Fountain to Gowalia Tank; glass negative, mid-twentieth century, Bombay; 25.4 x 30 cm. Accessioned: 1930–50.

20 FITZGERALD GAS LAMP

GAS lamps arrived in Bombay in 1833 after the Governor of Bombay, John FitzGibbon, saw that Ardaseer Cursetjee Wadia, a noted shipbuilder and the first Indian to be appointed a Fellow of the Royal Society, used coal gas to illuminate his house in Mazgaon.[1] Framjee Cowasjee, a cotton trader and philanthropist, was also among the first to use gas lamps at his residence in Mazgaon. However, the technology for purifying the gas did not exist at the time and during a dinner party, his guests were overcome by the smell.

A resolution was passed in 1843 to set up lamps on the principal streets in the city as a security measure, and the Government invited tenders for lamp posts. Within a decade, there existed fifty lamps in the city, which burned from dusk to midnight on all days of the year, except on the nights when moonlight was bright. The cost of gas lighting was approximately Rs 17 per lamp per annum.[2] In 1863, the Bombay Gas Company started laying out pipelines at Parel. By 1865, lamps were erected along Bhendi Bazaar, the Esplanade and Churchgate Street. On October 7, 1866, the *Bombay Builder* noted, 'A portion of the town was for the first time lighted with gas ... and as the lamp lighters went from lamp to lamp, they were followed by crowds of inquisitive natives.'

In the late 1860s, well-known citizens of Bombay presented the city with large ornamental lamps to be erected on public roads. The Fitzgerald lamp and fountain was erected in 1867 at the northern end of the Cruikshank Road (Dhobi Talao) in honour of Sir William Robert Seymour Vesey-Fitzgerald, Governor of Bombay from 1867 to 1872. It was designed and manufactured by Barwell and Co. at the Eagle Foundry in Northampton, England, as one of two identical lamps with ornamental fountains.[3] The first was installed in the market square at Northampton in 1863 to mark the matrimonial alliance of Prince of Wales (later King Edward VII) to Princess Alexandra of Denmark. The one in the Northampton square was dismantled in 1962 while the one sent to India was moved from its original location at Dhobi Talao to the grounds of the Dr. Bhau Daji Lad Museum in 1963-64. The photograph (opposite) of the gas lamp and fountain in front of the Robert Money School was probably taken in the early twentieth century and shows the fountain on a raised plinth with a spherical glass cover on top.

Special permission was granted by the Government to the Bombay Gas Company to lay pipes and fittings in the erstwhile Victoria and Albert Museum during the Bombay Exhibition in 1873 (see pp. 126-27) and the Museum was lit till 7 p.m. on February 15, when the exhibition opened.[4] Crawford Market was lit with gas lamps in 1882 after a brief experiment with electric lighting and the next year, the Municipal Corporation entered into an agreement with the Eastern Electric Light and

Sir Seymour Fitzgerald Gas Lamp and Fountain; cast bronze, 1867, Bombay; 1371.6 x 426.7 cm.
At the time of publication, the gas lamp was moved from the Museum garden back to its original location.

Power Company to lay electric cables along the important roads in the city. The lead pipes originally used by the Bombay Gas Company were replaced with wrought iron pipes that used lead joints. By the late nineteenth century, gas lamps were widely used in the city during important festivals such as Diwali. Coal purifiers were eventually fixed in 1906–09 and by 1910, there existed a total of 4,400 gas lamps in Bombay.

In August 1923, the Bombay Electric Supply and Tramway Company installed thirty-six electric lamps across the city. In fact, the BEST even received complaints from some of the city's inhabitants that the light from the lamps erected outside their homes came straight into their bedrooms and they petitioned the Municipality to cover the lights with shades! By December 1935, there were a total of 1,337 electric lamps lit for the whole night and ninety-six lit only till midnight. • RWB

Sir Seymour Fitzgerald Lamp and Fountain; glass negative, late nineteenth to early twentieth century, Bombay; 25.4 x 30 cm. Accessioned: 1917-18. The gas lamp was shifted in front of Metro Cinemas in the early twentieth century, following the demolition of Robert Money School.

KHADA PARSI GAS LAMP

Manockjee Cursetjee, a judge from Bombay, learned about a unique prize-winning gas lamp and fountain when he visited the 1862 International Exhibition in England. It was manufactured by Coalbrookdale Company, a well-known cast-iron manufacturer who produced the lamp for the Chilean Government circa 1840s. Cursetjee commissioned a duplicate to be installed in 'one of the most picturesque quadrants of Bombay' at an approximate cost of Rs 20,000.[1] The parts were shipped from England and assembled in India.

It has a Corinthian column with a bronze statue of his father—Shet Cursetjee Manockjee, who passed away in 1845—executed by sculptor John Bell. This iconic gas lamp with four fountains and the statue was erected in front of the Byculla Hotel, which was frequented by the city's elite. Shet Cursetjee Manockjee was regarded as a patriarch of the Parsi community in Bombay and held a prominent position in the Parsi Punchayat. He was the founder of one of the first schools for girls in Bombay, now called the Alexandra Girls' English Institution. It was believed that his great grandfather moved to Bombay when the islands were transferred from the Portuguese to the English in 1660s, learned English and became a prominent shipbuilder trading with Arabia and Bengal.

Ardaseer Cursetjee Wadia Gas Lamp and Fountain and Byculla Hotel; glass negative, late nineteenth to early twentieth century, Bombay; 25.4 x 30 cm. Accessioned: 1903–18.

On May 26, 1928, this gas lamp was moved from its original location at the junction of Nagpada and Bellasis Road to its present location near the foot of the Byculla Bridge with the consent of Shet Cursetjee Manockjee's family.[2] • RWB

21 THE ICE HOUSE

Top:
The Ice House; glass negative, late nineteenth to early twentieth century, Bombay; 25.4 x 30 cm. Accessioned: 1913–18.
•

Above:
Landing Ice at Bombay; engraving, J.I.V, *The Graphic*, volume XVIII, no. 466, November 2, 1878, Bombay; 20.1 x 20.6 cm. Accessioned: 2014.

THE Ice House of Bombay was built in 1843 in the Fort area, and stood next to the Great Western Hotel, opposite the entrance of the Government Dockyard. The history of the Ice House reveals the fascinating story of the consumption of ice in India and the trade with the United States. The first ice cream ever eaten in India was in the nineteenth century, made with ice from Massachusetts. The first ice was brought to Bombay from America in 1836.[1] Lesser known is the role of the erstwhile Byculla Club, which pioneered the steady import of ice to Bombay and the construction of the Ice House. Club members enjoyed specialty refreshments and cocktails served with crushed ice on sweltering days.

According to the *Bombay Gazetteer*, the first consignment of ice was received from America by the firm of Jehangir Nasawanji Wadia in September 1834. Sir Jamsetjee Jeejeebhoy pioneered the use of ice at dinner parties but a few days later, the *Bombay Samachar* reported that Sir Jamsetjee and his guests had caught very bad colds!

In 1839, the construction of an ice house was proposed and a movement for the regular supply of ice from America was initiated. A fund of Rs 10,000 was collected for building the Ice House, and an arrangement was made with Mr Tudor of Boston, USA, for the despatch of regular consignments.

Frederic Tudor (1783–1864), who was called 'The Ice King' in the nineteenth century, was an entrepreneur from Boston, who realised the profit to be made from harvesting, cutting and shipping ice from the lakes in America to tropical regions, where ice, if known at all, was a luxury product. He is single-handedly responsible for not only conceiving the idea of cutting, storing and shipping ice, but also for inventing the system and technology around it. He found a way to transform a merchant ship into a vessel for transporting ice by adding insulation with sawdust. His first shipment in 1806 was of about 130 tonnes. By the 1850s, more than 1,40,000 tonnes of ice were shipped from Massachusetts.[2]

However, by 1857, the lack of ships and the high freight costs caused the business to dwindle, eventually causing an 'ice famine' in 1877. According to the *Bombay Gazetteer*, a deputation of leading citizens in Bombay presented a memorial to the Governor of Bombay in 1877, asking the Bombay Government to 'institute a searching enquiry into the cause of the ice famine of 1876 and 1877, and to ensure a reliable and steady supply of that useful commodity'.[3]

Eventually, the introduction of ice-manufacturing machines, and other factors, such as the increasing expense of shipbuilding, adversely affected the ice trade. The Ice House now served no purpose and was used as a warehouse till its demolition in the 1920s. The K.R. Cama Oriental Institute, established in 1916, now stands on the same site. • PV

THE BYCULLA CLUB

The Byculla Club was founded in 1833 for the British residents of the area. The club's premises spread across the rectangular area marked by Club Road (M.M. Marg, Agripada) in the north and Bellasis Road to the south, and between Lamington Road (Dr Anandrao Nair Marg) to the west and Morland Road to the east. The grounds housed two tennis courts, a cricket ground, a clubhouse, members' chambers, servant quarters, stables, racing stands, a weighing room, a fern house and gardens.

The club provided a common meeting place for the British in Bombay to socialise. The activities of the club give an insight into the social life of the time. By the 1840s, the club frequently held balls, dinners and dances. Billiards and cricket were a regular source of recreation for the members.

Frequent dinners were held at the club in honour of the various high-ranking dignitaries departing to England. Some of the most illustrious figures for whom dinners were held at the club included Sir Bartle Frere, the Governor of Bombay (1862–67), and their Royal Highnesses the Prince and Princess of Wales (later King George V and Queen Mary) on their visit to India in 1905. The club was known for its food and drinks; the soufflé and cocktails being most popular.

As a trendsetter, the club observed elaborate norms of etiquette and devised ways of cooling water before ice was imported. It followed the 'traditional custom of dressing bottles in wet petticoats, fancifully arranged around the necks'. Port, claret and burgundy were usually dressed in wetted cloths of crimson with white flounces, while sherry and Madeira appeared in bridal white. Those were the days when a servant was essential to look after the cooling of water, but with the introduction of ice, the *abdar's* (head server's) importance began to wane, and by the 'forties, the ice age was fairly established'.[1]

The club played a key role in encouraging the import of ice. The *Bombay Times* of 1839 notes that 'the Society will be much indebted to the members of the Club, for their encouragement of this spirited undertaking, and we hope that measures may be arranged to give the public the full benefit of this important luxury'.

The same year, the construction of an ice house was proposed and the Byculla Club hoped to give Rs 500 to the fund being collected. However, this subscription met with some resistance from the club's committee. By April, as warmer weather set in, the reluctant members were persuaded and the proposal was approved unanimously. • PV

The Byculla Club, Cecil Burns; print, S. Sheppard, *The Byculla Club, 1833–1916, A History*. 1916, Bombay: Bennett, Coleman & Co. Ltd.; 24.5 x 16.5 cm. Accessioned: 1916-17.

22 BOMBAY SILVER RUPEE

IN October 1677, King Charles II authorised the East India Company to coin money at Bombay.[1] Governor Aungier, the most important of the early colonial officials and who is credited with instituting several progressive reforms to develop Bombay, established a mint in 1672. Until then, the Surat Rupee, issued in the name of Mughal Emperor Shah Alam II, was the prevailing currency of the Bombay Presidency. The mint was established to produce copper and tin coins to meet local industrial demands. The coins were minted in the Bombay Castle, now INS *Angre*, near the Town Hall. It was only in 1717 that the mint started producing silver rupees, once the Mughal Emperor Farrukhsiyar (r. 1713–19) granted permission to the East India Company to mint its first rupee coins.[2] These coins were hand-struck in a Mughal style and bore the name of the Emperor. This style continued until the unification of coinage in India in 1835.

The Museum has a diverse collection of Indian coins from the early historical (Western Kshatrapas, Indo-Greeks, second century BCE onwards) to the colonial period (Portuguese, East India Company, eighteenth century CE till mid-twentieth century CE). The East Indian Company (Bombay) collection was acquired in 1939–40. By the late eighteenth century, the Indian subcontinent had three types of coins: those issued in the name of provincial British Governors; those issued at mints under native control but subservient to the East India Company; and those struck at the Company's own mint.

The expansion and development of trade in the city necessitated the continued production and systemisation of coinage. The Company turned to the Soho Mint, London, to bring about major reforms in its coinage system, not only in England but across the colonies in which it operated. In 1829, the 'Old' Soho Mint was exported to replace the 'Old' Bombay Mint. The imported modern mint consisted of machine-presses that used steam for rolling, pressing and striking the coins, producing larger quantities more economically.

The present Mumbai mint was constructed between 1824 and 1830 by Captain John Hawkins of the Bombay Engineers. King William IV introduced uniform coinage across all the colonies in 1835. In India, the East India Company adopted the gold mohur as its principal gold coin along with the silver rupee and copper annas. The new coinage was in an English style, with the British King's name instead of the Mughal Emperor's on the obverse and the inscription 'East India Company' on the reverse.

This significant transition in currency is represented by the EIC silver rupee of 1835, from the reign of King William IV, in the Museum's collection. The obverse has the bust of King William IV, facing right, with the following lettering along the edge 'WILLIAM IIII, KING'. On the reverse, there are two laurel

Shivrai; copper, c. seventeenth century CE, Deccan; 3 cm (diameter). Minted during the reign of Chhatrapati Shivaji Maharaj (r. 1674–80). Accessioned: 1990.
•
Opposite:
One Rupee; portrait of King William IV on the obverse, silver, 1835, minted by the East India Company, Bombay; 5 cm (diameter). Accessioned: 1939–40.

branches crossing to make a wreath within which is written the value, 'One Rupee', in English and Persian. Outside the wreath, along the edge, are the words 'East India Company' and below them is the date, 1835. Silver coinage standardisation as a basic value throughout British India was introduced in 1835. It was argued that in a peasant economy, where small transactions were common, silver currency was more convenient, especially when it was reinforced by token copper coins.[3]

In 1858, the East India Company was dissolved and the control over the British Indian territories was handed over to the Crown. Currency was issued by the Crown instead of the East Indian Company. New coins were introduced in 1877 after Queen Victoria was declared the Empress of India. The coins were minted with the legend 'VICTORIA EMPRESS' and a new monetary system was introduced that became the foundation of the British Empire in India. • HK

23 WORLI ESTATES

THE Museum has one of the finest collections of rare maps of Bombay both in print and in relief. The relief maps of the Worli estates are remarkable as they show the topography of the area before and after the establishment of the city's iconic mills. Visible beside the mills are the dense residential quarters of the workers, which reflect the influx of migrants who came to Bombay to work in the cotton mills. The Worli area was carefully laid out, with the affluent housing at one end and the mills and quarters for the labour at the other end. Called Girangaon, this neighbourhood abuts the Museum, with the mill spires still visible. It represents the labouring heart of the city, which vigorously supported the protests for independence and where the powerful labour movements of the 1980s was born. The Museum acquired these dioramas in 1940 from the Bombay Improvement Trust to augment its collection on the modernisation of the city.

Situated within easy reach of the cotton-growing districts, Bombay proved well suited for the expansion of the cotton trade not only for the requirement of its own spinning factories but also for export to Europe, the United States of America, China and Japan. In fact, by the beginning of the twentieth century, Bombay was regarded as the largest cotton market in Asia.

After the Uprising of 1857, the town planners began an active programme of financial reorganisation and urban improvement to strengthen their rule, control the spread of epidemics, and organise trade. In the 1850s, as a result of the American Civil War, the export of cotton from Bombay increased manifold. The first Indian cotton mill, the Bombay Spinning Mill, was set up in 1854 by Cowasji Nanabhai Davar. In 1870, there were only ten cotton mills in Bombay, employing 8,103 workers. In the next two decades, rapid development took place and by 1890, there were seventy mills employing 59,139 workers.[1] The number of textile mills increased from forty-two in 1880 to an astonishing 136 by 1900. In 1911, 54 per cent of the city's mills were concentrated in the Worli–Byculla–Tadwadi area.[2] The workers required housing, preferably close to their work site, and the first *chawls* came up in 1899 on Bellasis Road in Byculla. By 1915, there were eighty-three mills in the city. The industry experienced a period of economic stagnation in the 1920s due to the plague and World War I. In the face of increasing competition from Japan and China, the mills declined and by 1953 only fifty-three mills were functional.

In the decade between 1933 and 1942, building activity reached its peak as the population grew from 1.16 million (1931 census) to 1.49 million (1941 census) and pressure on land escalated. The Bombay Improvement Trust opened up the lands to the north by reclamation and planning.

Governor Sydenham Clarke praised the trust for its 'excellent work' but believed that development had been undertaken without 'any harmonious plan', nor had it taken into account 'the relative urgency of the needs of the city' such as 'the future development of communications, or distribution of population'.[3]

By the 1940s the local merchants and industrialists stimulated commercial real estate growth by expanding into the suburbs. The Worli Before and After diorama is a depiction of the Bombay City Improvement Trust's proposal for the creation of residential areas with public amenities for the community. The Government scheme wanted to maximise profits by developing residential areas with a wide view of the spacious and sparsely populated bay. This changed the demographics of the Worli area and pushed the new business centres further north from the main town.

The textile mills formed the backbone of Bombay's industrial development and its commercial success. Almost every major industrial family of Bombay was involved in the textile trade, contributing to the socio-economic wealth of the city. The culture that was fostered around the textile industry became an intrinsic part of the city's identity. • HK

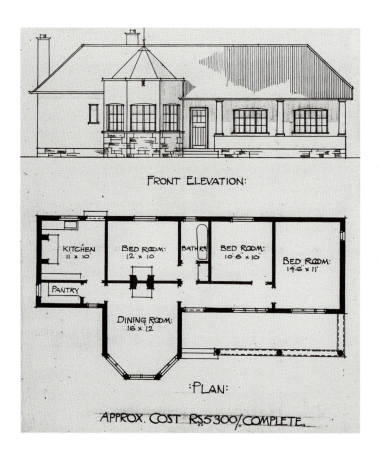

FRONT ELEVATION:

PLAN:

APPROX. COST RS.5300/-COMPLETE.

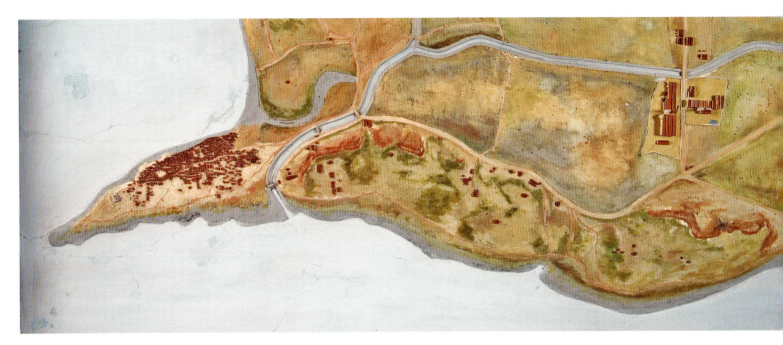

Top:
Worli Estates Before Development; plaster of Paris, pigments, wood, early twentieth century, Bombay; 76 x 174.5 cm. Accessioned: 1940.
•
Above:
Worli Estates After Development; plaster of Paris, pigments, wood, early twentieth century, Bombay; 76 x 174.5 cm. Accessioned: 1940.
•
Opposite:
The Cirrus Avenue Tenants Proposed Small-Cottage Scheme for West Agripada, approx. cost Rs 5,300, complete; glass negative, c. 1940, Bombay; 10 x 10 cm. Accessioned: 1940–50.

24 THE BOMBAY PLAGUE

THE Museum's collection of images about the infamous Bombay plague highlights the unfortunate aspects of urban life in the late nineteenth century. Known as the 'City of Gold', Bombay attracted migrants from across the subcontinent, which resulted in overcrowding and unhygienic conditions. The cramped housing put enormous pressure on the city's limited infrastructure, sanitation and health services. The prints show not only the horrors of the bubonic plague but also how traumatic the experience was for the migrants and working-class communities. The massive exodus of people due to the plague caused the city's economy to collapse.

The bubonic plague outbreak originated in China in 1894 and spread through the world via the ports used by British steamships across the Empire. The first official mention of the occurrence of the plague in Bombay was in the Mandvee area on September 23, 1896.[1] However, the British authorities were reluctant to admit the presence of the disease for fear of causing panic.[2] By the beginning of December 1896, the epidemic had rapidly spread through the other wards of the city. The suburbs of Parel, Sion, Mahim, Worli and Byculla were the most affected.

It is estimated that in 1896 alone, the death toll averaged more than 1,900 people per week. Business came to a standstill; trade was paralysed, and enormous sums of money had to be diverted from improvement works into efforts to combat the scourge. The plague drew public attention to the appalling living conditions of the town's working-class communities. A map of Bombay of this period shows that the port, docks, railways, mills and the business quarter, which collectively provided employment to most of the city's populace, were crowded together in the narrowest part of the island.

The population of Bombay in 1896 was approximately 800,000.[3] Once the authorities acknowledged the presence of the plague, they pursued a two-pronged strategy of disinfection and segregation. Houses where the plague had struck were marked, emptied, whitewashed and sprayed with carbolic acid. Their bedding was burnt. All those infected were taken to special plague hospitals and their relatives were isolated in camps. The authorities enacted the Epidemic Diseases Act in February 1897, which gave them extraordinary powers to curtail the disease.[4]

Fear and suspicion of the Government's interventionary measures to control the plague brought on an exodus of the working classes from Bombay back to their villages. Commercial activities came to a standstill and the disease began spreading to other towns. Plague doctors at the railway station would separate people into gendered queues for examination and there were arbitrary examinations on streets as well. These measures disregarded social customs, caste prejudices and religious sensibilities of the people. The loss of personal agency in these very public examinations created discomfort and growing resentment against the British among the local population.

Those who were suspected of infection were taken to segregated isolation camps, leading to loss of employment and steady income for many families. Isolated patients were frequently smuggled out and hidden within their homes or taken to search-free areas, making it difficult to stop the spread of the plague. The Government's resources were spent in placating people and quelling rumours as well as fighting the epidemic.

Waldemar Haffkine, a Russian bacteriologist, developed the vaccine for the plague in his laboratory at Bombay in 1897-98 and inoculations finally began. Working at Grant Medical College, Haffkine prepared bacteriological cultures from seven live patients suspected of harbouring the plague and three who had succumbed to it. As with earlier vaccines, Haffkine first proved its efficacy in animals and then its safety for humans by a clinical trial on himself.[5]

On January 16, 1897, Haffkine reported the successful outcome of his experiment upon himself. Over 8,000 volunteers came forward for vaccination in the next few months. However, it took some years to inoculate the public and stop the spread of the disease. On November 9, 1898, the Bombay City Improvement Trust was created by an act of the British Parliament. It implemented thirty-three vital schemes to improve the city's housing and planning infrastructure from 1898–1910. These included the building of *chawls* or working-class housing, and roads like Princess Street and Sydenham Road, which would channel the sea air into the more crowded parts of the town. The study by the plague commission (1907–11) helped to control the disease and led to its eventual decline by the 1920s, by which time it had caused more than 10 million deaths in British India. • HK

The Exodus from Bombay, Amedee Forestier; offset print, 1897, Bombay; 40.4 x 29.1 cm. Accessioned: 2013.

As the population of the city grew exponentially in the mid-nineteenth century due to an economic boom, new areas were developed to create housing to accommodate the influx of people. The making of foras, or reclaimed roads that cut across land reclaimed from the sea's flooding and the swampy areas between the islands, was the key factor that led to the development of central and northern Bombay. The first important road to be built was Bellasis Road. And the first *chawls* or working-class housing were built on Bellasis Road.

An inscription on the Bellasis Road bridge reads: 'This Bellasis Road was made in 1793 A.D. by the poor driven from the City of Surat in that year of famine, out of funds by public subscription, and takes its name from Major General Bellasis under whose order it was constructed.'[1]

A causeway built by General Bellasis at his own expense in 1793, as part of the famine relief effort, was instrumental in shaping the city. The causeway, called Bellasis Road, stretched from Malabar Hill to Mazgaon and opened the flatlands to the north of the Town of Bombay, leading to the development of Tardeo, Byculla and Kamathipura.

Byculla was earlier a low-lying swamp that was submerged at high tide. But after reclamation, affluent Europeans from Mazgaon started moving into the area and transformed it into a fashionable locality.

With the transformation of Bombay into an industrial city, the character of Byculla changed into a working-class neighbourhood. It was the first area to be affected by the devastating plague of 1896. The Epidemic Diseases Act of 1897 resulted in the development of *chawls* that are small apartments with common toilet facilities and shared verandas, and define working-class housing in Bombay. The architecture included a *chowk* (passage) to allow light and air into the building and a common courtyard for ventilation and recreation.[2] Long work hours and low wages meant that accommodation for mill workers and labourers had to be provided close to the docks or mills.[3]

Chawls spawned a distinctive communal culture and led to labour movements and mobilisation during the Indian independence movement. In 1911, the census of India estimated that 80 per cent of Bombay's residents lived in *chawls*.[4] Over time, the uses and context of the *chawls* changed, reflecting in a microcosm the city's social and working-class history.

The Municipal Corporation of Bombay donated the Bellasis Road Chawls diorama to the Museum. It depicts the various working-class housing typologies of early industrial Bombay, including *chawls*, two- and three-room apartments, and the landscaping to organise these buildings. The diorama was part of an effort to inform the public about city planning projects and demonstrate the Government's strategy of overcoming disease and congestion through creation of better housing facilities for the working class. Though the diorama was acquired by the Museum in 1954, it was probably made earlier, between 1899 and 1905. • HK

Bellasis Road Chawls; card paper houses on wood panel, pigments, painted grass, and metal details, late nineteenth to early twentieth century, Bombay; 28 x 113 x 142 cm. Accessioned: 1954.

LORD SANDHURST STATUE AND TROWEL

William Mansfield, Viscount Sandhurst, was the Governor of Bombay during 1895–1900. The Museum has three objects associated with Lord Sandhurst; a marble statue, a glass negative and a silver trowel that he used for the foundation stone ceremony of the first *chawl* built by the Bombay City Improvement Trust. Lord Sandhurst's statue was originally located at the corner of Oval Maidan.[1] The Bombay High Court, the University and the Secretariat buildings are visible behind the statue. Oval Maidan also had statues of Sir Richard Temple and Lord Reay, both Governors of Bombay.

Most of the colonial statues were moved to the Museum in 1965 during the Samyukta Maharashtra movement. Renowned sculptor George Edward Wade made the statue of Lord Sandhurst according to the principles of 'the new sculpture' movement.[2] Its distinguishing qualities were a new dynamism and energy as well as physical realism. The sculpture is depicted in a realistic mode, as if Lord Sandhurst is about to address a gathering, and props like those used in studio photography add volume to the sculpture.

In 1896, the city suffered a terrible plague epidemic, which first appeared in a *chawl* near Masjid Bridge, and spread rapidly, creating panic among the population. In an effort to stamp it out, Lord Sandhurst founded the City Improvement Trust in 1898. There was an urgency to provide hygienic accommodation for the poor and labour classes to improve the city's commerce.

The trowel used by Sandhurst is one of the most significant artefacts related to the modern history of Mumbai. The object marks the beginning of the transformation that took place to improve the housing and sanitary conditions of the city and is a marker of the signal change that encouraged the industrial development of the city.

The inscription on the trowel reads:
Trowel used by His Excellency, The Right Honourable, William Baron Sandhurst GCIE, Governor of Bombay, for laying the foundation stone of the first chawl undertaken by the Bombay Improvement Trust for housing the Poorer and Working classes.

• HK

Trowel; silver, 1899, Bombay; 7 x 30 x 9 cm. Accessioned: early twentieth century.

•

Left:
Lord Sandhurst (1855–1921); glass negative, early twentieth century, Bombay, 30 x 25.4 cm. Accessioned: 1903–20.

BOMBAY'S urban development was the outcome of the colonial administration's efforts to emulate ideas and systems that had been developed in Britain, specifically in London. The rapid population growth of the city had significantly increased the pressure on the existing infrastructure. By 1880, there were more than 800,000 people living in the city.[1] The booming economy led to overcrowding and various schemes were undertaken by the Government to improve the living conditions of the working-class population. One of the key concerns was drainage and sewerage to ensure that there was adequate hygiene.

Overcrowding and the ensuing unsanitary conditions led to epidemics and diseases, which resulted in high mortality rates. Worried that protests would lead to insurrections in the overcrowded parts of the city, the British Government overhauled the city structure physically and administratively. One of the first moves was the adoption of new civic policies regarding sanitation. During the

mid-nineteenth century, the idea of modernity was entwined with notions of hygiene and sanitation. This was based on new technologies like the hydraulic water supply and underground drainage, which required intensive use of new machinery and heavy expenditure. Historian Asa Briggs notes 'that the hidden network of pipes and drains was perhaps one of the biggest technical and social achievements of the Victorian age and the sanitary system was considered more comprehensive than the transport system'.[2]

One of the important people to leave an impact on sanitary policy in both Britain and India was Florence Nightingale (1820–1910). Born into an affluent British family, she vigorously pursued various health initiatives undertaken in India. She was consulted by officials coming out to India on matters pertaining to sanitation. And while she never visited India, she kept herself informed about the country, which was one of the recurring themes in her writings from 1862. In *Observations*, written in 1863, she commented on the water

supply and sanitary amenities of Bombay and the three Presidency towns. She noted that Bombay had water supply but no drainage, Calcutta had drainage and Madras had neither. She wrote many letters to Sir Bartle Frere, Governor of Bombay (1862–67), on sanitary issues.[3] She had a major impact on improving the sanitation and water systems in Bombay as well as in Madras and Calcutta in the late nineteenth century.

Bombay's climate added difficulties to the satisfactory solution of drainage problems. The high temperature caused quick decomposition and excessive formation of gas in the sewers, which could potentially lead to serious diseases. Consequently, special consideration had been given to the ventilation of sewers and to the materials used in the construction of the sewerage works. Open drains by the sides of streets and the yearly cleansing by the monsoon rains were to a large extent the drainage system that the city depended on in the early nineteenth century. The progress in education and economic prosperity created a demand for better sanitary conditions and surroundings. The lesson learned through various epidemics that hit the city pushed the Bombay Municipal Corporation to undertake improvement projects for better infrastructure.

Several schemes were conceived but it was only in 1882, under the guidance of Municipal Commissioner E.C.K. Ollivant (1881–1891) and executive engineer Rienzi Walton, that a proper drainage system for the city was executed. The 1882 relief map in the Museum collection, along with the drainage and sewage systems, also shows the geological features of Bombay. It shows the alluvium and other superficial deposits, the basaltic trap of Malabar Hill, freshwater beds, shales and flags, and a grey trap with shales interstratified, and the black rock of the Antop Hill. Its geological features present the ridges of basaltic rock on both the city's eastern and western sides; both these ridges are scarped towards the east, and slope downward towards the west.

During the tenure of Ollivant, Walton created the relief drainage map for the execution of the project. He had joined the Bombay Municipality in 1865 and worked there until 1872. He undertook several important public projects to improve the city's crumbling infrastructure, such as implementing the drainage system for the city, the creation of Tulsi Lake, a masonry storage reservoir at Malabar Hill. His main project however was the execution of the drainage and sewerage system of the city, which is depicted in detail in the Museum's relief map. • HK

Elevated Plan of the Island of Bombay (Drainage Map of Bombay), Surveyor Hurrischandra Rowjee; plaster of Paris, mixed clay and oil paint, 1882, Bombay; 12 x 274 x 99 cm. Accessioned: 1882.

27 RELIEF MAP OF GREATER BOMBAY

THE relief map of Greater Bombay illustrates the town's planning till 1923 and offers a glimpse of the future projects for the city. It shows the road and rail network, the aerodrome, water reservoirs, the dock and future sites reserved for industry.

The map was created by Sirdar S.L. Bagwe, an awarded architect and sculptor, who also made other dioramas in the Museum and helped with the restoration of some of the Museum's model collection.[1] Bagwe's original sketch of the map on paper is in the Museum's collection as well.

The map illustrates a period of great transition in the city. It indicates the setting up of railways, as well as the plan for the reconstitution of the Municipal Corporation into a 'Greater Bombay Council'. The expanded scope of the Municipal Corporation would enable it to preside over issues of road, transport, public health, water supply and drainage for the whole area. It attempted to integrate the municipal boundaries northward to include independent villages and municipalities such as Bandra in Salsette, and developing suburbs like Andheri, Malad, Parle and Santacruz. The municipal administration plan for 'Greater Bombay' was finally formalised only in the 1950s after Independence.

The road and rail network lines shown across the map defined the structure of the city, the value of land and the growth of commerce. The plan for the railways was in the works for several years before it materialised. The railway was one of the most significant developments in the country, connecting places and people, augmenting industrial development and the movement of goods. The impetus for developing railways was facilitated by the need for the movement of cotton following the failure of the cotton crop in America in 1846. The first train in India was started between Bombay and Thane on April 16, 1853, by the Great Indian Peninsula Railway Company.[2] The railway lines on the map show the extent of the development of the railway up to 1934. By this time, the city was connected by the railways on a north-south axis and also divided into the east and the west regions.

The aerodrome, situated in Juhu and set up in 1928, is also marked on the map. It was initially an unpaved airfield and was used for joyrides and flying classes by the Bombay Flying Club. It was only by 1932, two years prior to the making of this map, that the ground of the airfield became more developed. In October 1932, J.R.D. Tata, known as the father of civil aviation in India, made his maiden voyage from Karachi to Bombay via Ahmedabad, carrying airmail in a Puss Moth.[3] The Tata Airmail Services and Tata Airlines, which later became Air India, were established in the same year. Two runways were laid at the site only in 1936, which were concretised in 1937. The aerodrome served as the city's airport then and during World War II, up to 1948. • PV

Relief Map of Greater Bombay, 1923, Sirdar S.L. Bagwe; watercolour and pen on paper, Bombay; 36.3 x 21.5 cm. Accessioned: 1934.
Sketch made for the three-dimensional model of the map.
•

Opposite:
Relief Map of Greater Bombay, 1923, Sirdar S.L. Bagwe; mixed media, Bombay; 185 x 107 cm. Accessioned: 1934.

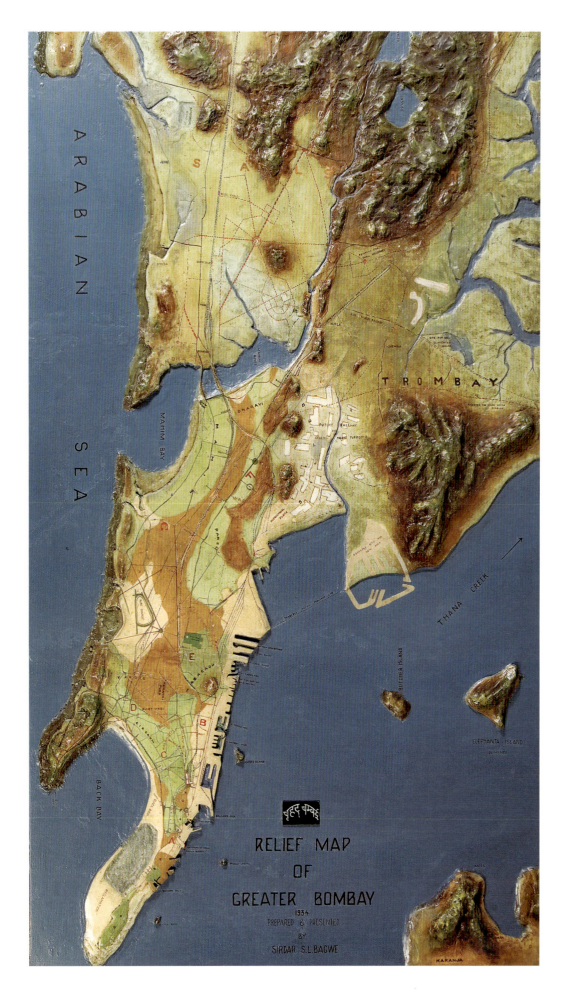

ARABIAN SEA

RELIEF MAP
OF
GREATER BOMBAY
1934
PREPARED & PRESENTED
BY
SIRDAR S.L.BAGWE

BY the 1930s, Bombay emerged from the ravages of the plague and famines, and the Great Depression with a new vigour and purpose. Ambitious new urban development plans, which included the famous Backbay Reclamation Scheme (1928–42), transformed a small Victorian town into a glamorous modern city. As the educated middle class flocked to the 'City of Gold'[1] in search of a better life, the need for housing resulted in the construction of many new buildings. The new, cosmopolitan Bombay embraced a fresh, modern style of architecture—Art Deco. One of the many concerns for the expanding city was health, and the new style—with its clean lines, central atriums and large spacious verandas that enabled healthy air circulation—was considered most conducive to reduce the impact of unfavourable weather conditions. Unlike the earlier Victorian style that declared imperial authority, the new architecture was the epitome of modern elegance. The city symbolised the aspirations of the transforming putative nation and designs symbolising modernity were interwoven with Indian motifs. American Art Deco in particular was valued as America represented independence from the colonial yoke and was seen as a young, dynamic nation. After Miami, Mumbai is believed to have the highest number of Art Deco buildings.

Between 1930 and 1950, wealthy princes and the business elite, in particular affluent Parsi entrepreneurs, embarked on an urban development crusade. These were people who had travelled across Europe and America and were eager to emulate contemporary Western trends.[2] Cinema houses were one of the first places to reflect Art Deco architecture. The prominence of American films and the picturisation of lavish lifestyles made the older theatres and entertainment places look dull and outdated. The new Deco theatres—Regal, Eros and Metro—were located at major intersections and became lively meeting places with ethnically diverse audiences. This was also the period when nationalism was at its peak, with the Civil Disobedience Movement (1930) and the Salt Satyagraha (1930) sparking much public engagement, making these places magnets for public participation and discussion.[3]

Eros Cinema, built in 1938, was located on newly reclaimed backbay land. Inaugurated by the Governor of Bombay, Roger Lumley, the grand opening included performances by Ida Santarelli's Orchestra, composed entirely of women, and dances by Les Cygnes. The single-screen movie theatre was described as the pride of the East and India's finest place of amusement in the *Bombay Chronicle*.[4] The Art Deco movement reached its pinnacle with the opening of Eros, which, like other Art Deco buildings in the city, appeared modern but borrowed from both Hindu and Islamic architecture.[5] The theatre was inspired and named after the Greek god Eros and built by the Parsi entrepreneur Shiavax Cawasji Cambata, who had spent five years planning it with specialists from around the world. The ziggurat-like structure was largely covered with sandstone from Agra. The building, 140 ft tall, was painted a light cream colour with red highlights to amplify the ornamental features of the facade. This colour interlocking contributed to the illusion of the building's height, establishing its prominence on the intersection where it is located. The building also housed Cambata's flamboyant modern residence on the two top floors. The luxurious interiors of the cinema featured murals of tropical vegetation and depictions of south Indian temples and the Taj Mahal. The elevator doors and auditorium entrances were decorated with a popular Art Deco motif, the frozen fountain, symbolising eternal life. By 1939, Bombay had nearly 300 cinema houses and more than 50,000 patrons went to the theatres in a week, making cinema houses places of extraordinary political and social significance.[6]

With the rise of the Swadeshi movement in the early twentieth century, Indian films emphasising national identity imbued with mythological vocabulary began to be made and screened in a variety of local places, including Art Deco theatres such as Eros and Liberty in Bombay. The Liberty Cinema, inaugurated in 1949, exclusively premiered only Indian films. Important Modern artists started their careers in cinema which continues to have a profound impact on artistic practice. Post-Independence, Indian films began to reflect the harsh realities of rural and urban India. Fantasy became an important trope that offered an escape from difficult circumstances. Films attracted people from all sections of society and Bombay soon became the entertainment capital of India and home to Bollywood, for which it is renowned today. • RJ

Opposite, above:
Eros Cinema; black and white postcard, c. 1938–50, Bombay; 10 x 15 cm. Accessioned: 2021.
Inaugurated on February 10, 1938, Eros was designed by Sohrabji Bhedwar, a partner at the architectural firm Bhedwar & Bhedwar, for prominent businessman Shiavax Cawasji Cambata. The interior of the cinema was designed by Fritz von Drieberg. The theatre was described as 'The Rendezvous of the East' in advertisements. In the mid-twentieth century, the building housed shops, a restaurant, offices, an ice rink and a ballroom. The cinema closed in 2016 after operating for seventy-eight years.
•
Opposite, below:
Eros Theatre, Bombay; colour postcard inscribed with 'Bhedwar & Bhedwar, F.F.R.I.B.A., B.A., L.C.E.'s, Chartered Architects, Bombay', c. 1940–50, Bombay; 10 x 15 cm. Private collection of Rajan Jayakar.

EROS THEATRE.

BHEDWAR & BHEDWAR,
F.F.R.I.B.A., B.A., L.C.E's,
CHARTERED ARCHITECTS,
BOMBAY.

Top:
Bombay Central (B.B. & C.I. Rly), Bombay; black and white postcard, c. 1930–50, Bombay; 10 x 15 cm. Accessioned: 2021.
Established in 1930, Bombay Central Station was designed by the firm Gregson, Batley and King and constructed by Shapoorji Pallonji. The building is marked with subtle Art Deco lines and motifs on the exterior. Located on the Western Line of the Mumbai Suburban Railway, it is a major station for local and long-distance trains today.

Above:
Marine Drive, Bombay; black and white postcard, c. 1940–50, Bombay; 10 x 15 cm. Accessioned: 2021.
In the early twentieth century, the Marine Drive precinct developed as part of the Backbay Reclamation Scheme, with most of the buildings facing the Arabian Sea assigned for residential use. Constructed between 1930 and 1950, the precinct adopted the Art Deco style. In order to preserve the uniformity and harmony of these buildings, design guidelines regulated the architecture of the area, which in 2018 was designated as a World Heritage Site along with the Victorian Gothic ensembles nearby.

Installation view *Silver Magic: Vintage Photographs of the Golden Age of Hindi Cinema, Portraits by J.H. Thakker*; curated by Ram Rahman, 2016. Kamalnayan Bajaj Mumbai Gallery, Dr. Bhau Daji Lad Museum, Mumbai.

Paddy Cultivation; half-baked terracotta, mixed
media, pigments, 1955-56; 65 x 102 x 218 cm,
figures: approx. 20-22 cm.
On view in the Kamalnayan Bajaj Mumbai Gallery,
Dr. Bhau Daji Lad Museum, Mumbai.

NATURAL HISTORY
Documenting the Exotic

BRITAIN emerged as the leading power in the eighteenth and nineteenth centuries in the competition for colonies and resources. This quest for riches was strengthened by the anthropocentric philosophy of the Enlightenment and the parallel quest for knowledge. Known as the Age of Reason, the 'long' eighteenth century saw the emergence of a new spirit of investigation due to which centuries of superstitious beliefs were unshackled through enquiry and logic.[1] The concept of reason opened up new ways of thinking about the world, employing the tools of science and empiricism to make sense of the unknown. Understanding the strange lands and peoples of the colonies required a frame of reference and 'nature' became the overarching empirical trope through which to grasp the incomprehensible. Empiricism demanded evidence and huge collections were amassed and explained in apparently 'scientific' terms during this period. Royal Societies mushroomed across Britain and in India to encourage the new antiquarian and natural history interests. Enlightened men and emperors vied with each other to collect the unusual 'specimen' from nature, the rare object, or artworks considered of great quality. 'Cabinets of Curiosities', *Wunderkammers* or 'Wonder Houses', as these collections were called, became a way of ordering and interpreting knowledge and defined an individual's status and intellectual compass.

Many of these cabinets became the nuclei of some of the major museums of the world. Emerging from similar interests and intentions, the erstwhile V&A, Bombay, and the Victoria Gardens where it was housed, were described to a gathering of Bombay's elite merchants as a 'House of Wonder in a Garden of Delight', in true Enlightenment tradition to attract potential donors who were not quite sure of its purpose. Governor Bartle Frere noted while laying the cornerstone of the Museum in 1862, 'The student in the Museum will thus find himself ever in the presence of nature in her richest and most varied forms. Such an association must be favourable, not only in supplying the materials of study, but in inducing the frame of mind in which the inquirer is most likely to reach the truth.'[2]

Gardens were an important trope of the Enlightenment and have been an enduring British passion. Colonial gardens filled with a vast variety of plants and ornamented with fountains, bandstands and elaborate statuary were, like colonial architecture, a declaration of the British regime's supremacy and superiority in India. The more varied and exotic the garden, the more it demonstrated the 'command' over nature and man's victory over the wild. Colonial gardens were as much a symbol of conquest as the pomp and pageantry that attended the Raj, and a subtle metaphor for the colonial civilising mission.[3] Observing, classifying and ordering the natural world would enable man to understand his purpose in the universe and to decipher God's writ through his creatures great and small. Eminent British philosopher John Locke's utilitarian philosophy, Charles Darwin's

Deep Time, Rohini Devasher; glass marker, acrylic, colour pencil and dry pastel, fossils, minerals and coral, 2016. Exhibition: *Speculations from the Field;* Origins of Mumbai Gallery, 2016–17.
Deep Time is a study of vertical time, of forms that suggest an accretion both of the temporal and the material. The evolution in the drawing creates a fossilised form that seems to turn into an extraterrestrial being as it spreads out and encroaches on the Museum wall. The artist recalls the original intention of the Museum as a natural history museum when it was the Government Central Museum. The drawing is juxtaposed with the Museum's reserve collection of fossils and minerals.

evolutionary theories and Carl Linnaeus's classificatory systems, among many others, provided the moral and ideological reasoning for conquest and exploitation. Both pleasure and purpose found expression in colonial museums and gardens.

Bombay had several public gardens, noted James Maclean in *Maclean's Guide to Bombay*, published in the 1880s. He lists gardens in front of the Town Hall, next to the University, by the Esplanade and adjacent to Crawford Market among others. But none were as visited as the beautiful Victoria Gardens. He elaborates: 'The grounds are appropriately laid out with raised paths and miniature ornamental lakes, and, being richly wooded with choice and rare kinds of tropical trees and plants, arranged botanically, present at all times a gracefully cool and refreshing aspect.' He describes an evening walk in the gardens, '... the gorgeous and varied costumes of the native ladies and gentlemen (who frequent the gardens of an evening by thousands), combining with the rich green of the surrounding foliage, add a feature of vivacity to the scene very charming in its effect, and present a kaleidoscopic study of endless interest to even the most ordinary observer.'[4]

The Victoria Gardens, like the V&A Museum, were fashioned by the passion of George Birdwood (see pp. 56-57) who was given charge of both. Birdwood approached his task with the zeal of a missionary. He collected, documented and nurtured a vast variety of exotic plants, vegetables, fruits, medicinal plants and trees for the botanical garden. He described their suitability for the Indian climate and soil, and painstakingly catalogued every example in his book *Catalogue of the Vegetable Productions of the Presidency of Bombay: Including a List of the Drugs Sold in the Bazars of Western India* (1865). He grew exotic vegetables to cater to the European palette, including endives, leeks, cos lettuce, Brussels sprouts and broccoli among others, which were sold to help maintain the gardens. He also encouraged resident Europeans to start their own kitchen gardens. He planted special 'exotic borders' around the Museum to engage his audiences and maintained an 'exotic shed' where plants from around the world were grown. He made detailed lists of the many vermin, including snakes, that ought to be destroyed to protect his beloved plants.[5] He conducted various experiments in the gardens to enhance the production of commercial plants like silk and jute, which were continued by his successors.

The same zeal and attention to detail characterises his organisation and presentation of the Museum collection which was at the time housed at the Town Hall as the Museum building was under construction. Like the botanical garden, the Museum was an attempt to gather as much information as possible about different Indian 'species': plant, animal and human. And Bombay, due to its strategic location and economic success, provided the perfect laboratory as well as the funds to conduct such experiments. In fact, Birdwood delineates the qualities a curator of the Museum must possess and notes that the ability to get the wealthy 'native' gentlemen of the city to donate to public causes such as the gardens and the Museum should be an important consideration in recruitment. He goes on to recommend a salary that would enable the curator to mix with the city's elite![6]

The Museum, Birdwood stated, would be a 'College of Inquiry' as distinguished from a university that was considered a 'College of Reading'. The former engaged in original research and towards this purpose, he proposed to hire five curators, 'practical experts in geology, botany, meteorology, chemistry and zoology, and each expert should give his whole energy to his specialty'.[7] The Museum's early collections reflect this bias towards natural history, the specimens of which were gathered in specially designed glass bottles, and included a large variety of stuffed birds, snakes, insects, dried fish and various grains, seeds, and dried plants, as well as a plethora of building materials, resins, gums and soils.[8] Birdwood noted that the geological collections were the most important and required a knowledgeable person to collate them and mourned the lack of such a person in Bombay.[9]

Opposite, top:
Museum in the Victoria Gardens, Bombay; black and white postcard, c. 1910–50, Bombay; 10 x 15 cm.

•

Opposite, below:
Interior view of the erstwhile V&A Museum, Bombay; print reproduced from a photograph, *The Journal of Indian Art and Industry*, London: W. Griggs and Sons, 1913; Showcasing the natural history collections at the Museum; 26.6 x 35.5 cm. Accessioned: 1913-26.

Museum in the Victoria Gardens, Bombay

Early colonial, exhibition and museum records are replete with information about the different minerals and stones of the region and their suitability for commercial exploitation. These were also important sections of the various local and international exhibitions. Birdwood particularly collected samples of agate as these were much in demand, and during the curatorship of Cecil Burns (1903–18) in 1909, a number of agate specimens from Cambay were added to the collection. These contained skinned and polished agates showing the various processes through which the raw stone passes until it becomes a finished article. In 1911, photographs were taken at Cambay of the different specimens, processes and implements that were used by the craftsmen in the agate cutting and polishing industry which were added to the case to make the collection more dynamic and improve the understanding of the collection. In 1922-23, a specimen of a mounted gun (cannon) made of agate, which was very popular in European markets, was purchased and added to the specially prepared agates case, to showcase how raw materials could be processed for commercial purposes.[10]

The early Museum at the Town Barracks emphasised this interest in natural history and the sciences. It contained a telescope through which people could see the stars, and a canal along the outside where a water mill functioned to illustrate a new technology and mode of power. At the entrance, it had fountains and a mini aquarium with aquatic plants and water tortoises.[11] The average attendance in 1866–67 was 75,796 when Bombay's population was 8,16,562.[12] Birdwood's vision and that of his colleague Dr Bhau Daji Lad for the infant Museum was expansive and encyclopaedic and he notes hopefully, in a report at the end of his tenure, that future citizens of Bombay will do justice to this vision by enhancing the capacity of the Museum.[13]

The focus on natural history was maintained even after the collection moved to the new building in 1872. The early displays were mostly of dried plants, stuffed animals and birds, with some 'economic products' or decorative objects, contributed by various princely states to the Museum. Many objects were bought at local exhibitions held annually across the country which had become a popular source of entertainment and marketing. Birdwood ensured that the Museum participated in almost every exhibition, both international and national, and a hoard of medals testifies to his exertions (see pp. 103). In 1890, an additional 15 acres were added to the original 33 acres of the botanical gardens to set up a zoo befitting Bombay. Besides lions and reptiles which were more common, two tigers, a few giraffes, zebras, a rhinoceros, and a hippopotamus were housed in specially prepared enclosures.[14] The relationship between the three institutions was organic and close. The Museum's curators carried out plant experiments in the gardens to explore their commercial possibilities.[15] Birdwood noted that a visitor should be able to see a tree in the garden and its product in the Museum.[16] This stress on the manipulation of raw materials through various processes to achieve a finished product was the essential premise on which the Museum was purposed. The models of artisans making objects in the Museum were fashioned not just to entertain but also to illustrate this idea.

Humans too formed part of this study of nature. The science of phrenology, in particular, was used as a means of determining generic traits and characteristics. In 1883, Tyrrell Leith, the founder of the Anthropological Society of Bombay, requested the Bombay Governor's permission to collect and display human skulls at the V&A Museum.[17] Such a display was to take place at the Calcutta International Exhibition and of course, Bombay wanted to show that it was as up to date with its science. The Society was formed 'for the purposes of promoting anthropological researches in India, by investigating and recording facts relating to the physical, intellectual and moral development of man, and more especially of the various races inhabiting the Indian Empire'.[18] However, permission to display skulls at the Museum was not granted due to fears that there would be a religious backlash from the public.

Prehistoric hand axes; stone, ~250,000 BCE, England; 14.4 x 3.6 x 10 cm (avg). Accessioned: 1933.
H.W. Seton Karr (1859–1938), was a British explorer and captain in the British army in Egypt. He collected prehistoric stone implements from expeditions to Somaliland and Egypt, as well as England and India. He distributed some of these artefacts to 200 museums across the world. The V&A, Bombay, acquired thirty stone implements from him.

The study of human skulls, however, was an enterprise across India and the Madras Central Museum's director, Edgar Thurston, would bribe visitors with money and *cheroots* to be allowed to measure their skulls.[19] Anthropological and ethnological surveys were a preamble to defining the races of the subcontinent as deficient and in need of a superior authority to govern them. Though the Museum was denied skulls, it did get an important set of masks of various Himalayan tribes (see pp. 112-13) from the famous Schlagintweit brothers. B.A. Gupte, who was assistant curator at the V&A Museum, Bombay, from 1875 to 1882, went on to work with Herbert Risley, the Director General of the Anthropological Survey of India. Gupte's papers show how completely he was co-opted into the colonial mission of defining tribals as lacking in intellectual acumen because of their smaller build (see p. 114), and castes or communities that resisted British rule as having latent criminal traits.[20]

The zoo, meanwhile, contributed a steady stream of dead animals to the Museum where a taxidermist cleaned, cured and stuffed them. In 1886, Dr Duncan MacDonald, the curator, reported that the department of mammals alone had 151 specimens, which included mostly skins and stuffed animals. In 1888-89, with the intention of bringing the Museum on par with the collections at the Indian Museum in Calcutta, it was decided to include skeletons in the display: '... a lioness, a gazelle, a sambar, a spotted deer, a monkey, two geese, one swan, one pea-fowl, one pelican, one emu ... The bones of the Gangetic crocodile ... were also set up and mounted'.[21] A whale that was stranded at Bassein was brought to the Museum and cleaned and cured. The skeleton was supposed to be put on display in the central hall but it proved too difficult to mount![22] Foreign animals were also stuffed and presented. An African lion and lioness were mounted in London, at great expense, by a renowned taxidermist, and shown within an appropriate setting in a large case at the Museum. An American bison and a black panther were among the several other exotic animals on display. Each year, more natural history collections were added, and the Museum was a veritable zoo with hundreds of stuffed animals, birds, reptiles, insects and fish on display.

Eventually, however, this practice was given up as the weather in Bombay made conservation an uphill task and funds were limited. With the zoo and the gardens next door, the Museum's displays looked forlorn and redundant. By the early twentieth century, with Bombay becoming an important trading hub, it made much greater sense for the Museum to focus on the city's modernisation and development, and its 'industrial arts'. • TZM

Medal, International Fisheries Exhibition, 1883; gold, London; 4.4 x 0.5 cm. Accessioned: 1883.
Inscription on obverse: *Victoria Regina*
Inscription on reverse: *International Fisheries Exhibition, 1883*

FROM its inception to the late nineteenth century, the Museum represented Bombay at national and international exhibitions, and received numerous medals for objects that were sent to be displayed. On May 12, 1883, the International Fisheries Exhibition opened under the patronage of Queen Victoria and Prince Albert Edward on the grounds of the Royal Horticultural Society in South Kensington, London. It was described as a 'scientific, cultural, and animal exhibition' that attracted an average of 18,545 visitors per day until its closing on October 31, 1883.[1] The Museum was awarded one gold and two bronze medals for examples of fish-eating birds and stuffed fish.

The exhibition was perceived as an exciting experience for learning, exploring and discovering marine and freshwater animals indigenous to the British Empire and other foreign nations. Displays were classified under six categories which included fishing equipment; fishing vessels, including steam carriers and boats; fishing nets; preserved fish for edible and non-edible purposes (e.g. fish oils, manure and other products prepared from fish); fresh stuffed or preserved specimens, casts, drawings of marine life such as algae, corals, molluscs and crustaceans and, lastly, history and literature of fishing.

The Museum's curator at the time, Dr MacDonald (1880–1903), selected a wide range of objects, classified under various divisions, which were exhibited at the show. The collection included seventeen types of fishing nets, ten types of hooks and traps, and baskets for storing fish. A range of boat models such as that of a fish canoe with paddles, a *batela* (trawler), and a *baqarah* (deep-sea dhow) were presented. Dr MacDonald states that while working for the exhibition, the Museum was able to secure specimens of natural history, fish, agricultural implements, including models illustrating how Konkan fishermen spun and dyed the fibre required for making nets, and of fishermen and fisherwomen from the Deccan, Konkan and Bombay. Attracting considerable attention were the models of the incarnations of Lord Vishnu, the Matsya (fish) and the Kurma (turtle) avatars. Types of garments worn by Bombay and Bassein fishermen such as caps, long *lungi* (*kobe* or lower garment), bodice cloth, waist belt and metal bangles were also added to the list of objects. The collection sent by the Bombay Government further included sixteen tins of dried and salted fish, and 216 specimens of stuffed fish, including the renowned Bombay duck or *bombil*. MacDonald sent a model of a *machwa*, which was described as the swiftest Indian sailing craft, to the Smithsonian Museum. This was among the ten models of fishing craft and four full-sized boats sent to the exhibition by Francis Day, Her Majesty's Inspector of Fisheries for India.[2]

The official catalogue for the exhibition declares that the Victoria and Albert Museum (Bombay) won awards under 'Jury 23' and 'Jury 26'. The first category of award 'G' was given to the Museum for its exhibit titled 'Case of Fish-eating Birds' under the section of Mammals and Birds. The award 'B' was given for two exhibits of stuffed fish, titled *Sparidae* or *kharva* and *Squalidae* or *mushi* under the Natural History section.[3] The front of the medal depicts the left profile of Queen Victoria and was designed by British engraver and artist Leonard Charles Wyon (1826–91). On the reverse, a juxtaposition of a lobster, eel, starfish and fish swimming in a net, is based on the designs of John Pinches (1825–1905).[4]

The Fisheries Exhibition was spread over 21 acres of land, and was as large as the Great Exhibition of 1851. Unlike general exhibitions, special exhibitions like this would attract groups with specialist interests. For instance, 'fishing gear and fishing craft of all nations' engaged the attention of fishermen and ethnologists; whereas 'life-saving apparatus of all kinds' held the interests of meteorologists, pharologists and philanthropists. Similarly, chemists and physiologists, and geographers and geologists would have benefitted from the displays of preparation, preservation and utilisation of fish, and the charts and relief models of the ocean. • HK

HORS CONCOURS MEDAL, 1867 EXPOSITION UNIVERSELLE

The Museum's medal, with the words 'Hors Concours', which means 'unrivalled', is a marker of the booming cotton trade between Bombay and the European markets in the mid-nineteenth century. It was awarded to the Government of Bombay for samples of raw cotton at the Universal Exhibition of 1867 in Paris.[1] The portrait of French Emperor Napoleon III graces the front of the medal and on the reverse, a pair of two-winged putti representing fame hold a cartouche above the French imperial eagle, and on the top is a laurel wreath. The cartouche is inscribed with the words '*Gouvernement de Bombay*'.

The abundant cotton trade from the 1840s to the 1870s produced the distinctive character of Bombay as the commercial capital of India. Before the arrival of the British, cotton cloth in India was manufactured through small-scale family-led establishments.[2] With the increasing demand in Europe, large-scale production of cotton was initiated by the British and many Indian farmers were forced to grow cotton instead of food crops. By the early nineteenth century, India was one of the major regions producing and exporting cotton.

The American Civil War (1861–65) was a boon for Indian raw cotton and India soon became the main supplier to the world. Bombay, located close to the cotton-growing districts of the Deccan and with the strategic advantage of a natural harbour, became the centre of the Indo-British cotton trade. The lucrative cotton business resulted in a frenzy of investment and speculation by traders, merchants, bankers and industrialists in Bombay. By 1865, when the American Civil War ended, Bombay had earned

Medal, *Hors Concours*; copper alloy, 1867, Paris; 5 x 0.4 cm. Accessioned: 1867.
Inscription on obverse: *Napoleon III Empereur, H. Ponscarme F*
Inscription on reverse: *Exposition Universelle de MDCCCLXVII a Paris, Gouvernement de Bombay, Hors Concours, H. Ponscarme F*

70 million pounds from cotton exports to Britain.[3] A new economic era dawned in Bombay with companies, dealing in reclamation, shipping, insurance and banking mushrooming all over the city.

Prominent merchant families such as the Sassoons, Ruias, Rungtas, Bajajs and Piramals built their fortunes in cotton export. In 1854, the first textile mill was established in Bombay; raw cotton was required for the burgeoning indigenous textile industry. This local demand facilitated the development of infrastructure, communication and transport in the city, and the railways was subsequently set up in Bombay to enable the swift movement of cotton. • PV

30 THE THANATOPHIDIA OF INDIA

by JOSEPH FAYRER

Bungarus fasciatus; chromolithograph, Joseph Fayrer, *The Thanatophidia of India: The Venomous Snakes of India*, second edition, London: J. and A. Churchill, 1874; 61.7 x 43 cm. Accessioned: 1880–1903.

SNAKES formed an important part of the Museum's natural history displays and fascinated the local people. The collection has many rare books on a variety of subjects relating to natural history. One of these is *The Thanatophidia of India*, a large folio book illustrated by artists from the Calcutta School of Art under the supervision of Sir Joseph Fayrer, an English physician interested in the study of ophiology. The edition was published in 1872, after Fayrer completed research on the subject with Dr Thomas Lauder Brunton and with the assistance of Dr F.C. Webb.

Fayrer pursued medical studies in Rome and received his M.D. in 1849. The following year he was appointed to the Indian Medical Service at Bengal as an assistant surgeon. His home in Lucknow was used as a hospital and a fortress during the Uprising in 1857.[1] Dr Fayrer wrote on many subjects connected to the medical practices in India. He became an expert on the health of Europeans in India and wrote extensively on the pathology of Indian diseases, the Indian climate and zoology.

During the late nineteenth century, the British administration started a campaign to reduce the number of deaths by venomous snakebites in the Indian subcontinent.[2] Fayrer made an extensive study of the venomous snakes of India, the physiological effects produced by their venom, and the treatment of snakebites. The Museum has the second edition of the book that was published in 1874 and printed by the Government of India.

The book opens with four quotes relating to the trauma and agony caused by snakebites from Shakespeare's *Antony* and Cleopatra, *King John* and *Hamlet*. Like other such documentary books of the period, art was invoked in the service of science. This is visible in the extraordinary skill with which the physical details of the snakes have been presented. The book enumerates the effects of nearly 500 experiments involving snakebites on various animals, and indicates treatments for each. It includes cases of snakebite from different parts of India during the year 1869–70, with their treatment as well as results, which illustrates the mortality rate of people bitten by venomous snakes.

Thanatophidia refers to serpents with poison glands and fangs, whose bite may or may not be fatal to humans. These serpents constitute two types—the viperine serpents or Solenoglypha, and the cobra-like serpents or Proteroglypha. Fayrer studied all aspects of snake poisoning and was responsible for many advances in finding the cure for snakebites. There are twenty-eight chromolithographs in the book, with detailed colour plates showing the variety of venomous serpents found in the Indian subcontinent. The painstaking precise illustrations with refined colouring and the intricate rendition of skin textures and physiological details would have greatly aided identification and underscored a scientific approach.

The Thanatophidia concludes with eight appendices, some of which contain an account of the use of snake venom in Ayurveda by the *kabirajes* (hakims) of Bengal, including a documentation of the four classes of snake-charmers found in the Presidency. The book is considered a pioneering work in the study of modern ophiology. A copy of the book was presented to Charles Darwin by Fayrer in 1874.[3]

The popularity of the book resulted in the production of a set of terracotta models of venomous snakes, made by renowned potter Hira Lal from Delhi in 1888 as educational tools in Government offices and museums.[4] Most museums in India had a strong focus on natural history at the time. Live snakes were displayed at the V&A Museum, Bombay, until 1887 when a staff member died following a snakebite, after which the practice was discontinued.[5] • HK

Ophiophagus elaps; chromolithograph; 61.7 x 43 cm.

PARAKEET

The Tuia tota or blossom-headed parakeet (*Psittacula cyanocephala*) is a famous bird of India. A model of the bird, along with thirty-two other specimens of garden and game birds common to the Indian subcontinent, is part of the Museum's natural history collection. The models, which are from Jaipur, are mounted on wooden bases and are made of paper pulp. Paper pulp was produced by beating together moistened paper with measured quantities of plaster, clay and glue.

Parakeets, also known as budgerigars, are a smaller species of the parrot family. An important component of fortune-telling in many parts of India, parrots have inspired poetry and painting in Indian culture since the Indus civilisation. In Indian mythology, the parrot is associated with Kamadeva, the god of love.

Tuia tota is also known as the plum-headed parakeet after the adult male bird's roseate, plum-tinged head. The male bird is further distinguished by a narrow black neck collar and a small red spot on its minor coverts (feathers). The model in the Museum accurately depicts different hues of the bird—the yellow of the bill on the top giving way to a dusky shade at the bottom, the deep green of the parakeet's wings and the bright yellow-green tone adorns its front and back. The adult female bird, whose model is also included in the collection, has a bluish-grey head with a subtle yellow collar.

Displaying models of birds was consonant with nineteenth-century European ideas about the study of nature in the pursuit of 'reason'. The Museum played a crucial role in furthering this scientific approach, especially with the establishment of the Bombay Natural History Society (BNHS) on September 15, 1883, which took place on its premises. The Society's monthly meetings were held at the Museum until January 1884. The Society aimed at exhibiting its natural history collection, which consisted of specimens of mammals and birds presented by generous donors, and encouraging scientific discourses on the subject. Dr Duncan MacDonald, curator of the Museum from 1880 to 1903, was one of the founding members and vice-president of the BNHS.[1]

In 1916-17, carcasses of different animals and birds, including the blossom-headed parakeet, were received from the Victoria Gardens' superintendent for the Museum's taxidermy collection.[2] Books such as *Oriental Memoirs* (1813), *The Illustrated Book of Canaries and Cage-Birds* (1878) and *Birds of an Indian Garden* (1924)

Plum-Headed Parakeet; coloured plate, W.A. Blakston, W. Swaysland and August F. Weiner, *The Illustrated Book of Canaries and Cage-Birds, British and Foreign*, London: Cassell, Petter, Galpin & Co., 1878, 22.8 x 31.4 cm.

made possible the study of birds, their diet, breeding patterns and bird-keeping. The subject became important as Indians and Europeans, both in India and abroad, increasingly fancied birds as domestic pets. Commonly referred to as 'foreign', Indian aviary birds such as bulbuls, mynahs and parakeets were popular with European keepers for their sweet notes and social personalities. A leading German ornithologist, Dr Karl Russ (1833–99), was known to have bred three generations of blossom-headed parakeets in his aviary. He later exhibited a young pair and its parents at the Crystal Palace Exhibition in 1877.[3] The Victoria Gardens, now the Veermata Jijabai Bhosale Udyan, is home to over 100 bird species today. It is India's largest aviary of exotic birds such as the black-crowned night heron, black-headed ibis, demoiselle crane, Japanese crane, painted stork, rosy pelican and the sarus crane. • IH

Common Mynah; paper-pulp, wood, 1925-26, Jaipur; 16.5 x 17.9 x 39 cm. Accessioned: 1925-26.

Blossom-Headed Parakeet; paper pulp, wood, 1925–26, Jaipur; 18.7 x 10 x 15 cm. Accessioned: 1925–26.

The Common Myna; coloured plate, T.B. Fletcher and C.M. Inglis, *Birds of an Indian Garden*, Calcutta: Thacker, Spink & Co, 1924; 23.7 x 17 cm. Accessioned: 2018.

31 ORIENTAL MEMOIRS
by JAMES FORBES

TRAVEL literature compiled by the artists and officers of the East India Company functioned primarily as documentation of explorations on geography and cartography, as well as sociocultural tracts. Of the many literary works on the Orient published in the nineteenth century, *Oriental Memoirs* by James Forbes (1749–1819) has secured special praise. The son of a London merchant, Forbes set sail for Bombay at sixteen as a writer (junior clerk or bookkeeper) for the Company. He arrived in India in 1766, where he would live for the next seventeen years. Forbes was a talented writer and artist and during this period he travelled extensively, documenting his journeys through the various towns and cities of the country. He was captivated by the abundant beauty, variety and fecundity of the natural life in India.[1]

The Museum has Forbes' monumental work that comprises four volumes compiled chronologically, beginning with his embarkation for Bombay (1765) via the Cape of Good Hope. The insights provided are plenty and informative. After brief layovers along the Malabar Coast (Cochin, Calicut and Goa), Forbes arrived at the Bombay harbour, which he describes as one of the finest in the world and accessible at all seasons. He outlines the topography of Bombay and its climate, from favourable conditions for sowing rice and grains to fertile soils for vegetation. He elaborates on plants (coconut trees), animals (jackals, squirrels, hedgehogs), birds (vultures, kites, hawks), and fish (pomfret, bumbalo or Bombay duck) indigenous to the city and its shores in a few chapters. These accounts are sometimes supported with Persian metaphors and poetry. Declaring an 'unprejudiced' approach whilst describing the social order, Forbes records, 'Many respectable Armenian merchants, with their families, as well as a few Persians, Turks, Arabians, and Jews, occasionally reside at Bombay; but the Hindoos, Mahomedans, and Parsees, form the great mass of the inhabitants.'[2] He further states, 'When I resided at Bombay, comfort, hospitality, and urbanity characterised the settlement, and early hours prevailed throughout the presidency and its subordinate settlements.'[3] The letters also highlight the important buildings in the city like the Government House, Mint, Treasury, Theatre, and Prison. The fourth and concluding volume touches upon the expansion of the Company's administration under Warren Hastings and other governors of India. He shares his thoughts on the spread of Christianity in India, an ideal he passionately advocated for as a devout Christian. The volumes comprise of a series of letters and drawings that total up to 52,000 pages.

The painting *Red, Blue and White Lotus from Hindostan* demonstrates Forbes' keen sense of observation and skill as a draughtsman. He expressed his appreciation of the lotus-covered lakes and their overshadowing banyan trees in poetic language. The flowers impart a cheerful and brilliant ambience, he says, one that he had not seen in the surrounding districts, in his letter describing the city of Brodera (Baroda) to a member of the council at Bombay, who had not visited Guzerat (Gujarat) and wanted to know more about the English *purgunnas* (an administrative unit) in the province.[4] Chronicled in January 1783, Forbes' letter narrates his three-week tour through the *purgunnas* under the jurisdiction of the Collector-General of Baroche (Bharuch). He describes the journey as delightful while suggesting the preferred seasons to visit Guzerat.[5]

Forbes employs an artistic narrative style that is both poetic and rich in detail in the *Memoirs*. His writing was influenced by the literary works of other European orientalists. With the improvements in printing technology from the eighteenth century in India, books had become more accessible. It's recognition as a language of antiquity encouraged translations from Sanskrit during the period. English translations of Kalidasa's Sanskrit play *Shakuntala* by Sir William Jones (*Sacontala* or The Fatal Ring), and the *Asiatick Researches* journal in 1789 made a great impact on Forbes' storytelling and his understanding of India.[6] Forbes describes the flora and fauna that he encounters by referencing anecdotes from the play *Sacontala,* for example, and Ahmedabad's architectural brilliance through Homer's *Odyssey.* Forbes' visual observations are interpolated by his notions of British sovereignty, which he perceives as a divine force of justice and goodness.[7] He remarks with fervour on the improved conditions of the Empire's most valuable colony, which was in an impoverished state at the hands of 'unworthy' Portuguese settlers.[8] Forbes' views in the concluding pages, on subjects outside the natural world, can be described as biased to a great extent. For instance, he indicates that Indian society would be significantly advantaged through Christianity and that a change in religious beliefs would help the people break away from superstitious traditions.

When he finally returned to England in 1784, Forbes collated his memoirs and published them in 1813. He brought over 200 specimens of seeds from Gujarat, including tamarind, custard apple, cotton, coffee, ginger and turmeric, which he grew at his conservatory at Stanmore Hall.[9] He was taken ill while at Aix-la-Chapelle (Germany) and died on August 1, 1819. • IH

Red, Blue, and White, Lotus of Hindostan, coloured plate, James Forbes, *Oriental Memoirs: A Narrative of Seventeen Years Residence in India, Vol. III*, London: White, Cochrane, and Co., 1813; 31.4 x 24.5 x 6.7 cm. Accessioned: early twentieth century.

Red, Blue, and White LOTUS, of Hindostan.

Above:
Bulbul or Indian Nightingale, on a Sprig of the Custard Apple Tree, James Forbes Vol. I; 31.4 x 25.5 x 7 cm.

•

Below:
Indian Squirrel and Tamarind, Vol. II., 31.5 x 25.5 x 6.8 cm.

VIEWS IN THE HIMALA MOUNTAINS *by* JAMES FRASER

Crossing the Touse, hand-coloured aquatint, James B. Fraser, *Views in the Himala Mountains,* London: Rodwell & Martin, 1820; 47 x 61 cm. Accessioned: 1939.

The East India Company mandated its officials to survey territories and to document their expeditions with a scientific approach. These explorations were crucial for British territorial expansion as they provided an understanding of the climate, people and local customs of regions that came under colonial rule. Of the many works of European artists that the Company commissioned, the ones by James Baillie Fraser (1783– 1856) are pioneering. Fraser arrived in India in July 1813. Two years later, he joined his brother William, an officer with the EIC armed forces, and embarked on a tour of the Himalayas from May to July 1815. It was during this period that Fraser extensively journaled and produced sketches of the topography he encountered while travelling through the unsurveyed regions of the lower Himalayan hill states. Besides being an excellent artist and writer, Fraser was also known as an adventurous traveller. During this journey, he set out to discover the origin of the two rivers, Jumna and Ganges.

The information gathered by the end of Fraser's expedition evolved into a voluminous account titled *Journal of a Tour,* which included thirteen appendices of 500 pages. He rendered the Himala sketches into watercolours that, along with the *Journal,* were published in a folio edition of twenty aquatints titled *Views in the Himala Mountains* in London in 1820. The Museum has in its collection a set of twelve lithographs. *Town of Rampore, The Junction of the Touse and Pabur* and *Crossing the Touse* are some of the prints from the collection. A visual vocabulary composed through these pictures would supplement Fraser's written accounts of the Himalayan villages, snowy ranges, flora and fauna and mineralogy. The notes and specimens collected during his Himalayan journey were sent to the Geological Society in London to be published in *Transactions of the Geological Society.*[1] In between the narratives of the countryside, Fraser documented local bazaars, houses and the inhabitants of the villages. These detailed observations became 'an amazing record of a region which remained little known until the twentieth century.'[2] • IH

THE nineteenth century marked a divergence in the European approach to knowledge production in India. Field-based surveys and observations were prioritised over text-based study.[1] An understanding of the geographical and economic potential of South Asia was crucial to the commercial interests of the East India Company. To fulfil this aim, German explorers and brothers Hermann, Robert and Adolph Schlagintweit were hired by the East India Company from 1854 to 1857 to conduct 'magnetic surveys' in India and High Asia (Himalayas, Tibet, Nepal) on the recommendation of Alexander von Humboldt, a leading contemporary German scientist. The brothers were inspired by the 'Humboldtian model' and compiled vast inventories of important geographical, topographical and meteorological data.[2]

The Schlagintweit brothers arrived in Bombay on October 26, 1854, and took different routes, travelling across India to Madras, Calcutta and the Himalayas. While in Bombay, they met Dr George Buist—an English geologist,

newspaper editor and the first curator of the Government Central Museum, later the V&A Museum—from whom they learned the technique of plaster casting.[3] Plaster casts were used by French anthropologists during Pacific explorations in the early nineteenth century. Dr Buist had learned plaster casting in Scotland and even made plaster casts of archaeological objects. The Schlagintweit brothers took casts of each other's faces, hands, feet and learnt to use the technique for ethnographic documentation during their travels.

It was a common German practice to take casts of well-known personalities upon their death as commemorative tokens.[4] The Schlagintweit brothers adapted this practice to take ethnographical casts of different 'types' of people in India. However, due to the varied funerary practices and superstitions associated with last rites across the country, creating casts of dead persons proved to be a challenge. Instead, they made bronze or copper casts of living people which were then mounted on wooden panels. The technique

involved making a gypsum mould of the face which was then cast in zinc and coated with a galvano-plastic deposit of copper of 'varied tint' as per the skin colour of their anthropological 'subjects'.[5] Since the process of making the initial plaster casts took 30–45 minutes, moistened paper cones were inserted into the nostrils of the men, women, and even children whose casts were taken. The plaster also caused skin irritations and people were most reluctant to undergo the process and had to be forcibly induced to do so. The brothers also enlisted the help of jail inspectors to take casts of prisoners.[6]

Over 200 such casts were made of ethnographical 'heads' or 'masks' and over fifty of hands and feet, divided into racial and geographical types. They offered a three-dimensional study of the anthropometry or physical features of different ethnicities in South Asia that photographic documentation could not. These were compared with other 'races' around the world to gain an understanding of human diversity.[7] The Museum's collection has two wooden panels, each with seven masks of men from tribes across Sikkim, Kashmir, Kulu, Bengal, Tibet, Bhutan and even Ceylon. Some faces are contorted into an expression of discomfort with lines visible at the corners of the eyes and forehead. These were shipped by Robert and Hermann to Bombay where they were housed along with the Museum's collection at the Town Hall and later displayed at the present site.[8]

Hermann and Robert Schlagintweit returned to Berlin in 1857 while Adolph, who took the overland route via Central Asia, was executed in Kashgar the same year. The Schlagintweit brothers' zoological, botanical and ethnographic observations and findings formed an important collection of specimens under the title 'The Schlagintweit Collections', and was housed at the India Museum in London as a holistic archive of India. It included over 800 botanical specimens, 160 preserved zoological objects, 281 textile and paper samples, over 700 original sketches and watercolours.[9] The results of this survey were to be published in eight volumes, with the ethnographic collections as the subject of volume seven. However, only four volumes were published and the rest of the material was archived in the India Office Records. Eventually, the collection was dispersed to other museums in London and some of the objects were even displayed at the 1874 International Exhibition at South Kensington, London. With the advent of photography, similar photographic documentation projects and surveys were taken up by the British Government, which were profoundly influenced by the Schlagintweit technique. • RWB

Casts of Trans-Himalayan Tribes, Robert and Hermann Schlagintweit; copper casts mounted on wooden panels, 1854–57, India. 11.5 x 40 x 11.5 x 398 cm. Accessioned: 1859.

Toda Man and *Toda Woman*, unknown photographer; photographic print, J.W. Breeks, *An Account of The Primitive Tribes and Monuments of the Nilagiris*, London: India Office, 1874; 33.5 x 26 cm. Accessioned: early twentieth century.

AN ACCOUNT OF THE PRIMITIVE TRIBES AND MONUMENTS OF THE NILAGIRIS
by JAMES W. BREEKS

Several ethnographic studies were made of the inhabitants of the Nilgiri forest in south India in the early nineteenth century. The Todas were among the groups most studied by different British administrators as the early anthropological theories identified them as the 'lost' tribes of the Levant.[1] The photos in this volume depict the front and side profiles of men and women of the Toda, Kota, Kurumba and Irula communities with anthropometric tools, such as a measuring stick and a graph behind the 'subjects', used as photography props. These instruments also indicate how phrenological and anthropometric studies were developed as 'science' in the nineteenth century to advance the British Government's economic and political agenda in India through policies that favoured their interests. Early anthropometric studies favouring the 'Aryan' racial type shaped and informed beauty standards of the colonial period.

In the mid-1860s, the Government of Madras commissioned a photographer from the Madras School of Art to document the indigenous groups living in the Nilgiri hills. Wax and bronze casts of the hands and feet of these 'hill tribes' were sent to the exhibitions held in Paris and London in 1867 and also to the major art schools in India.[2] The anthropometric measurements of hands and feet established a direct correlation with individual lifestyles, physical stature and medical history, which were interpreted as variables in the assumed racial hierarchy of the nineteenth century. The photographs were displayed at the 1868 Bombay Exhibition, held at Framjee Cowasjee Institute.[3]

In 1871, James Wilkinson Breeks, the first commissioner of the Nilgiris, began compiling photographs and information about the material culture of the tribes. The compilation was in response to a request from the trustees of the Indian Museum in Calcutta to document the 'primitive art' of the people of the Nilgiris before they came in contact with a 'foreign' civilisation. The Madras Government also suggested that a set be kept for the Madras Central Museum. The use of the term 'primitive' reveals the colonial attitude towards the indigenous peoples. • RWB

33 THE PEOPLE OF INDIA
by JOHN F. WATSON & JOHN W. KAYE

KUMHARS.
POTTERS.
HINDOOS.
LAHORE.
(223)

Kumhars. Potters. Hindoos. Lahore. (223), unknown photographer; photographic print pasted on paper. J.F. Watson and J.W. Kaye, *The People of India: A Series of Photographic Illustrations with Descriptive Letterpress of the Races and Tribes of Hindustan,* Vol. 4, London: India Museum, 1868–75. 33.2 x 24.4 cm. Accessioned: 2013.
The staged photograph depicts two potters with a wheel between them. The authors focus on the technique of producing pots while stating that most Indians do not use earthenware utensils to eat but chiefly for storage.

IN the aftermath of the Uprising of 1857, which was extensively reported in the British press, there was an urgent need for the British Government to analyse why the Uprising took place. The idyllic imagery of India from the previous century, depicted through sketches and travelogues by Europeans, was replaced by photographic documentation that would help the British better understand their colonial subjects.

The early technology of making and developing photographs was expensive, which limited its use to

Bustee. Hindoo. Hissar. (179), Vol 4; 33.2 x 24.4 cm.
Accessioned: 2013.
The men of the Bustee community were identified as
skilled swordsmen and 'athletic'. The photograph is
angled to show his sharp features, which the authors
go on to identify as 'Rajput'.

Scarf maker. Mussulman. Delhi. (188), Vol 4; 33.2 x 24.4 cm.
The scarf maker is identified by his profession and broad
religious adherence. He sits on the ground with a wooden
frame supported by trestles to embroider 'scarves' of
cashmere wool with silk threads.

commercial photography firms, the Indian and European elite
in photographic societies, and for Government purposes. The
first Viceroy of India, Lord Canning, took a keen interest in
photography when he assumed office in 1858 which resulted
in a Government memorandum to the provincial British
officers to photographically document the people living under
their jurisdiction.

Of the first round of hundreds of ethnological
photographs that were commissioned by Lord Canning, only
one known set of seventy-three albumen prints survives.[1]
Seventy-nine photographs from this collection were exhibited
at the 1862 International Exhibition in London, with a plan to
publish all as lithographs including descriptive texts, which
did not happen. By 1863, John William Kaye, the Secretary
of the Political and Secret Department, wrote to John Forbes
Watson, the director of the India Museum in London, about
widening the scope of this project. The aim was to create a
large publication from the prints available in the repository
of the India Museum that would act as an ethnological survey
of the various indigenous groups and communities across the
Indian subcontinent.[2]

*The People of India: A Series of Photographic Illustrations,
with Descriptive Letterpress, of the Races and Tribes of
Hindustan* was compiled in eight volumes and was meant
to be an encyclopaedic work. The preface to the first volume
credits fifteen photographers and describes how the
photographs were taken without a plan and as permitted
by the local circumstances of the different officers.[3] The
original negatives remained in India, with copies of plates
sent for reproduction to W. Griggs at the India Museum in
London. The eight volumes contained 468 albumen prints.[4]
The preface decrees it as an ethnographic work, devoid of
scientific research or philosophical investigations.

The eight volumes are divided based on the geographical
areas in India under British administration. That the work was
intended to document the attitudes and cooperativeness of
Indians with the British administration is evident as the first
volume opens with a critical note on the Santhal Rebellion
of 1855. The wide range of photographic 'subjects' includes a
combination of Indian tribes, communities, soldiers, persons
engaged in different occupations, religious mendicants, and
local rulers or chiefs in royal *durbars*. People are staged in
poses, usually in studios with props, that reflect the European
predilection with anthropometry that was believed to define a
particular community's or individual's degree of refinement.
The photos themselves are of varying sizes, from full-length
formal photographs to quarter-length portraits.

The photographs are arranged in a prescribed
taxonomic order with an accompanying label mentioning
the name of the community, caste, occupation and locality.
The only labels that carry the name of the individual
photographed are those of elite classes, religious leaders or
ascetics.[5] Occupational groups were photographed with the
tools of their trade. • RWB

THE ORIENTAL RACES AND TRIBES *by* WILLIAM JOHNSON

One of the earliest published ethnographic writings on India, that included photographs, was *The Oriental Races and Tribes, Residents and Visitors of Bombay* (1863–66) by William Johnson. This three-volume series, published in London, documented various communities and categorised them into different tribes, sects, occupations, races, etc.

Johnson was one of the founding members of the Photographic Society of Bombay in 1854 and served as the society's Joint Secretary, as well as co-editor of its journal. Trained as a civil servant, he practised photography extensively and in 1852 he opened a studio in Bombay, where he produced daguerreotypes and, later, albumen prints from wet plate collodion negatives. He was a significant contributor to the *Indian Amateur's Photographic Album* published by the society, and several of these photographs were reprinted in *The Oriental Races and Tribes*.[1]

The society was patronised by Lord Elphinstone, the Governor of Bombay, and had several influential citizens as members, including George Buist, William Crawford, Harishchandra Chintaman, Dr Bhau Daji Lad and Narayan Daji.[2] Dr Bhau Daji Lad, who was also the Secretary of the Museum committee, was one of the early members of the society along with his brother, Narayan Daji, who was an exceptional photographer. The photograph, labelled 'Vallabhacharya Maharajas' by Narayan Daji, was republished against a temple background in Vol. 1 of *The Oriental Races and Tribes* with a descriptive text. The original studio photograph of Vallabhacharyas also played an important part in the famous Maharaja Libel Case of 1862, which has been mentioned in the volume.[3]

The first volume documented the people of Gujarat, Kutch and Kathiawar; the second, the Maratha community; and the third is a miscellaneous collection. The series is a compilation of sixty-one photographs and each photograph has been labelled according to either caste, tribe, sect, or occupation. Several of the photographs in the volumes are photo-montages. The 'subjects' were photographed in the studio, often with props associated with their community, and later incorporated within appropriate outdoor locations. The descriptive text along with each print describes the community, its origin, apparel and lifestyle.[4] • **RJ**

Vallabhacharya Maharajas; albumen print, W. Johnson, *The Oriental Races and Tribes, Residents and Visitors of Bombay: A Series of Photographs with Letter-press Descriptions, Vol. 1. Gujarat, Kutch, and Kathiawar*, London: W.J. Johnson, 1863; 32 x 40.4 cm. Accessioned: 1910. Original photograph by Narayan Daji taken prior to 1863. Figures identified as (L to R): Gopkeshji, Jivanji, Maganlal, Gokuladhish, Chinmanji.

George Clarke Workshop Pottery (centre), flanked by
Ajanta pottery from the Sir J. J. School of Art, c. 1880–1926;
Bombay. On view at the Industrial Arts Gallery, Dr. Bhau Daji
Lad Museum, Mumbai.

INDUSTRIAL ARTS
A New Taste for Design

BOMBAY'S eminent citizens played a pivotal role in collecting objects and natural specimens for the Great Exhibition of 1851 in London. These came from all the districts of the Presidency, as well as the princely states of the region and beyond (see p. 12) and were sorted and organised by a selection committee comprising important British officials and Indian merchants. A large assortment of representative samples of a variety of crafts, vegetable and mineral products were dispatched to London where Indian crafts and design received high praise. *The Times* said, 'These remarkable and characteristic collections have a value that can hardly be overrated ...'[1] *The Official Catalogue* applauded the exhibits for expressing 'the management of colours, the skill with which a number of them are employed, and the taste with which they are harmonised ... Europe has nothing to teach but a great deal to learn.'[2] Several important British designers and artists, including Owen Jones and Richard Redgrave, were effusive in their praise for the Indian collections, which occupied the central axis of the exhibition in a display intended to portray India's riches to the world, and declare Britain as the most affluent and progressive nation. This was the first time that many of the visitors had seen such a vast variety and sumptuous display of Indian objects, including, among other things, the finest textiles, carpets, jewellery, especially the Kohinoor diamond, and even a stuffed elephant with a howdah atop it. London's design cognoscenti singled out Bombay Blackwood furniture (see pp. 134-35) for singular praise. Bombay Boxwork (see pp. 137–39) too commanded great attention for the delicacy of the intricate inlay work.[3]

The extraordinary display of Indian craftsmanship was intended to stimulate an appetite for Indian products and to demonstrate royal patronage, so as to set in motion a fashion which would become a pivotal trading advantage for Britain. Till 1857, when the Crown took over the governance of India from the East India Company, Indian decorative arts had depended mostly on the patronage of the Indian aristocracy. As royal patronage dwindled with the advent of the British and the dissolution of the Mughal Empire, artists, who acquired their skills over generations in an atelier, dispersed across the country in search of livelihood. The traditional methods of production changed in response to the altered circumstances and differing tastes. The new patrons—the local princes, the emerging merchant class, as well as colonial officials and European visitors who sojourned for long periods in the country, often taking up temporary residence—required furniture and furnishings or objects that were European in form and Indian in design, like chairs and tables, candelabra (see pp. 146-47) and tea sets (see pp. 165, 167). The ubiquitous import of European objects resulted in many artists copying these to appeal to the changing tastes of the elite Indian and European markets.

George Birdwood (see pp. 56-57) criticised this European influence, as did his colleagues in London and in India. As the first curator of the V&A Museum, Bombay,

Annexation, Jitish Kallat; painted black lead and steel, 2009; 183 x 150 x 130 cm. Exhibition: *Fieldnotes: Tomorrow Was Here Yesterday*; Industrial Arts Gallery, 2011. *Annexation* is an oversized black lead kerosene stove carved over with hundreds of gargoyles and animals that ornament the façade and interiors of the Victoria Terminus, now the Chhatrapati Shivaji Maharaj Terminus, devouring each other or grasping at food of various kinds. The churning turmoil depicted on the surface recalls the colonial grasping of territories as well as the fight for the survival of the people of the city today.

and as the commissioner for several international and Indian exhibitions, he attempted to influence public opinion by writing official catalogues for international exhibitions, detailing the beauty and history of Indian handicrafts.[4] He eulogised Indian craftsmanship for its exemplary design but insisted that Indian sculpture was monstrous and that fine arts did not exist in the country.[5] The objects he acquired for the museum and that he selected for the many exhibitions he organised reinforced this view and almost never included Indian painting or sculpture. This dichotomy created a schism both in teaching and practice, as was evident in the curriculum of the art schools established first in the Presidency towns and later across the country. Between the ideologues in London—including Henry Cole, John Ruskin, Owen Jones and William Morris—and the British bureaucracy in India, Indian craftsmanship was celebrated for its timelessness, its unchanging character, and its flat surface design and complexity. Its excellence arose, Birdwood and colonial officials argued, from repeating designs perfected over generations and from a pastoral devotion to the simple life.[6] In one stroke, by freezing the character of the art form, these men rendered any progress or change in the arts and crafts of India as anathema. They also denied the craftsmen any agency and attributed excellence to inherited skills. In fact, they were critical of the craftsmen's perceived lack of ability to transcend their particular inheritance and 'scientifically' understand the principles on which their designs and forms were based. It was these principles that the art schools set out to teach the students, using European logic and methods to improve their expertise and adapt it to new forms.[7] These discourses were to determine the trajectory of Indian art education and the understanding of Indian art in the West for many decades. The simple, beleaguered craftsman, however, was unfortunately not privy to this debate and in the quest to earn a living, produced what the market demanded.

British officials, especially Birdwood, lamented the import of cheap European goods that were responsible for the debasement of original Indian designs and the mongrel forms that appeared in the market as craftsmen experimented with different styles and techniques to appeal to their customers.[8] Their arguments reflected the bias of the Arts and Crafts movement in London that arose in the wake of the Industrial Revolution. It was felt that British goods were not competing successfully in the international markets due to the lack of creativity and imagination in design. Indian crafts were held up as an exemplar to be emulated and Owen Jones, the interior designer for the Great Exhibition of 1851, copied many Indian designs in his iconic book *Grammar of Ornament*. The efforts to control the deterioration of handicrafts, both in the metropole and the colony, were determined by Henry Cole's Department of Science and Arts in London, which oversaw the entire edifice of exhibitions, museums, art schools and industrial and technical schools across Britain and the Empire. Education policies developed in Britain were imposed unedited on the colonies. Art schools, museums and exhibitions became the central plank of the policy to ensure the improvement of the decorative arts, encourage good taste in craftsmen, patrons and merchants, and to provide a firm foundation for Britain's trading supremacy.[9] In the latter half of the nineteenth century and the early twentieth century, crafts, especially textiles, formed the backbone of the Indian economy along with agriculture.[10] But with cheap imports from Britain flooding the local markets and a policy that inhibited exports, Indian crafts suffered a major setback, and skilled craftsmen staved off starvation by migrating to other jobs or compromised on production to compete with the less expensive imports.[11]

Anxious that such rampant exploitation would lead to rebellion, the Government decided that art schools were the answer to the craftsmen's plight as British teachers would inculcate the 'principles' involved in the production of different crafts and help the artisans better adapt to the commercial pressures of producing objects that would appeal to the international markets.[12] In 1856, Sir Jamsetjee Jeejeebhoy (see pp. 62-63), one of the city's most generous philanthropists, was moved to put up funds to establish an art school in Bombay that would address the need for skill development in the Bombay Presidency. Madras and Calcutta had already established art schools earlier and Bombay urgently needed one as it transitioned from a small town into a major trading hub. In February 1857, the Sir Jamsetjee Jeejeebhoy School of Art was established in Bombay and opened at the Elphinstone Institute, for morning classes only, with forty-nine students.[13] The focus was on improving artisanal skills by teaching the students design principles and the basics of good draughtsmanship. Most of the students, however, did not belong to the artisanal class that the policy sought to address. Decades later, both John Griffiths and Cecil Burns, principals of the School, acknowledged this in an address to the Royal Society for the Arts in London.[14] In the early years, like the V&A Museum, Bombay, the School found itself struggling to survive. The colonial government was reluctant to spend money on educational institutions and it was the generosity of Rustomjee Jeejeebhoy, Jamsetjee's great grandson (1878–1931), that enabled the School to finally progress. The three founding teachers, George Wilkins Terry (see pp. 126-27), one of the first principals of the School and also curator of the V&A Museum; John Lockwood Kipling, father of the famous author Rudyard Kipling; and John Griffiths ran the School as best they could with limited resources, language constraints and the constant official refrain to produce traditional artisans and not modern artists (see pp. 315–17).

In 1890, once the building had come up and after several reviews and conferences to understand the impact of the schools of art and museums on the art education policy in the country, the Reay Art Workshops were started as an adjunct to the Sir J.J. School of Art, especially to train craftsmen. Six new ateliers in enamelling, woodcarving, silver and gold work, carpet weaving, brass work and copper work began in a makeshift shed.[15] Master craftsmen were employed in the different ateliers to teach the students craft skills, and the products were sold or sent to various exhibitions. In his annual reports, Griffiths records the names of students who were successfully employed in ateliers across the Presidency. These craftsmen spread their learning and the European Renaissance aesthetic principles of the School across the region. The School and the workshops declined due to the plague and were revived by Cecil Burns when he took over as the principal of the School in 1897. As he was also the curator of the V&A Museum from 1903 to 1918, there was a close association between the two institutions and some of the Reay Workshop objects, especially a fine collection of carpets, were acquired for the Museum.

International and local exhibitions were an important aspect of the cultural agenda of the city. These became sites for the display of technological emancipation, artistic virtuosity and political hegemony. The School and the V&A Museum regularly participated in these events, featuring decorative objects from Bombay, where many ateliers had sprung up. In fact, the Museum's earliest collection was the 'duplicates' of works sent to the Paris International Exhibition of 1855, though not much survives from then (see p. 12). The collection was most often replenished from these exhibitions and Griffiths made a significant purchase of objects for the V&A Museum at the grand 1883 Exhibition in Calcutta. It was Bombay, however, that took pride of place at most of the international exhibitions due to the efforts of Birdwood and Griffiths, and later Cecil Burns and Gladstone Solomon. In 1885, at the Antwerp International Exhibition, the Bombay Court represented India: 'At Antwerp, for the first time in the history of International Exhibitions, we find India represented not by an Imperial collection showing the products and manufactures of the whole of our Eastern possessions but by a collection made in Bombay and exhibited in a space known as the Bombay Court,'[16] the *Journal of Indian Art and Industry* noted.

In 1890, the visit of Prince Albert Victor provided a reason for the colonial municipal government to present an exhibition of advanced technology at the Museum, titled 'Products and manufactures of Western India.' A newspaper noted that there was '... a special section for Municipal exhibits that will be of exceptional interest to the towns of Western India which have drainage or water works on hand, or contemplate the equipment of a fire brigade provided with all the necessary appliances for dealing with conflagrations.' The Victoria Gardens were decorated and illuminated for the festive occasion, and the Bombay Art Society presented an elaborate exhibition on the arts and crafts of the region at the new School of Art building.[17]

From December 1904 to January 1905, the city hosted the Industrial and Agricultural Exhibition with great aplomb. Presented by the Indian National Congress, whose president, Dadabhai Naoroji, was a leading light of Bombay, the exhibition marked the coming of age of the city. Organised and funded by local merchants keen to show that they were modern and progressive, the template remained European in character, copying the architect Lyon Playfair's map for the Great Exhibition of 1851. The Art School's students were actively involved in constructing and decorating the pavilions and preparing decorative objects for the displays in a special court allocated for the School, under the guidance of Cecil Burns. Newspaper reports hailed the presentation as the 'greatest effort of the kind ever made in India.'[18] Centrally located at the Oval Maidan, a large green space abutting the important neo-Gothic institutional buildings of the city, the exhibition attracted 570,167 visitors over its six-week run.[19] Electric lights, which were a novelty at the time, lit up the sky, and cafes and amusements, like a water chute, were included to attract visitors. Several different courts advertised a variety of products from different parts of India. There was ivory carving and inlay work from Travancore and Mysore; pottery and brass work from the Jeypore School of Arts; elaborate stone carving from Rajputana and Gujerat; 'microscopic' painting from Delhi and Lahore; carved silver and gold work, including a beautiful Jain temple, from the south; a variety of engraved silver trays, tea sets and caskets by Oomersee Mawjee of Kutch; sandalwood from Multan; and pottery, brass work and enamel work from the Sir J.J. School of Arts, for which they were awarded a silver and two gold medals.[20] There was a vast variety of jewellery, textiles, furniture, furnishings and decorative objects to appeal to all tastes and budgets. The princely states of the Presidency presented the 'art and industry' from their regions. There was a Ladies Court and a Bombay Healtheries section, where the latest in sanitary ware and drain pipes were displayed. This was an important section of the exhibition as the city had recently emerged from a disastrous plague and healthy living represented modernity and progress. Another section of the exhibition presented raw materials like clays, resins and materials used for construction. A forestry section had different species of wood, and a mechanical section demonstrated the use of new types of pumps and ploughs. Models of ships, dairy farms and even a map of the Bombay islands were on display. Big companies like the Tatas had their own stalls. Lectures and talks explained the products and showed people how to use them. In form and method, the exhibition employed the same principles of display and engagement as museums and in fact some of the collections were donated to the V&A Museum, Bombay.[21]

The impact of the exhibition was unprecedented and there was a call from the city's eminent citizens to establish a large museum in Bombay, 'the second city of the Empire' (after London) which was the main entrepôt to the country and also its main market, to enable the display of India's great riches.[22] Lord Curzon, the Governor General of India at the time, had visited the Victoria and Albert Museum during his excursion to the Bombay International Exhibition, and though he commended the Museum for attracting almost a million people a year, the general opinion was that it was too far from the centre of town to be an effective site for marketing the country's products.[23] An effort had been made earlier in 1890 to transform the Museum into a 'Trades Museum' which would advertise the products imported and exported in the country, and would assist suppliers and buyers in determining quality and prices through its displays of the raw materials as well as finished products. Considerable deliberations took place but the idea was abandoned as it was felt that the Museum was too far from the commercial centre.[24]

The use of museums as a marketing strategy for social, political and commercial objectives, however, was now widely appreciated and private merchants began creating collections and setting up their versions of museums. One of the most prominent merchants of the city decided to create his own museum which was both a showroom and a collection, and was probably one of the first private museums in the country. Sheth Purshotam Mawjee, a wealthy merchant, had amassed a large collection of artefacts that included antiquities, miniature paintings, European paintings, Chinese artefacts, and an extensive collection of ivory, silver, brass, sculptures, jewellery and textiles.[25] Located at his residence in Walkeshwar, it welcomed visitors by appointment. The V&A Museum acquired much of its *bidri* collection from him (see pp. 160–63).

Museums, art schools and local exhibitions became the crucible through which to transform India's cultural milieu, by educating people's taste and inculcating a sense of refinement based on European principles and values. As Indians adopted British education and a European lifestyle, acquisition and display of objects became central to the expression of status. International exhibitions on the other hand were sites where India's culture could be marketed to the West. The success of the latter was visible in 'oriental' shops like Liberty & Co, which gained a reputation for presenting beautifully designed Indian products.[26]

The turn of the century, however, saw a reappraisal of Indian art with the rejection of Western principles of naturalism and realism by Indian scholars. Swami Vivekananda, whose speech at the Chicago Exposition in 1893 was a grand success and captivated the Americans, led the charge. 'Now what glory is there in merely imitating nature … ?' he said.[27] A.K. Coomaraswamy, the erudite Sri Lankan scholar who went on to become the keeper of Asian Art at the Boston Museum of Fine Arts, countered the claims of naturalism as high art, as he pronounced that it was based on materialistic principles. 'Beauty, rhythm, proportion, idea have an absolute existence on an ideal plane … in the mind, not in the detail of their appearance to the eye.' he said.[28] E.B. Havell, the principal of the Calcutta School of Art, went even further. He denounced the art school syllabus and its effects, saying, 'Indian Art cries out for bread; we give it museums, exhibitions and archaeology.'[29]

As the movement for independence strengthened, museums and art schools began to challenge the established colonial ideological framework and the form of the exhibition was deployed for the resistance efforts. Culture became an important instrument to expand the resistance movement.[30] The Indian National Congress employed the form of the exhibition to demonstrate their progressive mission and their solidarity with the craftsmen. Swadeshi markets rejected foreign goods and actively promoted Indian craftsmanship. The J.J. School of Art students designed posters for the resistance and competed with the best European artists for commissions. They won many prizes at the Bombay Art Society exhibitions despite colonial prejudices and found subtle ways to express their differences with the prevailing order.[31] Indian museums, including the V&A Museum, began collecting the work of Indian fine artists like Raja Ravi Varma, as well as ancient miniature paintings and manuscripts, as there was a reappraisal and recognition of Indian classical arts in the early twentieth century. At the 1911 Festival of Empire Exhibition in London, besides a generous selection of objects and artefacts, a section was devoted for the first time to miniature painting as well as modern Indian painting. Col. Hendley, who was the commissioner for the Indian section, included a large selection of different types of Indian painting, and Vincent Smith, a well-known archaeologist, in his introduction to the paintings, noted the refinement of the Mughal miniatures on display.[32] Centuries of prejudice were being slowly dismantled by Indian scholars and traditional Indian art found new admirers among the European and educated elite. • TZM

THE 1870s were a pivotal decade for exhibitions that were held in Europe, North America and other colonised countries to promote trade and an exchange of information. Advances in ship travel increased the mobility of people and goods across the world. These historic developments provided the context for the opening of the Victoria and Albert Museum, Bombay, on May 2, 1872, at its present site in Byculla. The Government put together a committee to plan an exhibition in Bombay in February 1873 which included George Wilkins Terry, the superintendent of the Sir J.J. School of Art, and other eminent personalities like Dr Bhau Daji Lad, Sir A.D. Sassoon, His Highness Aga Khan, Sir Jamsetjee Jeejeebhoy and Sir Mungaldas Nathubhoy. The main purpose of the exhibition was to review and select the exhibits for the international exhibitions to be held in London and Vienna later that year.

The committee decided to host the exhibition at 'the new and highly decorated building recently erected for the Victoria and Albert Museum.'[1] The popular Museum was frequented by almost 6,000 people in a single day as it was a novelty in the city. The exhibition would showcase the arts and crafts of the Bombay Presidency and would serve to build collections for the Museum as duplicates could be retained. The exhibition would also help to raise funds for the Sir J.J. School of Art through the sale of works from various ateliers of the School.

On November 1, 1872, Terry took charge of the Museum in addition to his responsibilities at the School. A set of tents were pitched on the Museum's grounds to store the Museum's collection which was not included in the exhibition. Wooden screens were built for hanging or displaying objects. A rotunda, whose construction cost approximately Rs 1,000, functioned as a cafe and was catered by a Mr Smith from Apollo Bunder.[2] The Government paid an advance of Rs 15,000, which was to be repaid from the proceeds of the exhibition.[3] Terry appointed an International Committee of Political Residents and Foreign Consuls connected to the Bombay Government, to represent the rank, wealth and position of the Presidency. Members from England, Germany, France, Austria, Italy, China and Japan were invited to select objects for display that would be commercially successful.

There was great interest around the exhibition and the newspapers claimed that it was one of the best produced in the country. On February 15, 1873, at 5 p.m., the Governor of Bombay, Sir Philip Wodehouse, inaugurated the exhibition with great pomp and ceremony with most of the prominent citizens present. A band of honour was organised to welcome the Governor who was met by the managing committee and Frank Souter, the first Police Commissioner of Bombay,

G.W. Terry, curator of the V&A Museum, Bombay (1868–79), superintendent of the Sir J.J. School of Art (1858–82); glass negative, late nineteenth century, Bombay; 15 x 10 cm. Accessioned: 1903-18.

at the entrance of the Museum in full uniform. The Governor walked through the Museum in procession and stood before the statue of Prince Albert to declare the exhibition open and address the guests.[4]

Special permission was taken to illuminate the Museum with gas lights until seven in the evening and the Bombay Gas Company installed the necessary pipes and fittings in the Museum building for the occasion. The central hall of the Museum was reserved for the members of the exhibition committee and arrangements were made in the gallery on the first floor for ladies and season ticket holders. Once the exhibition was declared open, the guests were permitted to mix and walk through the Museum. When the ceremonies were over, the Governor was escorted back to his carriage with a procession and a band of honour.

Principal Entrance to the Vienna Exhibition 1873; print, *Illustrated London News*, May 31, 1873, London; 15 x 35 cm approx. Image courtesy: Asiatic Society of Mumbai. The London International Exhibition of 1873 coincided with the Vienna World Fair, that commemorated the twenty-fifth year of the reign of Emperor Franz Joseph I.

The exhibition was kept open from 10 a.m. to 7 p.m. till April 27, 1873. Even the committee members were expected to purchase their tickets to view the exhibition. To encourage local families and women to visit, special omnibuses plied from St. Thomas Cathedral and Mumbadevi to Byculla. Wednesdays were reserved for women, and children under eight years of age were charged half. By mid-March visitors were only charged 8 annas and children 4 annas with the exhibition being kept open on Sundays and special bands were organised for public entertainment. The *Times of India* even appealed to keep the trains running till 7.30 p.m. to enable more visits.[5]

By the end of March 1873, several new exhibits were added.[6] Terry had requested patronage from the Chiefs of the Bombay Presidency, the Government of Gwalior, Indore, Bhopal, the Nizam of Hyderabad as well as the Raja of Travancore. They were promised that the objects purchased with their support would be permanently displayed at the Museum and their names would be acknowledged as 'a lasting testimony of their good wishes and liberality to the people of Bombay'.[7] However, only a few of the Indian nobility responded to this request.

Thousands of people visited the exhibition and the estimated total revenue raised was approximately Rs 15,000 through ticket sales and Rs 17,000 through subscriptions.[8] The exhibition was considered an outstanding success, attended by all sections of society, and Terry was not only able to expand the collection of the Museum but also raise funds for the School of Art. • RWB

WATCOMBE POTTERY

The Watcombe pottery exhibited in 1872-73, as part of the objects that were collected for the 1873 Bombay Exhibition, is an exceptional collection. The designs reflect an increasing international trend at the time of moving away from the exuberance of the Arts and Crafts movement to greater simplicity of form and pattern. Dr Wellington Grey, the Secretary and Curator of the Museum, mentions 'an interesting collection of pottery consisting of jugs, water bottles, tobacco jars, tea pots exhibited by the Watcombe Terracotta Company.'[1]

There was a ready international market and demand for mass-produced pottery and manufacturers began employing designers in order to achieve commercial success. Originally known as the Watcombe Terra-Cotta Clay Company, the firm was started in 1871 and used the red clay, rich in iron, found around Devon.[2] They manufactured plain and decorated, buff and red ware, which are the identifying characteristics of Watcombe pottery.

The designs and motifs on this pottery collection may be attributed to Christopher Dresser, an influential designer in Victorian England. Dresser and William Morris represented two ends of the Arts and Crafts movement that followed the Industrial Revolution. Morris emphasised the need for the revival of crafts with stylistic florals that covered every inch of the surface, while Dresser readily adapted his designs for machine production.[3] He used geometric repetition of design, even borrowing Egyptian and Etruscan patterns.

The Watcombe Terra-Cotta Clay Company eventually changed hands after the death of its founder and closed in 1962. • **RWB**

(L-R) *Jar*; *Ampulla*; *Water Pot with a Dish*; *Milk Jug*; unglazed terracotta, 1871-72, Torquay, UK; 18 x 9.8 cm (avg). Accessioned: 1872.

35 WONDERLAND ART POTTERY

BOMBAY School Pottery or Wonderland Art Pottery is one of the most important collections in the Dr. Bhau Daji Lad Museum. It was developed at the Sir J.J. School of Art from the 1860s, and production continued intermittently till the mid-1920s. Hugely popular as 'art wares' that were sold at the various international exhibitions held regularly in several cities across Europe, America, Australia and India, the production of this pottery was barely able to keep up with its demand. Though it started as an experiment in production and design for commercial purposes, the art form was adopted by the School and eventually became one of the most important scientific and technical design experiments to be carried out by the colonial administration.[1] A variety of shapes and styles were amalgamated to create a distinctive art form that influenced how Indian design was perceived in the West. Interestingly, however, the experiment did not achieve its original purpose to educate native potters in new designs and techniques, and to establish a flourishing output of art pottery for commercial purposes.[2] It soon became apparent to the colonial administration that the production of 'art wares' was ad hoc and expertise was family-based. The village potter, according to various colonial administrators' accounts, would travel with his wheel from village to village using local clay and making pots as required. The lack of an organised industry therefore impeded the progressive development of pottery as a refined commercial art form. In Europe, the art had been perfected in Meissen and at other regional centres. Britain had only lately joined this hallowed club with the establishment of Wedgewood and the Staffordshire potteries. Keen to develop porcelain and pottery in India for commercial purposes, the School of Art under George Wilkins Terry (1857–82), made a concerted effort to establish the pottery department as a part of its focus on Indian craftsmanship and design. Colonial officials were of the opinion that if India were to compete in the international trade of art ware manufacture, or 'industrial arts' as it was called at the time, the craftspeople would need to be organised and educated about production techniques and designs.[3]

In 1858, Terry took over as head of the School, a year after it had been established, and in 1865 was joined by two exemplary men who had been dispatched from London to consolidate the education programme of the School: Lockwood Kipling, the father of the famous author Rudyard Kipling, who was in charge of sculpture and ornamentation; and John Griffiths, who was in charge of decorative painting. Kipling had trained as a potter at Staffordshire and contributed significantly to Terry's growing interest in pottery.

Given the strategic importance of pottery and porcelain as an economic product, Terry had attempted to study local

Potter at a Wheel Showing the Second Stage of Pottery Manufacture; half-baked terracotta and pigments, 1912–14; made at the erstwhile V&A Museum, Bombay; 14.4 x 29.4 x 17.8 cm.

traditions and had started a small kiln at the School. The local *kumhars* or potters, who came from Gujarat originally, were not a highly skilled group, so he decided to bring in a potter from Sindh. Pottery from Sindh was admired for its beautiful forms and colours as well as its expert glazing. This pottery was influenced by Persian motifs and designs, though legend has it that the tradition started with a Chinese potter. A master potter by the name of Noor Mohammed was employed by Terry but he was reluctant to travel south and refused to part with his knowledge when he arrived as it was supposed to be a family trade secret.[4]

Another problem was that the local clay was of an inferior quality and it was surmised by the British that this was the reason a strong tradition of glazed pottery and porcelain did not exist in the region.[5] Kaolin, the soft white clay which is an essential ingredient in the production of porcelain and fine china, was not to be found in the Bombay region. Clay had to be imported from Sindh which posed another problem for the production of the pottery. Finally, after much trial and error, a combination of Kutch, Bombay and Malvan clays was used.[6] The local *kumhars* would throw the pots and once shaped, the students from the drawing and painting department would decorate the pots, both processes being guided by Terry and Griffiths. The head potter from Sindh would then glaze the pots, imparting to it beautiful 'earth tones'. This extraordinary enterprise, combining people of different religions, castes, traditions and expertise, produced a range of beautiful pottery that was in constant demand and always sold out in the first week of the exhibitions.[7]

Opposite:
Ajanta Pottery; glazed ceramic and pigment,
c. 1880, Sir J.J. School of Art, Bombay;
82.2 x 45.5 cm. Accessioned: 1894–1928.
•
Clockwise from left:
*Ajanta Pottery; Jar with Peacock Feather Pattern;
Jar Depicting Imagery from Ramayana;* glazed
ceramic and pigment, c. 1880–1900, Sir J.J.
School of Art, Bombay; 43.7 x 35.5 cm (avg).
Accessioned: 1894–1928.

Terry had hoped that the enterprise would become self-supporting; that its success would encourage students to join the pottery department; and that he would be able to expand it into a sustainable business. But he did not account for the reluctance of the head potters from Sindh or the caste hierarchies of the *kumhars*, something that bedevilled the School's stated aim of upgrading the skills of the craftsmen. Neither was the Government in London sympathetic to his cause and so he did not receive funding till much later. Terry therefore decided to set up a factory on his own, though he did use the resources of the School to supplement his efforts. Since he was superintendent and commissioner for several of the exhibitions, he used his clout to keep the enterprise going and personally supervised the execution of almost every pot.

Meanwhile, Griffiths, who became the principal of the School on Terry's retirement in 1882, had embarked on a major project to document the Buddhist caves of Ajanta, which had been discovered by Captain John Smith in 1819. The earliest caves date to the second century BCE and the later caves to about the tenth century CE. The paintings and murals represent the acme of Indian art and Griffiths was captivated by their beauty and refinement. From 1872 to 1885, he took his students to Ajanta to make copies of the murals and the decorative panels. These copies provided the inspiration for the decorative elements on much of the pottery.

The pottery designs were not restricted to copying the Ajanta murals. Natural floral patterns from Sindh were adapted and several new shapes and colours were added to the repertoire of the pottery production. The *Journal of Indian Art* notes that visitors to the School were amazed to see uneducated potters scantily clad skilfully working the clay on the wheel and producing a range of about 300 shapes and sizes.[8] Figures from the *Jataka Tales* and episodes from the *Ramayana* and the *Mahabharata* were frequently depicted on the jars and vases. The lotus was the most popular floral decoration on the pots and the style is copied directly from the Ajanta paintings, producing a refined and graceful effect. Sculptural representations of exotic fauna such as elephants, lions, parrots and peacocks were used to shape the handles or the base of the jars and vases. A particularly striking design of peacock feathers that has been much admired is in the collection of the Dr. Bhau Daji Lad Museum (see p. 131). It forms a *jali* or net pattern all over the pot, while the base and the handles are shaped like a peacock's fantails.

However, this serendipitous confluence of styles and shapes lasted only as long as Terry took a personal interest in the project. In fact, it was initially known as Terryware and only later acquired the exotic name of Wonderland Art Pottery. Its huge success as one of the most sought-after products ensured that it was dispersed across the globe. Collections of Bombay Pottery exist in museums across Britain and Europe as well as in the United States of America (notably at the Los Angeles County Museum of Art), in Australia (at the Melbourne Museum) and at the New Zealand Museum. John Forbes Watson, who was the Commissioner for Australia, was an old India hand and he purchased a large collection of Bombay Pottery from the 1886 Calcutta Exhibition for New Zealand and Australia.[9] The V&A Museum, London, which became the repository for objects collected for the India Museum set up by the East India Company, has the largest collection of Bombay Pottery. Some collections exist in Indian museums as well, including the National Museum, New Delhi; the Indian Museum, Kolkata; the Albert Hall, Jaipur; the Chennai Museum, and possibly others as well. Bombay Pottery was also showcased at many of the local industrial arts exhibitions, which had become popular across India and were held with great regularity.

Terry was appointed curator of the V&A Bombay, from 1868 to 1879. He made a great effort to build the collections of the Museum and promote Indian artware at various international exhibitions. He was allowed to continue the small factory he had established as he had invested a substantial sum of 2,000 pounds to keep the enterprise going.[10] Meanwhile, the Government took over the pottery kiln and class at the School in 1909 and given the popularity of Wonderland Pottery, decided to bring in a pottery teacher and establish an expanded pottery class as part of the Sir George Clarke Technical Laboratories and Studios, named after the man who inaugurated it. The Government invested over Rs 1,00,000 in this effort and 'offered the most decisive application of science to the problems of pottery production in Western India'.[11] The lab tested clays and set up new kilns and developed mechanised production systems. Ernest Fern, who was curator at the V&A, Bombay during 1918–30, was also superintendent of the Clarke Labs. He shifted focus from handmade products to mechanised mass-produced merchandise like pottery dishes, tiles, drainage pipes, etc. *The Story of Sir J.J. School of Art,* however, criticises Fern for being ignorant of traditional techniques and trying to modernise rather than appreciate 'the decorative qualities achieved by the traditional methods.'[12] • TZM

GEORGE CLARKE POTTERY

The Sir George Clarke Technical Laboratories and Studios opened at the Sir J.J. School of Art in 1909, to offer scientific and technical knowledge for the production of glazed pottery, including testing clays in the region, preparing glazes and building kilns. From 1913 the workshop started producing what in the early twentieth century was known as glazed 'Art Pottery'.[1] Ernest Fern, Superintendent of Pottery at the Sir J.J. School of Art and also the curator of the V&A, Bombay (1918–30), explains that the lab was set up to erect a demonstration pottery factory working in the vicinity of Bombay where all classes of students would receive training in the various branches of the pottery industry on purely commercial lines. However, by the 1920s there was a gradual decline in the demand for Bombay Pottery in Europe.[2] The trend shifted towards Japanese ceramic ware which became fashionable during the early twentieth century, and the lab closed in 1926.[3]

William Ault established Ault Pottery in 1887. Ault Pottery was best known for its inventive use of coloured glazes and produced the typical glaze-effect 'Art Pottery' of the period. Although Clarke Pottery shows signs of being influenced by Ault Pottery, the two have identifiable differences. A degree of stylised decoration on the surface of the pots is a characteristic of Ault Pottery, whereas the wares produced at the Clarke workshop were more spare and included a greater variety of forms and colours but used minimal decorative elements.

The well-known British designer Christopher Dresser had introduced a simplicity of form and design to Ault Pottery at Swadlincote, Staffordshire. Christopher Dresser was a pivotal figure in the Aesthetic Movement that influenced design during the late nineteenth century in Europe. He was a contemporary of William Morris but their styles differed significantly. Dresser strove to produce affordable, functional and well-designed domestic objects, whereas Morris' designs were more elaborate and inspired by natural forms. The Clarke Pottery collection at the Museum reflects design and form inspired by both these practices. • HK

 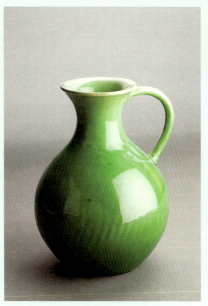 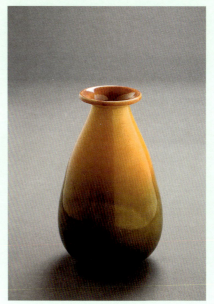

(L-R) *Vase*; *Jug*; *Vase*; glazed pottery, early to mid-nineteenth century, Clarke Workshop, Sir J.J. School of Art, Bombay; 19.6 x 13.5 cm. Accessioned: 1913–26.

WITH the increase in the number of East India Company officials and European visitors in Bombay, a unique style of furniture known as Bombay Blackwood became fashionable. Named after both the place where they were manufactured and the beautiful wood that was used, Blackwood sofas, chairs, tables, teapoys, brackets, cupboards and other items of furniture were popular with both the European and Indian elite. The Great Exhibition of 1851 in London, and the Paris Exhibition of 1855, made Bombay Blackwood famous globally and it won several awards at the exhibitions.[1]

India did not have a tradition of seated furniture and when the Europeans arrived, they found it difficult to furnish their houses in the manner they were used to. It became customary to bring pieces of furniture from Europe when setting sail for India. These were then copied by Indian craftsmen and, slowly, the tradition of Western-style furniture developed along the coasts and in the Presidency towns. Indian craftsmen were famous for being able to copy anything accurately, though in the case of furniture, their understanding of joinery was often a problem as they had neither used nor built seated furniture and copies were usually made from sketches or pattern books.

By the mid-nineteenth century, experienced craftsmen produced magnificent pieces that were an amalgamation of European form and Indian design. In Bombay, this coming together of two different idioms created a remarkable new style in which intricate Indian carving was matched with elaborate European styles which were produced in the dark luscious blackwood.[2] The early designs had less carving and were more elegant, but gradually the furniture acquired local flourishes as artisans added rococo touches and embellishments such as lions, elephants, serpents and birds, in their carving, which previously had typically British floral motifs.[3] Table-tops and flat surfaces were sometimes held up by cast images of animals and birds such as storks with their long, bent necks. Bombay Blackwood was usually carved in open filigree to the last fraction of an inch.[4] The craftsmen who worked the blackwood were predominantly Gujarati and Parsi migrants from Surat and Ahmedabad, where many had been employed for generations in building the grand havelis for local aristocrats and merchants. Many of them were skilled carpenters who were employed in shipbuilding, which was a major industry in Surat.[5]

The Parsi community of Bombay dominated the Bombay Blackwood trade. Most of the craftsmen and furniture store owners were Parsis and the workshops producing the furniture were located in and around the fashionable Meadow Street. The Parsis also patronised the furniture along with the Pathare Prabhus and Bohras, as they were among the most affluent communities of the city and lived in large spacious homes, essential to house Bombay Blackwood, which was heavy and ornate. Several European dealers in furniture also set up shop in India as this proved to be a highly lucrative trade. James Proctor Watson, proprietor of Watson and Co., Bombay, was an established furniture dealer across the country. By 1882, he had established a workshop from where he would supply Bombay Blackwood furniture across Europe.[6]

The American painter and designer Lockwood de Forest introduced East Indian craft to the flamboyant Gilded Age of America, where it received much appreciation from the American elite. He formed an alliance with the Indian philanthropist and art connoisseur Mugganbhai Hutheesing, and together they started the Ahmedabad Wood Carving Company in 1881.[7] Their furniture found buyers across America, including the famous industrialist and philanthropist Andrew Carnegie.[8] Unlike the art schools that attempted to reform Indian craft, de Forest provided patronage and encouraged excellence in his enterprise. He would provide a brief sketch and allow the artisans to imaginatively fill in the details. The results were unusual and outstanding. de Forest aggressively promoted the work at international exhibitions and in London and America. The company ran successfully for almost twenty years and de Forest sold it to Tiffany's Studio when he retired.[9]

As demand grew, the aesthetics were compromised, and the commercialisation of the furniture industry, as well as the rapidly changing fashions led to a decline in the demand for Bombay Blackwood furniture. Further, the Indian Forest Act 1927 declared the export of products made from the *Dalbergia latifolia* (blackwood) illegal. However, Bombay Blackwood furniture had by this time become synonymous with Indian design around the world, and was responsible for the revival of fine woodcarving in Ahmedabad and Bombay.

The Museum's elaborately carved Bombay Blackwood screen (opposite) has an intricate foliate design running along the borders with the three eagles perched on the top. The screen, which cost a princely sum of Rs 500, was presented to the Museum by Mungaldas Nathubhoy in 1859 in response to a request from George Birdwood. As there was no space to display it at the Town Hall at the time, it was added to the collection when the new Museum building was inaugurated in 1872.[10] • TZM

Opposite:
Bombay Blackwood Screen (above) and detail (below), carved blackwood, mid-nineteenth century, Bombay; 248 x 101 x 266 cm. Accessioned: 1859. Presented to the Museum by Mungaldas Nathubhoy.

MUNGALDAS NATHUBHOY (1832–1890)

Among the many merchant princes of nineteenth-century Bombay, Sir Mungaldas Nathubhoy was one of the most illustrious and generous. He was a member of the V&A Bombay Museum committee and donated freely to its fundraising efforts. He also presented the Museum with some artefacts, the most notable of which is the Bombay Blackwood screen.

Sir Mungaldas Nathubhoy was born on October 15, 1832. His ancestors had come to Bombay from Gujarat in the early eighteenth century. Ramdas Manordas, his grandfather, amassed a considerable fortune in land and houses, which Mungaldas inherited at the tender age of eleven due to the untimely death of his father. He studied at an English school and as he became increasingly preoccupied with his business, he hired a private tutor and took lessons during his leisure hours. Like many merchant princes of Bombay, he had a keen interest in learning and was a member of institutions like the Bombay branch of the Royal Asiatic Society and the Royal Geographical Society.

Nathubhoy built his fortune trading in cotton and became one of the largest landowners in Bombay. He was the head of the Kapol Bania caste of Bombay, and a local representative of the Hindu community in all public matters in the city. A well-known reformer, he assisted in establishing the Hindu Girls' School, gave fellowships to Bombay University, a large donation to the Indian Famine Fund, and donated more than Rs 500,000 to various charities during his lifetime.[1] He was nominated to the legislative council of Bombay and re-elected thrice in succession until 1874.

Nathubhoy made strenuous efforts to reform the caste system in India. He wrote a booklet and gave lectures on the subject. His research covered caste from Vedic times to the present and he notes, 'Thus each caste has been, as it were, a separate and stagnant centre of national life, isolated from the whole world: and what do we find at the root of all this mischief. It is the false theory of birth-right … '[2]

In 1872, he was made a Companion of the Order of the Star of India, and in 1875, the honour of Knight Bachelor was conferred on him, making him the first Hindu to be knighted by the Queen. In 1875-76 the Prince of Wales, later King Edward VII, attended Nathubhoy's wedding during his tour of India.[3] Nathubhoy died in Bombay on March 9, 1890, leaving behind a remarkable legacy. • TZM

Mungaldas Nathubhoy;
glass negative, c. late nineteenth to early twentieth century, Bombay;
15 x 10 cm. Accessioned: 1903–18.

NINETEENTH-CENTURY sources mention 'Bombay Boxwork' as an ivory craft practised in and around Bombay.[1] Elaborate micro-mosaic work which involved the binding of rods of various contrasting woods, horn, metal and ivory, with glue, was sliced and used as veneer patterns on wooden objects. *The Hobson-Jobson*, a glossary of colloquial Anglo-Indian words and phrases published in 1886, mentions 'Bombay Boxwork' as a well-known manufacture. 'Bombay Boxwork' objects included boxes, tables, card-cases, book stands, etc.

Bombay Boxwork was a popular craft, which became representative of India with many objects being sent for the great exhibitions in Europe. Bombay box makers exhibited about 750 examples of their work at the 1873 Vienna World's Fair. It was also in huge demand at stores like Liberty & Co. in London, who in 1885 brought a craftsman from Bombay to demonstrate the work at the Indian village set up in Battersea Park, London.[2] Ivory inlay work originated in Persia and travelled to Sindh, Surat and Bombay along the trade routes. It was introduced in Bombay in the early nineteenth century and there were about fifty master craftsmen with over seventy apprentices producing Bombay Boxwork by the mid-nineteenth century. The most popular craftsmen were Atmaram Vuliram, Framji Hirjibhai and Parshostam Chilaram whose atelier at Kalbadevi was among the first in the city.[3]

Above:
Portable desk; sandalwood, inlaid with ivory and *sadeli*, Indian (Calcutta), nineteenth century; 11 x 26 x 18.5 cm. © Victoria and Albert Museum, London. Acquired by the India Museum possibly after the 1855 or 1867 Paris Universal Exhibition and transferred to the V&A London in 1879.
•
Below:
Toilet Box; inlaid ivory and metal on sandalwood box, mid-nineteenth century, Bombay, 33.1 x 24.7 x 13.9 cm. Accessioned: c. 1858–1933. A workbox of a similar shape (see above) is in the collection at the V&A, London.

Most Bombay Boxwork objects in the Museum's collection were purchased in 1858 by George Birdwood through a donation by Juggannath Sunkersett.[4] Birdwood probably bought the objects from Atmaram Vuliram of Bombay, who was awarded a medal for his box that was exhibited at the Great Exhibition of 1851 in London.[5]

On ivory, art historian Ananda Coomaraswamy has commented, 'No other craft would throw more light on the history and migrations of designs in India than this'.[6] Similar to the ivory trade patterns, it is likely that Bombay Boxwork too originated in Surat and was introduced by the Parsis when they migrated to India from Iran around the tenth century CE. It is also known as *sadeli* in Gujarat. A majority of wood and ivory carvers migrated to Bombay from Gujarat, especially from Surat and its neighbouring areas which had highly skilled Gujarati and Parsi craftsmen.

The art form originated in a culture which had mastered geometry, and most of the mosaic wood objects depict repeated geometric patterns generated from a set number of points.[7] It bears a resemblance to the Persian marquetry of *khatam*, a craft that developed in the fourteenth century in Iran, and was patronised by the Safavid Dynasty (1501–1722).[8] Birdwood describes some of the common patterns as *chakar-gul* (round bloom), *katki-gul* (hexagonal bloom), *tinkonia-gul* (three-cornered bloom), *adhi-dhar-gul* (rhombus bloom), *horus-gul* (square matting-like), *tiki* (a small round pattern).[9] In 1912, the Museum acquired a set of forty-five specimens from J.P. Watson, illustrating similar patterns in inlaid woodwork.

The first step in creating an ivory mosaic is preparing thin rods by scraping lengths of ivory, bone or wood into the desired, usually triangular, shape. Artisans then glue these long thin rods together with animal glue, and slice them transversely to form a repeating pattern. To achieve variety and contrast, they used woods like ebony and rosewood, along with natural and green-stained bone and

ivory. They often introduced circular-shaped rods of silver, pewter or tin. Finally, they would glue the slices onto the surface of a wooden box, usually made of sandalwood. To achieve variations of patterns, they combined the materials in different ways.[10]

Persian and Indian makers of this exquisite decorative technique displayed an understanding of the qualities of the different materials they used. They combined materials which could expand and contract according to atmospheric conditions with others which were hard and unyielding. The result was a sharp definition of the lines and patterns which made the design most appealing. The shape of the early boxes was either rectangular or sloping at the front with a flat section at the back, reminiscent of English writing tables.[11] Artisans inlaid the borders with stylised floral scrolls and the centres with a single floral motif following a circular or oval symmetrical or asymmetrical pattern.

The history of ivory trade is linked to the development of Surat and Bombay, and indicates the shift of the commercial centre from Surat to Bombay. The west coast of India and the east coast of Africa were linked through an exchange of cotton textiles for ivory. Surat was the centre of trade till about the mid-eighteenth to early nineteenth century. However, the shortage of cotton from America during the Civil War resulted in the rise of Bombay as a centre for cotton trade and a major industrial city, attracting patrons and craftsmen from all over India.

As the city thrived and the population of Western and Indian elite grew, craftsmen started producing objects that catered to these markets. Victorian travel writer Mrs Eliot Montauban noted, 'For beautiful specimens of ivory, inlaid with silver mosaic, made into the most captivating work boxes, elegant baskets and seducing little nick nacks [sic] of all shapes and sizes and for every variety of purpose, the fame of Bombay has spread far and wide.'[12] • PV

Opposite:
Envelope Box; inlaid ivory and metal on carved sandalwood, mid-nineteenth century, Bombay, 24 x 16.4 x 14 cm. Accessioned: 1858–1933.

•

Right:
Rectangular Box; inlaid ivory and metal on sandalwood, mid-nineteenth century, Bombay; 6.9 x 15.4 x 10.7 cm. Accessioned: 1858–1933.

38 CARVED IVORY BOX

CARVED ivory boxes were popular gift items across centuries and cultures as they represented status and affluence. Between 1870 and 1915, Bombay became the world's third-largest market for ivory and was one of the main ports in western India through which ivory was imported from east Africa and routed not just to Indian production centres, but also to Europe, China and Southeast Asia in the late nineteenth century.[1] Surat, Poona, Nasik and north Canara were the centres where ivory craftsmen were located. Ivory articles were also sold at the Parisian Jewellery Mart, Swadeshi Stores, Sharda Stores, Khadi and Village Industries Stores in Bombay during the early to mid-twentieth century.

The craftsmanship was usually hereditary and catered to an exclusive clientele. Objects of daily use such as ivory combs and bangles were produced across major towns in India, but Delhi gained fame as a major centre for ivory carving in the 1900s with the Delhi Exhibition of 1902-03. European officials and tourists frequented the city, providing a ready market for the beautifully carved ivory objects that were praised as 'essentially Indian' with limited European influence.[2] Lala Faqir Chand's atelier in the *dariba* or main bazaar had a monopoly on the ivory trade in Delhi. By 1910, other producers, namely Shugan Chand and Lall & Co., competed with ivory souvenirs that were similar in design but cheaper. Craftsmen were the proprietors of their ateliers. About twenty to thirty ivory carvers worked in close quarters with sandalwood carvers and miniature artists in popular ateliers to meet the demands of the international markets. These highly skilled carvers could reproduce any design 'specifically ordered from even an unsatisfactory model or a photograph' and created bespoke pieces.[3]

Ivory veneer caskets and carved boxes, presented to high-ranking British officials, were among the most sought-after ivory articles during this period and cost anywhere between Rs 20 to Rs 200. The carved ivory box from Delhi that is in the Museum's collection was purchased in 1925 at a price of Rs 125. The surface of the box is decorated with an interesting mix of Islamic and European design. The ivory

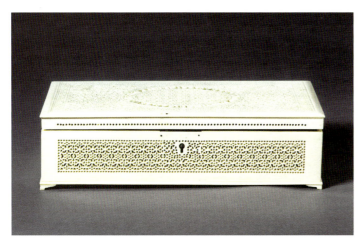

Above:
Address Casket; ivory, carved, c. 1899, Amritsar; 5.8 x 22 x 11 cm.
© Victoria and Albert Museum, London.

•

Opposite:
Box Depicting a Hunting Scene; carved ivory, wood, brass, late
nineteenth to early twentieth century, Delhi; 14.7 x 26.8 x 15.3 cm.
Accessioned: 1925.

•

Below:
Box; with perforated geometric design, ivory, late nineteenth to early
twentieth century, Delhi; 7.6 x 29.3 x 10.8 cm. Accessioned: 1925.
A similar box from Amritsar was presented to Lord Curzon in 1899
and was acquired by the Victoria & Albert Museum, London, in 1925
(see above).

panels carved in low relief depict hunting or shikar scenes in
an animated, sequential format framed with bold, engraved
foliate borders. The subject, style and treatment of the figures
on the carved panels resemble a Mughal miniature. Given the
popularity of Mughal miniatures in the European markets,
carvings resembling miniature paintings were being readily
adapted onto boxes and furniture by the second half of the
nineteenth century.[4]

There are two narratives of the hunt on the box. The
front and side panels depict a hunting party of archers and
a rider with a gun trying to shoot a lion attacking another
horse rider, with two mahouts on elephants in the distance.
The back shows high-ranking nobles on horseback, wearing
crowns with plumes, engaged in a deer hunt using falcons.
Falconry, using trained falcons for hunting prey, was a popular
royal sport during medieval times in the Middle East, India
and Europe. On all the four panels, the hunting party is
accompanied by dogs and hounds or jackals that were trained
to hunt.

The panels on the pyramidal lid depict architectural
drawings in perspective copied from European prints and
Indian miniatures. The nineteenth-century preoccupation
with the classical one-point vanishing perspective is
evident on the back panel, where the ramparts of a fort are

visible. The buildings have a combination of architectural elements: domes, arches, brick walls, palace terraces as seen in miniatures from Mughal and Rajasthani schools. What is most unusual are the palm trees across the panels on the lid, which are not seen in a north Indian landscape but are common on carved ivory boxes produced for an Anglo-Indian market in Vizagapatnam, a major trading port on the east Indian coast. The trend of depicting architectural drawings and landscapes on ivory boxes had begun in Vizagapatnam in the late eighteenth century and was probably adapted by the artisan on this box from Delhi. The combination of images from Mughal miniatures and postcard-like images of architectural styles provides a vignette of nineteenth-century India.

The port of Bombay, which was the main entrepôt to India, was thronged by tourists and merchants, and a substantial elite consumer class. It was the perfect market for consumers and sellers of luxury ivory items. A ban on hunting elephants in the late twentieth century led to the eventual decline of the ivory carving industry. • RWB

Above:
A Pleasure Boat of a Raja; depicting a nautch party in progress, carved ivory, early twentieth century, Mysore; 18.5 x 36 x 4.2 cm. Accessioned: 1930–33.
A similar pleasure boat from Berhampur was featured in *The Journal of Indian Art and Industry*, Vol X, 1904 and was sent to the India Museum collection.
•

Opposite:
Photo Frame; ivory fretwork on wood, early twentieth century, Vizagapatnam; 24.5 x 32 x 2 cm. Accessioned: 1939-40.

39 SOAPSTONE DISH

SOAPSTONE carving is one of the oldest surviving arts that is still practised and is still popular in Agra. Decorative stone carving evolved with the introduction of stone tracery and the famed Mughal art of *jali* work or fretwork stone carving during the medieval period. The art form evolved from large architectural applications to smaller soapstone artefacts both during and after Mughal rule. One of the key features of soapstone carving is its splendid floral and arabesque patterns which are in sharp relief. The soft stone allows for extraordinarily delicate details and intricate designs that are hard to achieve in other stone mediums. Although soapstone had been used for centuries to make a wide variety of ornaments, seals, implements and utensils, it was the Mughals who perfected the various types of soapstone ornamentation.

Soapstone, or *ghiya patthar*, is a talc-schist, a type of metamorphic rock that is relatively soft, making it ideal for carving. It is mined in Rajasthan and carved in Agra, one of the chief centres for stone carving in India. Soapstone artisans replicated the carving technique and geometric and floral designs of architectural elements to produce utilitarian as well as decorative objects such as plates, small boxes, miniature models of buildings, paper weights and inkstands. The art was passed down through generations and the same craftsmen also worked on marble inlay, which involved intricate carving

Opposite:
Carved Dish; soapstone, c. 1880–83, Agra; 30 cm (diameter). Accessioned: 1884.
•
Below:
Stone Carvers; half-baked terracotta and pigments, 1912–13, made at the erstwhile V&A Museum, Bombay, 15.3 x 23.4 x 15.7 cm.

and incising.[1] Soapstone artefacts, though fragile, gained popularity in the mid-nineteenth century among European travellers due to the low prices and elaborate designs.

The intricately carved soapstone dish in the Museum's collection is a blend of European motifs and designs executed with extraordinary Indian craftsmanship. The centre of the dish has a carving of the 'Green Man' face. The face is surrounded by foliage and a bunch of grape sprouts from his mouth. In late-nineteenth-century Britain, the image of the 'Green Man' enjoyed a revival, becoming popular with architects during the Gothic revival and the Arts and Crafts era. It started appearing as a decorative motif on many buildings and objects in Britain. The 'Green Man' has many variations and is found in many cultures across the ages. The myth of the 'Green Man' is related to various natural and pastoral deities and is primarily interpreted as a symbol of rebirth.[2]

The foliate design that emerges from the mouth of the 'Green Man' and is all around him is the Renaissance-style acanthus leaf pattern. This pattern was popularised by William Morris, the British designer associated with the Arts and Crafts movement in England in the nineteenth century, and was extensively used in the decorative arts of the time. It is also a famous Greco-Roman motif used in architecture. The Museum's Corinthian capitals, iron pillars and wrought-iron railings are also adorned with the ornate acanthus leaf pattern. The foliate design on the scalloped edges of the carved dish is a scroll in the palmette leaf pattern, which was also widely used as a neoclassical decorative pattern in the nineteenth and twentieth centuries.

The lithograph print of the soapstone dish from the *Journal of Indian Art*, Vol. I, 1886 strongly resembles the shape and motifs of the dish in the Museum's collection. This volume was edited by Lockwood Kipling who at the time was preparing for the Calcutta International Exhibition which opened in December 1883. The soapstone dish was probably purchased from the same exhibition from a craftsman called Nathu Ram or his brother Sewa Ram.[3] Nathu Ram and Sons was widely known for soapstone carving and stone inlay objects and had showcased its works at various exhibitions in the late nineteenth and early twentieth centuries.[4] In a report dated 1863, George Birdwood states that the carved soapstone ware of Agra was unknown in Bombay until the Museum received its first soapstone work in 1862 on loan. This was primarily due to the lack of trusted agencies to supply these artefacts to different regions.[5] With the initiative taken by the Government of India in 1883 under the 'Draft Scheme for the Promotion of Industrial Art' in the Bombay Presidency, the Museum gradually expanded its collection of decorative arts to include a greater variety of soapstone objects. • RJ

40 HORN CANDELABRA

THE Museum's horn candelabra is an important object in the collection that highlights the confluence of European and Indian design in nineteenth-century India. Made of bison horn in Ratnagiri, near Poona, which was a part of the Bombay Presidency, it shows how traditional craftsmanship quickly adapted to produce modern utilitarian wares for new patrons. The candelabra was probably made in the early 1880s. In Europe, elaborate candelabras were used primarily for aesthetic display of lighting in churches and aristocratic households.[1]

Ratnagiri and Sawantwadi in the Bombay Presidency were the two important centres for the production of horn objects. Buffalo and bison horn were most commonly used for this craft. Bison horn is more malleable than buffalo and hence lends itself better to intricate treatment. Bison horn was imported from Malabar and Cochin and finished objects were made at Vijaydurg, Malvan and Rajapur in Ratnagiri district.[2]

The horn candelabra in the Museum's collection has *nagas* (sacred cobras) entwined around the stem of the stand. The artisan has minutely engraved the outlines of the eyes, mouth and the scales on their backs. The *naga* is iconographically associated with Buddhism, Hinduism and Jainism and appears with several hoods in religious depictions behind deities, indicating divinity, royalty and protection.[3] Supporting the two arms of the horn are beautifully carved sunflowers and lilies. These are made from the translucent sections of the horn that were skilfully moulded by hand. The words 'Dadba jia' are visible on the stand and could be the name of the craftsman.

Horn objects were usually prepared by carpenters and metal workers in ateliers that housed several craftsmen who learned their craft over a period of time. This candelabra is very similar to the one mentioned in the official catalogue of Indian Art at Delhi, 1903, for the exhibition at the Delhi Durbar which is an even more elaborate version, and would have been created by the most experienced master craftsman of the atelier. Over thirty-five different types of objects were made in Ratnagiri, including cups, tumblers, combs, musical instruments, work boxes, powder flasks, bows and arrows, hukkahs, scent bottles, snuff boxes, and dagger and knife handles.[4] Craftsmen also created objects that were used during rituals such as bowls for pouring water over deities and for storing gunpowder.

The European demand for horn encouraged artisanal production, which gave a boost to the industry. The 1883 Calcutta exhibition catalogue states that traditionally only trays and caskets for the worship of idols were made in Ratnagiri but lately cups of various shapes and lampshades were being made to meet the demands of the Europeans

in India.[5] The catalogue of the 1903 Delhi exhibition states, 'A candelabrum or lampstand, of most artistic design and elaborate workmanship, was sold in Bombay'.[6]

In 1897, British civil servant Edward Hamilton Aitken wrote about Ratnagiri horn work: 'Even original and complicated pieces of work like this appear to be carried through without any model or design. The idea is in the workman's head, and the details grow under his hand.'[7] The horn objects from Ratnagiri had been exhibited at many local and international exhibitions.

By the early twentieth century, the production of horn objects experienced a decline due to the lack of patronage. Attempts were made by the British authorities to popularise horn objects in the international markets through exhibitions such as the British Empire Exhibition at Wembley in 1924. Despite such efforts there was a gradual decline in the manufacture and trade of horn work and it is not practised as a popular craft today. • HK

Above:
Horn Work Carried Out in the Konkan; print, G.P. Fernandez, *Report on the Art-Crafts of the Bombay Presidency*. Bombay: Government Central Press, 1932; 24.5 x 15 cm. Accessioned: mid-twentieth century.
•
Opposite:
Candelabra; buffalo horn, early twentieth century, Ratnagiri; 28.2 x 16.4 x 31 cm. Accessioned: 1922.

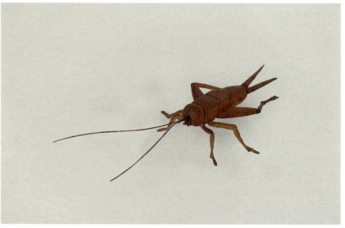

Left:
Crane (above); *Tiger* (below); horn, late
nineteenth to early twentieth century,
Trivandrum; 27.6 x 17.5 x 7.4 cm; 8.5 x 4.5 x 24 cm
respectively. Accessioned: 1939-40.

•

Right (top to bottom);
Lizard; *Cockroach*; *Beetle*; *Scorpion*; horn, late
nineteenth century, Ratnagiri; 7.2 x 4.4 x 3.5 cm
(avg) Accessioned: 1908-09.

41 SANDALWOOD PANEL

Carved Panel; inscription: *Gersari Water Falls*,
sandalwood, late nineteenth to early twentieth century,
Kumpta, north Canara; 33.5 x 23 cm.
Accessioned: 1913–14.

KUMPTA and Honavar in northern Canara, and Mysore were famous for producing carved sandalwood and ivory objects, and for the skill of the carvers. The art form was hereditary and largely practised by the men of the Gudigar community in the Bombay Presidency who had migrated to north Canara and Mysore from Goa in the sixteenth century to escape the Portuguese missionary zeal.[1] When young boys reached the age of twelve, they were trained in drawing for two years and then engaged in the carving ateliers.[2] In the late nineteenth and early twentieth centuries, carved sandalwood objects by Gudigars won medals at international exhibitions and were greatly admired by the Europeans. Objects included carved album covers, caskets, boxes and reproductions of picturesque images of Indian scenery from photographs.[3] While the Gudigars preferred to carve sculptures of gods and goddesses, the demand for 'souvenir' pieces for the European markets continued to increase. The practice of woodcarving was formally introduced at the Madras School of Art in 1877

The Falls of Gairsoppa, William Simpson; chromolithograph, J.W. Kaye, *India: Ancient and Modern with Descriptive Literature* (Vol. 2), London: Day & Son, 1867; 60 x 42.4 cm. Accessioned: 1900–18.

where artisans amalgamated carved sculptural forms as seen in the temples of Belgaum and Halebid, with European academic naturalism.[4]

In the early twentieth century, there were over 300 Gudigars making articles on demand in Kumpta.[5] The shortage of resources and raw materials hobbled the artisans' ability to keep a ready stock for sale and export in the markets in larger towns.[6] This, however, did not dent the demand and popularity of Kumpta work internationally.

The Museum records of the early twentieth century indicate the curators' interest in acquiring a range of carved sandalwood objects from Kumpta and Honavar.[7] The sandalwood panel depicted here was purchased by the Museum in 1914, along with another carved panel depicting jungle scenery. The panel depicts the scenery at the famous Gersoppa Falls (also known as Jog Falls) near Kumpta, which are among the tallest waterfalls in India. The Falls were a popular stop on the itineraries of the British officers, artists, writers and travellers visiting India.

Carved in high relief, the four waterfalls are at the centre of the panel and are surrounded by a lush forest and animated jungle scenery. On the right side we have intricate details of squirrels and monkeys climbing on trees, weaver birds with their nests suspended from the branches and a couple of tigers hunting deer. On the left side there are elephants bending tree branches with their trunks to reach the fruit and bears climbing the trees in an attempt to reach the honeycombs. The village homes are raised on plinths and have traditional sloping, tiled roofs typically seen in the high rainfall zones on the western coast of India. A few men dressed in *kurtas* (long traditional shirts) and *dhotis* (lower garments) are seen facing the waterfalls. A geometric design on the inner border and an elaborate scrollwork design on the outer, thicker border frame the panel. Interestingly, the words engraved on the stylised banner at the bottom read 'Gersari Water Falls', not Gersoppa Waterfalls, indicating the local variations of the name of the village where the falls are located.

William Simpson, a Scottish 'war artist' who visited India several times, also painted the 'Gairsoppa Falls', published as a chromolithograph in 1867. Simpson writes the following account of his visit to the Falls in his autobiography: 'In the rainy season these Falls form one mass of water, but in the dry period there are four separate and distinct falls. The latter is said to be the best time to see them … the mass of rock over which they pour is about 800 ft in height. The principal of these is "Maharajah" which drops for 828 feet without a break. Next is the "Roarer" so named from the noise it makes. The next is "Rocket" as the water comes down in sharp points. Fourth is "Dame Blanche" because the water spreads itself over the rocks producing the appearance of white lace.'[8] Today, these falls are known as Raja, Roarer, Rocket and Rani. • RWB

SANDALWOOD CASKET

Carved sandalwood caskets, jewel boxes, cabinets and writing desks made by the Gudigar community in Canara and Mysore were in high demand from British officers in the late nineteenth and early twentieth centuries. Sandalwood caskets and cabinets had become popular at Indian and international exhibitions and were also presented as gifts to Government officials.

The Museum's casket is from south India. It was probably purchased in Bombay where the local markets and salesmen would commission sandalwood articles from the artisans. Elaborately carved caskets took up to six months to create and commanded anywhere between Rs 250 to Rs 600.[1] Caskets made of two levels, such as the Museum piece, were first assembled, then taken apart to carve panels separately, and finally reassembled. The lower level is a shallow pull-out tray, with a knob and a box without compartments but with a keyhole indicating it was meant for valuables such as jewellery; the upper level has a hinged lid. Cabinets and caskets were supported on legs carved in the shape of animals. The Museum's casket has a mythical composite animal known as *makara* or a sea creature.

Monographs written by British Government reporters on the sandalwood carving industry in south India attribute the stylistic details on articles carved by the Gudigars to the Chalukyan-Hoysala temple ornamentation (circa the tenth to the fourteenth century CE).[2] Gudigars were known for their carvings in contrasting relief, and stylised scrollwork. The carvers were encouraged to execute European images depicting hunting scenes.[3]

The market for carved caskets gradually declined after the British troops left India. However, with the assistance of cooperative groups and state handicraft development programs, the trade revived after the 1960s. • RWB

Casket; sandalwood, late nineteenth to early twentieth century, south India;
45.7 x 35.8 x 32.8 cm.
Accessioned: 1898–1902.

ORNAMENTAL arms were prized possessions and gifts of choice for high-ranking nobility. The extent and skill of the decoration on armoury denoted the rank and wealth of the bearer. Till the nineteenth century most skilled craftsmen worked on producing extraordinary decoration on armoury to demonstrate their skills. This is evident in a range of decorative arts such as metal and ivory inlay, damascening and embellishment with gemstones on swords, shields and daggers. The Museum's first collection of Indian arms was presented by H.H. Gaekwad of Baroda and included both offensive and defensive weapons. In 1890, a range of weapons including swords, knives, spearhead, daggers and arrows were presented to the Museum by the Dewan of Palanpore, who had exhibited these at the Bombay Art Society's exhibition held in March 1890.

In the nineteenth century, British and European settlers and visitors were keen on collecting swords, daggers and battle axes. This interest was shared by the Indian nobility as well, who displayed their collections on the walls of their sumptuous palaces. The 1883 catalogue of the International Calcutta Exhibition notes that by the nineteenth century, the manufacture of Indian arms was limited 'almost entirely to supplying the demand created by collectors of curios'.[1] These were largely produced in Kutch, where craftsmen reproduced traditional designs and styles that were adapted for mounting on the walls of the homes of the Victorian and Indian elite.

Descriptions of armoury in the *Ramayana* and the *Mahabharata* (seventh to fourth century BCE) are among the earliest records in Indian texts of different types of weapons. Advances in technology and mastery over weapon-making were fuelled by the dynamic interplay of indigenous and exogenous forces throughout the course of Indian history. The resulting cross-cultural influences were a key factor in the evolution of sophisticated arms with extraordinary designs and workmanship. Styles were unique to particular dynasties who displayed their weapons with great pride. Duarte Barbosa, a Portuguese writer and officer appointed to India, mentions that the weaponry of the Mughal Empire in India was heavily influenced by Turkish weapons, which were imported at the beginning of the sixteenth century.[2] The *Baburnama*, the memoir of the first Mughal Emperor, Babur (1483–1530), mentions that a six-bladed mace, battle axes, broad axes and a javelin could be relied upon for causing damage in a single blow.[3]

It was a common practice in the Mughal courts to employ craftsmen, some of whom were invited from Persia and Turkey, to create and ornament their weaponry. Dagger handles or hilts made of precious materials such as jade and crystal, encrusted with jewels were also commissioned by the royal courts. The Museum's battle axe is an example of extraordinary workmanship mostly executed by a master craftsman in the late nineteenth century. The axe is also known as a Crow's Bill or Bhuj, and has a short, broad blade, the end of which is slightly curved into a point resembling a crow's beak. The hollow shaft, concealing a small dagger, is plated with silver and engraved with dense floral motifs,

with a brass elephant head abutting the blade. Red, green, and darker coloured gemstones are used for decoration on the elephant's eye and head. A part of the blade has a damascened floral design, typical of the arms from the northwestern provinces of India.

The Mughals had also developed an eight-blade mace known as *gargaz*, conceived in the shape of a flower with eight petals. The mace has a concealed spike on top and damascened floral motifs on the blades. This weapon was used to break the defensive armour of the enemy and was useful in close combat. The Mughal army introduced a change in the shape and quality of the sword in the Indian subcontinent.[4] A curved sword was much easier to wield in battle than a heavy broadsword. Curved swords had sleek, sharp blades made from damascened steel either imported from Persia or an alloy of iron. The dish-shaped pommel and basket hilt are characteristic of the changes brought about in swords or *talwars* during the medieval period and continued to be popular in the armouries of the Mughal and Rajput armies.

Another interesting weapon in the Museum's collection is a lance with a sinuous body, the broad end resembling the hood of a cobra and the narrow end or 'tail' tapering into a steel blade. This spear was a deadly weapon since it could be twisted into the enemy's body once pierced. The body of the spear is made of the curved horn of a species of antelope known as Kadu bull, native to south and central Africa. Arms and ammunition were often captured by the British army after suppressing rebellions. Musket bullets from the Second Anglo-Maratha War in 1803, and weapons captured by the British-Indian army from the different campaigns fought during World War I were presented to the Museum in the early twentieth century.[5] These were to be part of a Bombay War Museum which was never realised (see p. 205). The 103rd Mahratta Light Infantry (see pp. 228-29) played a crucial role in the Mesopotamian campaign. In the latter half of the twentieth century, a sword with a broad, single-edged curved blade and an ivory hilt was acquired by the Museum. This particular sword is typical of Malabar and was probably used by the Mopla community in the 1921 rebellion against the British during the Khilafat Movement. In 1973-74, the Government of India gave the Museum five weapons from the 1971 war. • RWB

Armoury Display and *Cannons* (foreground); metal, seventeenth to nineteenth century. On view at the Industrial Arts Gallery, Dr. Bhau Daji Lad Museum, Mumbai.

KOFTGARI SHIELD

A *dhal* or shield was the chief weapon for protection in the military. In Abu Fazl's *Ain-i-Akbari*, the shield takes first place in the extensive list that describes the various arms in the arsenal of Emperor Akbar (r. 1556–1605).[1] The circular and convex surface of the shield was designed to cause a lance head or arrow to glance off or slip when launched by the opponent during an attack. In India, shields were usually made with rhinoceros or buffalo hide, or hardwood, copper or iron, or a combination of these materials. The ornamentation of shields with lacquering and damascening is noted from the sixteenth century onwards. Exquisitely decorated and inscribed shields became a symbol of strength and valour.

The Museum has a collection of shields that were mostly manufactured in the nineteenth century. The shield on the opposite page was acquired in 1901 to showcase a regional Deccan variation in the armoury collection. It is representative of a small shield or buckler with an Indo-Persian style of decoration. Bucklers were used alongside shorter thrusting weapons such as a *khanjar* or *khukri*. By the late eighteenth and early nineteenth centuries, *koftgari* shields from the Deccan featured ornamentation imitating the best period of Persian art.[2] Symmetry and order were the hallmarks of design from this region. However, following the Uprising of 1857, the manufacture of arms (including shields) was curtailed by the British.

The Museum shield has a *koftgari* design and a raised thick snake-like body with its head and tail intertwined and circling the bosses. The use of the snake motif is possibly a continuation of a Classical style, where snakes were believed to embody the guardian spirit and evoke fear in the enemy. The use of gold and silver wire indicates an aristocratic patron. The four star-shaped bosses on the front served as fastening corners for hand straps on the reverse side of the shield, knuckle pad and hand straps. A garland of flowers embellishes the outer rim. It is likely that the shield was made to honour a royal ceremony or to be presented as a memento. In the late nineteenth century, shields were made for ornamental purposes and were showcased at the European and Indian exhibitions. • HK

Above:
Helmet; damascened metal with silver and gold wire inlay, c. late eighteenth to nineteenth century, Jaipur; 35 x 22 x 18.5 cm. Accessioned: 1932-33. The metal plate at the centre protected the area between the eyes as well as the nose. The tubes on either side and the top were meant to hold plumes, indicating that the helmet was to be used by royalty. The attached chainmail protected the head from all sides.

Opposite:
Shield; damascened iron with silver and gold wire, nineteenth century, Punjab; 5 x 53 cm. Accessioned: 1901.

43 KOFTGARI PAPER WEIGHT

THE art of damascening or *koftgari* originated in Persia and was brought to India by the Mughals in the sixteenth century. As war and conquest were the major preoccupations of the nobility during those times, the art was primarily used to embellish weapons. In India it was soon adopted by the Rajputs and the Sikhs in Punjab. Exquisite *koftgari* ornamentation can be found on swords, dagger hilts, scabbards, shields, helmets and other weapons. The term *koftgari* is derived from the Persian *kuft-gari* meaning 'beaten work'. The artisan is called a *kuftgar* or gilder. There are three types of *koftgari*: true *koftgari* or *Teh-Nishan*; shallow *koftgari*; and imitation *koftgari* or *Dewali* work.[1]

In the nineteenth century, with the advent of popular exhibitions and the focus on trade, the production of objects with *koftgari* decoration dramatically expanded to include a variety of domestic objects such as vases, candlesticks and decorative boxes. The official catalogue of the 1895 Empire of India Exhibition explains that gold *koftgari* of the Indian subcontinent was considered the highest form of luxury, and was 'bought for the most part by Europeans as curios'.[2] The 1857 Uprising was responsible for discouraging the

Above:
Koftgari Craftsmen; half-baked terracotta and pigments, 1912–14, made at the erstwhile V&A Museum, Bombay; 16.3 x 18.5 x 32.5 cm.
•
Below:
Paper Weight; damascened metal with gold wire inlay, c. mid-nineteenth century, Punjab; 4 x 27.5 x 8.6 cm. Accessioned: 1880–84.

manufacture of arms, but ornamental shields were made to showcase at European and Indian exhibitions. The demand for luxurious Indian decorative art products at international and local exhibitions enhanced the economic and social value of Indian craftsmanship.

The Museum has exquisite examples of *koftgari* works in its decorative arts collection, some of which were acquired in the mid-nineteenth century. Collected by George Birdwood, these aimed to introduce *koftgari* articles to the people and trade networks in Bombay. Among the most beautifully designed pieces is a gold damascened paper weight. An Urdu inscription 'Al Hafez – Kagazat Zabar' meaning 'preserving papers of the keeper of knowledge' is visible on the top of the paper weight, which is made in a unique elongated form with scalloped arches on both sides and a globular handle in the centre. Symmetrically designed, the central body depicts an intersecting vine pattern and is bordered with stylised leaves, tendrils and flowers. The inscription is placed at the base of the handle.

Floral motifs appear on much of the utilitarian wares manufactured in the Punjab, mostly in Sialkot which was a major damascening centre during the nineteenth century. Inscriptions were common, especially on weapons, but were also found on smaller utilitarian objects. Monograms, sacred characters, or poetic verses and charms were inscribed on tools and objects to protect the user from harm. Traditionally, these were meant to be on arms and armouries, but the custom was adapted for other prized, modern collectibles. At times, inscriptions would reflect loyalty to a king or God. However, traditional methods of production suffered due to the change in the type of objects in demand, which were mostly utilitarian. The ancient processes were modified by the artisans, and instead of incised and deeply laid damascene, they simplified the technique by using shallow, rapid incisions and hammering in fine gold wire by pressing it down with a tool.[3]

The paper weight was a luxurious object to keep loose folios pressed down and to organise them. Paper weights were often opulently designed to cater to the nineteenth-century taste for ornamentation. Glass paper weights initially appeared in Europe in the mid-1840s and gained popularity when they were displayed at the 1851 Great Exhibition, introducing a new fashion among collectors in Europe and America.[4] Paper weights were also produced in metal, marble, and other materials in varied designs. Letter-writing and copying ancient manuscripts were popular activities at the time, and paper weights became a fashionable way to showcase one's literary tastes and talents. • HK

ONE of the most appreciated art forms in India, the extraordinary craftsmanship of *bidri* dates back nearly 600 years to the mid-seventeenth century when the sultanates of the Deccan patronised it. The art reached its greatest perfection and beauty towards the end of the Bahmani period (early sixteenth century). By the late nineteenth century there were four centres of production which included Bidar, near Hyderabad, Lucknow in Uttar Pradesh, Purniah in Bihar and Murshidabad in Bengal.[1] Traditional manufacture of damascening and *bidri* ware included ornaments, swords, dagger hilts and scabbards, smoking utensils and inkstands.

The Museum has a fine collection of *bidri* ware, purchased in 1940 from Purshotam Vishram Mawjee, a well-known patron and art dealer who had a 'museum' at Walkeshwar in Bombay. It includes an unusual *tushta* (washbasin), also known as a *sailabchi*, with a *surahi* (ewer). The *tushta* has a perforated cover with a poppy flower motif inspired by Persian designs. Such vessels were commonly found in both the *zenana* (women) and *mardana* (gentlemen) sitting rooms. They were

Opposite:
Tushta and Surahi Set; *bidri* work, c. late nineteenth century, Bidar; 15 x 50.8 cm (*Tushta*), 29.6 x 35.2 cm (*Surahi*). Accessioned: 1940.
•
Below:
Bidri Craftsman; half-baked terracotta and pigments, 1912–14, made at the erstwhile V&A Museum, Bombay; 14.4 x 15.8 x 15.8 cm.

required for Islamic prayer rituals and handwashing before and after meals. The ewer, which has a lid, is densely decorated with a pattern of stylised foliage. The surface is interrupted by narrow rows of single fern-like motifs, running horizontally around the neck and lower part. These motifs are also realised on the 'S'-shaped handle and straight faceted spout. The elongated design of the spout allowed water to flow through it before being poured, adhering to Islamic religious beliefs of flowing water being considered 'clean'.[2]

There are different artisans involved in the entire process of making *bidri* ware, such as moulders, carvers, inlayers, etc. *Bidri* ware is made from an alloy of copper, zinc and sometimes lead. A lathe is used to make the clay mould and after smelting, moulding and turning, the designer traces and etches patterns on the surface with a small steel point. The carver follows his tracings and incises the patterns with delicate, finely pointed chisels of various sizes, working with a small hammer. The patterns are then filled with either gold or, more frequently, silver inlay. The work is polished with sandpaper, charcoal and coconut oil. The alloy is blackened by a solution of copper sulphate or sometimes saltpetre diluted with water, which brightens the silver against the jet-black background. The contrast thus created makes *bidri* ware so unique and lively. As *bidri* is made from an alloy, it does not rust or corrode. The value of the article depends upon the thickness and quantities of the precious metals used and the quality of execution.

The art of *bidri* declined in the 1800s due to want of patronage. However, this changed with the phenomenon of the large national and international exhibitions that began in 1851 with the Great Exhibition at London's Crystal Palace, which had a profound impact on *bidri* manufacture in India. The *bidri* articles from the subcontinent shown at the Crystal Palace were singled out for praise by leading art critics of the day as exemplifying good taste. Owen Jones in his *Grammar of Ornament*, published in 1856, included a plate of designs taken from *bidri hukkahs* shown in London in 1851 and 1855.[3] New centres developed in places like Surat in the Bombay Presidency, Aurangabad and Benares; and Bidar in particular received a boost in production which lifted it out of apparent decline.[4]

In the twentieth century, the art of *bidri* ware again showed signs of decay. The Nizam's Government tried to revive the industry in the early twentieth century and opened a department for *bidri* art in the Central School of Arts and Crafts, now the Govt. College of Fine Arts, Hyderabad. The changing demands in the twentieth and twenty-first centuries have led to the making of statuettes, ashtrays, walking sticks, USB drive holders, jewellery, vases, dishes and stationery items among others. • HK

Set of Betelnut Boxes (Pandaan) with Five Fish-Shaped Containers; *bidri* work, c. late nineteenth century, Bidar; 31 x 23 x 12 x cm. Accessioned: 1940.

•

Opposite:
Tushta (detail), *bidri* work, c. late nineteenth century, Bidar. Accessioned: 1940.

45 SILVER TROPHY CUP

'RAJ SILVER' represents a unique, hybrid style of silverware produced in the nineteenth and twentieth centuries that was different from the traditional silver objects produced by Indian silversmiths such as rosewater sprinklers, *attardaan* (perfume boxes), *paandaan* (betelnut boxes), etc. It was immensely popular among high-ranking Europeans, army officers, as well as the Indian elite. Silver articles were often ordered from European catalogues or customised by well-known firms like Peter Orr & Sons in the Madras Presidency and Oomersee Mawjee & Sons of Bhuj, Kutch, in the Bombay Presidency who catered to this elite market. Silver ateliers in Kutch, Poona, Bombay, Madras, Delhi, Kashmir, Cuttack, Calcutta, Benares and Burma produced objects suited to European tastes. The most sought-after objects were silver trophies, address caskets, tea services, cutlery, cigar cases, platters and decorative pieces meant only for display. Indian silverware was well received at the international exhibitions and *Primrose Record*, a British journal, commented that Britons would gaze avidly at the displays of Indian silver.[1]

The leading silver traders and firms had agents or branches in Bombay as it was the main centre for trading silver. The trade in Kutch silver developed with the encouragement given to it by Maharao Desalji II (1819–60), the ruler of Kutch who not only sent silverware to the Great Exhibition of 1851, but also presented articles to dignitaries on ceremonial occasions.[2] His successor, Rao Pragmalji Desalji II (1860–76) presented the Museum with a large coffee pot, a spoon and a tobacco pipe of Kutch silverwork in 1873-74, which was unfortunately stolen in 1876 during a theft at the Museum. From 1889 till 1932, the Museum's curators collected a rich variety of chased and repoussed silverware, representing famous designs and styles from across India, to showcase to merchants and traders. The Museum also acquired silver objects from neighbouring Asian countries of Burma, Siam and China, and Europe, indicating the established trade networks in the erstwhile Bombay Presidency.

Kutch silver is distinguished by its graceful, intricate, tightly executed floral design in shallow repousse against a frosted background. The typical scrollwork of encircling branches, floral patterns and animal figures that are repeated at intervals is visible in the trophy cup in the Museum's collection. Every inch of the article's surface is worked upon in the typical Kutch style, which was often compared for its profusion to Dutch silverwork.[3] There are two different hunting scenes depicted around the cup, one of a boar hunt with dogs in pursuit, and another of a lion preying upon an antelope. On the front is a small, blank space where the owner's name or coat of arms would be inscribed. There is a border of palmette leaves on the base of the cup above

Trophy Cup; silver, late nineteenth to early twentieth century, Kutch; 33 x 16.8 cm. Accessioned: 1889–1925.

Above:

Coffee Pot; *Milk Jug*; *Sugar Bowl*; *Tray*; silver, late nineteenth to early twentieth century, Dacca, Burma (tray): 18.8 x18.2 cm; 14.9 x 11.9 cm; 9.5 x 8.7 cm; 3 x 28.5 cm respectively. Accessioned: 1889–1925. The design depicting a *shikar* and the elephant-shaped knob on the lid reflect the Kutch style of workmanship. By the early twentieth century the silversmiths in India, Dacca and Burma produced silverware imitating styles across different regions of the Indian subcontinent.

•

Right:

Tea Kettle; silver, late nineteenth century, Kutch; 13.2 x 17.2 cm. Accessioned: 1889–1932. A typical Kutch silver teapot with its spout shaped like the trunk of an elephant and a small elephant knob on the lid, and four claw-and-ball feet. Tea-drinking as a ritual was introduced in India by the British and became fashionable among Indian royalty and the elite, leading to the production of many different tea services.

the stem. Pieces such as this were mostly commissioned to honour winners of a sporting event, such as a horse race, a polo match or even as a display piece.

American silversmiths like the Whiting Manufacturing Company of New York, took note of the popularity of the Kutch style and produced similar tea services, as evident in the teapot that is in the collection of the Dallas Museum of Art.[4] The style's international appeal can be attributed to the delicate foliate designs, and the high level of purity of the silver, which was between 96 and 98 per cent, well above the British Sterling standard of 92.5 per cent.[5] However, it is interesting to note that in spite of the global demand, the British Government imposed heavy import duty on Indian-made gold and silver plate.[6]

European department stores such as Liberty and Procter had set up ateliers in Bombay, employing jewellers from different regions in India. They produced designs native to their regions as well as a mix of European and Indian styles. By the late nineteenth century, there were over 2,800 jewellers in the city of Bombay alone.[7] Master goldsmiths were also skilled in silver repousse work, as is evident in the work of Oomersee Mawjee. The pre-eminence of Kutch silverware was due in part to his expertise and imagination. By the 1920s, an atelier of Oomersee Mawjee & Sons was also established in Baroda, which was patronised by the Gaekwad of Baroda. Kutch silver continues to be popular both with local and international patrons. • **RWB**

Above, left:
Silversmith; half-baked terracotta and pigments, 1912, made at the erstwhile V&A Museum, Bombay; 15 x 16 x 15 cm. Based on the sketch of a *Silversmith from Cutch*, Percy Brown (1902), *Indian Art at Delhi* (1903).
•
Above, right:
Silversmith, Bhuj, Cutch, Percy Brown, Assistant Director, dated July 26, (19)02; G. Watts, *Indian Art at Delhi, 1903. Being the Official Catalogue of the Delhi Exhibition, 1902–1903*, Calcutta: Superintendent of Government Printing, illustrations prepared and printed by Wiele & Klein of Madras; 24 x 15.1 cm. Accessioned: early twentieth century.

SILVER TEA CUP AND SAUCER

Kashmir has been famous for its crafts, such as beautiful embroidered and woven shawls and carpets, delicately painted papier-mâché and intricate woodcarving. The British had made a comparatively late entry into Kashmir, when the Maharaja was replaced by a state governing council in 1887. With the increase in the number of foreign travellers, Kashmiri silver became a popular tourist souvenir in India and began to be exported.

Silver articles in Kashmiri ateliers were produced by two categories of craftsmen: those who shaped the object and those who embellished it. One of the best-known patterns of Kashmiri silverware is the paisley. Other popular patterns are based on the flora that grows in the valley, such as the coriander or rosette pattern, the poppy flower pattern which is ubiquitous in Mughal art, and the readily recognisable and stylised chinar leaf pattern. Silversmiths in Kashmir often combined two or more patterns.

The trade in Kashmiri silver was concentrated in the hands of merchant middlemen—the customer and the artisan hardly ever met.[1] The well-known British jewellery firm Hamilton & Co., with branches in major Presidency towns, was famous for its selection of Kashmiri silver.[2] The Museum has several Kashmiri silver objects, either gifted or purchased at different times. The cup and saucer in the image have a traditional European form and an Indo-European confluence of design. Raised double paisleys are set against a ground of scrolling, stylised chinar leaf vines. The rims have an unusual Art Deco-influenced design, indicating an artistic effort to amalgamate two very different traditions. The parcel gilt inside the cup gives it a rich contrast effect. Both the cup and saucer have an empty space meant to engrave the name or coat of arms of the person to whom it belonged. • RWB

Cup and *Saucer*; silver, early twentieth century, Kashmir; 10 x 6.4 cm, 1.5 x 13.2 cm. Accessioned: 1921.

EUROPEANS had little knowledge of Indian crafts, especially silver, until the mid-nineteenth century advent of the international exhibitions where Indian silverware was one of the great attractions. With the opening of trade routes, Bombay became the main centre for the import and distribution of silver to the rest of the country as the trade in silver bullion was concentrated in the city, with shops and dealers right outside the Fort walls near Zaveri Bazaar in Kalbadevi (see pp. 70-71).[1] Indian silversmiths, responding to the demands of European clients, adopted a unique manner of embellishing the silverware with elaborate decoration that amalgamated Indian and European designs.

There was a distinction between the objects made for European use and traditional forms of Indian silver that had been produced for centuries in India. Objects such as *surahis* (water jugs), *paandaans* (betel nut boxes), *attardaans* (boxes for perfumes) and spice boxes were meant for Indians, while tea services, spoons, knives, dishes, salvers were used by Europeans and by the Indian elite who adopted a Western lifestyle. Silver plate, which is the term used to describe Westernised items, was much coveted by Europeans.

'Swami silver', from the Madras Presidency, was one of the most popular silverware. With its embossed figures of demigods or '*swamis*' from the Hindu pantheon, it presented an extraordinary adaptation of Indian design and European form. The images of deities were designed to fit within European shapes, and did not necessarily adhere to any prescriptive iconographic rules. In the mid-nineteenth century, Swami silver plate, with its focus on intricately chased 'deities', held an exceptional position both in India and abroad. While it captivated most viewers and consumers, it also invited strong criticism from others who considered it a sign of pandering to commercial demands.[2] George Birdwood (see pp. 56-57) was critical of the Swami style, commenting on a piece, 'nothing could be worse than the tea tray and teapot, and sugar and milk bowls, in this Madras tea service. The cups and saucers are unobjectionable perhaps, while the spoons, which are Hindu in character, are decidedly pleasing.'[3]

There are two main themes seen on Swami silverware: iconography from Indian mythology and the different occupations, which were featured in combination with ethnographic genre scenes and botanical representations.[4] Through artistic exchange and an assessment of British taste, the silversmiths working in the Swami style borrowed from multiple visual sources and created objects to cater to a variety of demands. These include themes that were borrowed from

Opposite:
Fruit Bowl; silver, late nineteenth century, Madras; 24.2 x 19 cm. Accessioned: 1896–1922.

•

Right:
Bowl; silver, c. late nineteenth to early twentieth century, Burma; 17.7 x 25 cm. Accessioned: 1900–26.

SILVER PITCHER

By the late nineteenth century, silver craftsmen from across India had migrated to Bombay which had become a great trading port. Silversmiths not only produced silverware in their typical traditional styles but also made hybrid silverware by combining eclectic regional styles. Poona, in the late nineteenth century, developed its own unique composite style of silverware due to its close association with Bombay. The silversmiths of Poona, influenced by Bombay's cosmopolitan eclecticism, used the Madras and Burma styles as their sources. They reframed the distinctive Swami silver iconography from Madras, and arranged it in the arched niches typical of Burmese silver work, producing a style of work which appealed to Indian patrons.

The *ghagar* or pitcher from Poona in the Museum's collection is in high relief and weighs 280 *tolas* (approx. 3.26 kg).[1] It portrays the ten avatars of Vishnu which are depicted in great iconographic detail. The traditional Swami-style imagery is organised within the scalloped arches typical of the Burmese style. The ten avatars are arranged in chronological order within two broad bands, one below the other, with each band having five niches. The first band has the Matsya, Kurma, Varaha, Narasimha and Vaman avatars. The second band has Parashurama (below Matsya), Rama, Krishna, Vithoba with Rakhumai, and Kalki. Since this piece was made in Poona, according to Maharashtrian traditions, it places Vithoba as the ninth avatar instead of Buddha. The avatars are set off with detailed landscapes such as trees, thrones, and other aspects meticulously rendered as per the *shastras*. A running scroll of leaves and flowers is placed in a band along the rim at the top, while the base is adorned with a palmette motif, both of which are typical of the Burmese style.

Poona silver works were sent for the Empire of India Exhibition in London (1895) and the Indian art exhibitions at the Delhi Durbar (1903).[2] The 1903 Delhi exhibition had exhibited a similar pitcher with the ten incarnations of Vishnu from Poona. • HK

Pitcher; silver, c. late nineteenth to early twentieth century, Poona; 32.2 x 30 cm. Accessioned: 1931.

Display of silverware from across the Indian subcontinent. On view at the Industrial Arts Gallery, Dr. Bhau Daji Lad Museum.

Company paintings, such as the depiction of people from different castes and occupations, as well as Hindu deities, temple complexes and processions, which show the image of a deity placed in a chariot or palanquin being taken through the streets of a town. The Swami style also borrowed visuals from Raja Ravi Varma's famous paintings and oleographs, including *Lakshmi standing on a lotus, Saraswati seated on a rock on the river bank,* or *Sage Vishwamitra rejecting the heavenly nymph Menaka.*[5]

The silver fruit bowl from Madras, which is shaped in the form of a lotus, is an elaborate example of the Swami style. Fruit bowls, as centrepieces, were a fashionable accessory on the dinner table in Victorian homes. The edge of the dish, raised on the stem of the flower, has fourteen canopied niches shaped like petals. Each niche depicts an embossed figure of a *gandharva* or mythological being who danced and played music for the gods. These figures are also seen around the stem

and the base. Three birds cast in silver, resembling the Great Indian Bustard, are arranged at the base. The rim around the base is decorated with stylised acanthus leaves.

The Swami silver industry in Madras was unique, as it was largely monopolised by Peter Orr & Sons, a European firm that employed local silversmiths. In other parts of India, silversmiths mostly worked independently or through merchants who acted as their agents. Silverware of the Swami style was presented by the Gaekwad of Baroda, the Maharaja of Cochin and the Maharaja of Indore to the Prince of Wales (later King Edward VII) on his visit to India in 1875-76, and was commissioned from P. Orr & Sons.[6] In Bombay, local silversmiths, who had migrated to the city from different parts of India, produced Swami silver tea service sets with Bombay's urban imagery executed on tea service sets.[7] The trade is still practised in several cities across India. • RWB

47 SILVER ENAMEL HUKKAH

THE *hukkah* is a traditional Indian smoking apparatus which was first contrived by the Mughal nobility during Emperor Akbar's reign.[1] It is a single, double or multi stemmed instrument, which has a base that contains water to filter tobacco before it is inhaled. Sometimes the tobacco was flavoured with honey or mint and other similar herbs. Occasionally cannabis or opium was used. By the early eighteenth century, smoking *hukkah* had become popular at the royal courts across India. British officers were introduced to the custom at these Indian courts.[2] Soon the practice became fashionable amongst the gentry as well. Beautifully embellished *hukkahs* denoted the status of the smoker.

This exquisite enamel-on-silver *hukkah* in five pieces was presented to the Museum in 1911 by Mr S.D. Smith, Assistant Collector of Excise, Bombay.[3] It is executed in the *champlevé* style attributed to Lucknow.[4] The *hukkah* is decorated with an intricate chinar leaf pattern, which at places has a coriander leaf pattern incised within it. It is enamelled in a colour scheme of green and blue, and has two peacocks attached to it, one on the lid of the *chillum* or the base, and the other on the pipe. The pipe of the *hukkah* is ornamented in scrolling bands of rosettes, enamelled alternately in blue and green. The base of the *hukkah* is adorned with cartouches which have a single delicately etched chinar leaf in the centre and a palmette leaf border.

The enamelling on this *hukkah* represents an ancient form of decorating objects, which was used on a variety of surfaces such as metal, glass, ceramic and stone. The ancient Egyptians are said to have applied enamel to stone objects, pottery and even jewellery. The ancient Greeks, Celts, Georgians and Chinese also used enamel on metal objects. The art of enamelling was introduced in India around the second century BCE.[5] Enamelling was widely used in the ancient world to embellish jewellery and votive objects. In the nineteenth century it began to be commonly used to embellish decorative objects as well.

The process of enamelling required deft fingers and a steady hand as intricate designs were enhanced through the use of different colours. Vitreous enamel is made by fusing coloured powdered glass to a substrate by firing between 750 and 850 degrees Celsius: the powder melts, flows, and then hardens into a smooth, durable vitreous coating.[6]

There are four main types of enamelling techniques. The first is where the enamel is simply applied to the metal as paint is applied to canvas. The second is called *cloisonné*, in which the pattern is raised on the surface of the metal by means of small strips of metal or wire welded on to it. Then enamel colour is applied to the outlined surface and the article is placed in the furnace until the glaze fuses; the wires prevent the fusion of colours during the heating process. The third type is *champlevé*, in which the pattern is cut out of the metal itself, by engraving, chasing or repoussing. The pattern is then filled in with enamel. The fourth is *quasi enamelling*, in which gold is fused onto a sheet of glass rather than fusing vitreous paste on to a metal.[7]

By the late nineteenth century, enamelling was being practised across India. Some of the main centres of the art form were Lucknow, Benares, Multan, Lahore, Kangra and Kashmir. But the most famous centre was Jaipur, due to the beauty and excellence of its enamelling, which was attributed to the mingled brilliance of colours, laid on pure gold by the enamellers of Jaipur.[8] Each centre had its own unique technique of enamelling. In Jaipur, the pattern was chased; in Kashmir it was repoussed; and in Lucknow, they used the *champlevé* technique. • TZM

Opposite:
Hukkah in Five Parts; enamel on silver, late nineteenth to early twentieth century, Lucknow; 79 x 24 x 57 cm. Accessioned: 1911.
•
Right:
Cup and *Saucer*; enamel on silver and parcel gilt, late nineteenth to early twentieth century, Kashmir; 6.7 x 11.2 cm; 2.4 x 13.32 cm. Accessioned: 1908–09. The cup and saucer are decorated in a typically Kashmiri broad-chinar-leaf pattern, enamelled in blue and turquoise blue in the *champlevé* technique using repousse. The interior of the cup is parcel gilt.

48 BRASS THAAL

THE versatile nature of a *thaal,* a large round dish, made it a significant item for production, collection and trade. It primarily functioned as a carrier for food, drinks and letters to royals and court officials. Large-sized *thaals* were usually displayed as decorative *objet d'art* in a formal setting of buffets in state dining rooms at royal palaces or stately homes. Based on the malleability of the material, a range of techniques was employed to produce the desired designs. While some *thaals* depicted scenes of hunting or 'oriental' patterns, others bore representations of Indian mythology inspired from sacred texts.

The sun god, Surya (see pp. 226-27), takes centre stage on this elaborate 'brass round dish with astrological figures' in repousse work from the Punjab.[1] Surya is seated cross-legged, riding a chariot drawn by his charioteer and a seven-headed horse. Surya's significance is widespread across India and in sacred Sanskrit texts such as the *Rigveda* and the *Mahabharata*. As the orb of light and heat, Surya brings the world light and dispels evil. His charioteer, Aruna, is described as the harbinger of day, and the seven-headed horse denote the rays of the sun.

The Museum's *thaal* is influenced by a work designed by Jaipur's leading repousse artist of the time, Raghunath. The craftsman was recognised as one of the best workmen for such work in Jaipur, which had become famous for its brass repousse or high-relief works.[2] A similar medallion of Surya and Aruna is observed in the centre of a coffee pot featured in the official catalogue of the Jeypore Museum in 1895. Mythological themed wares of this type were intended for decorative display or to help Europeans understand the signs and symbols of Indian astronomy.

Representations of Indian mythological figures in repousse on different metal objects had been popular since the late nineteenth century and greatly appealed to Europeans.[3] These were usually copied from the works of British orientalists such as Edward Moor (*Hindu Pantheon*, 1810), which served as a resource for students of Indian art. As Surya and other deities were widely worshipped, they were incorporated as elements of design in art schools where students would portray them following standard art school instructions.[4]

The craftsman or *tambat* (maker of large brass articles) has skilfully depicted the twenty-eight 'lunar mansions' or *nakshatras* and the twelve zodiac signs or *rashis* on the outer and inner borders of the *thaal* respectively. The niche borders of floral patterns are inspired by some of the tracery patterns observed in Mughal architecture.[5] The brass sheet would first be hammered or 'pushed out' from the reverse until the desired high-relief was achieved. All the finer details that the artisan visualised for the figures would be incorporated on the front with the help of a fine chisel, followed by polishing.

As a material, brass (*pittal*) was largely employed in India for producing domestic articles such as *kalash* (water jug), *thali* (dish), drinking cups, cooking pots and lampstands. It was one of the most frequently employed metals to make articles for domestic consumption, followed by bronze and copper. The large demand resulted in widespread production of and trading in brass in the subcontinent. The Bombay Presidency production was staggering at the beginning of the twentieth century. About 4,000 brassworkers and coppersmiths (*thateras*) were recorded in Bombay by 1900.[6] Vital raw materials were required for the smooth functioning of the centres. The manufacture of brass wares required rolled brass sheets or smelted copper, as brass is an alloy of copper, which local merchants imported from England, Germany and America. Well into the twentieth century, these imported sheets improved the quality of brass leading to diversified trade and consumption of both decorative and utilitarian brass wares.[7] • IH

Opposite:
Brass Thaal; ornamented with repousse work depicting the twenty-eight lunar mansions and twelve zodiac signs in Indian astrology; brass, late nineteenth to early twentieth century, Punjab; 3.3 x 78 cm. Accessioned: 1900–26.
•
Right:
Coppersmiths at Work; half-baked terracotta, paper pulp, and pigments, c. 1912–14, made at the erstwhile V&A Museum, Bombay; 16.5 x 42.2 x 69 cm.

49 LACQUERED LEATHER GANJIFA SUITE

GANJIFA cards first appeared in the sixteenth century in India and were more than a popular social amusement as they served as a symbol of the sociocultural hierarchy.[1] The game was complex, and only the educated and elite could attempt to master it. *Ganjifa* sets were exquisitely rendered, showing off the skill of the craftsman. Indian *ganjifas* are round, measuring 2–4 inches in diameter. The cards depict figures representing the royal court, mythological characters or deities that were meticulously painted by skilled artisans. The intricate compositions were influenced by miniature paintings and local traditions.[2] *Ganjifas* were made for the elite with expensive materials such as leather, ivory, or tortoiseshell (*darbar kalam*), and for the common man with pieces of cloth and palm leaf (*bazaar kalam*).

The etymology of *ganjifa* has mixed roots—*ganj*, Persian for 'treasure', and *chi pai*, Chinese for 'paper cards'.[3] The story of Indian *ganjifas* begins with the advent of the Mughals in the reign of Babur and then Akbar in the sixteenth century.[4] The game is mentioned with other favourite recreational activities such as chess, pigeon flying and wrestling in the *Baburnama* and the *Ain-i-Akbari*, the biographies of the Emperors.

The Museum's *ganjifa* suite has ninety-six cards and follows the Mughal card hierarchy, but the suite represents the adaptation of Mughal customs and games by the local Rajas. The suite is from Sawantwadi, a Maratha principality along the Konkan coast that was under the rule of the Bhonsles from the sixteenth century onwards. Several artists or *chitaris* settled in the region under the Bhonsles' patronage. In the mid-eighteenth century, Khem Sawant III (1755–1803) of the Bhonsle lineage was credited with sending playing cards to elite dignitaries like Nana Fadnavis of the Peshwa court and Kanhoji Angre, the Maratha naval chief. Even today, *chitari* descendants continue the tradition of producing cards at the Sawantwadi Palace.

The ninety-six cards in the Museum's pack comprise eight suites of twelve cards made of lacquered leather, which was one of the traditional materials used for making Sawantwadi cards. The *chitaris* painted the intricacies of the figures and borders using a fine-point brush and it was lacquered to protect it from damage. Each suite represents the departments of a court (treasury, clerks, gold and silver mint workers, musical performers, servants, swordsmen, etc.) and is recognised by the combination of symbols and coloured backgrounds. The reverse is usually painted plain red. The Museum's suite presents a Raja (seated in a chariot) and a Mantri/Wazir (on horseback; two riders being a sign of quality packs). The Museum deck is a *darbar kalam* suite.

The Museum set and box draw on the traditional *Chitrakathi* paintings. These were usually drawn on large

Ganjifa card; painted and lacquered leather, early twentieth century, Sawantwadi; 9.8 cm (diameter). Accessioned: mid-twentieth century. The card depicts Surya (Sun God) seated in a chariot pulled by a seven-headed horse, surrounded by attendants.

pieces of paper by the *chitrakathis* to narrate the Hindu epics, the *Ramayana* and *Mahabharata*. *Chitrakathi* translates to picture story and was a popular tradition in the Bombay Presidency.[5] It flourished in the seventeenth and eighteenth centuries in the state and was supported by the Rajas of Sawantwadi.[6] Pinguli near Sawantwadi is a famous centre for *Chitrakathi* art. The art form is distinguished by the profiles of humans and animals, and the ensembles of the Raja, by his *mukut* (crown), the Mantri's *pagadi* (turban), and the nautch girl's saree, nose ring and earrings, emulating the characteristics of the *Chitrakathi* figures. The bright colours of the cards and box are characteristic of Sawantwadi crafts.

The materials of the cards varied across regions. In Bishnupur and Orissa, artisan families made *ganjifa* cards with pieces of rag cloth (stretched, starched and glued together). In Jaipur, *ganjifa* cards were made of fish scales and Kashmiri *ganjifas* were made of papier-mâché. In some parts of the subcontinent, *ganjifas* were ritualistic gifts, especially for a new bride. The game is no longer popular, but survives as an artefact in private and museum collections. • IH

Top:
Coloured Ganjifa Cards; painted and lacquered leather, early twentieth century, Sawantwadi; 9.8 cm (diameter) each. Accessioned: mid-twentieth century.

•

Right:
Ganjifa Box with Sliding Lid; painted wood, early twentieth century, Sawantwadi; 12.2 x 17.2 x 12.2 cm. Accessioned: mid-twentieth century. Representing mythological scenes inspired by *Chitrakathi* art.

Box; papier-mâché, hand-painted and varnished, late nineteenth to early twentieth century, Kashmir; 5.5 x 21 x 15 cm. Accessioned: 1932-39.

•

Opposite:
Kalamdaan; papier-mâché, hand-painted and varnished, late nineteenth to early twentieth century, Persia; 21 x 2 x 3 cm. Accessioned: 1932–35. The beautiful *kalamdaan* from Persia is from the Qajar period (1789–1925) and is unique for its European-style painting. It tells the story of trade exchange of the nineteenth and early twentieth centuries. It showcases a scene from the birth of Christ and was presumably done for a European client. The painted, varnished surface of the pen case is inspired by Biblical imagery. The artist has painted some of the figures on the sides in oriental clothing, along with what appears to be the visit of the three kings, amalgamating European and oriental forms of representation.

KASHMIRI crafts became accessible across the country with the development of trade routes between the valley and the neighbouring province of the Punjab from the late nineteenth century. By the turn of the century, the popularity of Swadeshi exhibitions in Kashmir, Bombay, Delhi and Lahore, would set the stage for the steady exchange of goods from the valley.[1] The Kashmiri papier-mâché box in the Museum's collection is possibly a gift from the Maharaja of Kashmir, who participated in the 1873 Bombay exhibition, or was purchased by the curators in the late 1930s in Bombay along with a collection of Kashmiri objects.[2] It is decorated with lively florals and birds, typical of the Kashmiri aesthetic idiom, on a radiant gold ground.

The Kashmiri art of papier-mâché which involves moulding objects from paper pulp and painting and lacquering on the surface by specialised craftsmen, is known as *sakhtasazi* and *naqashi*. It was introduced to Kashmir from

Samarkand, Central Asia, in the fifteenth century during the reign of Sultan Zain-ul-Abdin, who ruled Kashmir during 1420–70. Some accounts suggest that the Sultan brought back artisans from Samarkand during his brief captivity there. Others mention that the Sufi mystic Mir Sayyad Ali Hamdani, who travelled to Kashmir from Central Asia in the fourteenth or fifteenth century, brought with him several followers, many of whom were artisans who specialised in shawl making, carpet weaving, woodwork and papier-mâché. It was around this time that the introduction of handmade paper from Central Asia made available a new malleable material for artisans to create decorative objects. Earlier, wooden objects such as bedsteads, doors and palanquins were painted in colourful designs.[3]

Kashmiri papier-mâché is distinct for its elaborate painterly designs, richly decorated with radiant gold and silver backgrounds and lively floral patterns, simulating gold and silver objects inlaid with colourful precious stones. Genuine gold and silver leaf foil were pasted on the surface of the object, which was then painted to incorporate the designs. Papier-mâché involves two kinds of specialised craftsmanship: the making of the object with paper pulp, known as *sakhtasazi*, and the painting of the surface, known as *naqashi*.[4] Different craftsmen carry out these processes. The papier-mâché object is made by building with softened paper, layer upon layer, within a mould. Pigments made with natural dyes are used to paint intricate patterns with brushes made from goat hair or cat fur. The surface is finally varnished.

Papier-mâché, a French term which means paper pulp, was known in Kashmir as *kar-e-qalamdani*, translated as 'pen case work', since originally it was used for ornamenting *kalamdaans* (pen cases) and book binding. It is also linked to the trade of Kashmiri shawls for the European market as papier-mâché boxes were initially made to hold shawls that were exported from Kashmir by French shawl agents in the nineteenth century. Across India, the highly decorated boxes may have also been used to carry *khillat* or royal gifts of cloth that were exchanged between important political officials in the Mughal and, later, the British India era. They were also sold separately and fetched high prices.[5]

By the mid-nineteenth century, papier-mâché work had become prolific in Kashmir, with intricate workmanship characterised by arabesque patterns, as well as the *butis* or paisley designs that were embroidered in a multitude of variations on Kashmiri shawls known as *jamavar*, *kaddar* and *buta*. Apart from the paisley, a variety of other decorative motifs were made on the surfaces of the box. The patterns are known to be drawn in freehand by the *naqash* (designer) who excelled in producing intricate forms and figures including illustrations of heroes from epic tales, animals and landscapes. The popularity of Kashmiri papier-mâché in the European market inspired a range of products—including trays, nesting tables, chess boards, candlesticks, picture frames, wall panels, screens, bowls and vases—which were produced for the European and the Indian elite. • PV

PAPIER-MÂCHÉ PANEL

Artwares from the princely state of Kashmir were often decorated by a characteristic design described as 'a teardrop with a bent tip' or *buta*, a literal translation of 'flower'.[1] By the 1850s, the abstract teardrop design would be labelled as 'paisley' after the Scottish town, Paisley, that manufactured Kashmiri imitation shawls with *buta* motifs.[2] The paisley motif evolved into an abstract shape around the beginning of the nineteenth century. It succeeded the naturalistic designs of the 1700s when flower bunches appeared with stems and sprouted from a vase. Various theories exist about the origins of the paisley design; however, its popular use in many different forms and in many mediums, each influencing the other, continues even today. For instance, the paisleys on the papier-mâché wares and shawls also influenced the silver ornamentation of the region.

The Museum's papier-mâché wood panel was presented by the Nazir of the Jumma Masjid, Bombay, and is crafted for decorative purposes (see p. 71).[3] It comes from the Punjab, which annexed Kashmir in 1819, during the reign of Maharaja Ranjit Singh (1780–1839). Many Kashmiri craftsmen and traders settled in the Punjab, and Kashmiri designs influenced the ubiquitous shawl production in the region. In particular, papier-mâché articles produced in the Punjab were decorated with shawl patterns.[4] Papier-mâché wood panels were made for ornamenting the ceilings and walls of sacred buildings in the Punjab.

The panel features paisleys in what is described as 'serpentine abstraction'. The paisleys frame four white *butas* that are connected to stylised stems in green. The forms contrast with the gold and red colours of the background, obtained from natural or mineral sources. The panel imitates designs of the Kashmiri *jamavar* shawls, where meandering paisleys and flowers are intricately embroidered on the entire surface of the shawl. • IH

Panel; papier-mâché, late nineteenth to early twentieth century, Punjab; 41 x 2 x 41 cm. Accessioned: 1897–1926.

51 LACQUER FRUIT TRAY

Fruit Tray; lacquer on wood, varnish, late nineteenth to early twentieth century, Sindh; 13.3 x 19.2 cm. Accessioned: 1889–1933. Decorated with *abri* work and flower motifs.

'CLOUD' and 'fire' are modest attempts to describe the complex artistry of lacquerware from Hala in Sindh which was a part of the Bombay Presidency.[1] The production of high-quality glazed tiles (*kashi ka kaam*) and lacquerware (*laky ka kaam*) established Hala's formidable standing as an artisanal centre. The crafts are an archetype of an ancient art that fostered not only inter-city and international trade relations but also a symbiotic relationship between town and countryside. Hala artisans relied on nearby villages located close to the rivers for raw materials such as clay, wood or lac, that were vital to produce their craft. The rural sectors relied on the markets of Hala to sell their finished products. By the seventeenth century, the town had become a prominent export centre.[2]

Hala is located 60 kilometres to the north of Hyderabad, Sindh. Its flourishing economy is largely credited to the establishment of *dargahs* (shrines) of famous Sufi saints who arrived in Hala as far back as the fourteenth century.[3] With every new shrine came the demand for Hala's glazed tiles that were used as building materials.

The Museum's collection of Hala lacquerware includes flower pots, fruit trays and round dishes. The objects are modelled in a range of colours from yellow, red, green and gold to neutral hues of brown, black and off-white. Different designs were employed by the craftsmen to accentuate an article's form. Artisans brilliantly interchanged or fused bold geometric or floral shapes, with limited or no representations of human and animal forms. The fruit tray (see p. 181) has a flower motif traditional to Sindh pottery and the mottled effect of *abri* or cloud work on the dark red ground.[4] Some of the finest specimens of *abri* came from Hoshiarpur (Punjab) and Sindh.[5]

Traditionally, lacquer was produced on a hand-powered lathe (*kharad*) by a turner (*kharadi*). *Kharadis* were important members of a community and were present in nearly every village in India. They were revered for their skill and talent that appeared in the creation of lacquered toys, boxes, furniture, etc. A *kharadi* sits on the floor and works on his spinning lathe, shaping the wood until the desired form is achieved. Once complete, the object is ready to be lacquered. The process involves pressing lac sticks (*battis*) across the object, which is also done on the spinning lathe. The heat produced by friction between the two surfaces facilitates the transfer of colour.[6] The term 'lac' comes from the Sanskrit word *laksha* meaning 'one hundred thousand', signifying the high number of insects required to obtain the lac. In India, insects that produce lac resin feed on *babul*, *palash* and *peepal* trees.[7]

The artisan applied lac sticks to create a variety of effects, namely *abri* (cloud-like), *atishi* (fire-like), or *nakshi* (engraved). Each piece involved a tedious process that earned the craft its reputation for uniqueness and ingenuity. Similar to medieval guilds, the ancient art of lacquerware was passed down from one generation to the next. A young apprentice would train under his father, an experienced or master craftsman, who, in turn, would have qualified under his father.

With the annexation of the Sindh to the Bombay Presidency in 1843, Sindhwork received newfound appreciation from British merchants and administrators settled in the Presidency. By the 1850s, merchants from Hyderabad in the Sindh began travelling to Bombay to extend trading networks in Western India and sell their region's local crafts. The merchants earned the title Sindhworkwallahs or Sindhworkies, and the goods thus became known as Sindhwork, an umbrella term for embroidery, quilts, lacquerware, woodwork and ornamental pottery produced in the workshops of the Sindh.[8]

Hala crafts were referred to as 'authentic' and 'great curiosities', and were highly sought after in the West, and popular at world expositions during the nineteenth century. At the Industrial Exhibition held in Karachi in 1869, Hala artisans were awarded several prizes for the superior quality of the wares; at the International Exhibition in London in 1871, Hala pottery received much attention in the exhibition's official catalogue.[9] By the late nineteenth century, the demand for crafts from the Sindh saw a decline resulting from depletion of raw materials, lack of patronage, changing fashions and consumer preferences. • IH

Right:
Wood Lathe Turners; half-baked terracotta and pigments, 1912–14, made at the erstwhile V&A Museum, Bombay; 18.7 x 19 x 31.2 cm.
•
Opposite:
Surahi; lacquer on wood, varnish, late nineteenth to early twentieth century, Sindh; 28.1 x 15.5 cm. Accessioned: 1932–1933. Decorated with *abri* work and flower motifs.

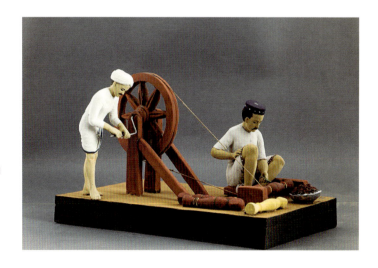

INDIAN pile carpets were prized for their skill and intricate traditional designs that appealed to the Western imagination of oriental splendour. There was a growing demand for Indian pile carpets in European markets by the mid-nineteenth century, which were prominently displayed at the international exhibitions. Carpet weaving was labour intensive and time-consuming, but had a high-profit yield. It was, therefore, one of the handicraft industries taken up for revival by the British in colonial India.[1] Pile carpet weaving was introduced in India around the sixteenth century during the reign of the Mughals. Prior to that, carpet weaving in India mainly consisted of flat weaves and durries. The major centres for pile carpets that were developed during the Mughal period were Srinagar, Amritsar and Agra.[2]

The Museum's carpet (see opposite) was made by the inmates of Yerawada Jail in Poona. It is a copy of a seventeenth-century Persian-style carpet, from the Archaeological Museum in Bijapur, which originally belonged to Asar Mahal, a religious shrine in the city. The carpets at Asar Mahal are believed to have been acquired in 1657 from Kashmir, during the reign of Mohammed Adil Shah. Some of the carpets from Bijapur were sent to the Yerawada Jail in the 1880s and 1890s to be repaired and lined.[3] It was most likely during this time that the carpet designs were replicated at the jail along with other Persian- and Central Asian-inspired carpet designs. The carpet was most likely acquired by Cecil Burns, curator at the Museum in 1904, from the Yerawada Jail superintendent. Another nearly identical carpet, also from Yerawada Jail, is in the collection of the Metropolitan Museum, New York.[4]

There was no pre-existing pile carpet weaving industry in western India prior to its introduction by the British.[5] The local industry consisted of rugs and flat, coarse-weave durries. However, the growing demand sparked the start of pile carpet making centres in western India, with designers, entrepreneurs and carpet weavers joining the fray. A new design sensibility emerged at these centres, that combined traditional Indian motifs and foreign designs. The major centres of carpet weaving in western India, and in the Bombay Presidency, in particular, were from an improbable source—the prisons. Carpet workshops had been initiated by the colonial government in jails across India including Jaipur, Amritsar, Bikaner, Lahore and Agra. The prison workshops were a Government initiative to meet the growing prison costs and to manage and discipline the prisoners. The carpets woven in jails were known as 'prison' or 'jail' carpets and were much sought-after by museums and private collectors.[6]

Jail officials had neither the art training nor the inclination to encourage the traditional crafts that were emerging from decline as a result of the increased attention on handmade products due to the international Arts and Crafts movement. Rather, they were driven by practical management issues, to earn money for the jails and to provide inmates a source of livelihood that could possibly be continued beyond the jail term. The jail carpet industry outshone external ones, not only because of the volume of productivity and labour, but also in developing a register for traditional design standards.[7] Jail carpets referenced traditional designs and used natural dyes.

By the 1880s, from a total of twenty-seven jails in the Bombay Presidency, nineteen jails contributed to the carpet-making industry. The prisons in Poona, Thana, Karachi, Ahmedabad and Hyderabad recorded the most employment. About 200 full-time prisoners were recorded at the Thana Jail, known for its quality carpets, cane-work and cotton weaving. The Thana Jail was equipped with forty to fifty looms that produced beautiful Persian and cotton carpets. Many were inspired by the design samples circulated by the Yerawada Jail.[8]

Considered a leader in carpet manufacture, the Yerawada Jail produced some of the best historical design carpets, sharing it's templates with other jails to copy. In addition to the recreating historical patterns, Yerawada Jail used only natural dyes, which produced more muted colours that appealed to the Western clientele.[9] The carpet in the Museum's collection has a pattern that is closely associated with Indo-Persian carpets. It has the characteristic symmetrical arrangement of vine scrolls and large palmettes in the field, as well as palmettes and the strap arabesque in the border. The palmettes are distinguished by the alternating use of pale yellow, ochre and blue. This all-over complex pattern is woven on a deep red ground to suggest an endless floral display. The images of a saddled and bridled horse, a small dog and two rams butting heads are seen repeated twice on two corners of the bottom edge of the carpet and are also found on the carpet at the Metropolitan Museum, New York.[10]

By the early twentieth century, the jails were unable to keep up production to meet the demand. By 1907, the Yerawada Jail had twelve looms in use, but the number of orders exceeded the production rate. Many jails continued to produce carpets even after Independence, with some including Yerawada Jail still producing durries. • PV

Yerawada Jail Carpet; wool on cotton, 1890–1904, Poona; 420.5 x 317 cm. Accessioned: 1904. On view near the grand staircase, Dr. Bhau Daji Lad Museum.

THE Indian subcontinent has been famous for its textile traditions for centuries. Greek historians Strabo and Arrian, both mention the trade in Indian fabrics that were exported to the Arabian coast as early as 130 CE.[1] The weaving industry established in the subcontinent is even mentioned in the hymns of the *Yajurveda*. The Indian epics, the *Ramayana* and the *Mahabharata*, also record a rich variety of Indian textiles.[2] The British assiduously documented the different fabric manufacturing processes so that the raw product could be sent to factories and mills in England, where industrialisation enabled cheaper costs of production.

However, the manual looms in India were still able to compete with the British mills as the looms produced cotton fabrics of greater strength and better muslin, which were highly valued by wealthy Indians.[3]

Among the most beautiful textiles in the Museum's collection is a Zoroastrian woman's bridal outfit. Elaborately embroidered, it consists of a loose-fitting *kameez* (blouse) worn over a voluminous *salwar* (trousers), and is probably from Yazd or Kerman, the two areas in Iran where the Zoroastrian community lived. The salwar piece is the part of one leg of a voluminous salwar. The Museum has another identical piece in its collection which would be the fabric of the other leg of the salwar, as well as the accompanying ochre embroidered blouse.

Life was difficult for the Zoroastrians in Iran as there were several regulations that distinguished them from the majority Muslim population. One directive included a strict dress code; for instance, Zoroastrian men (and sometimes women) were obliged to wear garments of yellow ochre or unbleached cloth. In addition, they were not permitted to buy cloth by the yard. As a result, shopkeepers would collect strips of leftover fabric and leave these in bins outside their shops for Zoroastrians to buy.[4] These were then laboriously stitched together to make garments such as the *salwar* and *kameez* seen here.

The embroidery on the two pieces suggests that they were meant for a bride to wear at her wedding. The peacocks in the panels of the *kameez* and the *salwar* are symbols of fertility and desire. The central panel contains a lattice-like arrangement with lotus flowers connected to each other by a single trellis with each ogival shape containing a peacock. The pieces on either side are filled with depictions of dancing peacocks and images of the sun—referred to in Persian as '*Khurshid Khanum*', a female representation of the sun (or the radiating sun), associated with Zoroastrian folklore.

Zoroastrian Iranians migrated to India to avoid the Arab conquest of Iran. They arrived in the mid-nineteenth century in Bombay. Shia Muslims and Baha'i Iranians were

Section of a Zoroastrian Woman's Bridal Salwar (detail, opposite); mid- to late nineteenth century, Yazd or Kerman, Persia; 51 x 92.3 cm. Accessioned: 1914. Presented by Mrs Meherbai Byramji Irani of Bombay.

Fig. 1: *Suzani* (detail); cotton, Shikarpur, late nineteenth to early twentieth century, Sindh; 179 x 105 cm. Accessioned: 1903–15.

Fig. 2: *Bandhani Saree* (detail); silk, late nineteenth to early twentieth century, Cambay; 431.5 x 144 cm. Accessioned: 1903–15.

Fig. 3: *Himroo Saree*; silk and cotton, late nineteenth to early twentieth century, Surat; 581 x 122.5 cm. Accessioned: 1903–15.

Fig. 4: *Embroidered Kurta* (detail); satin silk, late nineteenth to early twentieth century, Kutch; 109.5 x 99 cm. Accessioned: 1903–15.

Fig. 5: *Patola Saree* (detail); silk, late nineteenth to early twentieth century, Patan; 444 x 114.6 cm. Accessioned: 1903–15.

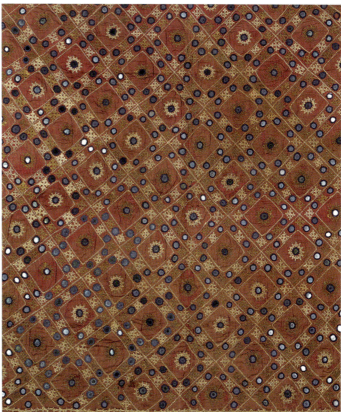

Fig. 6: *Chakla* (detail); cotton, late nineteenth to early twentieth century, Kathiawar; 85.1 x 85.8 cm. Accessioned: 1903–26.

also among the migrants fleeing persecution. Zoroastrians in India came to be identified as 'Parsis', from Persis (modern-day Fars). Ancient Persian texts note that the earliest Zoroastrians arrived on the island of Diu, on the west coast as early as the eighth century.[5] They inhabited various towns of Gujarat before migrating to Bombay by the mid-eighteenth century. Known for their acumen in education, business and politics, a few migrants who were skilled bakers set up what were known as Irani cafes that are popular even today. These cafes were introduced in the late nineteenth century, with the opening of the city's first hotels in response to the influx of foreigners. Famous for their hospitality and food, the cafes sport a distinct décor. High ceilings, large mirrors and a counter with glass jars stuffed with mouth-watering bakes is typical. Another classic element is the dark wooden bent-back chairs and marble table tops. In the 1970s and 1980s family rooms were very popular. Originally, they served continental food but post-Independence menus were adapted to include more Indian items. The cafes continue to serve traditional Parsi and Iranian dishes, including the famous snack *brun muska* (buttered bun) accompanied with Mumbai's famous '*cutting*' *chai* (tea). High real estate costs and changing fashions have witnessed the demise of several of these iconic cafes.

Fig. 1: Suzani, Shikarpur (Sindh), Bombay Presidency

Suzanis or *soznis* are vibrantly coloured, exquisitely embroidered pieces of cloth from Central Asia. They served as cradle covers, wrappers for gifts, bed canopies, curtains, tent decorations and wall hangings. Made by women, *suzanis* were an essential part of a bride's dowry. *Suzani* is derived from the word *suzan*, Farsi for needle. These cloths were famous in cities along the Silk Road: Bukhara, Samarkand, Shahrisabz, Tashkent and Ferghana, and the patterns were copied in Sindh. They were believed to contain magical properties related to protection and fertility. The large red roundels in this *suzani* are characteristic of the sun-disc motif, a central feature in *suzanis* created in parts of Uzbekistan. This *suzani* was presented to the Museum by former curator C.L. Burns.

Fig. 2: Bandhani Saree, Cambay, Bombay Presidency

Bandhani is derived from the Sanskrit word *banda* which means 'to tie'. It involves bunching together parts of the cloth and tying them with a thread such that they make a pinched circle, tied with a thread. *Bandhani* sarees are popular in Gujarat, and are made by the Khatri community of Kutch and Saurashtra. Bright red sarees were generally worn by the bride as red was considered auspicious for the married couple's life.

Fig. 3: Himroo Saree, Surat, Bombay Presidency
This is a brocaded fabric. It has an extra weft thread and is made on a throw-shuttle loom using cotton in the warp and silk in the weft. *Himroo's* speciality is that the silk threads used to form patterns on the surface of the fabric are collected in long loops that form a soft warm layer and is similar to the *kani* weaving in Kashmiri shawls. The fabric was patronised by and popular among the aristocracy and the elite. This red *himroo* saree from Surat has a pattern of small *butis* arranged in evenly spaced rows.[6] The *pallavs* (the loose end of the saree that hangs over the shoulder) has eight large *keri* (mango) shaped *butas*, each filled with small floral designs.

Fig. 4: Embroidered Kurta, Kutch, Bombay Presidency
This bright red *kurta* in satin silk is intricately embroidered with silk threads and small pieces of mirror (*abhala*). The front of the *kurta* is embellished in a fan-like pattern. The embroidery is executed in a dense chain stitch with running, straight and interlacing stitches. The mirrors are held together by buttonhole stitches. Such *kurtas* were worn by women at their weddings and were usually embroidered by the Memon merchants of Kutch.

Fig. 5: Patola Saree, Patan, Bombay Presidency
This saree's intricate pattern is achieved by tying and dyeing the warp and weft threads separately with mathematical precision. Motifs of flowers, jewels, elephants, parrots, tigers and dancing women are used in the border or in the central field, in a grid-like alternating pattern. The saree features a '*pan-bhat*' (pipal leaf) pattern, with the caterpillar, lotus flower and stars. *Patolas* were, and still are, very expensive. The designs varied for patrons from the Hindu, Jain and Muslim communities. While double-*ikats* were woven in Patan and Surat, single-*ikats* were made in Rajkot and Saurashtra.

Fig. 6: Chakla, Kathiawar, Bombay Presidency
Chaklas were auspicious coverings used for offerings to deities, or to wrap gifts at the time of a birth or marriage. The orange-coloured cotton ground of this *chakla* is embroidered with threads in darker shades of orange, white, blue and black. The lattice design is embedded with smaller squares, each holding a mirror and surrounded by mirrors. This geometry of squares was based on the idea of a sacred grid, symbolising creation—the sun and the moon, the day and night—and the passage of time. • PV

KINKHAB

Kinkhabs played a remarkable role in the fashions and lifestyles of the aristocratic elite of India and have long been famous as an important item of trade. Expensive and heavy, *kinkhabs* were handwoven pieces of silk cloth made with gold or silver threads, producing a regal effect. The British were fascinated with Indian textiles and Lady Curzon, Vicereine of India (1898–1905), is noted for sending Indian fabrics as gifts to her families in England and America. She also commissioned gold brocades and lace from master weavers.

The term *kinkhab* is believed to have originated from the Persian word *kam-khwab* or 'little dream'. In the West, it is broadly classified as brocade.[1] A range of outfits for both men and women were tailored using *kinkhabs* for formal occasions. The *kinkhab* pieces and *kinnars* (borders with gold and silver) in the Museum's collection come from Ahmedabad and Surat, famed centres of brocade production since Mughal times.[2] Neither of the two cities favoured a climate for sericulture. They imported large quantities of silk from Bengal and produced specialty silks such as *kinkhabs*. By the 1800s these were being exported to other parts of India, the Persian Gulf, southern Asia and Europe.

Maratha princes were known to shop for silk in large quantities to maintain their regal lifestyles. A royal bridegroom of Bharatpur in 1832 mandated his entourage of 8,000 men to dress in *pyjamas* made of the finest *kinkhab* silk.[3] The merchant class emulated these styles supporting artisanal production and trade.

The fascination with *kinkhab* was not only due to the gold and silver threads woven into it but also the richness of its patterns. A weaver could achieve a multitude of effects by varying the weaving technique on the loom, creating floral (*butedar*) or animal (*shikargah*) designs. Patterns of eye-flower (*chasamphul*), gold coin (*mohurbuti*) and mango (*keri*) are common in the *kinkhabs* of Ahmedabad and Surat.[4] *Kinkhabs* did not soil easily, making them valuable for ritual purposes, wedding trousseaus, gifts and later, for curtains and upholstery for the European elite.

By the mid-nineteenth century, *kinkhabs* were collected for design education and museum collections in England and Europe. Through these collections, a greater understanding of textile weaving, dyeing and embroidery was achieved, which was vital to replicate similar fabrics in European textile mills and gain the upper hand against competitive imports.[5] • IH

Embroidered Bedspread (detail); cotton, late nineteenth to early twentieth century, Kashmir; 221.3 x 150.5 cm. Accessioned: 1903–15.

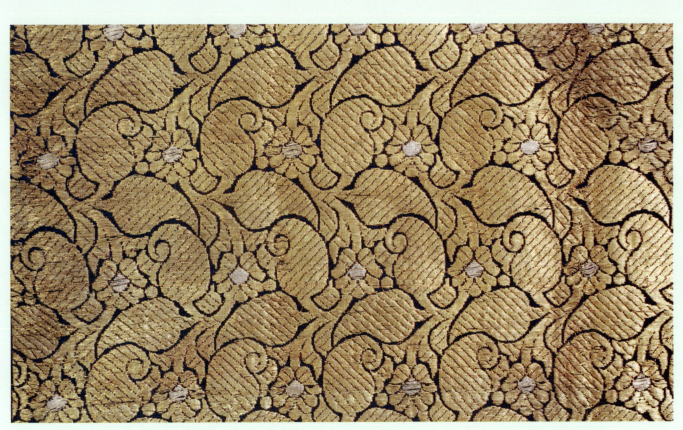

Kinkhab (detail); silk and gold wire, mid-nineteenth to early twentieth century, Ahmedabad; 82 x 74.8 cm. Accessioned: 1910.
The *kinkhab* depicts a woven pattern of the flower (*buti*) and mango (*keri*).

54 COCO DE MER DERVISH'S BOWL

A *kashkul*, or dervish's begging bowl, is associated with wandering Sufi dervishes from Central Asia, India and Iran. Sufi preachers were most active in India between the twelfth and fourteenth centuries. They spread the teachings of Sufi saints like Moinuddin Chishti, Hazrat Nizamuddin and saints from other Sufi Orders or *silsilahs*. The bowl functioned as the dervish's receptacle for alms, primarily coins and food, and as a drinking vessel. These bowls were ornamented with engravings of poetry, Quranic inscriptions, geometric patterns or representations of flora and fauna.

In Persian culture, the *kashkul* dates back to the ninth century. An empty bowl represents the traditional philosophies of Sufism which are the renunciation of worldly materials, the search for spiritual knowledge and communion with the Divine. 'Kash' translates to pulling, and '*kul*' to shoulder, and when combined describe an object that is pulled or carried over the shoulder as most dervish bowls, which have an attached chain, are.[1] Since the rule of the Safavid dynasties, dervishes wandered the streets with these bowls in hand, singing mystical poems in anticipation of offerings. Some *kashkuls* were inscribed with verses of Persian poetry or references to the twelve Shia Imams. These bowls were also used during the water-carrying rituals that mark *Ashura*, the tenth day in the month of Muharram, in the Islamic calendar.

The bowl in the Museum's collection bears intricate semantic patterns that run across the top rim. Elaborate low-relief inscriptions in the Nastaliq script of the 'Ayat-ul Kursi' from the Quran are revealed. The significance of the 'Ayat-ul Kursi' or 'The Verse of the Throne' is paramount throughout the Islamic world. The *ayat* (verse) establishes the 'eternal' and 'self-subsisting' nature of God or Allah, and is a verse from the second *surah* (chapter) of the Quran. Islamic scholars widely regard the chapter as a summary of the entire teachings of the holy book. Faith, kindness, charity and integrity are some of the topics discussed in great detail as ordinances for living. Below the Quranic verse in the eight cartouches of the bowl, are couplets from the poetry of Shams al-Din Muhammad Hafiz, the celebrated fourteenth-century Persian Sufi poet and Quranic scholar. Hafiz's poetry, described as refined and contemplative, centred on themes associated with Sufism—mystical devotion, wine (spiritual ecstasy) and love (divinity).

The Museum's beautifully calligraphed bowl was purchased in 1914 and is made from one-half of the shell of the Coco de Mer, a palm species endemic to the Seychelles. In the Safavid period, *kashkuls* were made from natural materials. Later these bowls were largely made from materials such as silver, brass and ceramic.[2] A bowl that was heavily ornamented with rich metals and engravings was intended for decorative purposes only. It would not be used by a devoted dervish as it would go against the primary principles of Sufi philosophy.

Coco de Mer shells were highly valued for their utilitarian qualities and traded via steamships from the Seychelles. After the opening of the Suez Canal in 1869, Aden, which was a part of the Bombay Presidency, served as an entrepôt between the islands and India. Coco de Mer shell carvings were also found in the Madras Presidency. These 'double cocoanut' shells depicted Burmese figures and peacocks, carved by prisoners of the Cannanore Jail where cocoanut carving was introduced as an industry around 1888 by the colonial government.[3]

The fruits of the Coco de Mer (*Lodoicea sechellarum*) washed ashore to India, Sri Lanka and the Maldives once they matured and dropped from the parent tree. The fruits have been associated with numerous legends and mysteries since they were discovered floating in the Indian Ocean by sailors. Originally the fruits were thought to grow on an underwater tree, hence the name Coco de Mer, which translates to 'coconut of the sea'. Numerous nineteenth-century European explorers and East India Company generals who visited the islands of Seychelles documented this natural wonder as a 'unique palm in the Seychelles' and the 'tree of knowledge of good and evil' in their travelogues.[4]

Bombay played an integral part in spreading Sufi teachings in western India from as early as the fourteenth century. Vernacular travelogues, namely *Jan-i-Mumbay* ('The Soul of Bombay'), highlighted popular Muslim pilgrimage places (*dargahs* or shrines) of venerated Sufi saints in Bombay during the fourteenth to the sixteenth century, including Makhdum Faqih Ali Mahimi (fourteenth century), Shaikh Misri (fifteenth century) and Shah Sharif (sixteenth century).[5] In present-day Mumbai, the *dargahs* of Sufi saints Haji Ali Bukhari (the fourteenth to the fifteenth century) and Makhdum Mahimi are the city's most well-known and visited Sufi sites by people of various faiths, attesting to the city's extraordinary integrative culture. The Haji Ali (Bukhari) Dargah receives approximately 15,000 visitors daily and is one of Mumbai's most famous sites. • IH

Opposite, top:
Dervish's Bowl; Coco de Mer half-shell, late nineteenth to early twentieth century, Bombay; 17.8 x 22.8 x 12 cm. Accessioned: 1914. Carved with inscriptions from the Quran in Nastaliq script and mystical poetry in Persian.
•
Opposite, below:
Dervish's Bowl (bottom).
Carved with arabesque ornamentation.

55 STONE FOO DOGS

LONG before the advent of the European powers on the subcontinent, India's trade with its Asian neighbours flourished. The opening of the Suez Canal in 1869 played an important role in the development of foreign trade, both European and Asian, particularly for Bombay, as much of the business was now routed through the port city. Vital new connections with other Asian countries that were a part of the European trade routes were established. These included Ceylon, Burma, Siam, Indonesia, China, Japan and Australia. The Museum has several artefacts from these countries as well as from Nepal, Tibet and the Middle East. The collection represents a modest attempt to showcase the crafts of other Asian countries for the interest and education of the local as well as the visiting population.

The most enduring and lucrative trade, among the Asian countries, was with China and that stretched back many centuries. By the time the British gained a foothold in India, the cotton trade with China was booming and when this declined in the early nineteenth century, opium took its place, though cotton continued to be exported to China in smaller quantities.[1] The trade with China in cotton and opium had created substantial wealth in Bombay and attracted people from all over the country even before the increase in the cotton trade because of the American Civil War in the late 1850s. The Parsis who were closely connected with British firms, and could travel abroad without restriction, dominated the cotton and opium trade in Bombay. They were also involved with the shipbuilding trade and that proved to be a significant asset in trading with China. Hindus were forbidden to travel overseas as it was considered polluting, so the Jews and Muslims, who were the other communities to participate in the trade, had a greater advantage. Many Hindu merchants, however, were involved in the local management and speculating in the trade which returned very high profits. British interest in Chinese trade revolved around the import of tea, for which there was an insatiable demand in England. The British Government also earned considerable revenue from the trade and levied taxes on every casket of cotton and opium bound for China.[2]

The most renowned Bombay merchants in this trade were Sir David Sassoon (see pp. 60-61) and Sir Jamsetjee Jeejeebhoy (see pp. 62-63) who had substantial interests in China. British-Indian traders bartered their opium with Chinese smugglers for a variety of goods, shipping them back to India for re-export to Europe.[3] Some of the goods that the traders brought back from China were intricately carved elephant tusks, ivory figures, lacquerware, textiles, vast amounts of porcelain, silks and embroideries, China figurines, lacquered furniture and sometimes portraits and jewellery.

The Museum's collection from China includes a stone river boat, stone dragons, mythological figurines, a vase, an ivory pagoda and a carved wooden horse saddle.

The other Asian country that developed a strong trading relation with India was Japan and by the early twentieth century, the trade was extensive. In 1930, Japan was the largest source of Bombay's imports after Great Britain and was also Bombay's largest consumer for exports due to its vast demand of Indian cotton.[4] Bombay imported brass, and a large variety of manufactured articles from Japan. The Museum's objects from Japan consist mostly of exquisite ivory work.

Among India's neighbours, trade with Burma expanded after the defeat of King Thibaw by the British in 1885. There was an influx of Indians into Burma at this time and they played a pivotal role in influencing the Burmese economic, social and cultural life. Parsis, Gujaratis, Sindhis, Punjabis, Chettiars, and others migrated to Burma for commerce. Ivory and silver constituted a dominant part of the trade and the Museum has some beautiful ivory and silver objects from Burma.

The north Indian railway system played an important role in the development of the Indo-Nepal trade. By the beginning of the twentieth century, Indo-Nepal trade relations entered a new phase with several railway lines being built to connect a number of towns situated along the borders of the two countries. The Museum has some beautiful statues and other objects from Nepal.

The shifts in the pattern of trading and shipping during the nineteenth and early twentieth centuries presented the Museum's curators with an opportunity to enlarge their scope for the collection. Asian objects that were acquired indicate a desire to explore the links between these cultures and India. Many objects were also gifted to the Museum by departing Europeans who were unable to carry everything back on the ship. • HK

Foo Dog; stone, late nineteenth century, China; 18.5 x 16.3 x 8.4 cm. Accessioned: 1926-27. Foo dogs or 'Guardian Lion' (Shishi) are important symbols in Chinese culture and are made in different sizes and materials. They represent prosperity, success and guardianship and are visible on the entrance and roofs of sacred temples, palaces and homes, as protectors of the buildings against evil spirits. According to Buddhist belief, the lion is the defender of the law and the guardian of sacred places. Contemporary writers have compared the appearance of a Foo dog with that of a Pekingese or Shih tzu ('lion dog'). Foo dog statues are usually made in pairs i.e. a male represented with an open mouth and a female with closed lips. The male figures are usually seen stepping on a ball, which symbolises earth, with a front paw.

56 STEAM SHIP SIAM

ON display in the Industrial Arts Gallery is a wood reproduction of the steamship *Siam* (SS *Siam*). The beautiful model recalls the romance of sea travel in the nineteenth century and the importance of steamships in the dispersal of colonial culture around the globe. The Industrial Revolution had initiated a remarkable development in the field of transportation technology. Centuries-old sailing ships were gradually replaced by much faster steamships.

The opening of the Suez Canal in 1869 further shortened the time taken to travel from Europe to India. By the 1880s, a journey from London to Bombay that would have earlier taken several months to conclude, sailing around the treacherous Cape of Good Hope at the tip of southern Africa, would be completed within twelve and a half days.[1] Owned by the Peninsular & Oriental Steam Navigation Company, popularly known as P&O, the SS *Siam* came into service in 1873, and sailed between London and Australia, via the Middle East and India, carrying passengers and cargo. The model of the SS *Siam* in the Museum was made in 1890 by an apprentice named Dayal Kanjee in the P&O Co. Bombay, when the ship was docked for repair work.[2] Inside the model you can see a big tunnel, two anchors, two masts and two lifeboats.

In 1837, the P&O Co., a British Shipping Company, was the first commercial shipping firm to win the mail contract between England and Egypt. By 1852 steam communication with Australia was established and in 1854 the Bombay mail service was started by the P&O Company for the East India Company.

In 1875, the P&O Company bought the SS *Siam*, which was designed to carry not only passengers but also a large amount of cargo, and of course, mail. It was employed for the route from London to the Middle East, then to India, and as far as Australia. It is likely that the ship carried the objects for the Melbourne International Exhibition which was hosted in 1880 at Carlton Gardens (Melbourne, Australia). The P&O Company frequently advertised its destinations at the international exhibitions. The objects sent from India included pottery, ivory inlaid boxes, ivory chess boxes, sandalwood paper knives, Kashmiri shawls, musical instruments and different types of metal wares.[3] The Indian Court at the Melbourne International Exhibition received much attention from visitors who were attracted to the novelty of Indian art and purchased authentic, and previously unavailable Indian souvenirs in Australia. Some of these objects are now in the collection of the Melbourne Museum.

In 1890, when SS *Siam*'s shaft broke while it was at Aden (Yemen) which was then a part of the Bombay Presidency, the P&O Company's alternate ship, SS *Canton* towed the *Siam* all the way from Aden to P&O's docks at Mazgaon in Bombay

International Exhibition at Exhibition Building, Melbourne, 1880: interior view showing the Great Hall at the Indian court, Ludovico Hart; *The Australian Photographic Journal*, March 20, 1896, p. 56; 23.4 x 29.1 cm. Source: Museums Victoria.

Opposite:
SS Siam, Dayal Kanjee; wood, thread, metal, 1890–97, Bombay; 82.2 x 60.5 x 17.2 cm. Accessioned: 1952.

where the necessary repair work was carried out. Five years on, Japan based company Nippon Yusen Kaisha bought the ship in 1895 and named it SS *Yorihime Maru*. It was used for the next seven years before being finally scrapped in 1902 in Japan.[4]

Unlike in the past, when people travelled by sea for trade or conquest, now, with the advent of faster, technologically advanced ships and shorter routes, common people curious to get a glimpse of the world were drawn to the sea. This new demand created an extensive shipbuilding industry for luxury passenger ships and various cruise liners. Travel by ship soon became a popular and luxurious way to see far off places. A network of port agencies was established along the routes to replenish steamers with fuel, fresh water and provisions. Advertisements from the late 1890s quote the fares to travel from London to Bombay to be approximately 55 pounds for first class and 37 pounds for second class.[5]

SS *Siam* was one of the many ships in the fleet of P&O, which became one of the first companies to exploit the potential of travel for pleasure. It soon joined the booming Victorian leisure industry and grew into the biggest shipping company of the world in the late nineteenth century. E.J. Kail (retired Deputy Manager of Alexandra Docks, Bombay) presented the ship's model to the Museum in 1952. • HK

Mumbai Communities, half-baked terracotta and pigments, 1908–12, made at the erstwhile V&A Museum, Bombay. On view at the Kamalnayan Bajaj Mumbai Gallery, Dr. Bhau Daji Lad Museum.

PEOPLE OF INDIA
Interrogating Identity

Tile as Archive (detail), Praneet Soi, 100 papier-mâché tiles, acrylic paint, 2016; 30.5 x 30.5 cm each. Exhibition: *Notes on Labour*; Kamalnayan Bajaj Special Exhibitions Gallery, 2017. This artwork narrates Soi's engagement with the craftsman Fayaz Jan in Srinagar. As the traditional Kashmiri patterns and designs of craftsmen are only passed on orally, Soi conceptualised an artwork that functions as an archive of the patterns, borders and floral tropes used within Kashmiri compositions; juxtaposed with a modern-day paver-block design.

BOMBAY in the late nineteenth and early twentieth centuries hosted an extraordinary variety of people who came from across the world to trade. Several writers noted the colourful Bombay bazaars, where people of all hues in traditional wear jostled and bargained, eager to strike a deal. The racecourse in Worli, where Bombay's social elite gathered on the weekends, was a curious sight for visitors, who unfailingly remarked on the resplendent variety of 'native costumes'. Edward Lear, the Victorian artist and nonsense verse poet, exclaimed on arriving in Bombay, 'Extreme beauty of Bombay harbour! ... Anything more overpoweringly amazing cannot be conceived!!! Colours & costumes & myriadism of impossible picturesqueness!!!'[1]

Bombay afforded the amateur anthropologist and ethnologist an extraordinary opportunity to document this great variety of 'races' and 'tribes' of the subcontinent, and museums as archival institutions became a part of the colonial government's massive knowledge-gathering and disseminating laboratory.[2] Lord Canning, the first Viceroy of India, initiated the collection of detailed information on all aspects of life in India through photographic documentation. The colonial government appointed John Forbes Watson, the first Keeper of the India Museum in London, and John Kaye, a senior Government official, to begin work on this mammoth task. They were among the earliest amateur anthropologists involved in an ethnological documentation of India. They produced the prodigious, photographic *The People of India* volumes, that would help to define the understanding of castes and communities in India (see pp. 115-16). Earlier visual histories, like those produced by James Forbes, Balthazar Solvyns, and other orientalists of the previous century were usually private enterprises undertaken for both 'scientific' and monetary gain (see pp. 108–11).

One of the earliest modes of documentation that captured the imagination of Europeans was the clay models of Indian castes, communities, occupations and even animals, that were being produced by Indian artists in Poona, at Krishnanagar in Bengal, and in Lucknow. By 1905, when the Museum's curator, Cecil Burns (1903–18), embarked on a detailed sculptural register of the sociocultural aspects of the Bombay Presidency, models and dioramas had become a popular means of illustrating Indian lifestyles in a 'realistic' three-dimensional form. They were considered an effective mode of both educating and 'amusing' the masses at the many international and national exhibitions. The Museum's collection of clay models and dioramas was also an important extension of the ambitious and controversial project by the colonial government to capture in minute detail, through 'scientific' parameters, the 'people of India'. One of the earliest public displays of Indian clay figures in London was at the 1851 Great Exhibition. Professor John Royles, Keeper at India House, London, and General Commissioner and Keeper for the India Section at the Great Exhibition, notes that the figures sent were 'admirable representations of the different castes and trades ...' that enthralled the public.[3]

The Museum's first collection of clay figures was ordered from Poona by George Buist in 1855-56, though they did not survive the Museum's many relocations.[4] The history of the evolution of clay figures from Poona is not well documented and the Museum's records reveal little about their provenance. Poona was an important artistic centre under the Peshwas, the powerful hereditary chief ministers at the court of the Maratha rulers. Poona's proximity to Bombay served it well during the rule of the East India Company, when many local *chitaris* ('artist' in Marathi) were employed to assist European artists who were travelling in India for commissions, and were especially interested in documenting the important cave temples of the region.[5] Sir Charles Mallet (1753–1815), the enterprising British Resident at the court of the Peshwas, had established an art school in 1790 at Shaniwarwada, the Peshwa's residence, that was run by the well-known British artist James Wales till his death in 1795. This was the first art school in the country. It is likely that 'realistic' sculptural modelling was taught by Wales as there is a record of an outstanding local artist, Gangaram Chintaman Tambat, modelling figures for Malet, and whom Malet called 'ingenious'.[6] European realistic painting had influenced Mughal artists in rendering the figure and European sculptural forms soon percolated to local levels by the mid-eighteenth century.

The tradition of clay modelling in Poona, however, predates the British intervention in teaching sculptural modelling, though undoubtedly visiting European artists impacted this tradition by emphasising Renaissance sculptural qualities. The potters in the Deccan, traditionally, commemorated historic military victories during Diwali (the festival of lights when the victory of good over evil is celebrated across the country). They created elaborate dioramas with clay models replicating the battle scenes of their chieftains.[7] This practice is followed even today, with many Maharashtrian households building or purchasing small castles with soldiers during Diwali. The clay modelling tradition of the region continues, most exuberantly, during Ganesha Chaturthi, which is celebrated with great fervour and pomp, especially in Mumbai, when clay sculptures, in various sizes, of the elephant-headed god Ganesha, Lord Shiva's son and the city's ruling deity, are taken through the streets in grand processions (see pp. 28-29).

Cecil Burns, who started the sculptural documentation of communities and professions at the Museum, and his successor Ernest Fern (1918–29), note that these displays attracted the most interest and the 'illiterate' ordinary people 'visited in great numbers' and were intrigued to see miniature, idealised representations of themselves.[8] The small figurines were also a favourite with European visitors as they provided a charming visual shorthand about Indian society. The *Bombay Gazetteer* of 1885 notes,

'Of the Poona figures, which include almost all castes and classes, perhaps the most interesting and characteristic are: A fully equipped elephant with a native prince and his attendants in the car or hauda; groups showing how Hindus cook and dine; a scene at a public well; a dancing party; a Hindu spinner, weaver, and goldsmith at work; a European gentleman carried in a palanquin; a Koli, or other highwayman waylaying and extorting money from a Marwari trader; a tiger-shooting scene; a prince or princess attacked by a tiger; a native fruit seller's shop; a native woman carrying water; a milkmaid; a Garodi or juggler with tame monkeys, snakes, goat, and mongooses; a Darweshi with a tame bear; a Gosavi or Hindu ascetic; a Fakir or Musalman beggar; a Brahman woman worshipping the sacred tulsi plant Ocymum sanctum [sic]; an astrologer telling fortunes; a Vaidu or wandering quack; a Parsi man and woman; a waterman with his bullock; a camel driver; a messenger; and the cholera or jarimari worshipper.'[9]

The models and dioramas in the Museum, however, are not merely a three-dimensional documentation of sociocultural practices and attires, but represent a unique art historical mode in the larger Company School genre (see pp. 206–08).[10] These figurines express a new form of popular art practice. They also reflect one of the most important tenets of the many art schools established across the country, which was to teach students and artisans how to produce a naturalistic representation of the human form, and sculpting models enabled that learning. Models and dioramas at museums and exhibitions also functioned as didactic props and were encoded with political significance as they presented a patronising, curious and exotic perspective. Produced in the early twentieth century under the tutelage of museum curators and art school officials, these essentialised forms, in distinctive categories, show us how Indians were being taught to view themselves and others through the new and progressive medium of the Museum.[11]

Colonial officials employed a Eurocentric and ethnographic lens to interpret Indian culture, and Indians were insidiously co-opted through the British educational system and colonial art schools to interpret their cultural roots and identity through these concepts.[12] Various systems of codification privileged certain community 'types' or degraded and even criminalised others.[13] The model and diorama collection, though beautifully rendered, is intent on capturing difference, which was one of the founding tropes of British rule. British administrators constructed an archaeology of dominance through visual narratives that codified divergence, variation, stratification and hierarchy. 'Scientific' theories redefined caste and custom through rigid distinctions and soon, Indians learnt to interpret themselves through such tropes.[14] For example, the notion that those who are tall and fair skinned are more refined, or the idea that the length and shape of the nose indicates a person's character, were the type of 'scientific' arguments used to provide moral justification for British rule over a 'primitive' race.[15]

In tracing the genealogy of the Museum's model and diorama collection, several artistic connections between the models and the various documentary traditions which preceded these in the subcontinent have been observed. European artists and writers who documented their travels to India in great detail were an important source for Company artists and model makers. The well-known F.M. Coleman (1860–1916), who was managing partner of the Times Press and had published hand-coloured versions of photographs taken by famous photo studios in Bombay such as Bourne and Sheppard, and the prolific James Forbes (see pp. 108–10), were used as direct references by the Museum curators in interpreting the identities of various castes and tribes as well as occupations (see pp. 209–13, 220, 222–24). Balthazar Solvyns (1760–1824), the enterprising French artist, was an important source for the models of palanquin bearers, sepoys, *coachvans*, *hukkabajs* etc. (see p. 231). The Museum's sculptural versions copy almost exactly the stance, clothes, facial features, and other accoutrements of the print versions. Coleman is the reference for many of the foreign community models, and Forbes for some of the models on music and dance (see p. 220). Watson and Kaye, the authors of the People of India volumes, were the source for the religious sects (see pp. 115–17); George Birdwood and Edward Moore's documentation of Indian deities influenced the rendering of the Hindu pantheon in the Museum (see pp. 226-27). Raja Ravi Varma's impact was prodigious and can be discerned in the models of Indian deities and in the religious dioramas (see pp. 251–253). The similarities between the Museum's models of Indian communities and the paintings and sketches of Rao Bahadur Dhurandhar, an eminent Bombay artist who went on to become the first Indian principal of the Sir J.J. School of Art, are also evident (see p. 211).

The new medium of photography contributed to the manner in which community types were represented. One can see, for example, that the model of the Parsi gentleman in the Museum's collection derives directly from the studio

Display depicting the headwears of the Bombay Presidency; glass negative, 1930–35, erstwhile V&A Museum, Bombay; 16.5 x 12 cm. Accessioned: 1930–35.

photograph of Parsis in William Johnson's *The Oriental Races and Tribes, Residents and Visitors of Bombay* (see p. 117). The Museum has a unique ethnographic album that features photographs taken in the adjacent gardens, which shows local people dressed as 'ethnic types', in much the same way that studio photography produced certain 'racial types' for the consumption of curious Europeans who were keen to share these exoticised images with friends back home. Many such images were used to help the model maker from Lucknow execute the various studies at the Museum (see pp. 210, 222–224). Postcards at the turn of the century drew on this image bank and greatly popularised and authenticated such interpretations.[16]

Most of the Museum's extraordinary collection of models and dioramas were prepared in-house, over a period of twenty years, by a master modeller from Lucknow, Shiv Prasad Balsing, about whom not much is documented except that he was very skilled.[17] Lucknow was famous for its 'realistic' clay models as these were the most Europeanised and coveted.[18] The Lucknow modeller was initially assisted by students from the Sir J.J. School of Art. It was felt that the practice of model-making would help the students in understanding the naturalistic representation of the human body. However, the Lucknow master modeller appears to have lost patience with the students as they were inexperienced and required training. Art historians of the period praised the Bombay clay models as being superior to the Calcutta figurines, which were covered with fabric and did not require much modelling skills.[19]

Colonial taxonomies prevailed in the ordering of this new section of the Museum. Burns found that there was little interest in the natural history section as the zoo had come up next door and it did not make sense to show stuffed animals any more. He decided to change the focus of the displays to include more models and dioramas.[20] Burns records that he used Watson and Kaye's The People of India series (1868–75) to guide his approach to the execution of the models. Equally important is the influence of Herbert Risley's book, *The People of India* (1908), as a system of ordering. The book was purchased by Burns for the Museum about the time the model collection began being developed and the book's contents pages read like the Museum's ethnographic section. Risley was one of the foremost British colonial administrators and the architect of the British ethnographic approach to Indian society. His long stint in India (including his work as the Census Commissioner and Ethnographic Commissioner for India), his detailed studies of the various tribes of Bengal, as well as his investigations into aspects of caste and its relationship to anthropometry had an overwhelming impact on the emerging field of Indian ethnography.[21]

In addition to the models, the Museum created a series of dioramas that would engage the public imagination. Duplicates of some of the dioramas had been sent to the various exhibitions held in the many European capitals to explain Indian society. These were also regularly loaned to local fairs and schools in Bombay as visual aids, till one of the dioramas came back damaged and the practice was stopped.[22] The history of dioramas during this period is fascinating. Large-scale theatrical performances with painted backdrops called panoramas evolved into scenes that involved the layout sometimes of whole villages, with live demonstrations, often accompanied with music and dance. These were presented at various international exhibitions, to cater to the insatiable curiosity about the exotic East. The frozen human tableaux produced at the Museum emerge from this tradition and such dioramas were a popular feature of the international exhibitions.

T.N. Mukharji, a Bengali scholar and assistant curator of the Indian Museum in Calcutta, who visited the Colonial and Indian Exhibition in 1886 noted the public fascination for such live demonstrations and his own discomfort at such displays, which were the equivalent of human zoos. The *Times* in London averred, 'At a single step the visitor is carried … into the stately splendour of that unchanging antique life of the East, the tradition of which has been preserved in pristine purity only in India.'[23] At the 1895 Empire of India Exhibition, George Birdwood and Imre Kiralfy, the Director General of the exhibition, recreated 'The Indian City', which showcased a street scene from Bombay and another from Hyderabad, as well as a Benares temple and a Lahore shop.[24] Another display was titled 'The Jungle', in which 'some thousands of specimens are to be seen, including elephants, rhinoceroses, tigers, leopards, buffaloes, bison, wild sheep, ibex, antelopes, gazelles, snakes, crocodiles, and a vast number of birds and butterflies and insects, arranged and grouped in a life like manner …'[25] Often, live demonstrations of native 'types' and of craft production were on display.[26] London's India Museum housed a large collection of such sundry 'types'.

During World War I, the Bombay Presidency's regiments played an important role in the decisive victory of the British in strategically important campaigns such as Mesopotamia (1914–18). A committee was set up to establish a War Museum in Bombay to commemorate these victories.[27] The committee called for contributions related to the War from the public. Trophies were collected between 1916 and 1925 and presented at the V&A Museum, Bombay, where the War Museum was temporarily housed.[28] Burns decided to create a diorama about the War at the Museum. He recruited the students at the Lord Reay workshop at the Sir J.J. School of Art to create a battle scene with 'a thousand small models of men in fighting attitude belonging to the armies of the Allies and the Enemy'. 'Zeppelins', 'aeroplanes', 'various flying machines' and 'guns of different calibres' were also crafted to present a realistic battle scene.[29] Military officials were invited to give suggestions to improve the display. Burns notes in his report that this presentation was very successful and was 'crowded every afternoon'. It is important to note the emphasis on the realistic and accurate depiction of the scene and the soldiers, but Burns does not tell us whether Indian soldiers were represented. Like the paintings and sketches of the period, the models and dioramas, though apparently innocuous, present a particular narrative. Unfortunately, the War diorama is no longer at the Museum and since it is not in the accession record, it is surmised that it was damaged and discarded. The War Museum never materialised due to financial delays and the increasing anti-British sentiment in India.

In revisiting the Museum's artistic historiography, this chapter not only highlights the uniqueness of the model and diorama collection, but also reflects on how identity is constructed, and how it mutates through political and social machinations. Visual archives like the Museum enable a nuanced reading of seemingly innocent facts. They demonstrate for us how the past is constantly shapeshifting as it inscribes itself onto the present, and helps us look afresh at who we are and how we might evolve. • TZM

Choor'rie Wallah
or
Native Ornament Maker.

As the British East India Company's trade links and interest in South Asia grew in the eighteenth and nineteenth centuries, many Company officials moved from England to India. A new style of painting by Indian artists, known as the 'Company School', evolved during this period, especially to cater to the tastes of the European patrons. The hybrid Indo-European style was marked by the desire to record and collect scenes of landscapes, streets, towns, lifestyles and occupations of the native people of the colonised regions. The style was an amalgamation of European painting, with its penchant for a three-dimensional perspective and naturalism, and the scale of Indian miniature painting. The local indigenous styles of painting did not appeal to the European patrons as Indian painting was considered 'primitive'.[1] Indian artists, therefore, began to produce paintings that blended European and Indian traditions. In addition to the Company officials, this genre also found favour with the local Indian elite. The term 'Company painting' encompasses large and diverse bodies of work from different regions, each with its own stylistic idiom. Mostly executed in watercolours, the characteristic features that link these styles of painting are their documentary nature and an attempt to objectively capture the various aspects of Indian life.[2]

Company painting is an important genre of Indian art and natural history, since it not only provided a record of the social and economic life of India, but also shaped later artistic developments that are evident in the Museum's clay model collection, influenced by the documentary aspect of this genre. Many of the prints and paintings in the Museum's collection include images of craftsmen, artisans and communities that are similar to the clay models in the collection. Among the most notable artists in this genre is Sewak Ram (1770–1830) from Patna. He was known for his sombre colour range of deep sepia, red ochre and dull white, indicative of a European influence that he probably acquired through exposure to prints and watercolours brought by the Europeans who often had Indian artists copy material. His works are known for a particular technique that required great skill, called *kajli seahi,* which involved painting straight away with a brush without using a pencil.[3] The image on the opposite page shows a bangle-maker at work, holding a tapered, wooden rod stacked with glass bangles of various sizes being fused with red lacquer over hot coals held in an earthen pot and placed over a traditional *chulha* (stove). Red bangles are customarily worn by married women across many regions of India, whereas green bangles are the norm in the Deccan region. The pierced heart with two arrows, a European sign for true love, is placed under the title 'Native Ornament Maker'. Colourful lacquer sticks are placed around

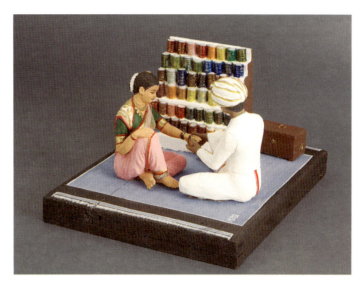

Bangle Seller; half-baked terracotta and pigments, 1914–15, made at the erstwhile V&A Museum, Bombay; 26 x 20 x 13 cm.
•
Opposite:
Choorrie Wallah or Native Ornament Maker, Sewak Ram; watercolour on paper, c. 1810-20, Patna; 21.9 x 17.6 cm. Accessioned: 2014.

the craftsman with wooden rods, holding more bangles, cooling against a low wall. The bangle-maker is seated on his haunches, on a low stool, seen even today in rural India.

Some of the major centres of this genre were Lucknow, Tanjore, Calcutta, Delhi, Madras, Patna and Benares, where the Company presence was concentrated. The Museum's collection includes paintings from most of these regions, the majority being from the Patna *qalam* (style), which was one of the most prolific styles. Artists of the Patna *qalam* earned a reputation for their depictions of festivals, occupations and scenes of everyday local life. Many artists from the Mughal courts and ateliers migrated to Patna, and were believed to be descendants of the celebrated miniature artist Manohar, from Emperor Akbar's court.[4] It was, however, in Murshidabad that many of the techniques that characterised the Patna *qalam* originated. Sewak Ram was one of the best-known artists of the Patna *qalam*.[5]

By the early nineteenth century, artists had devised popular themes for paintings and started creating sets comprising standard subject matter. The artists sold their paintings to tourists and locals in the bazaars, democratising the art form. Company painting began to decline with the advent of photography in the late 1830s. By the mid-twentieth century, the Patna *qalam* ceased to exist with the death of the last practising traditional artist, Ishwari Prasad Verma, in 1950.[6] • PV

MICA PAINTING

The Museum has a collection of twenty-three paintings on mica. Mica paintings were produced for the British by Indian artists and were executed in the Company style. Most of the works on mica in the Museum's collection were purchased in 1932 from Colonel Murray, a retired army officer posted in Bombay.[1]

Paintings on mica were valued for their transparent surface, enabling artists to use the transparency in different ways. The painted portions would render the surface opaque, and artists would leave a part of the space around the main subject or figure unpainted, giving the work an ethereal quality. Sometimes the ground below the main subject was shown as a horizon line and the rest was left unpainted. The unpainted parts represented a background, the sky, or an emptiness left to the imagination of the viewer. There are records of novel objects using mica, such as brocade boxes with a card which had painted on it a rug, a sky and floating limbs and head, without a body. Separate card sheets of mica with different costumes painted on the surface accompanied the box, and the mica sheets could be placed over the card to complete the figure, with the head, limbs and sky showing through the transparent mica sheets. It is believed that Queen Mary acquired such a card box from Benares during her visit in 1911.[2]

From the late nineteenth till the early twentieth century, mica painting flourished in Murshidabad, Patna and Benares in the east and in Trichinopoly in the south of India.[3] There were distinct stylistic differences in paintings from the east and the south. The paintings produced in the east had a different colour palette, with more reds and blues, compared to those produced in the south, where the colours usually took on hues of yellow, orange, brown and green. Paintings that captured different occupations were the most coveted collectibles for Europeans and visitors. Other popular subjects included depictions of festivals, processions, gods and flora and fauna of the region. The paintings in the Museum's collection are mostly from Patna and include a boot polisher, a snake charmer, a man ironing clothes, a lady dancer, a wandering minstrel, festival processions and palanquin bearers, among others. • **PV**

Man Polishing Boots; colour pigments on mica sheet, late nineteenth to early twentieth century, Patna; 14.8 x 11.8 cm. Accessioned: 1932.

Ironer; colour pigments on mica sheet, late nineteenth to early twentieth century, Patna; 15.2 x 12 cm. Accessioned: 1932.

Deccani Brahmin; half-baked terracotta and pigments, 1908-09, made at the erstwhile V&A Museum, Bombay; 6.5 x 23 cm.

Mahratta Brahman; reproduction of a hand-coloured photograph, F.M. Coleman, *Typical Pictures of Indian Natives*, Bombay: The Times of India Press, 1899; 24.2 x 18.4 cm. Accessioned: 2013.

THE clay model of the Deccani Brahmin (Brahmin from Deccan) in traditional attire was directly influenced from a coloured photograph titled '*Mahratta Brahman*', reproduced in F.M. Coleman's *Typical Pictures of the Indian Natives*, first published in 1897 by the Times of India Press, Bombay. Both the print and the model depict the gentleman — defined by his caste and region — in a four-part ensemble, representing the Deccan Brahman community. The lower garment is a *dhoti*, a loose garment made of silk or cotton, which is draped differently across various regions of India. Here it is depicted in the Deccani style typically worn in Maharashtra. His shirt or *kurta* is tied in the front, and draped over the shoulders is a plain white cloth with red edges and a gold *zari* border at the

ends, known as the *uparna*. The distinctive turban or *pagadi* was commonly seen worn in and around Poona in the Deccan. The clay model has two horizontal sect marks on his forehead, which was typical of the Brahmins in the Deccan, denoting his Shaivite caste affiliation. His shoes or *mojaris* have a distinctive upward twist at the toe. While the hand-coloured photograph is staged with the classic props of late-nineteenth-early-twentieth-century studio photographs, the clay model is accompanied by the figure of a Deccani Brahmin lady in the Museum's collection.

Typical Pictures is a collection of twenty-four hand-coloured studio photographs depicting the accoutrements of different Indian communities and occupations. Following the

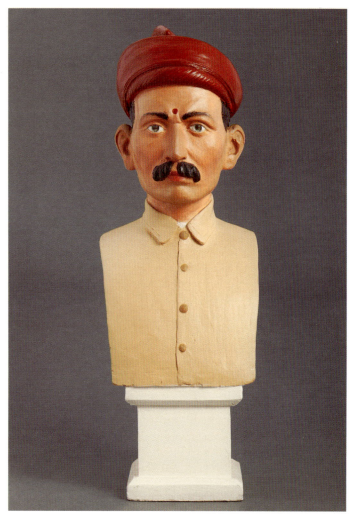

Deccani Brahmin; plaster of Paris and pigments, 1929-30, Bombay; 11.4 × 13 × 36.7 cm. It is directly influenced by the photograph of a Brahmin man taken outside the Museum. The facial expressions also match those of the person in the photograph.

Photograph Depicting the Attire and Headwear of a Brahmin Man; taken by the Museum Assistant, c. 1906–09, Bombay; 15 × 10.2 cm.

Uprising of 1857 in Bengal, photographers were commissioned by the British Government to document the people in different regions like the European naturalists had documented the flora and fauna of the newly established imperial colonies a century before. A firm grasp on the contemporary occupations and nuances of a person's attire, dictated by his or her intertwined caste or occupational standing, was crucial to understanding India's layered society. Professional artists from traditional royal ateliers found employment in photo studios to colour black and white images. Studio photographs and photo-type postcards depicting Indian castes and occupation types were highly coveted in the late nineteenth century in international markets and exhibitions,

and led to the acquisition of such miniature clay models for documentation and educational purposes.[1]

The original photograph reproduced in *Typical Pictures* may be attributed to Bourne and Shepherd, the famous late nineteenth century commercial photographers with studios across India and Europe. At the end of his description of the '*Mahratta Brahman*', Coleman notes with regret that 'the writer has to chronicle the death of the subject in the present picture' in the bubonic plague that spread across Bombay in 1897.[2] While the comment recognises that he was respected by people, the man's name has not been mentioned, indicating the symbolic, impersonal nature of the portrait as an example of his community 'type'. • RWB

PARSI COUPLE

Parsis migrated from western Iran or Persia to the Indian subcontinent in the second century CE for trade and again, in the eighth century CE following the Arab conquest of Persia. They settled in Gujarat and assimilated into the heterogeneous culture of the subcontinent. Known for their carpentry and shipbuilding skills, they were favoured by the British for their 'Aryan' genealogy and their business acumen. Their ships were often hired by the East India Company for trade between China, Africa and Europe.

As India rapidly industrialised from the eighteenth century onwards, the Parsis developed a symbiotic business relationship with the British.[1] They helmed many joint venture projects and carved out a unique identity to distinguish themselves from other Indian communities by adopting Western education, lifestyle, fashions, and Anglicised names. The British appointed English-educated communities, including the Parsis, in their businesses, creating a new class of Indian elite.

The image on the left depicts clay models of a Parsi couple in the Museum's collection

and the image on the right is a sketch of a Parsi couple by Rao Bahadur M.V. Dhurandhar. It is evident that Dhurandhar referenced similar contemporary photographs and drawings by Raja Ravi Varma Press and European artists to produce sketches, not unlike the process followed by the Museum curators and the clay modeller who was commissioned to create these figures.

The woman is wearing a traditional Parsi *gara* (embroidered saree). *Garas* are known for their sophisticated, fine silk embroidery. In the nineteenth century, trade with China was dominated by Parsi and Jewish merchants, which led to the evolution of hybrid Indo-Chinese embroidery patterns on either the entire *gara* or just on its border.[2] Parsi women's blouses were influenced by Victorian fashions. The models hold a parasol and a walking stick, which were popular accessories in the nineteenth to early twentieth century. The Parsi community continues to head important businesses in India even today and is known for their philanthropy. • RWB

Parsi Couple; half-baked terracotta and pigments, 1909-10, made at the erstwhile V&A Museum, Bombay; 9.3 x 9.1 x 22.5 cm.

The Parsees, M.V. Dhurandhar; Strip, P. and O. Strip, *The Peoples of Bombay*, Bombay: Thacker & Co., 1944; 24 x 16 cm. Accessioned: 1944.

59 SINHALESE

Sinhalese; half-baked terracotta and pigments, 1908-09, made at the erstwhile V&A Museum, Bombay; 9.6 x 22 cm.

Sinhalese; reproduction of a hand-coloured photograph, F.M. Coleman, *Typical Pictures of Indian Natives*, Bombay: The Times of India Press, 1899; 24.2 x 18.4 cm. Accessioned: 2013

THE MUSEUM'S collection of ethnographic studies in clay models of foreign communities attests to Bombay's abiding multicultural identity. The studies were assembled to communicate to visitors the variety and density of the city's population, reflecting its rapid growth as the largest port in Asia from the mid-nineteenth to the early twentieth century. Official census records and travelogues of the 1800s remark on Bombay's impressive variety of nationalities. The steady expansion of sea trade, railway networks and urban administration was an impetus to emigrating merchant and labour classes from interstate and foreign lands. The introduction of new municipal wards, housing schemes, construction of causeways and better roadways distributed a steadily increasing population across Bombay's northern, central and southern districts.

Many of the clay figurines in the Museum's collection are modelled on F.M. Coleman's *Typical Pictures of Indian Natives* (1899) and photographs taken at the Museum between 1906–09. The model of a Sinhalese man, native to Ceylon, is shown wearing a *comboy* (sarong), also known as *kambaya,* which is an ankle-length, light-weight skirt without pleats. The cloth piece was wrapped around the waist and fastened with a belt or a knot. A European-style button-down jacket with a band collar was a popular choice of upper garment. Sinhalese men were distinguished by the large hair-comb used to hold their long hair behind their forehead. Made of fine quality tortoiseshell, the comb was in the shape of a horse-shoe. Their long hair was tightly coiled and held high at the back of the head. Some men wore an additional comb just above their coiled hair; it was indicative of the wearer's high status in society.[1]

Ceylon, the 'Emerald Isle of the East' as Coleman described it in *Typical Pictures*, was an important hub of the East India Company's maritime trade in the mid-nineteenth century, with ships from the isle arriving frequently at the port of Bombay. Coffee, tea, cinnamon, sapphires, emeralds, pearls, and cat's eyes, in addition to ivory and sandalwood, were among the most lucrative items constituting the island's trade.[2]

Sinhalese, Arabs, Jews, Baluchis are some of the communities that made up the city's multicultural and multilingual ethnicity, most evident in Bombay's famous local bazaars that contributed to the city's economic growth. About eighteen bazaars, both big and small, were recorded in Bombay in the 1860s.[3] The rich symphony of various languages and the display of different costumes of both the shoppers and vendors added to these bazaars' diversity. They offered countless commodities, from seasonal fruits, vegetables, spices and sweets to Kashmiri shawls, brocade silks, gold and shellac jewellery. They catered to the resident and floating populations, including the English, Portuguese, Chinese, Arabs, Parsis, Hindus, Muslims and Christians. Along with the bustling bazaars, the neighbourhoods of Bhuleshwar, Kalbadevi, Girgaum, Kamathipura, Nagpada, Mandvi and Market (near the Jumma Mosque) boasted the inclusion of agiaries, churches, mosques and temples.[4] By the mid-nineteenth century, Bombay's multilayered society had forged a global reputation. • IH

ARAB

Arab merchants have traded in western India since antiquity. European colonisation and the development of an active sea trade between British ports in the Middle East and India increased Arab settlements in India. By the nineteenth century, Bombay witnessed a flourishing trade in pearls, dates, coffee, gums of various kinds, honey and ghee by resident and travelling Arab merchants. Some also exported Indian textiles to important Gulf ports.

The trade in Arabian horses was one of the most important features of the Arab presence in Bombay. The Arabian horse held a superior position in the British-Indian military and was purchased from open-air horse markets in Bombay. Each year, Bedouin Arabs brought Arabian horses to be sold in Byculla near the old racecourse. The influx of horse traders, who made their way to the city by sea, included Arabs from Saudi Arabia, Iraq and Kuwait, both from the affluent and bourgeois classes.[1] Byculla hosted the highest density of the resident Arab community, as recorded in the city's official census of 1906.[2] Some Arabs were major horse-racing enthusiasts and were known to own valuable studs in Bombay.

In Bombay, the Arabs were distinguished by their headdress, which consisted of a *keffiyeh* (head scarf) in plain white or the characteristic red and white print, and a buttoned, ankle-length *thawb* (outer coat). The model in the Museum's collection depicts an Arab man wearing a turban typical of Meccan Arabs from the nineteenth century, with his head scarf secured using thick, black *agal* (headbands).[3] • IH

Left:
Arab Man from Mecca; half-baked terracotta and pigments, 1908-09, made at the erstwhile V&A Museum, Bombay; 6.6 x 18.3 cm.
•
Left, below:
Photograph Depicting the Attire and Headwear of an Arab Man; taken by the Museum Assistant, c. 1906–09, Bombay; 15 x 10.1 cm.

60 THE COLLECTION OF TEXTILE MANUFACTURES OF INDIA
by JOHN FORBES WATSON

THE *Collection of Textile Manufactures of India* is a 'mobile industrial museum' of 700 Indian textile and fabric samples compiled by Dr John Forbes Watson from London's India Museum, which was established by the East India Company in 1801.[1] Watson first came to India as a surgeon in the British-Indian army in Bombay from 1850 to 1853 and assumed the role of the India Museum's director in 1858. Among his research and documentation projects was the compendium of textile samples meant to be a reference trade catalogue for British manufacturers and mills. When the American Civil War (1861–65) abruptly halted the steady supply of cotton to English mills, a reeling British economy began urgently seeking a solution for the mass unemployment that ensued.[2] British mills increased cotton purchases from India and manufacturing imitations of popular Indian fabrics in the textile looms at Lancashire, which were then exported back to India. Watson was aware that finer Indian fabrics such as muslins, silks, or embroidery that were being replicated in England for sale in India were far inferior in quality to those available in India and the production costs were much higher.[3]

Twenty sets of this work were produced, thirteen of which were distributed across the manufacturing towns in England. Only seven were sent to Indian cities where textile trade took place, to be distributed among the town halls, art schools or chambers of commerce in Calcutta, Madras, Bombay, Karachi, Punjab, the North West Provinces and Berar. The set in the Museum's collection was forwarded by the Secretary of State for India to the Bombay Chamber of Commerce in 1867-68.[4] The Museum, then located at the Town Hall, with a focus on economical and industrial collections and greater access to the public was considered an ideal repository for the set.

The collection enabled British agents in India to study the samples and recommend fabrics that could be produced by the looms in England. Each volume consisted of mounted and classified 'working samples' of Indian textiles.[5] Each page was numbered and labelled with detailed information: material, the quantity and quality purchased by buyers, the community that commonly wore specific patterns and fabrics, the length, price, weight, provenance, and place of purchase of the fabric. The opposite page shows a piece of fabric thickly embroidered with gold thread, iridescent elytra or the hard casing of beetle wings. The pattern is a dynamic mix of floral roundels and diagonal lines with vine embroidery. By the nineteenth century, beetle-wing embroidery was in vogue and practised extensively in the Madras Presidency from where it was exported to the international markets.

An accompanying volume, *The Textile Manufactures and The Costumes of the People of India*, was published in 1866 to guide the British manufacturers on how different kinds of clothes were worn or draped in India. It includes several coloured plates borrowed from Watson's other encyclopaedic project, *The People of India* (see pp. 115-16), detailing the variety of traditional attires and modes of dress. It was also meant to draw the manufacturer's attention to the 'steadiness' of Indian fashion which was seen in contrast to seasonally changing European fashions.

The textile samples in the sets include turban cloth, garment pieces for men and women, *dhoti*, *sarees*, calicos, muslins, silks, woollens and 'piece goods'. The volumes on woollens and plaid samples were thought to be advantageous to English manufacturers as they could be easily replicated. George Birdwood criticised the catalogue in the 1870s for its narrow understanding of Indian textiles and generalised classification. • RWB

Embroiderer; half-baked terracotta and pigments, 1912–14, made at the erstwhile V&A Museum, Bombay; 13 x 18 x 14.5 cm.
•
Opposite:
Muslins, thickly embroidered, Madras; fabric embroidered with gold thread in beetle wings, mounted on paper in leather-bound volumes, J.F. Watson, *The Collection of Textile Manufactures of India*, London: India Museum, 1866–67; 34 x 19 cm. Accessioned: 1869–70.

Prov. No. 515.

No. 277

INDIA FABRICS.

MUSLINS THICKLY EMBROIDERED.

Length 1 yard 29 inches; width 1 yard 13 inches.   Weight 12 oz.

From MADRAS.

EMBROIDERER

Textile production and trade is an ancient industry in India, employing a range of artisans. The rich diversity in styles of embroidery is an important aspect of Indian sartorial elegance. Every region in India has its unique embroidery tradition, from the *kashida* work of Kashmir, the *chikankari* of Lucknow, the *kantha* work of Bengal to the *Chamba rumals* of Himachal Pradesh, *phulkaris* of Punjab and the *kasuti* work of the Deccan and south India. Fine embroidery was considered a refined art form and compared to a detailed painting. While women were at the forefront of embroidering and stitching in private homes, men were engaged in producing embroidery for the commercial markets.[1]

The Museum has eighteen clay models depicting the various stages of textile manufacture from cleaning cotton, weaving, dyeing, making gold and silver spangles, block printing and embroidering. The image below shows two embroiderers executing *zardosi* work (gold thread embroidery) on a piece of fabric that was typically stretched over a wooden frame to enable the craftsmen to sit on the ground and embroider. The attire of the craftsmen consists of a *jama* or *kurta* (upper garment) worn over cotton pyjamas with a turban and a cap, signifying they are from north India. The figure to the right is Muslim as distinguished by his cap. There are shallow dishes placed next to each embroiderer, containing gold and silver thread and perhaps sequins.

The model draws inspiration from the image in the *Journal of Indian Art*, reproduced below, which depicts four embroiderers from the erstwhile Bombay Presidency. Master embroiderers from Sindh and Delhi settled in Bombay after the decline of royal patronage in the nineteenth century. The cosmopolitan nature of the city, brisk trade and the business opportunities it afforded made it an attractive destination for many craftsmen. A shop in Kalbadevi, an important market even today, employed almost 200 workers by the late nineteenth century. The four embroiderers are shown working on the different types of garments that were commercially popular: caps, garment borders and large pieces of fabric. Silk from China and France was extensively used for embroidery in Bombay.[2] Surat and Sawantwadi were the other major embroidery centres in the Bombay Presidency.

Popular motifs included regional flora and fauna, arabesque patterns and designs evoking the idea of fertility and prosperity, which was especially seen in embroidered fabrics presented to brides. Pearls and precious stones were embroidered onto the fabric for royal patrons and even onto carpets. The most famous example is the pearl carpet commissioned by Maharaja Khanderao Gaekwad of Baroda, first displayed at the Art Exhibition held in February 1868 at the Framjee Cowasjee Institute, Bombay.[3] • RWB

Embroidering; half-baked terracotta and pigments, 1912–14, made at the erstwhile V&A Museum, Bombay; 23 x 13 x 15.5 cm.

Bombay Embroiderers at Work; photo-lithograph by W. Griggs, *The Journal of Indian Art*, Vol. II. London: W. Griggs and Sons, 1887; 36 x 27 cm. Accessioned: 1900–10.

61 REPOUSSE CRAFTSMEN

CLAY models of craftspeople in the act of producing finely crafted objects and representing over twenty Indian 'industries' are displayed alongside the objects in the Museum. These models not only showcase the stages of production of an article but also ensure that visitors from all backgrounds understand the details of the manufacturing process. The models, which were created in the early twentieth century, have an ethnographic focus on the body of the craftsperson, including indicating markers of his caste, community and region, and an emphasis on manual labour that was typical of colonial documentation projects.[1]

The clay models of repousse craftsmen depict two artisans hammering designs onto a copper vase using small, handheld chisels and hammers. The model on the left wears a round, black *topi* (cap) with embroidered designs, while the model on the right wears a *pagadi* (turban), both typically worn by men in the Deccan. Both are dressed in long-sleeved, white shirts worn over cotton *dhotis* (lower garment). The model was based on an illustration from the *Journal of Indian Art and Industry* depicting craftsmen at the Reay Art Workshop.

Sons of craftsmen of the Kasar (brassworker) and Tambat (coppersmith) communities, who were engaged in hereditary practice in the Bombay Presidency, enrolled at the Reay Art Workshop when it was established in 1891.[2] The ornamentation or repousse work, as seen in both the model and the illustration, was done by *nakashawallahs* or craftsmen specialising in ornamentation work. Repousse work includes raising design in relief on the metal from the reverse, using hammers and small round, flat or chisel-headed punches as seen among the instruments laid out next to the craftsmen. This technique is used to ornament malleable metals such as copper, silver and gold, and applied to decorative panels on walls, doors, utensils, jewellery, etc.

The vase depicted in the illustration was 3 ft tall and 2 ft 10 inches in diameter, and made of two sheets of copper.[3] The exterior of the vase was lightly layered with a mixture of mud and ash to enable tracing the design. The vase was filled with a mixture which hardened and designs were traced on a paper and punched out till the ornamentation was raised in relief. The vase was finally polished once the core had been melted out. Large vases were mostly used for storing water or grain while the smaller ones were only used for storing water.

Designs were carved into wood and then hammered onto an overlaid metal sheet in Punjab, Kashmir, Jaipur and Moradabad. At these centres, glass paint was fused into the hammered designs to produce enamelled brassware. In the Bombay Presidency, Poona was known for its bold repousse work with natural, floral, even mythological motifs, while Kutch was known for its delicate, shallow repousse.

Repousse work from the Bombay School of Art won medals at important exhibitions in India and abroad.[4] Objects such as pitchers, jars, salvers and decorative panels were executed at the School. By the mid-twentieth century, there were over 100 students being trained at the Reay Art Workshop, and working on commissioned artworks. The Sir J.J. School of Art continues to teach repousse work as part of the Fine Arts degree. • RWB

Top:
Repousse Craftsmen; half-baked terracotta and pigments, 1913-14, made at the erstwhile V&A Museum, Bombay; 19.8 x 17.6 x 25.3 cm.
•
Above:
Vase — Hammered Copper at the Bombay School of Art; lithograph of sketch executed by Vithal Keanthad when J. Griffiths was the principal, *Journal of Indian Art,* Vol. I, London: W. Griggs & Sons, 1886; 36.5 x 27 cm. Accessioned: 1900–10.

BOMBAY SERVANTS

In nineteenth-century India, a familiar scene in a British household was the organised bustle of domestic helpers. It was recorded that smaller British families required up to ten to twelve servants, while larger homes hired a cadre of thirty servants.[1] Caste and community hierarchies were attributed to the need for such a large number of servants. Social conditions limited duties such as sweeping floors and handling meat to specific castes. Duties were systematically assigned and seldom overlapped to maintain an orderly imperial culture. F.M. Coleman lists a minimum of five servicemen hired by the smallest of households, seen in his painted photograph titled *Bombay Servants*. From the left, featured here are a *sevak* (butler), *hamal* (cleaner), bearer, cook, *masaulchee* (torch-bearer) and *ghorawallah* (syce). A larger retinue was hired for the households of high-ranked military officers, viceroys, and also rulers of the Indian princely states.

To manage and hire their attendants, British men and women relied on guidebooks such as Charles D'Oyly's *The European in India* (1813), John Murray's *A Handbook for India* (1859) and Flora Annie Steel and Grace Gardiner's *The Complete Indian Housekeeper and Cook* (1888). The publication of guidebooks or etiquette books, particularly during the late 1880s to the mid-1920s, indicates the growing number of the British elite and bourgeois class that travelled to and lived in India.

In the photograph, standing in the centre, is the bearer. He ranked in the 'upper' servants category and earned up to Rs 30 a month in the late nineteenth century. Of all domestic staff, he was the most experienced and was in charge of numerous duties around the house, including overseeing other servants. Bearers were known to have English-speaking skills, which made them valued interpreters between their employers and subordinate staff. A bearer often served the master of a household as his valet.

Next in the social order of servants were cooks. They were solely responsible for meal preparation; at times, this included purchasing supplies from the market. Coleman states that the bearer and cook in the photograph are Goan. In Bombay, a large number of early Goan emigrants worked as cooks, butlers and domestic servants for the British.[2] It was common to hire Goan Catholics for kitchen duties as they were not bound by religious customs that forbade them to serve wine and handle meat. Hindus whose caste permitted them to handle alcohol and meat also filled these positions.

Cooks worked closely with *khidmatgars,* who were waiters or servants employed to fulfil other kitchen tasks. They both earned up to Rs 15 to Rs 20 a month. *Khidmatgars* were often skilled confectioners and cooks themselves; however, their primary duties involved setting up and waiting at the table during meals, cleaning dishes, polishing silverware and preparing tea. The term *khidmatgar* alternated with 'boy', the anglicisation of *bhai* (brother), often used generically to indicate house help.

To the bearer's left is a *battiwallah,* also addressed as *masaulchee,* who was in charge of lighting kerosene lamps and candles for meals and across the house as well as cleaning and maintaining the lamps. Globes were to remain spotless at all times; reservoirs filled with kerosene and wicks cleaned or replaced as required. The *masaulchee*'s duties also extended outside the quarters of the house to guide the *ghorawallah* at night. Running by the side of the horse, he held a lighted torch that he continually maintained from a bottle of oil tied at his waist.

A *ghorawallah* or syce, as he was known in Bombay, was responsible for the upkeep of horses, saddlery and harness. He could handle from one to three horses. Ensuring the horses were well fed and groomed before their riders took them out was one of the syce's primary responsibilities. The syce is usually depicted holding a *chowri* (fly whisk) to ward off flies. Appearing on the right of the bearer is a *hamal*, holding a dusting cloth. The dusting of furniture, tabletops and books was his duty.

In addition to roles and responsibilities, staff appearance played a part in establishing and maintaining colonial ideals of discipline and sophistication. Keeping up appearances through appropriate attire was mandatory. A turban, a loose-fitting, knee-length *angrakha* (upper garment) paired with a waistband and trousers, at times a *dhoti* (cloth tied around the waist by men and tucked in the centre), was a standard mode of dress adopted by servants. Some even sported their employer's regimental badges on their turbans. The service of the *khidmatgars* earned them the trust and praise of their employers, encouraging correspondence between them long after Independence.[3] • IH

Left to right: *Sevak* (butler), *Ghorawallah* (syce), *Battiwala* or *Masaulchee* (torch-bearer) and *Coachvan* (coachman); half-baked terracotta and pigments, 1912–14, made at the erstwhile V&A Museum, Bombay; 9.5 x 23 cm.

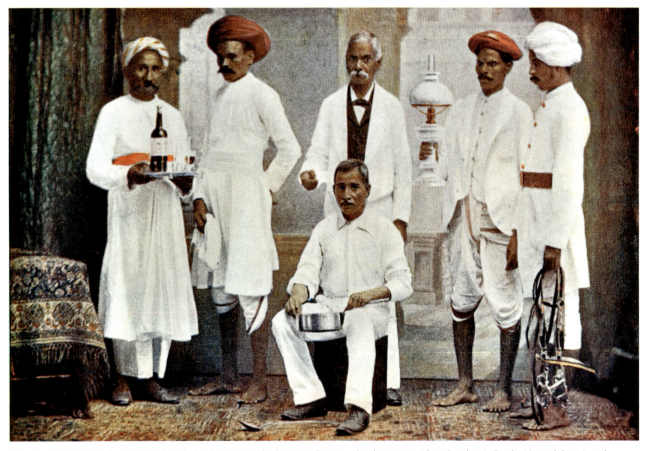

Bombay Servants; left to right: *Sevak* (butler), *Hamal* (cleaner), Bearer, also known as 'dressing-boy', Cook, *Masaulchee* (torch-bearer) and *Ghorawallah* (syce); reproduction of a hand-coloured photograph, F.M. Coleman, *Typical Pictures of Indian Natives*, Bombay: The Times of India Press, 1899; 17.2 x 24.5 cm. Accessioned: 2013.

Dancer and Musicians; half-baked terracotta and pigments, 1908-09, made at the erstwhile V&A Museum, Bombay; 22.3 x 23.7 x 23.7 cm.

Dancing Girls and Musicians, James Forbes; engraving, *Oriental Memoirs: A Narrative of Seventeen Years Residence in India*, Vol. II, London: White, Cochrane & Co., 1813; 31.5 x 25.5 x 6.8 cm. Accessioned: early twentieth century.

BOMBAY'S commercial success in the mid-nineteenth century attracted musicians and dancers who arrived in the city from neighbouring regions of the Presidency and other princely states. *Nataks* (musical plays) and *baithaks* (seated performances) were popular forms of entertainment and it soon became a mark of cultivation to have a music teacher. New audiences and elite patronage encouraged many musicians and dancers to settle in Bombay to perform and teach different musical styles.[1]

The clay model of a dancer and her accompanying musicians represents a typical form of popular entertainment in the Presidency towns during the eighteenth and nineteenth centuries. Elite patrons employed a nautch (dance) party to celebrate special occasions such as weddings or in honour of esteemed guests, usually English ministers and Nawabs. The party would consist of one or two lead dancers and musicians, usually a *sarangi* and a *tabla* player. The more established the dancer, the greater the number of accompanying musicians. Nautch parties were regularly invited to English homes by

the end of the eighteenth century, beginning a tradition that continued throughout the nineteenth century.[2]

Nautch dancers arrived in Bombay from Goa, Gujarat, Gwalior and Hyderabad. A nautch girl was a trained singer and composer in addition to her being an accomplished dancer. Known as *Kalavatis* ('women possessed of the arts or *kala* of dancing and singing'), nautch girls in Bombay were either Hindu or Muslim and were well-versed in singing in Marathi and Hindustani.[3] Also popular in nautch soirees were *thumri* and *ghazal*, two semi-classical music genres that have links to Kathak. The performance involved simultaneous storytelling through singing amorous couplets and rhythmic hand and feet movements. The tinkling bells of the dancer's anklets coupled with the *sarangi*'s melody and the beat of the *tabla* created a sought-after pleasurable experience.

Nautch girls dressed modestly, in a fitted bodice, leggings and an *odhni* (shawl) draped around the waist and over the shoulder or head. The garments were made of rich fabrics such as silks and velvets and were embellished with shiny trimmings and borders. Dancers adorned themselves with flowers as hair accessories, gold and pearl jewellery, including toe rings, and perfume. They reflected a genteel demeanour to their audiences who were often enamoured by their charm and beauty.[4] Successful nautch girls revelled in a 'star status' with their numerous patrons and followers and lived an opulent lifestyle.[5]

For the European orientalists and Indian luminaries of the eighteenth and nineteenth centuries, Hindustani music and dance were essential subjects to be surveyed and enjoyed. Historically, Hindustani music flourished under the patronage of Mughal *darbars* (courts) and were passed down to successive generations following the Empire's disintegration. This tradition formed a prestigious system of cultural pedagogy in the post-Mughal era. These legacies developed through hereditary apprenticeship which became the foundations of schools called *gharanas* (music styles). The term '*gharana*' has its roots in the Hindi word for home. *Gharana* disciples memorised and preserved their *gurus*' or *ustads*' (masters') teachings through classical singing or dance performances. *Gharanas* were named after the various cities they were founded in like Gwalior, Indore, Baroda, Jaipur, etc., and were differentiated by their unique styles of composition, singing and presentation of ragas. The 'Bhendibazar Gharana' emerged in 1890 in Bombay. It was established by the brothers Chhajju Khan, Nazir Khan and Khadim Hussain Khan, singers who had migrated from Moradabad (Uttar Pradesh) around 1870 and lived in the Bhendi Bazar locality.[6] This *gharana* was centred on a particular rhythmic classical singing style called *khyal*.

Towards the end of the nineteenth century, nautch dance forms became corrupted and were stigmatised by the British and Indian educated elite who were influenced by puritanical Victorian morals. The formidable reputation of many dancers was compromised and they were labelled as 'impure/immoral', pushing both artists and patrons to end engagement with the art form.[7] • IH

TAUS

A *taus* or *mayuri* is a stringed folk musical instrument associated with Hindustani music of Punjab. Its distinguishing feature is the wooden body in the shape of a peacock. Some models of the *taus* are adorned with real peacock feathers, a lacquered representation, or painted in hues that suggest the bird. Like the violin, the *taus* is held in the left hand and played using a bow in the right. The instrument is mainly used in devotional music performances.

The *taus* in the Museum's collection reflects rare traditional craftsmanship. It is built using *tun* wood (Indian mahogany) and embellished with ivory near the four main *kuntis* (tuning pegs), eyes and crown. The *tabli* (soundboard) is covered with goatskin. The *taus* typically has a finger-board or a neck fitted with four main metal strings and twenty metal frets.

The instrument was acquired in 1910 to be displayed along with four other Indian stringed instruments; the *tanpura*, *shruti veena*, *rabob* and *swarmandal*. The *taus* takes its name from the Persian word for peacock, and is known to be a precursor of the *dilruba*, another bowed, stringed instrument that is also a part of the Museum's collection.

During the nineteenth century, instruments such as the *tanpura*, *sitar*, *dilruba* and *taus* were mostly produced in north India in Rajasthan and Uttar Pradesh, and in West Bengal. The Bombay Presidency, until 1860, only produced single-stringed accompaniment instruments like the *tamboori*.[1] It was only after the mid-nineteenth century, when Bombay developed into a town and music performances became fashionable, that multiple-stringed instruments emerged in the region. • IH

Taus; wood, ivory, goatskin and metal, late nineteenth century, north India; 107 x 16 x 43 cm. Accessioned: 1910.

63 VASUDEV

Vasudev; half-baked terracotta and pigments, c. 1907–26, made at the erstwhile V&A Museum, Bombay; 11.5 x 6.5 x 24 cm.

Vasudev; photograph, taken by the Museum Assistant, c. 1906–09, Bombay; 15.5 x 10.9 cm.

ONE of the significant factors that led to the 1857 Uprising (referred to by the British as the Indian Mutiny) was the widespread discontent among the Indian sepoys (soldiers) due to the ill-informed policies of the British army. To redress this, Queen Victoria issued a proclamation in 1858 instituting a policy of non-intervention in the local population's social and religious affairs. It became crucial for British officers to gain a deeper understanding of the various religious sects and their ideologies to prevent future conflict. Religion in India, particularly Hinduism, evolved into different sects and sub-sects over many centuries. Rituals, ceremonies, mannerisms varied considerably, and people showed their sectarian association by their dress as well as marks and signs on the forehead or neck.

The Museum's collection of about ninety clay models of religious sects includes adherents of Vaishnavism,

Shaivism, and Shaktism and their sub-sects, as well as practitioners of Buddhism, Jainism, Sikhism and Muslim *fakirs*. These clay models were added to the collection between 1907 to 1926 and became popular among the local population as they were familiar with these communities.[1] People from different sects were photographed at the Museum and placed together in an album that served as a template for the preparation of these models.[2] Several ethnography books such as *The People of India* by John Forbes Watson and John William Kaye were also consulted as a reference. In 1928, the book *Monograph on the Religious Sects of India among the Hindus* by the Museum's assistant curator D.A. Pai was published. It offered extensive details on various religious sects, sect marks and the different practices with reference to the Museum's collection.

Worshipper of Shiva as Bhairava; half-baked terracotta and pigments, c. 1907–26, made at the erstwhile V&A Museum, Bombay; 9.5 x 24.3 cm.

Worshipper of Civa (Shiva) as Bhairava; photograph taken by the Museum Assistant, c. 1906–09, Bombay; 15 x 10.5 cm.

After the Bombay plague, the British became suspicious of beggars as they were perceived to be spreading diseases. The 1902 City Police Act criminalised a range of activities which were considered a disturbance in the public sphere. The police were empowered to regulate as well as prohibit activities such as begging, singing, playing music, displaying images, etc. in public spaces, and to levy fines and make arrests. Several communities and sects that lived on alms were termed as 'beggars' under colonial rule and identifying and understanding their practices became important.

Vasudev, a community of worshippers of Krishna, lives on alms. They sing devotional songs and verses extolling the names of several kings, deities and saints who believed in charity, usually in Marathi. In exchange for alms, they also share anecdotes from Krishna's life. They carry a wooden flute around their neck, and two attached cymbals in one hand, and a *khartal* (wooden clapper) in the other. They are seen singing and dancing early in the morning on the streets and open their bags for food, money, or clothing. Dressed in a white *kurta* and *dhoti*, their conical headgear adorned with peacock feathers with a brass top dramatically distinguishes them. Before beginning their practice every morning, they worship their peacock feather coronet. Vasudev, Krishna's father, is believed to have worn similar headwear. The worshippers are initiated into the community by a priest as a child. Typically, they wander from one location to another, halting at the temples, and are highly respected among the Marathi-speaking communities. Once seen frequently on the streets of Bombay, the sounds of the vibrant Vasudev tradition are slowly disappearing with greater urbanisation. • RJ

FAKIRS

Fakirs are religious ascetics who have withdrawn from worldly desires. They are considered holy and believed to have miraculous powers. Originally *fakirs* were of Muslim descent, but later the term was also extended to members of several Hindu sects. In order to strengthen their will and spiritual power, several *fakirs* place themselves in excruciating physical difficulties, fatal fasts, self-inflicted pain, etc. *Fakirs* travel from one holy site to another on pilgrimage, typically in large groups. During their visits, they reside in the local *masjids* (mosques) and live on alms provided by others. Each sect follows different beliefs, dresses differently, and practices specific routines such as singing songs of the fifteenth-century poet Kabir, performing religious rites, acrobatic stunts, playing instruments, etc. In the nineteenth and early twentieth centuries, *fakirs* were highly regarded among the local population and were often consulted on illness and misfortunes caused by what was considered 'the evil eye'. The British were wary of *fakirs* and wanted to restrict their movements and activities. Common people would often disguise themselves as *fakirs* in order to extort money or commit crimes. With the rise in the cases of theft, extortion, and the number of beggars on the streets of Bombay, the Government viewed *fakirs* with great mistrust and passed laws restricting their movements.[1] • RJ

Fakir; half-baked terracotta and pigments, c. 1907–08, made at the erstwhile V&A Museum, Bombay; 9.2 x 21.5 cm.

Photograph of a Fakir, taken by the Museum Assistant, c. 1906–09, Bombay; 15 x 10.5 cm.

SECT MARKS

It has been a customary practice among Hindus to wear marks on the forehead, also known as *tilaka* in Sanskrit, or popularly as *chappa*, in accordance with one's sect. These markings symbolise their devotion to their deity. Devotees believe that by wearing such markings they are under the protection of the deities they represent. Typically, these sect marks are painted by hand or are applied using metal stamps. Some devotees also used heated stamps to cicatrise their body parts.[1] Sect marks are most widely used by the followers of Shiva and Vishnu.

Each stamp bears symbols or a script which can be immersed in a paste and applied to the forehead, shoulders, arms, stomach, etc. after the devotee has undergone a purifying morning bath.[2] Different marks have different attributes and meanings. Marks made on the forehead, for instance, draw attention to the power and potential of the human mind.[3] The name of the deity and various *mantras* (phrases) are chanted while applying these marks.

Vaishnavites (Vishnu worshippers) are typically seen with two vertical lines on their foreheads resembling the letter 'U', representing the feet of Vishnu or his incarnations. This principal mark, also known as *Urdhvapundra*, is used by various sects of Vaishnavism with minor variations. The Ramanandi sect wears a similar *tilaka* with a semicircle at the root representing the feet of Rama and a red line in the centre representing Sita. In the Vallabhacharya sect, Krishna's footprints are indicated by two lines on the forehead that join at the bottom with a red dot representing Radha. These sect marks are typically crafted from sandalwood paste or *gopichandan* (white clay). • RJ

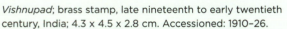

Vishnupad; brass stamp, late nineteenth to early twentieth century, India; 4.3 x 4.5 x 2.8 cm. Accessioned: 1910–26.

Vaishnavites (Vishnu worshippers) are commonly seen with the footprint mark representing the feet of Vishnu or his incarnations. The footprint stamp or Vishnupad in the image has within it iconography associated with Vishnu, such as the conch shell represented by the spiral on the right foot and the lotus flower on top of the left foot. The conch shell signifies the cyclical nature of life. Vishnu's feet are often referred to as lotus feet since the lotus symbolises purity.

Sect Mark Worn by Shaivites; brass stamp, late nineteenth to early twentieth century, India; 4.4 x 2.2 x 2.7 cm. Accessioned: 1910–26.

Shaivites (Shiva worshippers) anoint three parallel horizontal lines, known as Tripundra, across the forehead. The symbol in the centre of the Shaivite sect mark, as seen in the image above, typically signifies Shiva's third eye. This sect is often marked by other symbols such as Shiva's *trishul* (trident), the crescent moon or triangular markings. These sect marks are painted with a paste made of either ash, red sanders wood, or *rudraksha drupe* (the fruit of *Elaeocarpus ganitrus*). *Shaktas* (Devi worshippers) usually wear a triangular mark or big red dot made with red turmeric or vermilion on their forehead.

Surya; half-baked terracotta clay with pigments, 1910-11, made at the erstwhile V&A Museum, Bombay; 47 x 20 x 36 cm.

THE collection of Indian deities at the Museum corresponds to engravings from two publications of the nineteenth century: *The Hindu Pantheon [Sri Sarva Deva Sabha]* (1810) by the East India Company's Major Edward Moor, and *The Industrial Arts of India* (1880) by George Birdwood (see pp. 56-57), former curator of the Museum. Both publications were present in the library and would have served as source material for the modeller, Shiv Prasad Balsing, who prepared the models under the direction of curator Cecil Burns. The deities include Shiva, Brahma, Vishnu, Ganapati, Kartikeya, Hanuman, Shiva–Parvati, Vishnu–Lakshmi, Parvati, Durga, Saraswati; the Vedic gods Indra, Soma, Surya, Agni, Yama and Kubera, and the Jain Tirthankara and Buddha.[1] Balsing also referenced popular prints of Ravi Varma and other artists to produce this unique group of models.

The Hindu Pantheon by Edward Moor was one of the first didactic books that described Hinduism to an English audience. Moor was fascinated by philosophies and iconographies of Hinduism and his book, which

consisted of 105 illustrated plates, was largely based on paintings and sculptures that he collected in Bombay as well as those that he borrowed from Company friends. Moor lived in Bombay for over ten years, where he was a member of the Literary Society of Bombay and was instrumental in the establishment of the paper *The Bombay Herald*. In 1864, the book was republished by Rev. W.O. Simpson, and was referenced by archaeologists, collectors, scholars and administrators for Hindu iconography, particularly in the context of Indian arts and crafts. The illustrations in the book were drawn by prominent British artists Matthew Haughton and Moses Haughton the younger.[2] The Edward Moor collection of nearly 600 sculptures and paintings of Indian deities was exhibited at the Indian Court of the Festival of Empire in 1911 and was later acquired by the British Museum in 1940.[3] Birdwood's *The Industrial Arts of India* provides a brief overview of several Hindu gods and their avatars, as well as the many ways in which they are venerated by different communities

(L to R): *Chandra* (Moon God), *Kubera* (God of Wealth), *Agni* (God of Fire), *Indra* (God of Heaven, Thunder and Rain), *Yama* (God of Death), *Kartikeya* (God of War) and *Surya* (Sun God); half-baked terracotta and pigments, 1910-11, made at the erstwhile V&A Museum, Bombay; 29 x 19.2 x 29 cm.

Surya and Chandra, Matthew Haughton and Moses Haughton the Younger; pl. 89, etching on wove paper, engraved by John Dadley. E. Moor, *The Hindu Pantheon (Sri Sarva Deva Sabha)*, London: Thomas Bensley for Joseph Johnson, 1810; 24.5 x 19 cm. © Royal Academy of Arts, London.

across the country. The book includes eighty-five sketches of gods and goddesses, some of which were reprinted from *The Hindu Pantheon.*

In the skilfully executed clay model of Surya (the sun god, opposite), as observed in Moor's *The Hindu Pantheon*, he is seated on a chariot, holding a spiral conch that symbolises infinite space which is ever expanding, and a wheel as a representation of the cycle of life and death and the daily rotation of the sun. His charioteer, Aruna, is depicted riding a seven-headed horse, an exemplification of bravery, grit and determination. Surya's body is adorned with ornaments. A halo of rays emanates from behind, covering cardinal directions and emblematic of the creation of life. Surya was worshipped by Hindus across the Bombay Presidency on different days, solar eclipses and important festivals such as Ratha Saptami, which falls in the month of January or February according to the Gregorian calendar.

The models are made in the European style while keeping in mind traditional Indian iconographies. The modeller, Balsing, was from Lucknow which was a major centre for clay modelling. In the late eighteenth century, the Nawab of Oudh, Asaf ud Daulah, had employed Italian sculptors under the guidance of celebrated savant Claude Martin, Major General of the East India Company, and Superintendent of the Nawab's arsenal, for the decoration of his palaces and gardens in Lucknow.[4] The admiration for this style had an impact on the production of clay models across the country. The process for creating these figurines in clay employed an Italian template that used a circular base and a metal armature inside, with details executed with the help of tooling and carving.[5] Stylistically, the Lucknow figures display an Italian-style fluidity in their dress which is also visible in the Museum's collection.[6] The figures were popular with European tourists and renowned both in India as well as internationally.[7] • HK

65 THE MAHRATTA REGIMENT

THE British control over the Indian subcontinent increased in the seventeenth century due to the political turmoil in different parts of the subcontinent with the decline of Mughal supremacy. To support its commercial activities and ensure territorial hegemony over lucrative lands, the Company started raising small military brigades. Soon, it entered into treaties and alliances with various Indian kingdoms to gain absolute control over the subcontinent. Renowned British historian Bruce Lenman states that 'the real key to the subsequent military success of the British East India Company … was the sheer size of the sepoy infantry force it raised.'[1] The Company and its British soldiers began interacting with Indian soldiers who were different in all aspects—of attire, weaponry and military tactics—from their British counterparts. Many British travelogues and journals are replete with colourful descriptions of the different types of Indian soldiers. In the seventeenth and eighteenth centuries, Indian soldiers used weapons such as swords, spears, lances and daggers, as opposed to European weapons such as muskets and sabres.

The British used caste and religion as a strategy for raising Indian regiments and units post 1857. They would recruit members of a specific caste, sect or tribe for a particular regiment. The British-Indian army was a collection of regiments, and each community provided a group of divisions. Using their military expertise, the British attempted to create a distinct identity for each unit. Every regiment was given its own home (depot) to foster distinctive customs. A system of hierarchy and differentiation was established through uniforms; each regiment had its distinct uniform, like the Governor's Bodyguard, Bombay (right), which depicts a colourful cavalry horseman in a red and white uniform, with a distinct *pagadi* (turban) and a moustache, who is carrying a flag. The regiment was formed in 1865 from part of the 1st South Mahratta Horse. Like its counterparts in the Governor of Madras's Bodyguard and the Governor General's Bodyguard, the Bombay force was an Indian equivalent of Britain's Household Cavalry.[2]

The clay models of Indian regiments were produced at the Museum in 1915-16, with the finest details visible, many of which resemble the illustrations in *Armies of India* by Major McMunn, published in 1911. One of the most extensively described and illustrated infantries in the book is the Mahrattas. Major McMunn states that the Mahrattas had a reputation for great wiriness and endurance. The 103rd, 105th, 110th, 114th and 116th infantries were Mahratta regiments, each enlisting six Mahratta companies and two companies of other classes.[3] Their uniform consisted of a red upper coat with blue pants, leather shoes and waistbands, both plain and

Governor's Bodyguard, Bombay; half-baked terracotta and pigments, 1915-16, made at the erstwhile V&A Museum, Bombay; 8 x 21.5 x 20.2 cm.

•

Opposite:
Indian Regiments; half-baked terracotta and pigments, c. 1915–20, made at the erstwhile V&A Museum, Bombay. On view in the Kamalnayan Bajaj Mumbai Gallery, Dr. Bhau Daji Lad Museum, Mumbai.

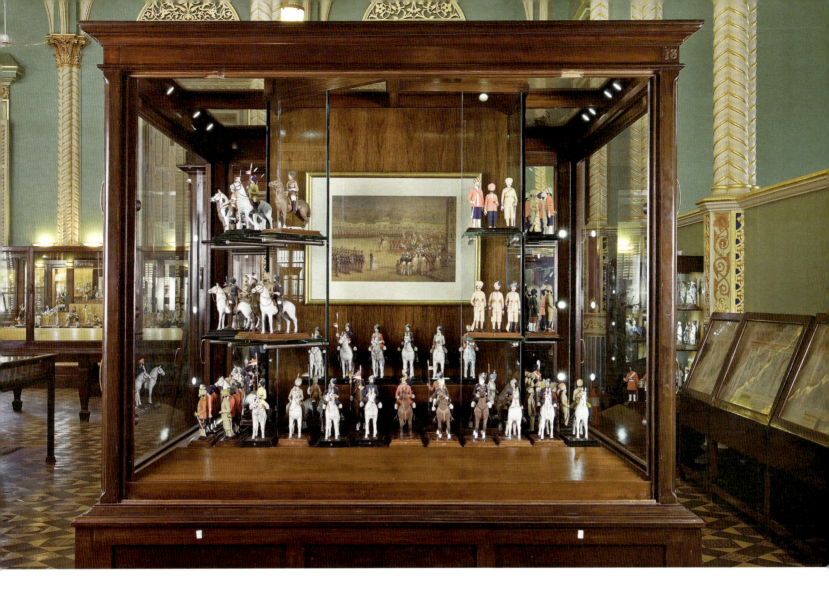

103rd Mahratta Light Infantry, 102nd King Edward's Own Infantry, 101st Grenadiers; half-baked terracotta and pigments, 1915-16, made at the erstwhile V&A Museum, Bombay; 22.9 x 12.5 x 28. 6 cm.

patterned. Additionally, the upper coat was detailed with laces and facing colours; a silver lace was added in 1812; a gold lace in 1832; blue facing in 1888 and black facing in 1885. The 1913 regulations added a typical light infantry button of bugle horn with '103' between the surmount and strings.

The regiment consisted primarily of recruits from the former Mahratta Empire, who were drawn from the present-day state of Maharashtra and from the Marathi-speaking areas of Andhra and Karnataka. In 1922, all the battalion regiments were amalgamated into the 5th Mahratta Light Infantry Regiment. These Mahratta Light Infantry Regiments fought in several engagements, including the Third Anglo-Mysore War (1790–92), Fourth Anglo-Mysore War (1798–99), Second Anglo-Sikh War (1848–49), the Expedition to Abyssinia (1868), the Second Afghan War (1878–80), World War I (1914–18) and World War II (1939–45). • HK

KELAT-I-GHILZIE

The Museum has an exclusive collection of war medals awarded to Indian soldiers by the colonial government during the nineteenth and twentieth centuries. The earliest medal in the collection belongs to the famous Battle of Seringapatam (1799), fought between the British East India Company and Tipu Sultan, the ruler of Mysore. Other important medals are associated with battles fought by the British army in Burma (1824–26), Canton (1842–60), Punjab (1848-49), Persia (1852–95), Waziristan (1894-95), Egypt (1887–89) and Tibet (1903-04).[1]

One of the most significant medals in the collection is the Kelat-i-Ghilzie, made in silver and issued to honour bravery during the First Anglo-Afghan War (1839–42). It was designed by renowned engraver William Wyon.[2] The design on the obverse is a laurel wreath with a mural crown at the top and a shield in the centre. The reverse has a trophy of arms on top of a plaque bearing the inscription 'INVICTA MDCCCXLII' (Undefeated, 1842). The medal is suspended by a pin and engraved with the name of the recipient on the edge when issued to British personnel but the indigenous troops were given medals without the honour of their names. The Afghan wars have a direct link with Bombay as the Bombay Sappers and Miners fought in them. The Afghan Church in Colaba was built between 1847 and 1865 as a memorial to commemorate the British-Indian regiments that fought in the two wars.[3]

For the courage displayed by the garrison in the First Anglo-Afghan War, which included the regiments of Shah Shuja's 3rd Infantry Battalion, three companies of the 43rd Bengal Native Infantry, forty European gunners, sixty Bombay Sappers and Miners, and eight British officials at Kelat-i-Ghilzie, located between Kabul and Kandahar, the East India Company, on October 4, 1842, authorised the medal to be awarded to all troops who participated in the protracted siege. • HK

Kelat-i-Ghilzie, 1842; silver, First Anglo-Afghan War (1839–42); 3.6 cm (diameter). Accessioned: 1903–11.

INDIGENOUS SOLDIERS

भाट सैनिक बंगाल

Bhaut (left), *Sepoy* (right); half-baked terracotta and pigments, 1921–22, made at the erstwhile V&A Museum, Bombay; 24.5 x 9.5 cm.

In 1921-22, clay models of indigenous soldiers depicting their mode of dress and arms were made at the Museum, copying the images in Edward Orme's *The Costume of Hindostan*, published in 1807, and F.B. Solvyns' *Les Hindoos*, published in 1808–12. Solvyns described several types of indigenous soldiers but singled out the Bhat or Bhaut as one of the 'tribes' whose profession was to flatter and puff up their seniors and spread reports commending those who employed them. The Bhauts played a significant role in the local militia for the chieftains as protectors of families and personal attendants during public events. They were in service to proclaim titles in elaborate and ostentatious language. The book *Oriental Memoirs* by James Forbes, published in 1813 (see pp. 108–10), states, 'Many of them have another mode of living; they offer themselves as security to the different governments for payment of their revenue, and the good behaviour of the *Zemindars* and public farmers; they also become guarantees for treaties between native princes, and the performance of bonds by individuals.'[1] The clay model of the Bhaut is dressed in the typical 'Hindoo' domestic dress; the handle of his dagger is visible in his cummerbund or waistband.

Solvyns describes sepoys as native soldiers who wore their original country attire and notes that the word is of Persian origin, derived from the word *sepahi*, meaning 'infantry soldier', and it was anglicised to 'sepoy' by the British. Sepoys were mostly employed by the native princes as they were sturdy and courageous. The clay model of a Bengal sepoy is based on Solvyns' engraving. He is holding a musket in his right hand, wearing a *pagadi* (turban), a *lungi* (loincloth) and waistband. There were regional variations in the uniform of the sepoys, modified by the *mansabdar* (military commander) who recruited them. Their fighting tactics included crowding and with European influence, they started forming battalions. Sepoy divisions were started by the East India Company in Bombay and subsequently in Madras and then in the Bengal Presidency in 1757.[2] After the Uprising of 1857, which was sepoy-led, the British amended their Indian army recruitment procedures and based the divisions on ethnicity and religion to keep communities separate and to encourage loyalty through competition. • HK

Traditional Indian Games; showcasing *Wagh Bakri* (game of tiger-goat), *Fugdi* (dancing in circular formation), *Patang* (kite flying) and *Atya Patya* (game of feints), half-baked terracotta and pigments, 1922–25, made at the erstwhile V&A Museum, Bombay; 242.6 x 117 x 52.6 cm.

INDIA has a rich tradition of games and sports, many of which are rooted in broader religious and ritual contexts and are played not just for recreation but also for improving mental and physical health. Games such as Ludo and Snakes and Ladders, which are played across the world, originated in India.[1] These games were adopted by the British and reintroduced in their modern versions.

Colonial administrators considered Indians to be physically weak.[2] It was believed that the implementation of physical education in the country would help to develop discipline and a good 'moral character' towards the Empire, among the subjects.[3] The Indian Education Commission, or the Hunter Commission, was set up in 1882 to investigate the existing state of elementary education and to recommend the measures required to improve it. The commission was appointed by Lord Ripon, then Viceroy of India, and supervised by

Sir William Hunter.[4] In several primary and secondary schools especially in Bombay, Western sports such as cricket, tennis, football, etc. were introduced to inculcate discipline, loyalty, obedience and Western attitudes. Indian sports such as *viti-dandu* (tip-cat), *kho-kho* (tag game), *atya patya* (game of feints) were also adopted as part of the curriculum. Since most of these sports required players to simply follow the captain's commands, it was assumed that the implementation of organised team sports would help to inculcate civic sense and self-control.

The outbreak of plague and diseases such as cholera and smallpox in Bombay strengthened the British resolve to expand physical education and fitness programmes in villages and towns in the early twentieth century.[5] Several schools for girls were also established, with physical education integrated as part of the curriculum. Numerous sports grounds, clubs, *vyayamshalas* (gymnasiums), *akhadas* (sports arenas), etc.

Songtya (Indian Backgammon); half-baked terracotta and pigments, 1922-1925, made at the erstwhile V&A Museum, Bombay; 20.2 x 17.5 x 9 cm.

Chor Sepoy (chase game); half-baked terracotta and pigments, 1922–25, made at the erstwhile V&A Museum, Bombay; 20.2 x 20.2 x 11 cm.

Ganjifa (card game); half-baked terracotta and pigments, 1922–25, made at the erstwhile V&A Museum, Bombay; 20.2 x 17.5 x 9 cm.

also opened in many regions over the years, adding to the popularity of Western and Indian sports and games. These clubs not only served recreational purposes but also became important places to interact and socialise outside home and work.

Outdoor games were introduced to boys from a young age to develop strength and stamina. However, physical activities for girls were limited to playing indoor games, dancing and romping exercises, etc.[6] Since women were primarily involved in household work, developing strength through games was not considered relevant. On specific occasions and festivals, women were part of various intense physical activities and games involving dancing and singing, as part of rituals.[7] The celebration of Mangala Gaur is particularly significant, as numerous games and folk dances are held to celebrate a newly married woman. Games such as *fugdi* (dancing in circular formation),

kombda (imitating rooster's gait), etc. are played during the celebration. In several areas of Maharashtra, Mangala Gaur is still observed on Tuesdays in the month of Shravan which falls in July–August according to the Gregorian calendar. Board games such as *songtya* (Indian backgammon), *buddhibal* (chess) and *ganjifa* card games (see pp. 176-77) were popular among both men and women. These board games enhanced strategic thinking and were an integral part of court cultures throughout India. References to many of these games are found in Indian mythologies, sculptures and court paintings.

Indian games were a popular leisure activity in villages and were studied to understand the routines of daily life and the social structure of village communities. Traditional Indian games gradually declined in the towns and cities due to the introduction of Western games like cricket, with only a few played at festivals such as Diwali and Holi today. • RJ

HUNTING was a favourite pastime of the nobility in India and of British officials, who often accompanied their Indian acquaintances on such expeditions. The Museum's diorama depicting the Emperor Jahangir (r. 1605–27) on *shikar* (hunt) is an elaborate tableaux of forty courtly figures, who are in various poses of royal attendance, modelled in clay. Jahangir is seated on an elephant, guided by a *mahout* (elephant rider), and his accompanying huntsmen, carrying swords and shields, are on horseback and foot. The scene is set in a dense field of trees and shrubs near a water body. The entourage surrounds a wounded lioness, documenting the details of a *shikar* orchestrated for the Mughal Emperor Jahangir. The diorama is a faithful representation of a seventeenth-century miniature painting in the collection of the Indian Museum in Kolkata (see opposite page). The folio belonged to a manuscript album, now dispersed. In Jahangir's ateliers, artists were ordered to paint events as they occurred, building a visual documentary, later compiled into albums. The painting recounts the event when Jahangir showcased his hunting skills to Rana Karan Singh (r. 1620–28), the eldest son and heir of Maharana Amar Singh, ruler of Mewar.

The Museum records reveal the diorama was made in 1927-28 by Sivaprasad Balsing, under the curatorship of Ernest Fern (1918–30). A few years later, the showcase containing the diorama was rearranged and repainted. The display was paired with installations of 'Durbar and Court scene' reproductions, prepared at the Museum. Dioramas themed around classical Indian history were introduced into the Museum's collection, following their mass appeal. Hunt stories, coupled with the Mughal ideals of scientific inquiry and royal privileges, made valuable exhibits.[1]

Emperor Jahangir Showing his Lion Hunting Skill to Rana Karan; gouache on paper, seventeenth century, Mughal School; 47.1 x 31.6 cm. Image courtesy: Indian Museum, Kolkata.

•

Opposite:
Emperor Jahangir on Shikar; half-baked terracotta models, mixed media, 1927-28, made at the erstwhile V&A Museum, Bombay; 275 x 183 x 63 cm, avg height of figures: 22–24 cm.

In March of 1615, Maharana Amar Singh succumbed to the attacks of Prince Khurram (later Emperor Shah Jahan) and pledged his allegiance to the imperial court of Jahangir; the court was earlier at Agra and had moved to Ajmer in 1613. The chain of events that followed led the Maharana to send his son Prince Karan Singh as his envoy to Ajmer, in the company of Prince Khurram. The Emperor was a generous host and showered the Rajput prince with lavish gifts, including jewel-encrusted swords and daggers, an expensive robe of honour, royal falcons, horses and elephants.[2] Jahangir's generosity underlines a political strategy to strengthen newly formed alliances in return for loyalty. It also displayed Mughal wealth and etiquette to his new allies who were dazzled by the rich courtly lifestyles. Before Karan Singh was to depart from Ajmer, a royal hunt was arranged. Jahangir narrates the episode in his memoir, *Jahangirnama* (1605–24). When he heard that a lioness had been spotted in the nearby hunting grounds, Jahangir, accompanied by his huntsmen and Karan Singh, set out. He explains how gusty winds and his frightened elephant made it challenging for him to aim and shoot. Against all odds, he fired a bullet straight between the lioness' eyes and succeeded in his attempt to impress Karan Singh, depicted on elephant back to the left, with a hand raised over his head in amazement.[3]

In the diorama, Jahangir wears a turban adorned with feathers and is seated atop an elephant, replicating the image of the Emperor in the painting. Other details that copy the painting are the Mughal-style attire of a turban, robe and girdle; Jahangir's *toradar* (matchlock); and the *mahout*'s *ankush* (elephant goad). The matchlock was Jahangir's preferred hunting weapon. He was as passionate a hunter as he was a naturalist. His memoirs elaborate on his hunting escapades from his favoured hunting grounds to the number of animals captured live or killed by a bullet. Mountain sheep and goats, wild asses, nilgai, antelopes were common prey for Mughal Emperors. Hunts of big game such as lions and tigers were deemed heroic and a royal privilege. All kills were accurately described and recorded in royal registers to commemorate the Emperor's skill and bravery. Jahangir was particularly conscious of his kills' size and weight, the largest of which were at times painted by the artists in his ateliers.[4]

Game captures were a result of a combination of tactics. One was a 'ring hunt', *qamargha*, which involved the hunting group closing in on the prey in a shrinking circle, as seen in the diorama. The Mughals also made use of decoy animals, such as antelopes. These were used to attract bigger game. Some victories were carefully planned manoeuvres. Emperors devoted many days, at times months, on their hunting expeditions. They travelled with their princes, the harem of ladies, and attendants to exclusive game reserves selected by their court advisers. Exclusive locales provided privacy to scrutinise political matters, away from the prying eyes at court. Hunting was an elite Mughal sport that involved skill and strategy and was often a declaration of prowess. • IH

DIORAMAS that presented improved farming systems and technological innovations in agriculture were made at the Museum between 1907 and 1930 to educate the masses in new methods of sowing, improved tools and implements, various types of water lifts and crop production techniques to optimise the output of agricultural land. It was under the guidance of Cecil Burns in 1904 that several display cases were prepared containing a range of new agricultural implements.[1] The specimens included ploughs, levellers, clod-crushers, harrows, soil stirrers, bullock hoes, seed drills and hand implements such as spades, sickles, axes, bill-hooks, winnowing sieves and scoops, as well as models of different kinds of water lifts, such as the Persian wheel, the scoop lift, the *mohote* and the lever lift, which were prepared in clay and their use displayed for public knowledge.

Burns' successor, Ernest Fern, had maps and charts prepared that showed the geological condition of the soil in India, the seasonal and the annual rainfall, and the extent of cultivation of the principal food grains, oil seeds and cotton.[2] There were also maps showing steamer routes, marketplaces where cattle were available, tracks for bullock carts, high and low ground, and land suitable for gardening or for growing fruit and cotton. One of the early displays had specimens of soils from various districts in the Bombay Presidency and samples of fertilisers and manure.

Fern also ensured that the agriculture diorama cases were illustrated pictorially to provide a context for the displays. The models were made to scale to demonstrate the advantages resulting from terrace farming, fencing fields, introducing ridge plantation, raising embankments around open wells, and opening out narrow roads. These exhibits, besides bringing a new dimension to the collection, demonstrated the advantages of modern-day implements over older ones in saving time, labour and costs.

Realising the potential of land was imperative for the British Government. In order to acclimatise exotic crops for

Top:
Agricultural Improvements under the Taluka Development Association; half-baked terracotta, mixed media, pigments, 1931-32, made at the erstwhile V&A Museum, Bombay; 50 x 240 x 107 cm, avg. height of figures: 20–22 cm.

•

Above:
Paddy Cultivation (detail); half-baked terracotta, mixed media, pigments, 1955-56, made at the erstwhile V&A Museum, Bombay; 65 x 102 x 218 cm, avg. height of figures: 20–22 cm.

•

Opposite:
Agricultural Implements; diorama, half-baked terracotta, wood, mixed media and pigments, 1914-40, made at the erstwhile V&A Museum, Bombay; 218 x 102 x 65 cm.

production in India and to maximise commercial benefits, the Royal Botanic Gardens (1787) and the Botanical Survey of India (1890) were established to guide these efforts.[3] A survey report of 1893 on the 'Improvement of Indian Agriculture' was commissioned by the British Government under the direction of Dr John Augustus Voelcker, Consulting Chemist to the Royal Agricultural Society of England, to investigate and guide the improvement of Indian agriculture by scientific means.[4] Efforts were made to develop commercial crops such as sugarcane and to introduce new crops such as tea in India. This led to the establishment of the Central Department of Revenue Agriculture and Commerce in 1871, which was followed by various regional departments in the 1880s to guide policies for agricultural improvements.[5]

Several famines occurred in India during the nineteenth and twentieth centuries, which had a hugely adverse impact on agriculture and daily life.[6] Dependency on the monsoon often meant lengthy droughts and combined with British policy failures, the impact on agriculture was disastrous. Lord Curzon, who was Viceroy of India during the severe famines of 1899–1900, ordered the administration to concentrate on problems in the agricultural sector to overcome the damages caused by regular famines. As a result, the Agriculture Research Institute (now the Indian Agricultural Research Institute or IARI) was established in 1905.

The agricultural sector was an overwhelming factor of the Indian economy in the nineteenth and early twentieth centuries, providing over 68 per cent of the labour force.[7] The intrinsic approach of the British was to regulate Indian agricultural policies to the benefit of Britain. For the British, the Indian agrarian economy was a source of raw products for their businesses, which led to the steady decline of farmers' incomes. Peasant movements against the British erupted due to high taxes and colonial economic policies that resulted in the destruction of underestimated traditional methods of agriculture as well as other livelihoods such as handicrafts. • HK

THE British Government employed various methods of publicising new schemes and initiatives. Village guides, magic lanterns and, later, films, dramas, songs, gramophone records, press, coloured pictures and posters mounted in public places, leaflets, handbills, public meetings and lessons in schools were some of the efforts to reach the largest number of people.[1] Another powerful method was the use of miniature dioramas and exhibitions at *melas* (local fairs).

In the nineteenth century, the colonial administration focused on two major concerns regarding the spread of disease. The first was that disease was transferred through physical contact and the other that disease could spread through the environment by water and air. High rates of mortality due to waterborne diseases were a major concern during the nineteenth century. Renowned social reformer

Florence Nightingale focused on sanitary conditions after the 1857 Uprising. She suggested the creation of a Department of Health in every Presidency and stated rhetorically, that 'what was wanted was to drain India, to water supply India, to cleanse India, by something more than surface cleansing.'[2] She was active in the debates to set up a Royal Commission to address the health conditions in India as a quarter of the British army was stationed there and mortality rates were very high. In 1874, she wrote a pamphlet, *Life or Death in India*, which reported the progress of sanitary measures, and called for the British Government to continue providing aid to local government leaders in bringing public health initiatives to their areas (see pp. 86-87).[3]

The diorama showcasing improved water sanitation depicts a 'before and after' scenario of the well-water

system. The diorama was accessioned in 1935 but appears to have been made earlier. Between 1892 and 1940, over ten million people died of the plague and over 15 million died of cholera, which prompted the British administration to undertake various initiatives to increase hygiene and sanitation awareness. The Museum diorama is an example of such efforts.[4]

The left side of the diorama illustrates how poor health conditions arise from the unhygienic use of well water. The right side shows how clean water can be obtained through the proper design of wells and the use of an advanced pulley system for bringing up clean water. Two different types of wells are depicted, the old and the new. The old shows the ancient step-well system, near which people are washing their clothes and even bathing. The proximity of the people and their actions in the diorama appear to be an exaggeration to enforce a point. In most villages and towns in India, activities such as bathing, washing clothes and utensils were done in flowing water to avoid contamination.

On the right, in front of a smart new house, a woman with her hand on her head is bemoaning the ignorance of the villager who is bathing by the well. It is an interesting juxtaposition of the educated woman and the rustic villager. By using a familiar gesture and an affluent, educated woman, the message is reinforced. At the new well, the washerwoman's platform and the well wall prevent contamination and the waste water is recycled for a vegetable garden. The old traditional well used buckets or a *charsa* which needed four bullocks and four men to operate, which was time consuming. The new well has a Persian wheel, with galvanised iron buckets, and requires only two bulls.

The diorama also shows a roof over the well to keep out leaves and bird droppings, a properly built platform, a masonry drain around the well to collect waste water, and a common bucket so people will not use their own vessels every time to take out water. It closely resembles the descriptions in the book by F.L. Brayne, advisor of Indian Affairs to the Director General Welfare, Government of India, published in 1937.[5] • HK

Village Water Sanitation Improvement;
wood, half-baked terracotta, mixed media and pigments, 1935, made at the erstwhile V&A Museum, Bombay; 56 x 219 x 106 cm, avg. height of figures: 22–24 cm.

AN IDEAL INDIAN VILLAGE

The outbreak of plague in India in 1896, coupled with the presence of other contagious diseases, led to the establishment of Government departments dedicated to improving sanitation and housing in urban centres and villages. Through the Town Planning Act of 1915, regulated planning schemes were first adopted in Bombay and eventually in other Indian cities. Better housing conditions in both cities and villages were recommended as essential for the 'moral' upliftment of the underprivileged classes. The Town Planning and Valuation Department also published a *Pamphlet on the Principles of Housing, Planning, etc. as applied to Villages* in 1935 as the villages were also slowly transforming into towns.[1] The diorama of an *Ideal Indian Village* (see below) was based on a *Plan of a Model Village* obtained by the Museum curator in 1940 from the Director of Rural Development, Bombay Province.

The pamphlet acknowledged that the villages in the Bombay Presidency remained unsurveyed and the Government recommended several improvement measures. Wide roads and village thoroughfares that turn at angles to allow easy access to public spaces were proposed to reduce traffic congestion. The village is provided with a local village office, a school, a temple, and a playground for children at its centre from where the roads radiate outward to residential and commercial *bazaar* (market) areas. An open *kaccha* (dirt) roadside

is meant to contain the drainage system. The pamphlet suggests that either brick or mud houses be built in the residential areas as per the occupants' economic status but they should be raised on a plinth to avoid vermin infestation. 'Ideal' villages were characterised by houses of brick with tiled roofs, as seen in this diorama, arranged in concentric circles and at a distance from each other to allow ventilation and sunlight through the windows and to curb the spread of contagious diseases. Verandas and latrines are provided in larger homes and public toilets built on the fringes of the residential quarters for those who could not afford larger houses. A *mori* (washing area) and flue are shown in every kitchen to ensure hygienic cooking practices. Separate stables are suggested for cattle at a distance from the house. Public amenities like manure pits, tanks, wells, a post office and a threshing floor are also mapped out.

The diorama was meant as a visual aid and educational tool for the visitors to the Museum about the reforms introduced in the villages.[2] Between 1943 and 1957, various dignitaries from Multan, Calcutta and the Department of Broadcasting and Information who visited the Museum were impressed by the diorama and requested the plan. The 'ideal' layout of this diorama, while seemingly democratic and socialist, belies the nuanced socio-economic realities of individual village communities. • RWB

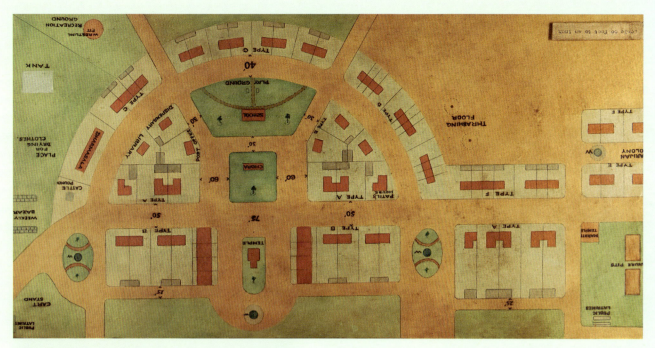

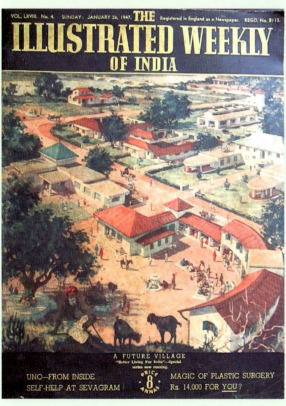

Above:
Plan of the Model Village; reproduced by
B.C. Mehta, ink on paper, 1944; 28.6 x 55 cm.
Accessioned: 1940.

•

Left:
A Future Village – Better Living for India
series, *The Illustrated Weekly of India, Vol. 36*,
India: Times Group, January 26, 1947.
Source: Public Domain.

•

Opposite:
An Ideal Indian Village; wood, half-baked
terracotta, mixed media, pigments, 1943–44,
made at the erstwhile V&A Museum, Bombay;
22 x 218 x 104 cm.

Avatars of Vishnu; half-baked terracotta, pigments,
1910, made at the erstwhile V&A Museum, Bombay;
30 x 33.5 x 23 cm.
On view at the Kamalnayan Bajaj Mumbai Gallery,
Dr. Bhau Daji Lad Museum.

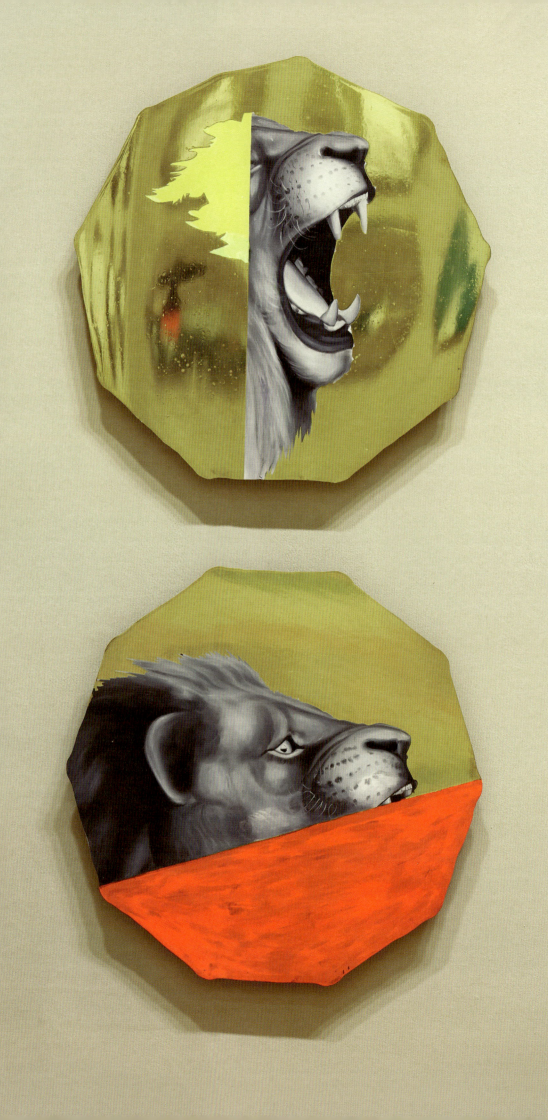

RAJA RAVI VARMA
The Influence of a Master

RAJA Ravi Varma, the extraordinary artist from the royal family of the erstwhile state of Travancore in south India, had an enormous impact on Indian visual culture in the late nineteenth and early twentieth centuries.[1] Much has been written about his paintings and his glamorous life at the courts of the various maharajas who were his patrons.[2] But his profound impact on craftsmanship and objects has received less attention.[3] Varma was a self-taught artist who successfully adapted the European Salon painting style for an Indian audience. Presenting mythological and religious themes, he created the Indian equivalent of the grand history paintings that were considered the acme of European 'fine art'. He rescued Indian painting from European prejudice as it had been derided for lacking empathy and refinement.[4] Varma's protagonists evoked a sense of tactility and immediacy that had not been observed in Indian painting earlier. By humanising his characters, who traditionally were idealised beyond reach, especially his women, he engaged his viewer in the denouement he captured in his paintings. His deep scholarship and knowledge of ancient Indian texts and his acute sense of observation enabled him to create paintings that strongly resonated with Indians of all classes. European governors, maharajas and the educated Indian elite pursued him relentlessly with commissions.[5]

The artist and his younger brother, Raja Raja Varma, who worked closely with him and was an accomplished artist himself, were captivated by late nineteenth-century Bombay. The city, with its rich intellectual life, theatre and music (which the Varmas were particularly fond of), its many shops and other forms of entertainment (like parades along the Esplanade), excited the brothers and they made repeated visits, staying for long periods, so much so that it was almost a second home for them.[6] Ravi Varma knew about European museums through catalogues and spoke wistfully about their importance.[7] He would work to create the first gallery dedicated to a single artist's works in Travancore, though this only fructified after his death in 1935.[8] In a letter written to persuade the Dewan of Travancore to support the establishment of a museum to showcase his works, he says that it would be 'a repository of historical information, a learning ground for local artists and equally a symbol of a progressive state'.[9] Though there is no record of Ravi Varma visiting the erstwhile Victoria and Albert Museum, Bombay, one can surmise that he did so as his brother, Raja Raja Varma, notes in his diary that they stayed at a house very close to the Museum on Clare Road in Byculla on one occasion, and on another that they were going to visit the Victoria Gardens, where the Museum is located, to hear the governor's band play in the evening.[10]

Raja Raja Varma does however record that the brothers visited the School of Art as part of the Maharaja of Travancore's entourage on January 5, 1895. Ravi Varma was unimpressed with the students' work. His brother notes, 'There is nothing to stimulate them to exertion and fire their imagination. What they want is national art

Walk of Life—Dashavatar, Thukral and Tagra; 120 paintings on brass with lacquer, 2015; 61 x 61 cm. Exhibition: *Games People Play*; Kamalnayan Bajaj Special Exhibitions Gallery, 2015. Conceptualised as a board game, the artwork is inspired by the original sets of *Ganjifa* cards in the Museum's collection. Imaginatively elaborating each of the ten avatars of Vishnu into ten sets of twelve paintings, each defined by abstract symbologies, a total of 120 paintings on shaped brass plaques interpret the myths of the Dashavatar as the evolution of life.

galleries in the Presidency towns with good collections of works of acknowledged merit, representing different schools, ancient and modern ...'[11] Later, Ravi Varma's son and nephew would study at the School and go on to establish their own School of Art in Mavellikera near Trivandrum, that would reproduce the Ravi Varma style.[12]

Bombay was the city in which Ravi Varma chose to stage his accomplishments as a painter of repute. He was one of the very few Indian artists who had achieved international accolades, and the only one to be awarded the Kaiser-e-Hind by the British. He held several exhibitions at the Bombay Art Society and won several medals. His paintings were praised in the newspapers and he was a regular at the Bombay soirees. In 1891, he showed fourteen large paintings at the Bombay Art Society. These had been commissioned by the Gaekwad of Baroda for his palace and were inspired by myths and legends from the *Puranas* (ancient Indian texts) to arouse in Indian audiences a sense of their own traditions and history. The exhibition caused a sensation and was visited by thousands over a two-month period from December 1891 to January 1892.[13] In 1893, Ravi Varma was invited to present his work at the Chicago International Columbian Exposition, one of the most famous and well attended exhibitions in America. Sayajirao Gaekwad of Baroda supported the commission of ten paintings, which were briefly displayed at Thacker and Co. in the city.[14] They presented the private lives of women from different social strata and from various communities, reflecting India's great diversity. The commission won many awards at the exposition.[15]

In 1894, invigorated by the adulatory response the exhibitions had received, and imbued with nationalistic fervour, Varma established the Ravi Varma Fine Art Lithographic Press to produce high-quality oleographs of his paintings. This initiative would enable him to reach a mass audience and make him a household name across the country. Varma was friends with several nationalists in Bombay, including Dadabhai Naoroji, the president of the Congress Party, and Bal Gangadhar Tilak. In fact, the Ravi Varma Press printed images of nationalist leaders like Tilak and others for mass circulation as part of the Swadeshi movement, which was a call for Indian independence.

The press was a fraught business venture that required Varma to spend many months in Bombay. In the early days, the artistic process was managed by M.V. Dhurandhar (see pp. 254, 322-23) and M.A. Joshi.[16] The plague that engulfed Bombay from 1896 to 1905 had a devastating impact on the business and Varma moved the press to Malavli, a hill station near the city. Eventually, after many tribulations, Varma sold the press to his assistant, Fritz Schleicher, in 1903. The impact of almost a decade of the press, however, was far-reaching, and Varma's images defined a new consciousness of Indian identity and culture that heightened nationalist Hindu sentiments. By 1911, the Pune Chitrashala Press had partnered with the Ravi Varma Press and continued to produce prints and oleographs of Ravi Varma's paintings for many years.[17] Varma's pre-eminence would be challenged soon after his death by a younger generation of nationalist artists and critics, especially E.B. Havell, Sister Nivedita and Ananda Coomaraswamy, who reviled Varma's submission to European aesthetic principles and decried the sensuality of his works.[18] Rabindranath Tagore, India's Nobel laureate poet, admitted that he found Ravi Varma's paintings compelling. However, his nephew, Abanindranath Tagore, who was a student of E.B. Havell, would create works that especially challenged Ravi Varma's aesthetics.[19]

Undoubtedly, however, Varma's realism and voluptuous figures entered the visual lexicon of everyday objects created for elite consumption and tourism. They became a powerful visual reference as they were used in advertisements and on mill and matchbox labels.[20] The impact of Varma's influence on the decorative arts is apparent in the work of Oomersee Mawjee, the reputed silver merchant from Kutch, who sold his wares across the country. His workshop included drawings that were used as reference for the decorative embellishments on the silver objects, including

Swami work from Madras and Poona silverware that were taken directly from Ravi Varma's oleographs (see p. 170).[21] Similar references are visible in the Museum's collection of wood and ivory carving. Ateliers often had the same craftsmen working on different materials at the same time. However, the greatest impact of the artist on the Museum's collection is visible in the models and dioramas of Indian deities and mythological scenes that clearly used Varma's works as a visual aid. The Museum purchased fourteen photographs of Ravi Varma's paintings to put up in the case alongside the deities, and recorded that they 'added considerably to the attractiveness of the case'.[22]

Ravi Varma stands at a moment of artistic transition in the country and was among the earliest 'modern' Indian artists.[23] He crafted a visual language that permeated artistic mediums and impacted not only painting but also craft traditions across the nation. His influence on Indian cinema, especially on notions of Indian femininity, was profound.[24] The craze for European-style Indian paintings among the country's elite would produce a reaction from the Bengali artistic intelligentsia who rejected mythological paintings for a local and secular narrative as the nationalist movement progressed. Ravi Varma, however, was the first Indian artist to achieve the fame and notoriety that European Renaissance artists had done earlier, strengthening the impetus for individual artistic achievement and recognition in India. • TZM

AMONG the collection of Indian deities at the Museum, the most compelling is a group representing Vishnu's *Dashavatar* (the ten incarnations of Vishnu), which was made at the Museum in 1910-11. Each region of India has its own variant and interpretation of the myths associated with the *Dashavatar*. However, no list can be presented as standard; the most well-known is that from the *Puranas*.[1] The ten widely accepted avatars are Matsya (the fish), Kurma (the tortoise), Varaha (the boar), Narasimha (the man-lion), Vamana (the dwarf), Parashurama, Rama, Krishna, Vithoba (in Maharashtra) and Kalki (the future avatar).

The concept of an avatar is based on the notion that when evil rises on earth over a period of time, the ultimate power will incarnate and manifest to triumph over evil. An avatar can be interpreted as the diffusion of spiritual ideas for the upliftment of the soul and to liberate the good from the cycle of birth and death; or it could be a warning to bring about change in the life of the people. The *Bhagavad Gita* states in chapter 4.7–8. 'Whenever dharma declines and adharma flourishes, then I create myself ... for protecting good people and destroying evil, for establishing dharma, I come into being in age after age.'[2]

The fourth avatar of Vishnu, Narasimha, who is half-man and half-lion, is one of the most frequently represented images of the *Dashavatar*. In the legend, the demon king Hiranyakashipu was in a never-ending war with Vishnu, one of the supreme deities of the Hindu pantheon. Hiranyakashipu wanted to avenge the death of his brother, Hiranyaksa, which was caused by Varaha, a previous avatar of Vishnu. Hiranyakashipu undertook austere penance to please the god Brahma, who granted him a boon—he could not be killed on earth or in space; by fire or water; during day or at night; neither inside or outside; by human or animal—making him immortal. Hiranyakashipu's son, Prahlad, was a great devotee of Vishnu and this angered his father who asked him that if Vishnu was all-pervasive, could he be found in the pillar in front of him. At that moment the pillar split and Narasimha emerged from it and killed Hiranyakashipu. He came out at twilight (neither day nor night), and on the threshold of the palace (neither inside nor outside), put the demon king on his lap (neither earth nor in space) and killed him, thus making the boon futile.

The Narasimha clay model is based on an 1899 painting by Raja Ravi Varma. Like the painting, the model depicts the moment of denouement as the four-armed Narasimha plunges two hands into Hiranyakashipu's belly and rips out his organs. The terror of the avenging moment and Narasimha's immense anger is a symbol of deterrence against wrongdoing. The expressive ferocity, iconographic representation, blood spillage, seated position, clothing and crowns of Hiranyakashipu and Narasimha bear a resemblance to the painting. The painting also portrays Prahlad and Lakshmi pleading with Narasimha to calm down. The Chitrashala Press established in Pune in 1878 had earlier produced prints of Narasimha which Ravi Varma likely referred. The Museum's model appears to reference both images as well. Several of the other *Dashavatar* clay models in the Museum's collection like Parashurama, Rama and Krishna also share a resemblance with the oleographs of Raja Ravi Varma.

The legends of the Dashavatar have been performed through dance and theatre for centuries in villages across the south Konkan regions which were part of the erstwhile Bombay Presidency. This Marathi folk ballet was known as Dashavatar or *bohada*. The plays, which are still performed today, are several hours long and are often enacted by seasonal farmers and labourers from October to March. Traditionally, it was only men who participated as the plays were shown in temples. In the nineteenth century, as people from the Konkan region started migrating to Bombay to work in the mills, they carried the folk art with them, and the art form soon became popular in the city. • HK

Narasimha, Raja Ravi Varma; oil on canvas, 1899; 30.5 x 20.3 cm. Image courtesy: Rupika Chawla.
•
Opposite:
Narasimha; half-baked terracotta and pigments, 1910, made at the erstwhile V&A Museum, Bombay; 26 x 19 x 16 cm.

DATTATREYA

With an increase in ethnographic documentation, religious idols were collected, classified and displayed at museums and colonial exhibitions as artefacts in the nineteenth and early twentieth centuries. Dattatreya is considered an embodiment of the three Hindu deities—Brahma, Vishnu and Shiva—and was worshipped in the Bombay Presidency. The earliest references to him can be traced back to the *Puranas*, the *Ramayana* and the *Mahabharata*.

Dattatreya or Sri Datta first emerged as a teacher of yoga with tantric traits and was portrayed with one head. Over time, the iconography of the deity altered, and the three-headed portrayal of Dattatreya emerged after the mid-sixteenth century as a representation of the composite form of the Trinity.[1] Over the years, Dattatreya has been revered as an immortal guru, yogi and avatar of the Trinity in Gujarat, Maharashtra and Karnataka.

Dattatreya is commonly depicted dressed as an ascetic, signifying his detachment from worldly pleasures. He is portrayed holding elements associated with the Trinity, such as a *gada* (mace) indicating pride, *kamandalu* (water pot) symbolising the cosmic energy through which the universe is created, a lotus stem signifying purity, and a *shankha* (conch) denoting the sound of creation. In the most popular representations, he is shown with a *trishul* (trident), a symbol associated with Shiva. The cow behind the deity is a metaphor for Mother Earth who provides nourishment. A significant aspect of the iconography is the four dogs in different colours representing the four Vedas—*Rigveda, Yajurveda, Atharvaveda* and *Samveda*. The Vedas are a collection of religious texts containing hymns, poems, prayers and mythological accounts that form the basis of Hinduism.

The imagery of the clay model in the Museum's collection shares a strong resemblance to Raja Ravi Varma's oleograph of Dattatreya. Ravi Varma's inspiration for the print was probably the Dattatreya temple which was located near his residence in Girgaum, Bombay. Raja Raja Varma's diary also cites a record of his visit to the Elephanta caves, where there is a sixth-century depiction of the Trinity, another possible source for his imagery.[2] An illustration similar to the painting was published in the book *Hindu Holidays and Ceremonials* in 1919 by B.A. Gupte, assistant curator at the Museum from 1874 to 1882.[3] • RJ

Dattatreya; plaster of Paris and pigments, c. 1919–22, Bombay; 30.5 x 37 x 19 cm. Accessioned: mid-twentieth century.

Dattatreya; independent oleograph, c. 1910, Karla, Lonavala: Ravi Varma Press; 35 x 50 cm. Image courtesy: Wellcome Collection. Attribution 4.0 International (CC BY 4.0).

Embassy of Shri Krishna; half-baked terracotta models, 1909-10, made at the erstwhile V&A Museum, Bombay; 81 x 193 x 81 cm.

THE diorama, based on the imagery of Raja Ravi Varma's painting *Krishna Shisthai* (Sri Krishna as Envoy) depicts one of the most crucial moments of the epic *Mahabharata* which concludes in the great Kurukshetra war between the two clans, the Pandavas and Kauravas.[1] Yudhistira, the eldest of the Pandavas, requests Krishna (an avatar of Vishnu) to act as an envoy between the warring clans to negotiate peace and prevent the devastation of war. However, when he enters the court of Dhritarashtra, the father of the Kauravas, Krishna is treated with contempt. The Kauravas further attempt to take him captive by trying to bind him in ropes. This infuriates Satyaki, Krishna's devotee, who draws his sword to defend Krishna. Krishna puts out his hand to hold back Satyaki and eventually reveals his *Vishwaroopam* or Supreme form to everyone (see pp. 296-97). The painting depicts this particular dramatic scene between the Kauravas and the furious Satyaki, while Krishna is seated, bemused and calm. This episode represents the last attempt at peace by the Pandavas before war was declared.

Ravi Varma painted mythological characters and deities dressed as princes, typically against the backdrop of a palace. The iconic compositions of his mythological paintings were often referenced from the English, Parsi and Marathi proscenium theatres, which he attended with his brother during their time in Bombay.[2] The expansive gestures of the characters, the curtain, and the classic pillars depicted against an opulent background reflect parallels to a staged theatrical scene. The painting, also known as 'Krishna's Embassy to Duryodhana', was commissioned by the Maharaja of Mysore, Krishnaraja Wadiyar IV, along with eight other *Puranic* paintings to be exhibited at the Durbar Hall in the Jaganmohan Palace, Mysore. Ravi Varma labelled *Puranic* paintings as those that depicted literature's dramatic and pivotal incidents that invoke a sequence of events.

The exquisite brocade that adorns Krishna's shoulder in the painting is a replica of the brocade gifted to Ravi Varma by the Maharaja of Mysore. It is represented by a pink fabric in the diorama. In order to create a familiar visual image, Ravi Varma synthesised elements of court attire and elaborate jewellery from different regions. Krishna is portrayed in his peacock plume headdress wearing a precious *Basra* pearl necklace.[3] The eldest of the Kauravas, Duryodhana, is depicted dressed in an *angrakha*, a common attire worn by Indian princes in the nineteenth century. His rage is portrayed by large, bulging eyes, influenced by Kathakali, the classical dance of Kerala.[4] The courtiers are portrayed in traditional attire, and wearing turbans ornamented with a *sarpech* (aigrette).

The Indian mythological imagination in the late nineteenth century was shaped by the popularity of theatrical productions based on the *Ramayana* and the *Mahabharata* and the availability of affordable prints. The realistic portrayal of characters revived classical Hindu mythology and found great acceptance across India. Over the next century, the influence of these prints was visible in Indian cinema, television, comics and printed literature. The popular television shows *Ramayana* and *Mahabharata*, which aired on Doordarshan in the 1980s, captured viewers with their grand theatrical settings and costumes that were directly influenced by Ravi Varma's paintings. • RJ

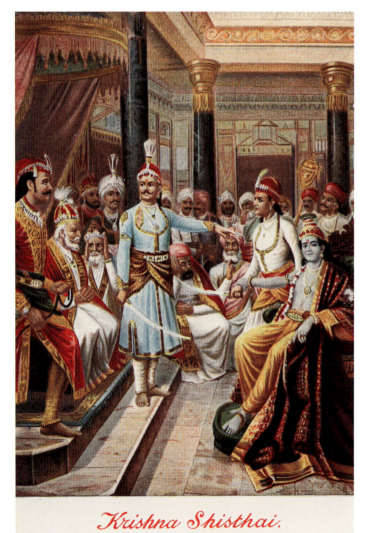

Krishna Shisthai.

Krishna Shisthai; print on postcard, c. 1910, Malavli, Lonavala: Ravi Varma Press; 13.7 x 8.7 cm.
Accessioned: 2018. Gifted to the Museum by Omar Khan.

SITA IN ASHOKVAN

Ravi Varma's painting *Sita in Ashoka Grove* (1894) portrays a dejected Sita sitting under an Ashoka tree in the gardens of King Ravana's palace in Lanka, surrounded by dark-skinned demonesses who are trying to distract her. It captures a poignant moment in the *Ramayana*.

The painting highlights the ordeals of Sita, wife of Lord Rama, prince of Ayodhya, who has been abducted by the demon king Ravana. The diorama at the Museum is a close interpretation of the painting and replicates the mood and the gestures as well as the lush foliage of the exotic gardens in Lanka depicted in the painting. The bare-breasted women that encircle Sita are the demonesses who guard her in the Ashoka grove. Their dark skin tones and partly clad, sensual bodies provide a visual and contextual distinction to the lamenting, demure Sita who is draped in a white saree. The painting is one of the many important mythological episodes that epitomise Ravi Varma's series of *Puranic* paintings, including *Ravana Dressed as a Mendicant Arrives with the Intention of Abducting Sita* and *Ravana Carrying off Sita and Opposed by Jatayu*, based on Valmiki's *Ramayana*.[1] • IH

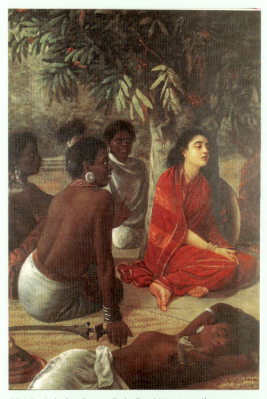

Sita in Ashoka Grove, Raja Ravi Varma; oil on canvas, 1894; 101.6 x 76.2 cm. Image courtesy: Roohi and Rajiv Savara Family Collection/The Savara Foundation for the Arts, New Delhi, India.

Sita in Ashokvan; half-baked terracotta, pigments, mixed media, 1909, made at the erstwhile V&A Museum, Bombay; 57 x 118 x 72 cm.

IN the late nineteenth century, Indian art schools adapted the naturalistic representation of the human figure as portrayed in European art. The movement reached its peak with the increase in popularity of prints by Raja Ravi Varma, particularly in Bombay. His influence extended to the Sir J.J. School of Art, where surface decoration with the realistic portrayal of gods and mythological scenes began to be taught in response to popular demand.[1] Varma's painting style as well as subject matter was adopted by several students of the School, including M.V. Dhurandhar (1867–1944). Like Ravi Varma, Dhurandhar was much sought after by royal families for commissioned portraits and mythological paintings. He was skilled in the Western academic style and painted Indian subjects that were influenced by Varma's composition and style but differed thematically. Dhurandhar was interested in the ordinary life of people whereas Ravi Varma focused on religious themes and mythical narratives. Dhurandhar did execute a few paintings on mythological subjects and Varma's stylistic influence is apparent in these in the treatment of the subject's ornate jewellery and sumptuous apparel.

Dhurandhar was first exposed to Ravi Varma's works in newspapers and magazines while growing up. In 1896, he met Ravi Varma for the first time at the Bombay Art Society's exhibition. Ravi Varma was not only intrigued by Dhurandhar's work but also purchased the latter's painting *The Music Lesson*, which was used by the Ravi Varma Fine Art Lithographic Press for mass-produced lithographs.[2] Thus began Dhurandhar's long-standing association with Ravi Varma and the press. Both men were active members of the Bombay Art Society and often exhibited there. Established in 1888, the society played a central role in promoting art in the city and encouraging young artists, particularly the students of the Sir J.J. School of Art. Varma also presented Dhurandhar with two small watercolours depicting scenes from the *Ramayana*. Over the years, several paintings by Dhurandhar were used by the Ravi Varma press for lithographs.

An ivory sculpture based on Dhurandhar's painting *Ramrajyabhiseka*, which depicts the scene of Rama's coronation after his return from fourteen years of exile and his victory in Lanka over Ravana, who had abducted his consort, Sita, is part of the Museum's collection. It is the end of part six of the *Ramayana*, called 'Yuddha Kanda' (Book of War). It features Rama and Sita seated on the lion throne, while Rama's brothers Lakshmana and Shatrughna, stand on either side with their hands folded. Bharata, another brother, is depicted carrying an ornate umbrella. Two *rishis* (sages) stand beside Rama, performing the *abhishek* (purification ceremony) by pouring sacred water. Hanuman, an ardent devotee of Rama, is shown kneeling at his feet in worship,

and Vibhishana and Sugriva, who assisted Rama in his victory, are shown standing beside the throne on either side, waving *chamaras* (fly whisks). The elongated crown and ornamentation of the figures are stylistically similar to such representations in the Tanjore paintings of south India.[3] Dhurandhar's *Ramrajyabhiseka* closely resembles Ravi Varma's *The Coronation of Rama* in the posture of the figures, the facial features, the layering of the pearl necklaces and the luxuriant use of gold. *The Coronation of Rama* was among the first paintings to be printed as lithographs and circulated by the Ravi Varma Press. • RJ

Ramrajyabhiseka, M.V. Dhurandhar; oleograph on paper, c. early twentieth century, Karla, Lonavala: Ravi Varma Press; 71.6 x 50.8 cm. Image courtesy: Swaraj Art Archives.
•
Opposite:
Rama's Coronation; carved ivory on wooden pedestal, early twentieth century, Trivandrum; 24 x 29 x 12.2 cm. Accessioned: 1948.

VISHNU ON GARUDA

Vishnu is regarded as the preserver and protector of the universe in Hinduism. The ivory sculpture of *Vishnu on Garuda* in the Museum's collection is based on the painting *Vishnu Garuda Vahana* by Ravi Varma, painted c. 1880–90, which depicts Vishnu with his consorts, Sridevi and Bhudevi, sitting beside him on the eagle Garuda, his *vahana* (vehicle). Sridevi is another name for Goddess Lakshmi, while Bhudevi is the goddess of the earth. Garuda, Vishnu's vehicle, is the king of birds and a protector and destroyer of evil, which is symbolised by the serpent. Vishnu is shown holding a *shankha* (conch), *chakra* (discus), *gada* (club) and *padma* (lotus) in his four hands (see p. 276). The sect mark resembling the letter 'U' on Vishnu's forehead is also worn by his devotees (see p. 225). His consorts are portrayed wearing red sarees with golden borders, and holding *chamaras* (fly whisks). An image of Vishnu and Lakshmi on Garuda is also illustrated in the book *The Hindu Pantheon* by Edward Moor, published in 1810, which was one of the sources for Ravi Varma's early imagery. The Museum's ivory is a close copy of the Ravi Varma painting with the sculptor adding a European style nimbus and extending the wings for a grand effect.

Many mass-produced commodities imported from Europe in the early twentieth century featured pictures of Hindu deities in an effort to appeal to Indian audiences.[1] The print *Vishnu Garuda Vahana* was published in calendars advertising popular products of that period, such as jam by C&E Morton Ltd in 1930, Madura Mills Co. Ltd. in 1956 and soap by Sunlight, a brand under British Lever Brothers (Hindustan Unilever) in 1934. The Lever Brothers in India distributed thousands of calendars featuring the image.[2] Matchbox labels manufactured from Sweden in the 1930s had similar imagery. With the growth of textile mills in Bombay, the Ravi Varma Press in Lonavala began printing textile labels, along with postcards, matchbox labels and advertisements.

Varma's works were popular across Travancore, including in the School of Arts at Trivandrum, where ivory carving was the most important subject. Several of his works were also on display at the Trivandrum School of Arts until 1935. Neelakantan Achari, a skilled

Vishnu Garuda Vahana, Raja Ravi Varma; oleograph, c. 1880-89; published in Sunlight Soap calendar of 1934; 65 x 50 cm. Image courtesy: Jyotindra Jain, CIVIC Archive, New Delhi.
•

Opposite:
Vishnu on Garuda; carved ivory on wooden pedestal, early twentieth century, Trivandrum; 19 x 13 x 15.4 cm. Accessioned: 1948.

craftsman and friend of Ravi Varma, played a significant role in the development of ivory carving in Travancore. His style was deeply influenced by Ravi Varma.[3] Ivory objects from Trivandrum were exported in large quantities to Bombay and sold at elite shops as well as the Swadeshi emporiums, from where this piece was acquired in 1948. • RJ

Saraswati; porcelain, early twentieth century, Calcutta Pottery Works; 10.5 x 8 x 21.2 cm. Accessioned: early twentieth century.

•

Opposite, left:
Lakshmi; porcelain, early twentieth century, Calcutta Pottery Works; 11 x 8.5 x 20.5 cm. Accessioned: early twentieth century.

•

Opposite, right:
Damayanti; porcelain, early twentieth century, Calcutta Pottery Works; 16.2 x 6.4 x 24 cm. Accessioned: early twentieth century. Inspired by the oil painting *Damayanti and Hamsa* by Raja Ravi Varma.

THE Museum collection has three porcelain figurines based on the quintessential imagery of two Hindu goddesses, Saraswati (the goddess of knowledge) and Lakshmi (the goddess of wealth), and a mythological princess, Damayanti. The figurines display the maker's mark, C.P.W. (Calcutta Pottery Works), at the bottom. C.P.W. was a private enterprise set up in 1907 by Maharaja Maninder Chander Nandi, Baikuntha Nath Sen, and Hemendra Nath Sen to provide the Indian market with 'Swadeshi' alternatives to imported porcelain in response to the nationalist Swadeshi and Boycott movement that swept through the country in 1905–11. Under the supervision of Satya Sundar Deb, reckoned as the pioneer of Indian ceramics, Calcutta Pottery Works became very successful. With inexpensive, high-quality, locally procured raw materials (feldspar), latest technology, economical fuel and easily available skilled labourers, the factory thrived and produced affordable porcelain. Teacups, saucers, jars, teapots, insulators, inkpots, dolls and images of gods and goddesses were some of the commodities made by the manufacturer. These wares competed with imports, particularly from Japan and Germany.[1]

The porcelain figurine of Saraswati corresponds to a commercial print of the goddess produced by the Calcutta Art Studio established in 1878. Since its establishment, the earliest and most lucrative prints produced at the Studio featured religious and mythological subjects. The aesthetic culture of the Studio was credited to the artistry of former students of the Calcutta School of Art (set up in 1854) who were employed at the Studio. By the late nineteenth century, the Studio's coloured lithographs of gods and goddesses significantly controlled a market previously dominated by Kalighat *pats* (scroll artworks) and Bat-tala wood-engravings. The Studio's published prints were also duplicated by its English competitors, who sold them in India in large quantities for a fraction of the regular price. However, this business takeover would last only until the 1920s, when prints from the Ravi Varma Press became widely accessible and dominated the market.[2]

The broad appeal of prints from the Calcutta Art Studio and the Ravi Varma Press lay in their 'realistic' representations of traditional Indian mythological themes. With the arrival of photography, the demand for 'realism' when depicting popular subjects grew. It reflected the shift in tastes of Calcutta artists and collectors alike, who were greatly influenced by the standards of Western neoclassical and allegorical paintings. Compared to the Kalighat and Bat-tala pictures, described by British art critics and collectors as 'crude' and 'folkish', the new adopted 'realistic' style revealed perspective and volume. The artists at the Studio and Ravi Varma Press, already well-versed in Western art principles

and proficient in portraiture, life-study, and landscape painting, realised their subjects amidst mountains, forests, and lakes, giving them a tactile, 'life-like' quality. The Western perspective of depth dramatically altered the flat allegorical paintings, making them more desirable and fashionable.[3]

The 'new Indian' iconography and popular visual culture generated by the Calcutta Art Studio and Ravi Varma Press was not confined to the mass-printed medium only but also materialised in decorative collectibles such as porcelain figures. The trio of figurines represent the most popular themes resulting from the sociopolitical context in the last decades of the nineteenth century when Indian nationalism was on the rise. The Indian appropriation of Western techniques applied to the goddesses Saraswati and Lakshmi was deemed the most successful imagery produced by the Studio since its establishment. The figurines represent three independent narratives and reflect an idealised iconographic representation of Indian women as 'devi.' The long, open tresses and pose of Saraswati and Lakshmi are thought to possibly be modelled on the classical

depiction of the goddesses in Renaissance-era paintings. Later in the century, Ravi Varma's chiaroscuro and theatrical settings captured the 'life-like' quality of the *nayika* (female protagonists) in the depiction of Damayanti. This is evident in the expressive facial features, execution of the skin tones and graceful expressions. Critics have suggested that Varma's female figures possess a palpable sentimental quality inspired by the prevailing salon painting norms in Europe. However, others have extolled his depictions of Hindu gods and goddesses as evoking a *bhava* or 'feeling and expression' in a unique assimilation of European realism and Indian tradition.[4]

The porcelain Saraswati's saree is devoid of richly coloured embellishments to portray a symbolic sense of purity and wisdom. The representations depict the *veena* (musical instrument) in the goddess's right hand and a manuscript in her left hand, along with her *vahana* (vehicle), a white swan and a blue water body at her feet. Despite their mythological symbolism, the porcelain models reflect the influence of European porcelain figures that were the rage among the urban elite. • IH

AMONG the objects influenced by Raja Ravi Varma's artworks in the Museum's collection is a sandalwood sculpture of Parvati, consort of Lord Shiva, holding their son Ganesha or Ganapati on her left hip with her arm wrapped around him. The sculpture recalls the celebrated painting *There Comes Papa*, painted in 1893, depicting Raja Ravi Varma's eldest daughter, Mahaprabha (1872–1919), holding her son Marthanda Varma on her left hip. The gaze of the child and the pet dog follow Mahaprabha's right hand raised in a gesture, perhaps pointing towards her approaching husband. *There Comes Papa* was one of the ten paintings sent to the 1893 International Exhibition in Chicago, where Raja Ravi Varma's artworks won two medals. The visual consonance between the sculpture and the painting highlights the extraordinary story of Lord Shiva's first meeting with his son. According to legend, Ganesha was born while Shiva was away and when he returned home, he was unable to recognise his own son and beheaded Ganesha in a rage. Confronted with his wife's anguish, he promised to restore their son by imbuing him with new life. The first creature he encountered was an elephant and he replaced Ganesha's severed head with that of the elephant.

The art schools established in the Presidency towns under the British Government emphasised the Western style of academic realism in paintings, which was emulated by nineteenth-century Indian artists including Raja Ravi Varma, who was heavily influenced by Raphael's *Madonna*.[1] The mother–child theme, depicting unconditional love, was universal and highlighted the prevalent ideal goal of a woman as a mother. He made several paintings of Yashodha and Krishna that mirrored versions of *Madonna and Child* executed by European painters in the high Renaissance period (fifteenth to early sixteenth century). The preoccupation with Renaissance language in Indian art at this time is exemplified in the theme of the mother-and-child, the contrapposto figure of Parvati, the fall of her garment and her facial features. The detailed attention to jewellery and the style of the saree drape seen in the sculpture is characteristic of Ravi Varma's paintings. His *nayikas* (female protagonists) were modelled after members of his own royal family of Travancore or well-known singers, as he had a great interest in music and theatre. The back of the sculpture is elaborately carved, delineating the folds of the saree, worn in the Maharashtrian style popular in Bombay, and the flowers ornamenting Parvati's hair. The peacock, considered sacred in Indian mythology and a symbol for Kartikeya, Ganesha's elder sibling, is poised behind Parvati in the sculpture.

Sandalwood was expensive, as it was regulated by the Government, but it was preferred by carvers due to its soft and malleable nature. Carvings from north Canara in the Bombay Presidency and Mysore in the Madras Presidency were popular in Bombay's markets and emporiums. The sculpture of Parvati and Ganesha was acquired by the Museum from an emporium months before Independence in 1947, along with carved panels showcasing other figures from Indian mythology, indicating a purposeful shift towards showcasing Indian traditions and narratives in the Museum. • RWB

There Comes Papa, Raja Ravi Varma; oil on canvas, 1893, Trivandrum; 124.46 x 81.28 cm. Image courtesy: Travancore Royal Family, Kowdiar Palace, Thiruvananthapuram.
•

Opposite:
Parvati and Ganesha; sandalwood, early to mid-twentieth century, Bombay; 41.5 x 21.2 x 15.2 cm. Accessioned: 1946-47.

JEWELLERY BOX

In the early twentieth century, there were about twenty carvers creating sandalwood boxes in Surat, known as *pettigaras* or box carvers. The box bears a striking resemblance to the ones made by one of Surat's finest woodcarvers Chunnilal Mancharam Pettigara. He won medals for his well-designed jewellery boxes depicting *Puranic* imagery inspired by Ravi Varma's lithographs.[1] The box in the Museum was purchased from Sharda Stores in Kalbadevi but was probably made by the same carver or his atelier.

This exquisitely carved box depicts a reproduction of Raja Ravi Varma's portrait of Maharana Pratap Singh (1540–97), the thirteenth ruler of Mewar. Known for his valour and resistance to Mughal expansion in northwest India, Maharana Pratap's portrait was executed in 1901 when Raja Ravi Varma stayed in Udaipur under the patronage of Maharaja Fateh Singh (r. 1884–1930). A 'tall, Rajput man' dressed in Maharana Pratap's armour and helmet and carrying a sword in its scabbard posed for the portrait as there was no readily available photograph or image of Maharana Pratap.[2] This portrait has been replicated in exact detail on the lid of the carved box.

The artisan adapted the portrait to recount the narrative of the king—on the far left, with a halo around his head—who is commanding his army from his fortress on a hill that is surrounded by a forest. The foliage resembles a sandalwood forest with wild animals and birds carved in great detail. The soldiers advancing with their swords drawn, as if heading into battle, mirrors the theme of a predator attacking its prey. The soldiers are carved in individual, successive layers, each wearing different facial expressions. The scene is framed with scrollwork characteristic of sandalwood carving. The lid has a mirror attached on its inner surface, while there are smaller boxes within—each with a carved lid and miniature knobs—meant to hold valuable jewellery. • RWB

Jewellery Box; sandalwood, brass handles, mirror, early to mid-twentieth century, Surat; 30.9 x 41.1 x 16.4 cm. Accessioned: 1940-41.

•

Opposite:
Maharana Pratap I, Raja Ravi Varma; oil on canvas, 1901, 236 x 144.7 cm. © Maharana of Mewar Charitable Foundation, Udaipur. Image courtesy: Media Office, The City Palace, Udaipur.

औद्योगिक कला दालन
Industrial Arts Gallery

(Foreground) *Bronze display*, (left) *Sandalwood display*, (rear, right)
Brass Thaals display, late nineteenth to mid-twentieth century. On
view in the Industrial Arts Gallery, Dr. Bhau Daji Lad Museum, Mumbai.

CLASSICAL ARTS
Commodifying Culture

WITH the plague now a memory, there was a boom in trade during the interwar years and the budding middle classes had much to entertain them in the city, especially a new museum that was established to commemorate the visit of the Prince of Wales (later King George V) in 1905, after whom it was named. Located near the Gateway of India, the building was inaugurated in 1922, and was especially built to house Indian antiquities which were being excavated with great zeal across the country. Archaeology and anthropology were new disciplines birthed by the antiquarian and orientalist societies in London and Europe. These gave rise to similar institutions in India, the earliest being the Asiatic Society of Bengal, established in 1784 by the English scholar and Supreme Court judge in Calcutta, William Jones. It not only published treatises and presented scholarly lectures on Indian culture, but amassed a large collection of objects which became the nucleus for the Indian Museum in Calcutta. The Asiatic Society of Bombay followed in 1804 and by 1840, it started admitting Indian scholars, among the earliest of whom was Dr Bhau Daji Lad. The study of Indian culture was, from the beginning, an important political objective of the colonial government.

Both the disciplines of archaeology and anthropology matured in India around the 1930s. The Archaeological Survey of India, which was founded in 1861 under the leadership of Alexander Cunningham, lapsed for a while after his departure, and was revived by Lord Curzon in 1902, apparently on the advice of George Birdwood, the V&A Bombay's first curator.[1] Much of the material that came into the early museums was distributed from the excavations conducted by the Archaeological Survey. Much of it also left the country as part of a flourishing illicit trade in antiquities that was endemic to the buccaneering ethos of the East India Company, which continued during the Raj. This curiosity about the exotic past, which in the nineteenth century became the mark of a cultivated personality and generated copious amounts of documentation and collections, created an appetite among foreign visitors and the Indian elite not only for paintings and prints, but also for free-standing sculptures and handcrafted objects. A pervasive culture of acquisition and display filtered down to the bazaars creating local hybrid versions of classical forms.[2]

Henry Cousens, the Superintendent of Archaeology for Western India (1891–1910), had carried out excavations at several sites in the Deccan and in Sindh. He had urged the Bombay Government to create a new museum to house the artefacts that were stored at the Town Hall, as the V&A Bombay did not have the space and it was far from the city centre. The city's pundits decided that the new Prince of Wales Museum (now the Chhatrapati Shivaji Maharaj Vastu Sangrahalaya) would house antiquities and that the V&A Bombay would focus on industrial arts and local history.[3] The Government consulted Ernest Fern, the V&A Bombay's curator, seeking his views regarding the transfer of the archaeological collections to the Prince of Wales Museum. Fern had a prejudiced view of the masses that thronged

0+0=0-0, L.N. Tallur; wood, electric grinder, sensor, saw dust, 2011; 221 x 99 x 56 cm. Exhibition: *Quintessential*; Nineteenth Century Mumbai Paintings Gallery, 2011-12. Collection: Rajshree Pathy. The sculpture, a life-size, purpose-built androgynous wooden figure, looks traditional without being identifiable within a specific style or period. The figure is well advanced in destroying itself by taking an angle grinder to its head. Tallur employs the human figure as a site of decay to comment on the wilful negation of ideals and values. In the context of the Museum, this work takes on a particular resonance as it symbolises the extraordinary neglect of our cultural heritage.

the Museum from the nearby 'native' areas—13 lakh in 1924, at a time when the Bombay Presidency's population was about 1.4 crore! Fern felt that the British and Indian merchant elite would be better served by the other, more centrally located museum, and he willingly agreed to give away the V&A Bombay's remarkable archaeological collection stating that such artistic objects would not interest the Museum's visitors who belonged to the uneducated masses and were only interested in the more 'popular' sections of the Museum.[4]

In 1924, the Government decided that the large collection of antiquities from the V&A Bombay would be handed over to the Prince of Wales Museum to enhance its archaeological collection. This included a group of rare Gandhara sculptures bequeathed to the V&A Bombay by Henry Hardy Cole, who had been sent to India in 1868 to find exotic material for the India Museum in London.[5] Hardy Cole was the son of Henry Cole, the man in charge of the first Crystal Palace Exhibition and director of the Department of Arts and Science that oversaw the entire edifice of colonial art institutions. The younger Cole spent a year in India as an archaeological surveyor, visiting various excavations and collecting the best pieces to take back with him to London. What he could not carry back, he distributed to the museums established by the colonial government in the country.[6] The V&A Bombay's collection also included '10 beautiful slabs from ancient Assyria' that were gifted to the Museum by the Governor, Lord Falkland.[7] Sir Henry Rawlinson, the renowned British orientalist, had gifted these to Bombay in 1847. This was not

Below, left:
Head of Buddha; glass negative, possibly photographed by Henry Cousens in 1900 at the erstwhile V&A Museum, Bombay; 16.5 x 12 cm. Accessioned: early twentieth century.
The schist sculpture was from a lot of Graeco-Bactrian or Gandharan sculptures given to the Museum by H.H. Cole in 1885-86 from excavations at Yusufzhai district.

Below, right:
Radha–Krishna; ivory on wooden pedestal, early twentieth century, Honavar; 23.5 x 13.9 x 7.9 cm. Accessioned: 1930s.

Opposite:
Mahishasuramardini; brass, late nineteenth to early twentieth century, Poona; 16.5 x 19.8 x 32.4 cm. Accessioned: 1925. Poona was an important centre for manufacturing brass, copper and bell metal articles in the nineteenth and twentieth centuries.

the first time the Museum had to part with its archaeological collections. Earlier, objects from the collection were dispatched to the Sir J.J. School of Art during Cecil Burns' tenure as principal, as there was not enough space at the V&A Museum to accommodate these, and Burns wanted to build the small collection housed at the School museum. Objects were also distributed to the Lord Reay Industrial Museum (Mahatma Phule Museum), Poona, the Barton Museum at Bhavnagar, and later to the National Museum, New Delhi. For many years the V&A Bombay and the Prince of Wales Museum worked together, sharing information and exchanging artefacts, and at one point there was even a proposal that the two would be governed by a single authority.[8]

The colonial art schools, meanwhile, were encouraged to make drawings, paintings and plaster casts of the antiquities that were being discovered, to send to institutions abroad and in India to facilitate an understanding of Indian culture. Like anthropology, the science of archaeology enabled the British to create an Indian historiography and grasp what seemed a strange and unfathomable culture, albeit through a European prism. Major projects were undertaken by the art schools to document monuments and sites. Perhaps the most famous of these was the expedition led by John Griffiths, principal of the Sir J.J. School of Art, who spent nearly two decades along with his students, camped for months at the Ajanta caves near Aurangabad, documenting the paintings on the interior walls. An early set of paintings of a few caves were displayed at the V&A Museum in 1872 when it opened.[9]

Sets were sent to museums in England and in India, and a copy was later acquired by the V&A, Bombay.

Artists trained at the art schools took pride in their skills in rendering spatial templates and the human anatomy accurately, that being one of the foremost objectives of the schools. The naturalistic depiction of form became a pervasive notion to determine artistic excellence and was incorporated into the production of sculpture and architectural models as well as exotic objects to suit elite tastes. The idealised forms of traditional deities that earlier followed prescribed norms of execution governed by the tenets of the *Shilpa Shastras* (Hindu principles of art), evolved in the early twentieth century into sensuous, Europeanised figures that were often given a more popular demeanour.[10] The Museum's ivory sculpture of Radha–Krishna from Honavar (see p. 268) depicts Radha as a water carrier with Krishna, in a Europeanised, secular manner, without the iconographic attributes that usually accompany the representation of deities. Radha wears her saree in the modern style that was popularised by the Indian nationalists. The students of the Reay workshop at the Bombay School of Art regularly carved deities as designs for doors and pillars but rarely made religious objects.[11] The department stores, markets and bazaars were full of such souvenirs of Indian deities and models of temples (p. 282).

The sculptures in the Museum reflect this intersection of several different contingencies.[12] Unlike archaeological or temple collections that have a completely different genealogy, these works portray an emerging modernity and popular visual culture that reference tradition but refracts it through a modern, Europeanised lens. Among the many styles that influenced the new visual codes were the paintings of Raja Ravi Varma and the popularity of his oleographs, which would completely transform the traditional paradigms of classical Indian art. Several exhibitions conducted by different organisations like the Bombay Art Society, the Art Society of India, the Indian Merchant Chambers in Bombay, and the Indian National Congress, would encourage the spread of the new 'bazaar' forms.[13] Indigenous craft production was an important part of the strategy to resist the British and therefore, the display and sale of artisanal products was encouraged by these organisations through regular exhibitions which were visited in large numbers.[14] The nationalists prevailed on local businessmen to display and patronise Indian crafts as was in evidence at the 1904 Bombay Exhibition (see p. 124).[15]

There had been a reassessment of Indian art in the early twentieth century by Ernest Binfield Havell, the superintendent of the Calcutta Art School and by the Tagore family.[16] The erudite Sri Lankan scholar Ananda Coomaraswamy defended Indian aesthetics as denoting spiritual values, and wrote several books challenging the colonial understanding of Indian art (see p. 125). In an important essay in the *Journal of Indian Art and Industry* on the Festival of Empire in 1911, he had criticised the Government for '… making Indians strangers in their own country.'[17] He encouraged Indians to appreciate and understand Indian classical art.

These changing attitudes are reflected in the collection of the Museum. In 1930, D.A. Pai was appointed as the first Indian curator of the V&A, Bombay. He had been the assistant curator since 1905 and he introduced a new focus on Indian art through the expansion of the collection and its redisplay. Most of the classical Indian collection at the Museum was built during his tenure and the tenure of his successor, Dr S.C. Upadhyaya, a noted scholar of Indian art. Curator Fern made the first purchase of miniatures on ivory for the Museum in 1929, probably on the advice of Pai (see pp. 300-01). He notes that the miniatures are among the finest being produced at the time.[18] He also notes that displays of important events about Indian history were being considered to educate the masses.[19]

Many of the objects in the classical collection of the Museum were a part of a purchase from Lt Col. Howard Murray made by Pai. Murray served in the Mesopotamian War and was awarded the Companion of the Indian Empire for his service. In 1931, he retired from the army and became a merchant in Bombay.[20] Departing British officers were known to make collections which they sold at exorbitant prices in London. Occasionally, if the collection was too large or deemed not sufficiently valuable, it was disposed of in India. Murray's ill health resulted in his selling much of his collection to the erstwhile V&A Museum, Bombay. After his death a few years later, his wife gave the Museum the remaining articles as a bequest. These included brass and copper works, lacquer objects, Tibetan and Chinese pieces, Indian armour, ivory paintings, paintings of Navagrahas (nine planets personified), and Ashtadikpalas (the eight cardinal points of the compass) and old Tibetan and Persian illustrated manuscripts.[21] The Murray Collection was the first large collection of Indian miniatures that entered the Museum and included Mughal (see pp. 290-91), Pahadi Kangra (see pp. 296-99), Rajput, Deccan (see pp. 292-93) and Sikh miniatures. These were on display in the Old Indian Historical Pictures room which was very popular.

The resistance to British rule strengthened in the early twentieth century with the Swadeshi movement which called on the people to boycott British goods and buy Indian-made products. Bombay played a significant role in motivating people to join the resistance under the leadership of M.G. Ranade, G.K. Gokhale, and B.G. Tilak, among others. Thousands participated in the meetings and activists also organised a number of 'swadeshi bazaars' at which 'country-made' goods were sold. The middle classes of Bombay, especially small merchants, shopkeepers, clerks, teachers, students and journalists, were ardent supporters of the movement.[22]

Cultural nationalism became an important facet of political and economic nationalism. The Museum acquired many of its objects in the 1930s and 1940s from the emporia and Swadeshi stores which were set up as part of the resistance. In 1930, Kanaiyalal Vakil, the art critic for *The Bombay Chronicle*, wrote a scathing criticism of the Bombay Municipality's lack of interest in promoting Indian craftsmanship for trade and education at the V&A Museum. He called upon the Municipality to project the Museum and its collection as 'an active instrument and power for the promotion and a systematic advancement of Swadeshi' and said that it 'must now function as the school and laboratory for the children and students in the city and as the showroom and also the salesroom for the articles of Swadeshi manufacture'.[23]

In 1942, Mahatma Gandhi declared the Quit India movement from the Gowalia Tank in Bombay. The entire Congress leadership was put in jail and the city responded with strikes and riots, making it almost impossible for the Government to function. There was much political ferment and in December 1945, just prior to Independence, the opening of the Vikram Exhibition of Indian Culture, at the Bombay University's Convocation Hall, caused considerable excitement. Called the 'Glory that was India' by Karl Khandalavala, the noted art historian, the exhibition attempted to provide a comprehensive view of Indian art. It featured modern Indian artists' paintings, murals, Ajanta frescoes, miniatures, manuscripts, sketches of earlier fashions and costumes, among other things. The Museum loaned the exhibition nine industrial artifacts and ten plates of Indian embroidery designs. The exhibition had a thirty-five-day run and visitors thronged to see it.[24]

Dr Upadhyaya had become the V&A Museum's curator in 1939. He reorganised the display to emphasise classical Indian art and this section at the Museum was expanded. Labels were prepared in four languages—English, Marathi, Urdu and Gujarati—to ensure visitors understood the displays.[25] Despite its remote location, the Museum continued to be very popular with the masses, and *The Bombay Chronicle* reported in 1936 that the most popular site in Bombay was the V&A Museum, with 3,600 visitors a day.[26] Upadhyaya added to the existing collections to increase the assortment and depth of both sculpture and miniature paintings, and to give the Museum a nationalistic artistic direction which would enable Bombay's audiences to gain a new understanding of their history and culture. • TZM

THE kingdom of Travancore, with its capital at Trivandrum, emerged as a primary centre for ivory carving in the nineteenth century. Since ancient times, the goldsmiths of Travancore were known for their idols and palanquin decorations in ivory.[1] The art enjoyed royal patronage under Raja Swathi Thirunal Rama Varma (1813–46) and subsequent rulers who maintained private ivory ateliers that employed several carvers. Travancore ivory carvers gained international fame when an ivory throne was presented to Queen Victoria and showcased at the Great Exhibition of 1851 in London. To meet the growing demand for Travancore ivory carvings among the European and Indian elite, and to benefit from the great commercial profit, the colonial government decided to establish a department of ivory carving, locally known as '*Dantha Appis*', in 1872-73.[2]

In order to encourage the development of the craft, the Trivandrum School of Art was established in 1888 along the lines of the Madras School of Art, and the ivory department was integrated with the industrial branch of the School. So successful was the trade that the School dedicated a separate space for ivory carvers—a pandal with a thatched roof and bamboo trelliswork on all sides—in the middle of the School's courtyard. This enabled the carvers to work in the natural air and light that was necessary for detailed work.[3]

Tusks were packed in wet cloth and kept for several days till they became soft enough to carve. Carving required great skill as the depth and background of the object had to be first cut with a drill and saw, and then smaller details incised without letting the ivory crack. Articles made from a single piece were limited in size to the width and length of the tusk. The principal objects cut from solid ivory were small. Numerous small pieces of ivory were joined together to create a large article or ivory plates fixed with ivory rivets or cement were used on large sculptures created from wood. Finished articles were sometimes dyed or bleached and then polished once dry.[4]

The art schools encouraged students to employ European naturalism in their treatment of the human form. However,

Opposite:
Radha–Krishna; carved ivory on wooden pedestal, early twentieth century, Trivandrum; 15.5 x 8.4 x 32 cm. Accessioned: 1954–55.

•

Right:
Shiva and Parvati; carved ivory on a wooden pedestal, early twentieth century, Trivandrum; 16.9 x 10.9 x 39 cm. Accessioned: 1957-58. This is a classic example of Travancore ivory carving, depicting a four-armed Shiva on a hill, with a halo behind his head, embracing Parvati, whose figure is shown on a smaller scale. Nandi, Shiva's bull, is seen at their feet. The fluidity of this carving and the slight curve suggests that this was carved from a single tusk.

British art critics also advocated a return to conventional Indian subjects and mythological scenes to optimise commerce.[5] Students at the Trivandrum School developed a signature aesthetic assimilation that depicted traditional subjects using European modes of representation. This style was eventually copied by other artisans. Thirteen ivory carvings in the Museum's collection depict the Trivandrum School style, which is characterised by tall, graceful figures of Hindu gods and goddesses. Krishna, Shiva and Saraswati were the most popular subjects.

The carving of Radha–Krishna (see p. 272) is a typical Travancore depiction of a Hindu deity adorned in traditional attire yet employing European ornament. The dancing figures of Radha and Krishna are reminiscent of the French Salon painting style which, at the time, was considered the highest form of art. Radha's balletic pose, her drapery, the cooing doves and romantic foliage, as well as Krishna's halo, showcase the influence of Western art on work produced in India. Unlike the traditional depiction of the god's consort on the left, Radha is depicted on the right, holding Krishna's flute which alludes to their intimacy.

Travancore was known for its high-quality ivory and it did not import raw material, unlike other ivory centres which depended on imported tusks from Africa that were transported via Bombay.[6] While there was an abundance of elephants in the forests, only hunters appointed by the royal court were allowed to hunt. Heavy punishment was meted out to unauthorised hunters. The high quality of ivory, coupled with the training at the Trivandrum School of Art, enabled Travancore to attain the 'foremost position among the ivories in India'.[7] The most popular articles for the European market were knife handles, paperweights, photo frames, round boxes, billiard balls, keys of musical instruments, chess pieces and thin plates for miniatures, while bangles, mirrors and combs were meant for the domestic market. Many popular shops in Bombay stocked and sold ivory articles from Travancore and southern India well into the 1950s and 1960s.[8] The ivory trade was completely banned in India in 1986. • **RWB**

Nataraja with Eighteen Arms; carved ivory on wooden pedestal, c. early twentieth century, Trivandrum; 17.4 x 9.5 x 38.5 cm. Accessioned: 1958. Shiva, also known as Nataraja or the Lord of Dance, is depicted performing the celestial dance or *tandav*, signifying destruction, stability and regeneration, ensuring the balance of the universe.

MAHARAJA KHANDERAO GAEKWAD II OF BARODA (1828–70)

Maharaja Khanderao was the eighth Gaekwad of the princely state of Baroda and ruled from 1856 to 1870. He aided the British in suppressing the Uprising that broke out in 1857 by sending his army to assist them in the revolting states. The Gaekwads' allegiance to the East India Company arose out of the need to safeguard Baroda against the Peshwa expansion. The Peshwas had extracted heavy sums from the Gaekwads to recognise the legitimacy of their heirs in the eighteenth century.

H.H. Khanderao Gaekwad was a connoisseur of art and jewellery, and was a generous philanthropist. In 1863, he donated Rs 5,000 to the proposed botanical gardens and the V&A, Bombay.[1] He commissioned a marble statue of Queen Victoria by the famed sculptor Matthew Noble in 1864, which was originally intended to be placed on a terrace in front of the Museum (see p. 51).[2] He also donated a large sum of money in 1870 to build the Royal Alfred Sailors' Home to accommodate visiting sea men and officers. It is now the headquarters of the Mumbai Police.

The miniature ivory statue of H.H. Khanderao Gaekwad of Baroda, made in Delhi, was probably commissioned by him and presented to the Museum between 1863 and 1870. The ivory carvers of Delhi were known for being able to render any image or photograph in sculpture. The statue is modelled on an old black-and-white photograph of the Gaekwad seated on a chair, flanked by his attendants. A connoisseur of jewellery, the Gaekwad possessed a large collection of state jewels, including the internationally famous diamonds 'Star of the South' and 'English Dresden'. Here he is shown wearing the ceremonial collar necklace studded with rose-cut diamonds, pearls, cabochons and drooping emeralds. Apart from the sword in his left hand, he also has two pistols and a dagger in his cummerbund. The Gaekwad *pagadi* or the royal headwear that he wore was originally 38 metres of narrow *Chanderi* fabric with pearls at the end of the tassels. The carver has depicted the headwear without the traditional turban ornament or *sarpech*. The chair he is seated on is exquisitely carved with lion heads as the arms and paws as the feet. • RWB

Maharaja Khanderao Gaekwad II of Baroda; carved ivory, nineteenth century, Delhi; 10.6 x 11.2 x 8.5 cm. Accessioned: 1863–70.

WOODCARVING is a long-practiced art in India. The rich forests of teakwood, sandalwood, ebony and rosewood, especially around Trivandrum and Mysore, gave rise to an enduring tradition of high-quality woodcarving. Teakwood was used for carving furniture, architectural brackets, lintels and screens, while rosewood was mainly used for carving figurines of elephants and Hindu deities, bookends, boxes, cabinets with ivory inlay as its rich colour and density exuded a much-prized aura of luxury. The range of articles produced in rosewood is limited as the material is best suited to deep relief or sculptural work rather than low relief carving.[1]

Temples in south India provided a ready reference for woodcarvers. Mythological figures, elephants and miniature models of temples were popular articles purchased by European travellers and Indians. Figures of deities were also carved in and around major religious centres to cater to the demand of pilgrims for both worship and as souvenirs.[2] The Padmanabhaswamy Temple in Trivandrum is one of the most important pilgrimage centres for the followers of Vishnu, worshipped as the Preserver of the Universe. The main deity in the temple is known as Lord Padmanabha or Ananta, which are names for Vishnu when he is depicted in a resting position on Shesha (the celestial serpent) with a *padma* or lotus emerging from his navel (see pp. 242-43). Vishnu is also known as Narayana or Hari when he is not depicted in a reclining position.

The Lakshmi–Narayana rosewood sculptures in the Museum's collection are identified by their iconography. Narayana is depicted with four arms holding four attributes: a *gada* (mace) symbolising strength and knowledge; a *padma* (lotus) symbolising purity; the *Sudarshana Chakra* (spinning disc) that destroys evil and symbolises *dharma* or duty; and the *Panchajanya* (conch) that was used during the epic battle of Kurukshetra, and represents control over the five elements of the universe. Lakshmi is the goddess of wealth and prosperity and the consort of Lord Vishnu. Both her hands in the front are raised in *mudras* (gestures) symbolising blessing and prosperity while those at the back hold lotus buds. The sculptures have been carved in great detail both on the front and the rear, with Lakshmi's braid detailed till below her torso. Both figures are standing on fully blossomed lotuses, an important iconography of the Vaishnavite cult. The elaborately carved sashes represent the traditional style of detailing prevalent in south India. The sculptures are placed on pedestals similar to those of ivory figures from the Trivandrum School of Art (see pp. 272–274, 257).

The adulatory response and demand for woodcarving from India at international exhibitions encouraged the establishment of woodwork classes at the Schools of Art.

Classes were introduced at the Madras School of Art in the late 1880s by Superintendent E.B. Havell, who employed a master craftsman, Meenakshi Asari, from Ramnad (Tamil Nadu), to teach the students woodcarving. At the J.J. School of Art, the headmaster, G.W. Terry introduced wood engraving in 1857. When the Reay Art Workshops were established in 1891 at the Bombay School, woodcarving was one of the first ateliers that was set up and offered a three-year course. The focus was on creating architectural and sculptural work using traditional methods of production.[3] Most of the students were sons of hereditary craftsmen from the nearby regions of Surat, Nasik, north Canara, Belgaum and produced doors and wall panels, windows, chairs, tables, teapoys, among other things.[4]

Merchants and salesmen in Bombay commissioned customised articles in a variety of woods from artisans in south India to sell in the markets in Bombay and abroad.[5] The Lakshmi–Narayana sculptures on the opposite page were purchased from Sharda Stores, a part of the Swadeshi Market in Kalbadevi, Bombay. The Swadeshi markets were set up to promote indigenous crafts as a part of the economic resistance to colonial rule. Post-Independence, woodcarving that was carried on in a traditional manner by artisan units, was defined by the Government as a 'cottage industry' for economic and policy support.[6] In the late 1960s, concentrated efforts were made to boost the woodcarving industry and provide skill development and market exposure to the artisans in Kerala with the establishment of a formal training programme at Sree Moolam Thirunal Shashtiabdapoorthi Memorial and a chain of Government emporiums known as 'Kairali'.[7] • RWB

Lakshmi–Narayana; rosewood, early to mid-twentieth century, Trivandrum; 20.8 x 15 x 55.7 cm. Accessioned: 1950.

25/2

25/1

77 PARVATI

THE Museum has a magnificent bronze figurine of Parvati, the consort of Shiva, which was acquired in 1961 from south India.[1] It was probably produced in the mid-twentieth century at Swamimalai, Tamil Nadu. The ancient art of making bronze statues is practised even today in a few clusters primarily in Swamimalai. The sculptors follow the traditional lost wax process of metal casting according to the injunctions of the *Shilpa Shastras* regarding proportions and iconography.[2] However, slight variations occur. As the eminent scholar A.K. Coomaraswamy explains, each maker of an icon achieves a pure mental state, *citta-sanna*, and then visualises the icon as per given canonical prescriptions.[3]

The *sthapatis* or icon makers of south India follow specific procedures required for casting. The process, known as *madhuchchhisthavidhana*, is described in the south Indian text *Manasollasa*.[4] There are three categories of idols: purely art pieces; *utsava murtis*, festival images that are taken out in ceremonial processions; and original idols, which are for temple sanctums and must remain inside the temple where they are worshipped.[5] There are four main stages in the production of icons: wax model making; preparing a clay mould for the wax model; casting the metal icon in the clay mould; and lastly, finishing the icon with engraving and polishing.[6] The *sthapatis* maintain that metal deities for processional worship in temples should never be hollow cast because that would be inauspicious.[7]

The Museum's Parvati stands in a graceful triple bend or *tribhanga* pose, where the body is 'broken' at two points to produce three bends in the body. The right hand is raised in *kataka mudra*, in which fresh flowers or other venerated objects are inserted. The left is in *lota hasta mudra*, where the hand is facing forward and fingers point to the earth in a gesture of bestowing a boon. The figure's voluptuous

form, ornamentation and the lotus pedestal are symbolic of prosperity and fertility. The goddess wears an intricate lotiform or lotus-patterned *dhoti* and jewellery, including necklaces, armbands and anklets, as well as the sacred thread. A *kirtimukha*, the icon of victory and bounty, is placed at the centre of her waistband. Her face is serene with a slight smile and elongated eyes. On her head is a diadem and conical headdress with a *chakra* (halo) behind. The stylistic features of this bronze Parvati exhibit a continuation of the Chola dynasty traditions.

The Cholas were the dominant power in south India for more than four hundred years, from the ninth to the thirteenth century. During the golden age of the Cholas, the arts of sculpting and bronze casting reached new heights. Deities were worshipped as living entities who participated in various rituals and festivities. Portable images of the deities were required to be able to perform these rituals.[8] The temple bronzes of south India developed as a response to this tradition. The Cholas are credited with building one of the largest temples (Brihadeshwara) in south India. Numerous bronzes of Shiva and his consort Parvati are found in Chola temples and *sthapatis* take inspiration from these to continue the bronze sculpture tradition.

Parvati's mythology is treated as the ongoing story of Sati, born to lure the aloof and lone ascetic Shiva into marriage.[9] Parvati does not appear in Vedic literature. Textual evidence for her existence appears directly in the epic period (400 BCE–400 CE). Both the *Ramayana* and the *Mahabharata* present her as the consort of Shiva. In the *Puranas*, she is introduced as the daughter of Himavat and Mena, and as a reincarnation of Sati, Shiva's first wife.

The collection in the Museum includes bronze sculptures of several gods and goddesses, most of which were collected post-Independence and reflect the museumisation of votive objects and their transformation from religious into secular objects for the purposes of display of the finest traditional craftsmanship. The 1948 exhibition 'Masterpieces of Indian Art' at the Rashtrapati Bhavan, which was the first major exhibition of classical Indian art in Delhi and formed the nucleus collection of the National Museum in Delhi, had a powerful impact on the collection and display of classical sculptures.[10] This effect can be seen at the V&A, Bombay with the acquisition of nineteenth century copies of sculptures executed in the classical style. It indicates a change in the direction of the Museum's visual and historical narrative and distinguishes the bronze collection from the Art School sculptures in wood and ivory, collected earlier, which were influenced by European concepts of art (see pp. 272–74, 276–77). • HK

Parvati; bronze, mid-twentieth century, south India; 17.2 x 17.2 x 58.4 cm. Accessioned: 1961.

SUDARSHAN SAHOO is a well-known master craftsman and artist from Orissa, who has worked towards reviving the age-old art of stone carving. Sahoo combines art school naturalism with traditional *Shilpa Shastras*. The Museum acquired some of his sculptures possibly between 1990 and 2003, including the Nabakeli, which is similar to the *Nauka-lila* tradition popular in north India. It describes an episode in Krishna's life where he is disguised as a boatman to trick Radha and the *gopis*. Sahoo hails from the city of Puri, which is the epicentre of arts and crafts in Orissa. In 1952, he began his career as a sculptor, training under Guru Bhubaneshwar Mohapatra and Guru Kunai Moharana. He founded Sudarshan Crafts Museum, Puri, in 1977 and Sudarshan Arts and Crafts Village, Bhubaneswar, in 1991 to raise awareness about the art of traditional sculpture. Sudarshan Arts and Crafts Village, established with the assistance of the Government of Orissa, is a training and production centre for traditional sculptures in stone, wood and fibreglass.[1] The atelier follows the principles of the *gurukul* system of learning, showcasing the living heritage of Orissa's arts and crafts. Sahoo was honoured in 1988 with the Padma Shri, the fourth highest civilian award in India, for his contribution to the field of arts and crafts. In a career spanning over six decades, he has exhibited his sculptures in India and abroad and has won several awards, including the 1981 National Stone Carving Award and the 2006 Shilp Guru Award.[2] In December 2018, Sahoo had a solo art exhibition at the Jehangir Art Gallery, Mumbai.

The red stone sculpture by Sudarshan Sahoo depicts the scene of 'Nabakeli'. The boatman in the sculpture has a halo and a U-shaped mark on his forehead—*naman*, a symbol representative of Krishna or Vishnu. The central female with a veil or *ghunghat* and adorned beautifully, may be assumed to be Radha. This depiction of Krishna sailing with female cowherds or *gopis* has many regional variations as commonly seen in various paintings and sculptures. In this myth, Krishna appears at the helm of a boat in the guise of a boatman, and agrees to ferry the *gopis* with butter in their pots across the river Yamuna.[3] He holds an oar dipped in the river, depicted as wavy lines. Krishna, Radha and the eight *gopis* are adorned with sumptuous ornaments. The swan boat in the sculpture is also highly embellished.

Boats are an important part of early literature, poetry and folklore in eastern India. Orissa's rich history of maritime trade has inspired artists to depict various types of boats in sculptures and paintings for many centuries.[4] The earliest representation of boats in Orissa can be seen in sculptures from the Brahmeswara temple, Bhubaneswar, c. the eleventh century, and Bhoga Mandapa of the Jagannath Temple, Puri, c. the twelfth century. Similarly decorated boats whose prows are carved in the shape of a swan's head are seen across Orissa during various festivals.[5]

The story of 'Nabakeli' can be seen throughout Orissa in songs, plays, rituals and poems, as well as in theatre, where a couple dressed as Krishna and Radha sail on a lake. This story is performed every year at the Dhanu Yatra Festival in the town of Bargarh in Orissa.[6] The story is also narrated in the famous and widely popular poem *Nabakeli*, written by the seventeenth-century Oriya poet, Dinakrusna Das.[7] Radha–Krishna stories are elaborately narrated in the twelfth-century poem *Gita Govinda* by Jayadeva, a Sanskrit poet from Kenduli village in Orissa. *Gita Govinda* contributed to the rise of the Bhakti movement throughout India.[8]

Sudarshan Sahoo created his own style by integrating different techniques from temple carvings from all over the country. In his practice, he follows and teaches the rules of the *Shilpa Shastras*, which can be seen in his works in the depiction of *mudras* (gestures) and ornamentation. • RJ

Saraswati, Sudarshan Sahoo; *tenali* stone, c. 1952–2003, Orissa; 21.4 x 11.1 x 45.6 cm. Accessioned: 1990–2003.

•

Opposite:
Nabakeli, Sudarshan Sahoo; red stone, c. 1952–2003, Orissa; 22.2 x 23.4 x 9.3 cm. Accessioned: 1990–2003.

THE 'picturesque' visual documentation of India through sketches and postcards culminated in systematic archaeological surveys and documentation across the British provinces in India in the nineteenth century. The monographs, art journals and travelogues produced during this period include sketches of ruins as well as drawings of architectural and design details, which reflect an attempt at a preconceived classification, based on a European historiography, of the built environment of India. Sketches executed by trained artists and students of the Presidency art schools as well as plaster casts and models of architectural details were made and shipped to exhibitions and museums in England and around the world.[1]

These 'studies' aimed at building an 'archive' of India and were meant to validate the European view of the country as a 'mystic' land of great antiquity and spirituality. This view was projected primarily onto the city of Benares, which had long been chronicled as the spiritual core of India. The temples and ghats of Benares were portrayed in many travelogues and sketches by British artists, and those by James Prinsep especially have contributed to an enduring image of the city in the Western imagination. Prinsep, who deciphered the ancient Brahmi and Kharosthi scripts, resulting in a breakthrough in Indian history, was appointed as an 'assay master' or the quality-checker at the Benares Mint in 1820.[2] Though trained as an architect and draughtsman, his weak eyesight had initially prevented him from pursuing an architectural practice. However, during his time in Benares, he took great interest in surveying and documenting the city, its temples, mosques, mansions of well-known merchants, and its festivities. He created a map of the city based on his survey. His sketches and watercolours were eventually published in London between 1830 and 1834 as *Benares Illustrated, in a Series of Drawings*.

The brass model of the Kashi Vishwanath temple in the Museum's collection was based on an original woodcut print by Prinsep.[3] It was part of the British art collector Lt Col. H. Murray's private collection of Indian antiquities, which the Museum purchased during the curatorship of D.A. Pai, the Museum's first Indian curator (1930–39). The temple is built in the Nagara style, typical of north Indian temple architecture and is dedicated to Lord Shiva. The brass model is displayed alongside a pith model of the Meenakshi temple at Madurai, built in the south Indian style and dedicated to Goddess Meenakshi, consort of Lord Shiva. This juxtaposition demonstrated to Museum visitors the two main styles of temple architecture of the Indian subcontinent.

The model was made in Benares, which was considered to be the foremost centre of brassware production due to the variety of designs executed, the superior casting of the metal, and the rich colouring that gave it a 'gold-like lustre'.[4]

A Benares Brassworker Practising His Craft; print from a photograph by Johnston & Hoffman (active 1882–1950), *Indian Pictorial Education*, Bombay: Times of India Press, 1930; 28.5 x 3.5 x 39 cm. Accessioned: mid- to late twentieth century.

•

Opposite:
Model of the Kashi Vishwanath Temple in Benares; brass, mid to late nineteenth century, Benares; 83.5 x 75.5 x 51.7 cm. Accessioned: 1932.

The most skilled brassworkers made chased and perforated reproductions of famous buildings in and around Benares. Such models were popular at international exhibitions and were sometimes decorated with gemstones or enamel work. Brass reproductions of this scale were valued at thousands of rupees and commissioned or purchased by visiting Europeans. They were also presented to high-ranking British officers.[5] A bequest notice of Lord Edward Bulwer-Lytton (1803–73), the Secretary of State for Colonies, specifically mentioned a model of an Indian temple and his mother's diamond ring as his most prized possessions.[6]

The city of Benares has been a seat of high culture and learning in the Indian subcontinent for centuries and also identified as the sacred pilgrimage site 'Kashi' in religious texts. Kashi also means the 'city of lights', derived from the ritual *aarti* (worship) of Ganga, believed to be the holiest river in Hinduism, on the *ghats* (steps) near the river at dusk. According to the legends in Indian religious texts, Shiva captured Ganga as she fell with great force from heaven towards the earth. Shiva captured her in his dreadlocks, taming her fall to Earth. The Kashi Vishwanath temple, dedicated to Vishweshwar or Lord of the Universe as Shiva is known, was built on the western banks of the river which is at a higher elevation, protecting it from floods. The temple is one of the twelve most important *jyotirlingas* or phallic stones believed to be the aniconic form of Lord Shiva, located in the temple's sanctum. Devotees believe that a visit to the temple at Kashi and a dip in the Ganga will wash away their sins from all past lives and enable their soul to be freed from the cycle of rebirth and achieve spiritual enlightenment.

The present structure of the temple was commissioned by Ahilya Bai Holkar of the royal family of Indore in 1780. The temple complex consists of smaller shrines for other gods associated with Shaivite practice. The *shikharas* or towers surround a dome in the centre. The Kashi Vishwanath temple is also popularly known as the 'Golden Temple of Benares' after Maharaja Ranjit Singh of Punjab donated the gold to plate the temple's dome. • **RWB**

Shiva Temple; teakwood, mid nineteenth century, Gujarat; 32.3 x 48.5 x 59.7 cm. Accessioned: 1862-63. The model was gifted to the Museum by Maharao Pragmalji II, the Rao of Kutch and resembles the Koteshwar temple in Kutch which was built in 1820.

MEENAKSHI TEMPLE

Pith models made in Tanjore and Trichinopoly of famous temples located within the erstwhile Madras Presidency were popular at international exhibitions in the nineteenth century.[1] *Sholapith* is a type of tree found in the Deccan and the eastern parts of India, and the wood from this tree is used to create religious items such as sculptures of Indian gods and goddesses or decorative items. The wood is delicate and well suited to be carved in great detail with minimal tools.[2] Miniature models of people, artificial flowers for decoration, hats, jewellery and models of Mughal tombs or Muharram *taboots* are created out of *pith*.

The model of the Meenakshi temple in the Museum was made in Madurai, known as the 'City of Temples' in India. Meenakshi translates to 'a goddess with eyes like fish'. She is worshipped as an avatar of Parvati (see pp. 278-79). Meenakshi is the sister of Lord Vishnu and is married to Lord Shiva. This amalgamation of the two sects is reflected in the Shaivite and Vaishnavite sculptural iconography within the temple. The temple's construction began during the reign of King Kulasekara Pandya (1190–1216 CE) of the Pandya dynasty and continued under the rule of Vishwanatha Nayak (1529–64 CE), founder of the Madurai Nayak dynasty.

The atelier where the model was produced was located near the Meenakshi temple complex in the West Paniyan Agil Lane and probably catered to Indian pilgrims as well as European tourists looking to buy souvenirs in the mid-twentieth century.[3] Great attention is paid to the details in this model, including the representation of the deity in the sanctum, which can only be viewed by looking through the main entrance of the model. It was acquired by the Museum to showcase the south Indian style of temple architecture, with its tall *gopurams* (entrance towers). The model is rendered with accurate architectural details, and even has electric wires underneath with thirty-six miniature bulbs to light the lamp posts around the periphery of the temple and the windows in the *gopuram*, indicating that it was probably created in the mid-twentieth century. • RWB

Meenakshi Temple, T.K. Mahalinga Rao; *pith* wood, mid-twentieth century, Madurai; 31.44 x 31.44 x 30.4 cm. Accessioned: 1959.

Miniature paintings; gouache, ink, watercolour on paper, late eighteenth to early twentieth century. On view in the Industrial Arts Gallery, Dr. Bhau Daji Lad Museum, Mumbai.

80 FLOWER STUDY

EVEN before the establishment of the Delhi Sultanate (1206–1526) in the thirteenth century, cross-cultural exchange of commodities and ideas had prevailed due to the Indian overseas trade along the Red Sea and Levant sea routes.[1] By the turn of the next century, the Delhi Sultanate had strengthened ties with foreign cities, particularly with Persia via the ports at Hormuz. These cities were also prime centres of Islamic culture and there was an active cultural exchange.[2] Indian sultanates treasured Persian epics which were widely emulated by local artists, both Indian and Persian, and circulated to royal and non-royal patrons. Records suggest that, for instance, manuscripts and books produced in Iran were commissioned or exchanged as gifts between the Bahmani court of the Deccan and the Timurid court in Shiraz during the first half of the fifteenth century.[3] The apex of this cultural collaboration was achieved when the Mughal Emperor Humayun (r. 1530–40 and 1555-56) returned to India in 1554 concluding his royal exile and refuge at Tabriz, in the Safavid court of Shah Tahmasp I (r. 1524–76). While at Tabriz, Humayun was greatly influenced by Persian concepts of calligraphy and painting and returned to India with several Persian masters.

Of the many genres in Persian miniature paintings, flower studies were among the most popular and the most appreciated. These appeared widely in the *muraqqa* (albums) of Islamic empires from the sixteenth to the eighteenth century, particularly of the Safavids and the Mughals. The era exemplifies the confluence of Persian and Mughal styles, reflected in the miniature paintings of the period. The paintings displayed various themes such as portraiture, pastoral scenes and studies in flora and fauna.

Miniature paintings originally formed a part of manuscript illustrations or albums. But with the Ottomans conquering Tabriz in 1548, the *kitaab-khana* (royal library and workshop) set up by Shah Tahmasp soon dissolved, and Persian painters sought to sell single-leaf miniatures outside the royal courts. As a result, individual miniatures became widely available. The affordability of these pictures, as compared to albums, encouraged a wider network of collectors. However, many artists and master artisans dispersed from Persia, seeking patrons and work opportunities in Istanbul, Kabul and the Deccan.[4]

The painting in the Museum's collection is in the Qajar style (1794–1925). It is a single-page flower study, marked by the artist's signature and numbered in the Siyaq script at the bottom of the folio. European techniques of foreshortening and shading greatly influenced Qajar painting. Individual botanical studies were often inspired by European printed books and prints that made their way to Persia from

the seventeenth century through European diplomats and traders. Shah Abbas is credited with establishing unprecedented commercial and diplomatic ties between Persia and Europe. The period is marked by experimentation with European concepts by Persian artists that would continue in the succeeding Qajar period.[5]

The painting represents a mallow plant with two flower blossoms and leaves with stems. The soft colours, the contouring and the suggested venation of the plant add volume and impart a natural form that is a distinctive feature of the Qajar style. Flowers, as a central or supporting decorative motif, were integral to Persian visual culture. By the turn of the nineteenth century, the iconography of roses, irises and mallow flowers appeared in abundance on Persian carpets, textiles and pottery.[6] A decorative frame of calligraphy panels alternating with motifs of the 'flower and bird' or *gul-o-murgh* completes the composition.

Persian artists would adapt and appropriate foreign themes to suit Persian sensibilities.[7] This is effectively conveyed through the Persian script on the border of the painting. The couplets are from Nizami's poetry found in *Iskandar-Nameh* or *The Book of Alexander*. Nizami Ganjavi (1140–1202) is considered the greatest romantic epic poet in Persian literature. His *Iskandar-Nameh* is the concluding poem in his epic pentalogy, *Khamseh*, that comprises 30,000 couplets. A select twelve couplets are added to the panels in decorative cartouches and recall Alexander's campaign against Russia. Nizami portrays Alexander not only as a conqueror but also as a prophet and a wise man.

'All musky of mole (bepatched) and anklet-wearing,
The tip of the tress twisted above the ear:
Head to foot, in royal jewels;
Neither the foot the runner, nor the hand endowed with power:
With those languid feet of strained power,
What army can Sikandar defeat?
If on them fall the head (the point) of a needle,
(wide) like a window they open the mouth (in lamentation).
They wage war by date and the kalendar (of happy omen);
Delay a month in calculation:
Not of this sort, are those soldiers that, on the day of battle,
Bring forth the dust (of destruction) from a broken clod:'[8]

• IH

Flower Study; inscription: 'Sayyid; Raqam No. 20', gouache and ink on paper, Persian School (Qajar), 1325 (AH)/1907 CE, Persia; 27.4 x 18.4 cm. Accessioned: early twentieth century.

81 MUGHAL COURTIER

IN seventeenth-century Mughal India, the subject of portraiture achieved new standards. Extensively illustrated on small-sized folios, portraits narrated important and accurate accounts of the royal court and truthfully revealed the sitter's individual qualities. The courtier portrayed in this miniature painting is Mir Abu'l-Ma'ali, a close associate of Emperor Aurangzeb (r. 1658–1707) and father of Khan Jahan Bahadur Kukaltash. The latter, for whom the Emperor had great regard, was a high-ranking military commander in the imperial army.

He is represented in side profile, sitting upright and in a pose of supplication that is characteristic of portraits of Mughal courtiers. He is attired in white in a fashion that was popular at the court of Aurangzeb; a *jama* (full-sleeved robe) and *pajama* (trousers) along with a *pagadi* (turban) and a long piece of gold brocade or *patka* (waist belt) with floral motifs on the two ends. A similar ensemble is seen in many of the compositions of the Emperor himself.

The painting achieves a high level of artistic resolution through the arrangements of its formal elements—a sword positioned beside the courtier that establishes a linear hierarchy with the *jali* and the carpet; the colouring of the bolster and cushions against which

Mughal Courtier; gouache and ink on paper, late seventeenth to early eighteenth century, Deccani School; 19.1 x 12.6 cm. Accessioned: 1941–42.

he sits and his serene profile. A sense of subtle lavishness is achieved by the use of gold paint for the sides and borders of the cushions, on his waist belt and turban. Other compositional elements, such as the floral carpet and white *jali* (perforated screen), add textural flourishes. The stylised florals on the carpet correspond to a lattice-and-floral pattern that was popular in woven carpets in the mid-seventeenth century.[1] The light yellow colour of the carpet enlivens the painting yet enables the artist to achieve a restrained palette. *Jalis* were structural elements widely used in palaces and tombs for ornamentation, providing light and breeze inside rooms and along the pathways around mausoleums. The white colour of the *jali* alludes to the marble that was extensively used in Mughal architecture since the reign of Emperor Shah Jahan (r. 1628–58). The open sky is also highlighted with streaks of pink and gold,

adding a touch of vibrancy to the overall austerity of colour. Gold was applied in the final stages of painting and represents the influence of the Deccan Sultanate style of painting which was popular during Aurangzeb's reign, as the Mughals annexed the Deccan with the conquest of Bijapur and Golconda in 1687.

The softness in line and shading observed in this painting reflects attributes of Hunhar, a Mughal artist active during the mid-seventeenth century. Royal portraits by Hunhar are found in 'The Shah Jahan Album', initiated by Jahangir and passed down to his son, Emperor Shah Jahan, and finally to Emperor Aurangzeb. The artist who produced the Museum's painting is possibly from Hunhar's atelier or influenced by it. The Mughal courtier's portrait assimilates Mughal realism with Deccani stylistic treatments of the late seventeenth century. • IH

Shahjada; ink and watercolour on paper, late seventeenth century, Mughal School; 43.4 x 30.3 cm. Accessioned: 1941–42.

SHAHJADA

The princely portrait is set against a saturated green background, a typical trend observed in individual Mughal portraits since the early seventeenth century. The standing portrait of the young Shahjada, which literally translates to 'son of a Shah', could have been dispersed from a royal album that was commissioned to record distinguished personalities of the court. The prince is idealised by a halo, which also serves as a marker of his royal status. The representation of garments and accessories establish the subject's stature and the period.[1] Following Emperor Aurangzeb's conquest in 1687 of the Deccan, nobles and princes adopted styles that were influenced by Deccani forms. In the painting, the prince wears a short stole around his neck, a long, full-sleeved flowered *jama* (long robe), a plain overcoat tied at the waist and *juti* (footwear). An embellished *pagadi* (turban) with a plume of feathers, a golden *patka* (sash) around the waist, *shalwar* (trousers), and ornaments such as a pearl necklace, armband and rings define his aristocratic status. A hallmark of Mughal portraiture was to realise the individuality of the subject.[2] The circular shield, bejewelled sword and dagger fitted in the *patka* indicate the prince's military prowess as an officer in the Emperor's army. • IH

A *sanyasi* (ascetic) sitting cross-legged in a meditative pose is centrally positioned in this miniature painting, which is an artistic strategy to emphasise the meditative mood of this composition. The ascetic, wearing hooped earrings and wrapped in a *dhoti* (lower garment), sits on a tiger skin, in front of a shrine, beneath a *peepal* (fig tree) in deep meditation at the hour of dawn. Ascetics frequently appear in Indian miniature paintings as they were an integral part of traditional Indian culture. They live in remote places, in austere simplicity, renouncing worldly pleasures. Their purpose is usually self-realisation and often they live with other ascetics, meditating, preaching or practising penance, attracting many devotees.

From the sixteenth century to the nineteenth century, miniature painting flourished across three regions of the subcontinent—the northern regions governed by the Mughals, the Rajasthani states under Hindu maharajas, and the southern sultanates under Deccani princes.[1] As Mughal power waned and patronage declined, artists from the Mughal court sought out other patrons, absorbing regional traditions and creating paintings that were an amalgamation of styles from multiple schools. This began during the reign of Emperor Aurangzeb (r. 1658–1707), under whose austere rule artists relocated especially to the Deccan courts, modifying their art practice according to their new patrons' demands and tastes.[2]

This painting presents various influences, a mark of mid-eighteenth- to nineteenth-century works. Its dominant aesthetic is Deccani, but it includes strong Rajput influences. It appears to be a leaf from a *Ragamala* folio from the Deccan. *Ragamala* (garland of musical modes) miniature paintings are pictorial representations of Indian music performed during different times of the day. The miniature in focus evokes a *Bangali Ragini* in a Deccani style of the mid-eighteenth to early nineteenth centuries. The *Ragini* falls under the principle *Bhairav Raga*, which is performed early in the morning. *Bangali Raginis* are characterised by a meditating ascetic, male or female, placed inside or around a small shrine. They are represented holding a string of beads in their right hand. Deccani paintings are an amalgamation of Persian, Mughal and Rajput idioms. Such a hybridity of styles reflects the Deccan's history of political reconstruction under the Mughals, its close ties with the Safavid dynasty (1501–1722), and ancestral connections with Hindu, Ottoman and Turk communities since the fifteenth century.[3]

The composition's airy landscape with mauve-orange clouds in the background, the extensive use of light green, and the piles of rock-like motifs in green and pink are typical of landscape paintings from Rajput schools (Bikaner, Bundi and Kota) produced in the late seventeenth to late eighteenth centuries. Rajput-style miniatures famously feature ash-grey streams of water or lakes, which are always seen in the foreground, with white birds pictured nearby or in the stream. Architectural elements and buildings are usually white. The use of gold is spare, reserved only for utensils (the ascetic's pot), and a few architectural details such as the finial here. Deccani colour palettes are dominated by hues of pink, purple, mauve and green. The colours bring to life abstract clouds, plains and rock-stone surfaces in the composition. The stylised trees and the pink strip of Persian-derived rock-stone surface are typical Deccani features. Unlike refined Mughal paintings, Deccani compositions are described as exaggerated and dramatic.[4] The figures appear languid and lack the formal precision characteristic of Mughal works. Beyond the folio's edges, Deccani dramatisation is extended by an outer border of marbled paper. The use of marbled paper or *ebru* for folio decoration became popular in India, particularly in the Deccan courts, around the seventeenth century.[5]

Another significant Mughal influence is observed in the decorated *hashiya* (border). Margin painting was developed in the last quarter of the sixteenth century by the painters of Emperor Akbar's atelier. Margins became an integral part of miniatures and album painting. The brown margin of the miniature is decorated with single *peepal* leaf *butis* (motifs) in gold ink that connect it to the *peepal* tree featured in the picture.

Over the centuries, *ragas* continued to be painted and performed with great fervour across different Indian regions, each developing their signature style or *gharana*. In the late nineteenth century, theatre was the rage in Bombay, and raga-based songs formed an essential part of musical performances in Parsi and Marathi theatrical productions. The establishment of the 'Bhendibazar Gharana' in Bombay in the 1890s led to a greater appreciation of Hindustani classical music. The *gayaki* or singing style of this *gharana* was characterised by its slow open throat singing and the improvisation in *ragas* of Hindustani and Carnatic music. Disciples received training focused on voice and breath control.

A variety of public spaces offered audiences new listening experiences. *Baithaks* (seated performances) and *sangeet nataks* (musical plays) were organised in music halls, auditoriums and gardens across Girgaum and Malabar Hill. Anjanibai Malpekar, an eminent artist of the *gharana*, a disciple of Nazir Khan (one of the founders of the Bhendibazaar Gharana) and the muse of Raja Ravi Varma and M.V. Dhurandhar—she modelled for several of their paintings—debuted at Muzaffarabad Hall (Girgaum) in 1899. The Victoria Gardens was another popular venue, which hosted open-air live Indian classical music concerts and radio performances transmitted through wireless amplifiers.[6] • IH

Ascetic; gouache on paper, mid-eighteenth to early nineteenth century, Provincial Deccan School; 38.3 x 26.8 cm. Accessioned: 1941-42.

RAGAMALA, which translates to 'Garland of Ragas' in Sanskrit, is a unique amalgamation of art, poetry and music. It is a set of miniature paintings depicting *ragas* or melodies from Indian classical music (see p. 292). Each *raga* is associated with a specific season or time of the day during which it is performed. This is also reflected in the paintings, which usually depict lovers, either human or divine, that are emblematic of spiritual devotion. The painting tradition was first established in the second half of the fifteenth century as a specific genre of miniature painting and became the favoured subject for illustration among Rajput patrons. The genre expanded to include the wives of *ragas*, called *raginis*, and their sons and daughters, called *ragaputra* and *ragaputri* respectively. The loose-leaf paintings were assembled in an album typically thirty-six or forty-two in number and circulated within the inner court circles. The commissioning of a *Ragamala* was a symbol of the patron's refined taste, and viewing it became a pleasurable shared experience for courtiers and visitors. By the nineteenth century, with the loss of aristocratic patronage and the rise of British rule, the art declined.[1]

The term *raga*, which means colour or passion, denotes a musical mode. It is a melodic framework based on a scale with a given set of notes and has unique characteristics. The earliest mention of *ragas* can be traced back to between the fifth and seventh centuries in the *Brihaddeshi* treatise. As early as the fourteenth century, poets began adopting these *ragas* in their works and described them with detailed verbal imagery. These early verses or *dhyanas*, or poetic elaborations along with traditional imagery of many deities in painting and sculpture, became the template for artists to paint *Ragamalas*. Emotions such as melancholy, passion and serenity in the *ragas* were portrayed visually through the gestures and postures of the figures. The resemblance between a *raga* as a musical mode and its painting is unique. Every *raga* is sung on a specific scale and follows a certain set of universal rules. Similarly, *ragas* in paintings are composed of compulsory elements that are common in all schools. While the style of painting is influenced by the regional culture, the wealth of the patron, and the expertise of the painter, certain emotions and iconographic characteristics remain the same.

Between the sixteenth and nineteenth centuries, *Ragamala* paintings were being produced by various Indian courts, including in Rajasthan, the Pahari regions in the Himalayas, and the Deccan. The early Deccan style of miniature paintings was strongly influenced by the Mughal style as the Delhi Sultanate gradually fell to the Mughal army in the seventeenth and eighteenth centuries. During this period, several Rajput nobles also moved to the Deccan as military commanders for the Mughals and were accompanied by their court artists. The migration of artists and the presence of these Hindu rulers across the Mughal Empire contributed to the cross-fertilisation between the Rajput and Mughal styles of painting. It also resulted in the dissemination of *Ragamala* iconography from the north to the south. This confluence of different styles resulted in the development of new hybrid schools such as Hyderabad and Jaipur.[2]

The Museum's collection of *Ragamala* paintings from Hyderabad was made in c. 1760–1800, during the Asaf Jahi dynasty, when a significant number of stylistically similar *Ragamala* sets were being painted. The chief patrons were the Nizams and their Muslim and Hindu nobles. These sets portray better perspective views of architecture with semi-naturalistic vanishing points. Another defining feature of this period includes architectural elements painted white and buildings with tall storeys and small pavilions.[3] The female figures were heavily ornamented, wearing short blouses with a transparent *odhni* or veil, and depicted with elongated eyes and pointed chins. Lilac, violet, dark green, and light colours of sage green were commonly used in Deccan paintings. Gold was also used in abundance and the skies were typically rendered in a palette of blue and pink, as seen on the opposite page. The open terraces with elaborate architectural details in the background of the miniatures illustrate the vastness and wealth of the Indian courts.

Showcased here are *Raga Bhairava* (left) and *Ragini Vibhasa* (right). The musical mode, *Raga Bhairava*, is performed early in the morning just before sunrise. The scene is set on a terrace outside a pavilion and Krishna is painted in deep blue, a colour usually used in Deccani-style paintings. The central female figure, his lover Radha, is portrayed in the *ragamala* rubbing Krishna's right hand with sandal paste and a maid is shown preparing the sandal paste in the foreground. *Ragini Vibhasa* is typically sung at dawn. The painting portrays a couple on a bed, awakened by the crowing of the rooster at the break of dawn. The early morning denotes the inevitable separation for the lovers, and the male figure is shown pointing an arrow at the rooster in protest. • RJ

Opposite, left
Bhairava Raga; watercolour on paper, c. 1760–1800, Deccani School; 41.8 x 31.4 cm. Accessioned: 1940-1941.

•

Opposite, right:
Vibhasa Ragini; watercolour on paper, c. 1760–1800, Deccani School; 41.8 x 31.4 cm. Accessioned: 1940-41.

84 VISHWARUPA DARSHANA

THE *Vishva-Rupa* or *Vishwarupa Darshana* is described as 'the manifestation of the Universal Form' in the *Bhagavad Gita*, which is the most widely read Hindu holy scripture.[1] The *Bhagavad Gita*, known popularly as the *Gita*, narrates the philosophical discourse between Lord Krishna, the supreme deity of the universe, and Arjuna, a prince of the Pandava clan, whom he is leading into battle as his charioteer. The discourse takes place before the beginning of the battle of Kurukshetra, which is between the Pandavas and their cousins, the Kauravas. The story of this heroic battle is narrated in one of the great epics of India, the *Mahabharata*.

The episode in the *Mahabharata* in which Lord Krishna reveals himself as the *Vishwarupa* or the Supreme Form, is found in the eleventh chapter of the *Gita*. Arjuna is overcome by grief and confusion about going to war against the Kauravas, who are his own blood. He is distraught by the idea of the violence and devastation of war. Arjuna seeks his charioteer's guidance and Krishna, who is in human form, reveals himself as the Absolute, the source of all creation. Krishna reminds Arjuna that his *dharma* or 'duty' is to fight to establish truth and righteousness, without attaching himself to the outcome of his actions.

The miniature painting's otherworldly form—which displays multiple heads, eyes and hands wielding numerous weapons—presents the artist's interpretation of the original text of Lord Krishna's *Vishwarupa Darshana*. The chapter commences with Arjuna's request to see the Lord, the Creator of all things, in his cosmic form. 'Behold my forms,' says Lord Krishna, 'by hundreds, and by thousands, various heavenly, diverse colours and shapes. See wonders, in numbers never seen before.' Of this divine manifestation, says Arjuna, 'O God, within thy body I see all the gods, as also all the varied hosts of living beings and the Lord Brahma seated on his lotus throne, and all the Rishis, celestial snakes.' He further describes all the wondrous forms with many arms, stomachs, mouths and eyes on all sides, including the Lord's crown, mace, discus, as a mass of glory and 'darting refulgent beams around.'[2]

The concept of *Vishwarupa* appeared in sculptures as a cult icon in Mathura around the fifth century CE and in Shamlaji, Gujarat, in the sixth century CE. However, the images evolved over the centuries and continued to be produced and worshipped in north India until the eleventh century.[3] Images of deities for worship were made in strict accordance with *Shilpa Shastras* rules. The painting or sculpture had to indicate to the worshipper the recognisable attributes of the deity, becoming a symbol to focus his devotion. For instance, a large number of hands represented the numerous attributes of the deity. *Vishwarupa* is identified by the realisation of numerous arms, on the right and left, each holding a weapon or a recognisable pose.

This symbolism is integral to Hindu religious imagery and remains essential to all forms of representation connected to worship and rituals. The painting style is similar to other *Vishwarupa Darshana* paintings from the Pahadi School of the early nineteenth century. In the Museum's painting, the Lord is depicted wearing a bright yellow loincloth, standing tall with his legs taking a rock-like form of mountains. All the twenty crowned heads bear countless animals and birds. The arms to the right and left balance the composition, carrying weapons and Lord Krishna's signature attributes—the *kamal* (lotus), *trishul* (trident) and *gada* (mace). Other conventional components of the painting are the Sun and the Moon with human faces on his chest, and on the belly, the *Brahmanda* or Vishnu reclining under the Sheshnaga as Krishna himself is an avatar of Vishnu. Goddess Lakshmi, Vishnu's consort, is shown at *Brahmanda*'s feet and a seated Brahma depicted on the upper chest of the Lord. Arjuna stands on the right with his hands pressed together in a *namasakaram*, expressing his admiration and devotion to Lord Krishna. The horse, shield and sword, which are the attributes of battle, are left unattended in the foreground, drawing attention to the interaction between Arjuna and the Supreme Lord. The miniature's borders are in the characteristic Pahadi Kangra style from the mid-eighteenth century with the application of gold paint to create delicate, decorative florals.

Most rulers of the states in the Pahadi regions were patrons of religious Pahadi paintings. Although a large portion of royal commissions centred on individual portraits of the rulers or scenes of grandeur from their courts, themes of religious mythology or poetry formed a vital genre for the Hindu patrons.[4] By the seventeenth and eighteenth centuries, patrons included members of the ruling family, other than the raja himself, Muslim rulers, merchant families, and devout women who worshipped Krishna.[5] By the 1920s Pahadi Kangra miniature paintings were collected by Europeans and this painting was a part of the Colonel Murray bequest (see p. 271). • IH

Vishwarupa Darshana; gouache and gold paint on paper and border, c. early nineteenth century, Pahadi Kangra School; 39.3 x 27.2 cm. Accessioned: 1932–35.

THE Pahadi Kangra School of miniature painting originated during 1744–73 under the patronage of the Rajput rulers in the Kangra Valley in the lower Himalayan region. The Kangra School drew on both Mughal and Rajasthani influences as artists migrated from the Mughal to Rajput courts due a decline in Mughal patronage and the changing sociopolitical landscape. A distinctive style evolved and flourished in Basholi, Guler, Chamba, Mandi, Bilaspur and Garhwal.[1] The Kangra School produced a substantial number of miniatures during the reign of Rajput King Sansar Chand (r. 1775–1823), who was an ardent devotee of Lord Krishna. There was a revival of the *Bhakti* (devotion) movement among the Vaishnavite sects in this region between the fourteenth and fifteenth centuries inspired by the renowned poets Sur Das, Tulsi Das and Tan Sen.[2] Legends of Krishna's life became a popular subject for Kangra miniatures as Sansar Chand commissioned artists to produce miniatures with a distinct Vaishnavite theme.

While the Mughal miniatures portrayed the lifestyle of the court, the martial exploits and histories of kings and emperors, and the natural world, the Kangra miniatures borrowed from the Rajput School and depicted idealised narratives from Indian mythology but retained the technique of the Mughal School.[3] The principal figures are repeated in a Kangra miniature in continued, sequential actions to depict the entire narrative in a single frame. The fine lines were achieved with brushes made from squirrel hair and traditional tempera technique with natural pigments. Once the sketch was drawn, the landscape and figures were coloured, with the artist outlining the figures again as a final step. A majority of the Kangra miniatures are unsigned as one artist sketched and another artist from the atelier or family painted the same miniature. Often, the artists moved between courts and the practice evolved within families through generations.[4]

The Museum's collection includes twenty-two Pahadi Kangra miniatures depicting a series of mythological stories of Krishna's life from his birth to adulthood derived from the *Bhagavata Purana*.[5] The paintings were possibly executed in Garhwal and are derived from the styles of a few prominent master artists of the Kangra idiom. A few folios bear resemblance to those by Chaitu (c. 1810–1860s), who belonged to the family of prominent Kangra artists Nainsukh and his older brother, Manaku. Chaitu worked in Kangra and moved to Garhwal by 1829, where he established his own workshop.[6] There are stylistic similarities in the colour palette, composition, the use of grey in the interior spaces, the facial features of men and women, and even the style of turbans in those executed by Chaitu's workshop and the ones in the Museum's collection. The hardened outline of figures, pale skin, mass of hair instead of the earlier line by line delineation, along with the straight linear facial features with elongated eyes indicate that the Kangra miniatures in the Museum's collection were probably produced in the mid nineteenth century. The shape of the sloping, tiled roofs, of homes rendered in white or pink are also a key feature of mid-nineteenth century Kangra miniatures. The earlier variations of the Kangra miniatures were framed by a red monochrome border which was replaced by a floral border on darker colours by the mid-nineteenth century, as seen in the miniatures at the Museum.

The painting (opposite) showcases the celebrations at Gokul, a village in the Mathura district that is associated with Krishna's legends, shortly after the birth of Krishna. Yashoda, King Nanda's wife, raised Krishna as her own child and is shown feeding him in her chambers while female musicians play for her just outside. On the terrace male musicians accompany dancers in the courtyard to provide entertainment for the king and courtiers. Nanda, dressed in a *jama* (tunic) and trousers in the Mughal style with a turban worn in the *atpati* (Akbari) style, is shown receiving the *doob* (sacred grass offering), giving alms to the assembled crowd and visiting his wife's chambers to see the baby. Celestial figures are depicted showering blessings on Nanda, a feature seen in the Kangra paintings created in the mid-nineteenth century. The miniature is composed of interlocking planes and diagonals to connect architectural spaces such as balconies, terraces, walls and a courtyard to compartmentalise the activities illustrating a narrative sequence. The architectural details and the brightly coloured notes of the crowds appear to be derived from the works of Purkhu, a Kangra artist who produced works until the 1820s.[7]

The Kangra School eventually declined due to lack of court patronage with the annexation of the Kangra Hills into the administrative province of the Punjab by the British. By 1888, J.L. Kipling, the principal of the Mayo School of Art, records the existence of *Kangra ki Qalm* as a rarely seen style of work.[8] The disastrous earthquake of 1905 in the Kangra Valley resulted in the near end of the Kangra idiom as many painters died or moved away from the region. In the early twentieth century Ananda Coomaraswamy focused international attention on the Pahadi Kangra School of painting when he exhibited miniatures in 1910 in Allahabad.[9] The Kangra School is now being revived with state support to train a handful of artists who continue to practice this art today. • **RWB**

Krishna's birthday celebrations; gouache on paper, mid-nineteenth century, Pahadi Kangra School; 23.5 x 30.5 cm. Accessioned: 1935.

PORTRAIT painting on ivory was popular among elite Indians and Europeans from the late eighteenth century until the advent of photography. Corresponding to European miniature portraits, this genre of the Company School was lucrative for both Indian and British artists. Enshrined in ornate frames, brooches, or pendants, these miniature portraits made exquisite diplomatic gifts and souvenirs to mark special events. Charles Napier (1782–1853), commander in chief of the Bombay army (1849–51) had his portrait painted by Ghulam Husayn Khan, an artist from Delhi c. 1850.[1] Small portraits made on paper or cards to fix on to turbans was a practice that had existed among the Mughal nobility, and became especially fashionable in Shah Jahan's court. By the eighteenth century, with the breaking up of the Mughal Empire, artists who specialised in miniatures began to lose their royal patronage. They soon found ways to adapt their painting skills to the demands of the new patrons, the European visitors and the Indian elite. Portrait painting in the miniature style on ivory resulted as an influence of Western portrait painting, which had become popular during the British rule. As Company Painting developed, British residents and travellers would

Mumtaz Begum; watercolour on ivory, Company School, mid-nineteenth to early twentieth century, Delhi; 15.3 x 12.5 x 1 cm. Accessioned: 1929.

Opposite:
Jodhabai; watercolour on ivory, Company School, mid-nineteenth to early twentieth century, Delhi; 15.3 x 12.5 x 1 cm. Accessioned: 1929.

show the portraits that they had carried from Europe to these artists to copy and to commission new portraits.

The process of painting on ivory required skills involving stippling and watercolour tinting, which were different from the usual miniature painting techniques of line drawing and colour filling. Artists, who were used to working on miniatures, using thin brushes, were able to adapt and create beautiful paintings on ivory. Europeans preferred to collect subjects that depicted local themes. Especially sought after were paintings of the Mughal monuments and Mughal kings and queens and heroic warriors like Prithiviraj Chauhan the Rajput King (p. 302). The Museum's collection of paintings on ivory reflects this fashion. The collection includes paintings of monuments such as the Taj Mahal, Diwan-e-Khas and the Golden Temple as well as of Mughal emperors and empresses.

The image of Jodhabai (c. 1542–1623), wife of the Mughal Emperor Akbar, painted on a small oval piece of ivory, depicts the public iconography of Mughal royalty. It is interesting to note that the portraits of women were not realistic, but rather idealised female types, unlike those of the men.[2] Many of the smaller portraits were oval in shape and multiple portraits were mounted with a glass covering within ornate carved wooden frames. The ivory paintings reflect the incorporation of Western techniques of representation, visible in the perspectival delineation of the monuments. Most of the monuments have been executed using the photographic perspective of Western paintings rather than the symbolic and narrative style of traditional miniatures. Often paintings were traced from photographs. The process involved tracing the photograph on mica and then retracing the opposite side with transfer ink. Once the drawing was transferred onto the ivory, it was painted with watercolours.[3]

The middle third of the elephant tusk was the only usable part to create a surface for the paintings. The ivory piece was split vertically through the centre, and then filed and sandpapered to smoothen the surface. The piece was then further sliced into thin veneer sheets for the painting. Before painting, to make the surface ready, the artist would rub the surface with cuttlebone or *samandar jhag* ('foam of the sea'), which would make the ivory surface smooth as paper.

Ivory miniatures were highly sought after in the souvenir trade and many were sent to exhibitions in London in the 1860s and 1870s. Delhi was the main centre of production as Mughal artists were concentrated there.[4] Ivory painting continued until the late twentieth century till the ban on ivory hunting and trade. Craftsmen and artists then adapted miniature painting to camel bone, which is considered superior in quality as compared to other cattle bones, by the early twenty-first century. • PV

JACOB (1849-1921)

Alexander Malcolm Jacob, born in Diyarbakir, Turkey, was an enigmatic figure who inspired memoirs and novels by English travellers and authors in the late nineteenth and early twentieth centuries. Frequently described as a spy, double agent, magician and a mystic who held seances and elaborated on 'Eastern philosophy', he was a trader in jewels and antiques. Jacob's shop on the Pall Mall in Simla—packed with miniature paintings, illustrated manuscripts, silver and damascened objects, books, jewellery and artefacts from across Asia—provided the backdrop for the mysterious 'Lugran Sahib's Spy School' in Rudyard Kipling's *Kim*, published in 1901 in London. Jacob is fictionalised as the double agent Lugran Sahib in this novel that was set against the political intrigue of the Great Game.[1]

Jacob arrived at Apollo Bunder in Bombay in 1865 and gained employment in the court of Hyderabad's Nizam, Afzal ud-Daula, as apprentice scribe. Jacob left Hyderabad soon after Nizam's death and worked at Calcutta's famous jewellery firm Charles, Nephew & Co., as well as the princely courts of Dholpur and Jaipur. In 1876, Jacob established his antiquities and jewellery business in Simla, which had been declared as the summer capital of the British Indian Government in 1864. Here, he found a ready market among the wealthy British officers who spent up to six months every year in Simla and gained popularity in British society, even befriending the Viceroy, Lord Lytton. His curio shop became an unmissable stop on the itineraries of British officers and brought him to the notice of the local police and intelligence services.

Jacob developed an immense network of contacts and informers in the British military and Government as the majority of his customers were army officers nearing retirement who invested in jewellery and antiquities with the hope of selling them at greater profits back home in England. While it is believed that Jacob presented his favourite customers with his own miniature portrait in signet rings, the one in the Museum's collection is the only known portrait of him.[2] The finely executed miniature (opposite) shows Jacob dressed in finery like a nobleman with embroidered trousers and jacket over a white *jama* (upper garment worn by Indian nobility), with an embroidered Cashmere shawl draped on his right arm. A dagger and a pistol are tucked in his cummerbund (waistband). He holds a sword in his left hand and wears an amulet around his waist as he was known to be

Prithviraj Chauhan; watercolour on ivory, Company School, mid-nineteenth to early twentieth century, Delhi; 10.8 x 7.8 cm. Accessioned: 1929.
Prithviraj Chauhan (r. 1178–92) was one of the favourite subjects of portrait painters.

superstitious. The detailed work suggests that the portrait was created by a master artist in north India's miniature ateliers. The portrait is framed in an exquisite *koftgari* (damascened) frame.

Jacob catapulted to infamy in 1891 when a deal to sell the Imperial Diamond to the richest Indian noble, Mahboob Ali Khan, the Nizam of Hyderabad, fell through, and the Nizam filed a court case against him. This case marred Jacob's reputation as a jeweller and made the British Empire wary of him. The Imperial Diamond later came to be known as the 'Jacob Diamond' and it was eventually purchased by the Government of India at the turn of the twentieth century.

In 1903, Jacob moved back to Bombay, first staying at Waterloo Mansions and then at the Watson Hotel's Annexe. Most of the articles from his shop were auctioned and later sold in Bombay at much lower prices in order to pay his legal fees. Jacob died in Bombay in 1921 and was buried at the Sewri cemetery. This portrait of Jacob was in the possession of collector Lt Col. Howard Murray and presented to the Museum by his widow in 1935 after Murray mysteriously disappeared from the ship while on his way to Australia.[3] • RWB

Jacob; miniature on ivory,
Company School, late
nineteenth century, Delhi; 24.7
x 16 x 1 cm. Accessioned: 1935.

AN important painting collection of *Navagrahas* (nine planetary deities) and *Ashtadikpalas* (guardians of the eight directions) hangs in the Museum's library. These were acquired from the royal palace of Tanjore by Lt Col. H. Murray and Mrs Murray, who donated it to the Museum in 1935. During the late seventeenth century, Shahaji Bhosale, father of Chhatrapati Shivaji Maharaj, conquered much of the territory of south India. Shahaji Raje's elder son, Shri Venkoji Bhosale, ascended the throne of Tanjore in 1675. The city served as the capital of the Maratha kingdom until 1855. The Maratha monarchs were reputed as patrons of the arts and

during the reign of Shivaji Maharaj of Tanjore (r. 1833–55), there were eighteen artist families residing there.[1] Many of these artists are credited with the elaborate murals and stucco decoration of the Durbar Hall in the Maratha palace.[2] The main themes depicted are deities and portraits of the Bhosale rulers of Tanjore.

The Tanjore or Thanjavur style of painting flourished from the seventeenth century with the reign of the Marathas in south India. Richly painted surfaces, vibrant colours, simple composition and gold foil that add a sumptuous look to the paintings are the characteristic features of Tanjore

Navagrahas and Ashtadikpalas (Surya); seventeen paintings with natural colour pigments and gold foil on wood, late nineteenth to early twentieth century, Tanjore; 90 x 75 x 9 cm. Accessioned: 1935.

The Navagrahas (nine planetary deities): In many south Indian temples, Surya (Sun) is placed at the centre while the eight planets face the eight cardinal directions: Shukra (Venus) faces north, Chandra (Moon) north-east, Mangala (Mars) east, Rahu south-east, Shani (Saturn) south, Ketu south-west, Brihaspati (Jupiter) west and Budha (Mercury) north-west. The directions correspond to the eight-part division of the day which emanates from Surya. The Navagrahas in the Museum's collection are depicted riding their *vahanas* (vehicles).

(Above and opposite) *Ashta* means eight, *dik* means quarters and *palas* means rulers. The Ashtadikpalas are the rulers or guardians of the eight quarters of the universe and are usually depicted in the *mandapas* (hall) of the temples. These divinities are part of the Hindu pantheon and originated in the Vedic period. The epics and *Puranas* differ in the names and number of the *dikpalas*; most of them indicate four but gradually the figure increased to eight as the divisions of quarters increased. The Museum collection reflects the interpretation of the *Puranas*.

paintings. The paintings are created on solid wooden panels and thus locally referred to as *palagai padam*.[3] The Tanjore style is a hybrid of classical and popular traditions.[4] By the mid-seventeenth century, many types of decorative objects and paintings were produced by the court artists for sale in the bazaars.[5] Tanjore paintings are one of the earliest manifestations of commercially available framed pictures in India.[6]

'Reverse glass' paintings—known for their distinctive style comprising simple layouts, a muted colour palette and minimal backgrounds—were relatively inexpensive and popularised the Tanjore tradition of painting in south India. Artists trained in this style were crucial to the development of the chromolithograph aesthetic for Ravi Varma and later of calendar art.[7]

Apart from painting temple murals and sculptures, and making portraits, Tanjore artists produced sacred icons on wood panels. The panels, often embossed with gold as well as silver and studded with jewels, were used to adorn temples, community prayer halls, and shrines. Tanjore paintings, such as the Museum's collection of *Navagrahas* and *Ashtadikpalas*, were produced in response to a growing demand from worshippers and collectors. Painted with natural pigments on plain backgrounds, each painting bears the name of the deity written in English. Its layout resembles the large-scale Tanjore palace murals. The main murals are in the ornate Durbar Hall. The palace walls are embellished with murals depicting scenes and themes from mythology and several deities, as well as portraits of the Maratha rulers of Tanjore. The realistic representation of human and animal figures reflects the artists' command over anatomical drawing and their understanding of the European concept of 'naturalism'. This could be due to the influence of the Company School painting style that flourished in Tanjore during the late seventeenth century. The British realised that Indian artists were highly skilled in adapting European techniques to local needs and quickly assessed the demands of the market.[8] The iconography was derived from ancient texts like the *Rigveda* and the *Shilpa Shastras*, which is apparent as all the planet and guardian figures are depicted with gold shields on their chests and appropriate weapons in their hands. The architectural elements in the composition of the *Ashtadikpalas* paintings, especially the arches, are two-dimensional representations of shrines. These artworks belong to a special genre of painting that fuses the religious and the popular as well as the Indian and European aesthetic to create a new language of artistic representation. • HK

INDISPUTABLY the most celebrated work in Persian literature, the *Shah Nameh* or 'Book of Kings' was written by poet Hakim Abul-Qasim Firdawsi Tusi over a period of thirty years and completed in 1010 CE. With sixty-two stories, 900 chapters and over 50,000 rhyming couplets in three parts, the *Shah Nameh* blends myth, legend and historical fact as it narrates the story of the Persian world from the moment of its creation to the Arab conquest of the Persian Empire in the seventh century CE.

Firdawsi (940–1025 CE), an aristocratic Muslim from Tus in the north-eastern Iranian province of Khorasan, wrote his epic poem under the rule and patronage of the Samanids, a local dynasty. In an effort to assert their cultural identity and independence from the Abbasid caliphate in Baghdad, they encouraged a revival of pre-Islamic Persian tradition and thought.[1] In drawing upon pre-Islamic sources and choosing modern Persian over Arabic as his literary medium, Firdawsi preserved the history of *Iranshahr*, or the Greater Iranian people, in their own language. A thousand years after it was written, his *Shah Nameh* remains an enduring symbol of Persian cultural and literary identity, and a masterpiece of world literature.

A work of remarkable complexity and variety, the *Shah Nameh* covers the reign of fifty mythical and historical kings. It follows the lives, exploits, victories and very human struggles of the kings and heroes, fathers and sons; with its universal and timeless themes celebrating justice and the ultimate victory of good over evil, Firdawsi's *Shah Nameh* appealed to and influenced cultures far beyond its time and place. As it emphasises the divine right to rule, the *Shah Nameh* has also been widely commissioned in symbolic efforts to legitimise kingship across the Persianate world.

In India, copies of the *Shah Nameh* find mention as early as the fifteenth century, but few folios from these manuscripts are known.[2] The Mughal Emperor Babur (r. 1526–30) brought with him to India a famed copy of the *Shah Nameh* produced in Herat, Afghanistan, in the mid-fifteenth century. Now in the collections of the Royal Asiatic Society of Great Britain and Ireland, the manuscript was a treasured possession of the Mughal imperial library and is marked with the seals of five emperors, including Shah Jahan (r. 1628–58) and Aurangzeb (r. 1658–1707). There is some evidence to suggest that the manuscript inspired Akbar to commission his own copy; intriguingly, the Akbari *Shah Nameh* is yet to be discovered.

Whilst gifts of the *Shah Nameh* from Iran were prized in the rich, eclectic Mughal courts, copies commissioned in the royal ateliers were rare. In contrast, the *Shah Nameh* was widely produced in the popular Mughal tradition at the provincial courts of Mughal nobility and officials.[3] The production of *Shah Nameh* manuscripts spread as far north as Kashmir, where it became the most popular Persian text illustrated in the regional style from the seventeenth to the nineteenth centuries, intended for trade and wider, bourgeois consumption.[4]

The *Shah Nameh* (opposite) is one of two illustrated copies in the Museum's collection, bequeathed by Irene Murray, widow of Lt Col. Howard Murray, in 1935.[5] It comprises 492 folios of text in the Persian Nastaliq script, organised in four columns, with forty-five illustrations in Kashmiri style. Kashmiri manuscript paintings of the eighteenth and nineteenth centuries indicate a fusion of styles from various painting schools. Distinctive features include a bold colour palette of ultramarine blue, orange, dark purple and moss green. The figures are characterised by their prominent, outlined eyeballs and shorter bodies that appear in frontal, side, or three-quarter views. In general, the rendering of landscape and figures lack perspective, thus appearing flat. Architectural forms are minimal and simplified.

The tales of Rostam, bravest of the brave, form a large part of the heroic section of the *Shah Nameh*. In the featured image, Rostam is an older man fighting against his young son, Sohrab. The painting depicts the moment of denouement. Rostam is recognised by his symbolic tiger skin and fierce demeanour. The valour of young Sohrab is no match for the experienced Rostam. He is defeated as he is pushed to the ground and stabbed by Rostam's sword. The dying Sohrab exclaims that his death will be avenged by his father, the legendary Rostam, for whom he has been searching. Until this point father and son were unaware of each other's identity. The revelation causes Rostam great shock and agony. Sohrab lifts his arm and reveals the onyx on his armband as he learns the identity of his estranged father. Rostam recognises the precious stone as the token he had given to Princess Tahmina, Sohrab's mother, several years ago. The startled soldiers, the horses of Rostam and Sohrab in the foreground, the flags and soldiers at the top, frame the two protagonists and contribute to the symmetry of the painting. The vivid colours heighten the sense of drama and tragedy. The broad bands of blue, purple, orange and green express the sky, fields and mountains across the manuscript's painted folios, providing a visual consistency to the text. These form a quintessential Kashmiri interpretation of a traditional Persian classic. • **AS**

Shah Nameh; manuscript, gouache and ink on paper, eighteenth to nineteenth century, Kashmir; 9.1 x 30.7 x 50 cm. Accessioned: 1935.

89 ASHTASAHASRIKA PRAJNAPARAMITA

FOR the past few centuries, Tibetan manuscripts have provoked much interest among the historians of South Asia. Tibet was an unexplored region until the twentieth century, and museums and universities had small Tibetan collections. There was a rise of political interest in Tibet due to its central position in Asia in the mid-nineteenth century. The continuous failure of the British to establish diplomatic relations with Tibet, and rumours of Russian interest, led to an expedition called the British invasion of Tibet in 1903-04. The mission was led by Francis Younghusband, and was known as the Younghusband Mission. The beginning of the twentieth century was also a period of intense interest in the collection and display of oriental artefacts as ethnographic departments in museums proliferated. Interest in Tibetan manuscripts grew due to research on Tibetan and Sanskrit languages. Orientalists were intrigued by the possibility of finding the original Sanskrit palm-leaf manuscripts which were carried from India by Buddhist monks to establish Buddhism in Tibet around the seventh century.[1] The upsurge of interest in oriental studies led to considerable demand for acquiring such artefacts for personal and institutional reasons and became the priority during the mission. This resulted in many officers unofficially taking artefacts and manuscripts for personal benefit. John Claude White, political officer of Sikkim, who accompanied the expedition took several photographs which were presented along with his paper on *The Arts and Crafts of Tibet and the Eastern Himalayas* at the Royal Society of Arts in 1910. The discussion piqued the interest in Tibetan arts and crafts in the metropole. George Birdwood, who was in the audience, expressed handsome praise for Tibetan architecture.

The illustrated folio from the Tibetan manuscript in the Museum's collection is based on *Prajnaparamita Sutra*, the fundamental text of Mahayana Buddhism. The *Prajnaparamita* is regarded as the embodiment of supreme wisdom that leads to enlightenment and is not only read but also worshipped. The folio is from the Tibetan manuscript *brGyad stong pa* or *Ashtasahasrika Prajnaparamita* in Sanskrit. *Ashtasahasrika Prajnaparamita* translates to 'The Perfection of Knowledge in Eight Thousand Lines' (*slokas*), and is one of the earliest Mahayana scriptures. *Prajnaparamita* has gradually changed over the years, varying from several shorter and longer versions. *Ashtasahasrika Prajnaparamita*, originally written in India between the first and second centuries CE, was translated into several languages and became popular in Mahayana Buddhism. Mahayana, meaning 'greater vehicle', is one of the main branches of Buddhism—the others being Theravada and Vajrayana Buddhism. The first translation of *Prajnaparamita* in Tibetan was made about the ninth century.[2]

Bodhisattva Vajrasattva, the Buddhist deity of enlightenment, is important in Vajrayana Buddhism. He is shown illustrated in the centre of the first folio (opposite). Vajrayana, also known as *tantric* or esoteric Buddhism, became popular in India during the Pala Empire in the eighth century and was later introduced in Tibet.[3] An extension of Mahayana Buddhism, it advocates new *tantric* practices to facilitate progress along the road to enlightenment. Vajrasattva is shown seated on a lotus in finely rendered garments with a scarf that drapes around his shoulders in elegant loops. Surrounded by a multicoloured circular aureole, he carries in his right hand a *vajra* or thunderbolt held near his chest. *Vajra*, the diamond sceptre, symbolises compassion, indestructibility of knowledge and the nature of reality, important requisites for enlightenment in esoteric Buddhism. *Siddhasana*, or the adept pose, which is sitting with the right leg on the left thigh, is another significant iconographic feature. Vajrasattva is illustrated with gold accessories such as bracelets, anklets, necklaces, earrings and a crown ornamented with jewels. Confident outlines and subtle shading are used to add a sense of scale. The colours are more luminous than those typically seen in Pala or Nepalese illuminations. Rich blues and deep magenta reds make the miniature strikingly vibrant. Both in workmanship and style, these illustrations are painted in an idiom that flourished in western Tibet from the eleventh to the thirteenth century, and are likely to have been produced during that period.

This manuscript, consisting of loose paper folios, is handwritten in *Uchen* (*dbu-can*) script in black ink. The script is written with a 'head', a horizontal stroke of various lengths on the upper part of the letter. The animated illustrations between the lines do not illustrate the text but are created as auspicious symbols to protect the book, the reader, and the person commissioning the manuscript. There are two circles on each page of the manuscript, marking the holes which would have been punched to hold the leaves together in the old manuscript from which it was copied. The loose papers, held together by boards, are probably made from the bark or roots of local poisonous plants. Poisonous plants were probably used to make the paper resistant to insect attack and thus long-lasting.[4] The manuscript was acquired by the Museum in 1932 from retired Lt Col. Howard Murray of the British Indian army.[5] • RJ

Ashtasahasrika Prajnaparamita; ink on handmade paper, c. eleventh to thirteenth century, western Tibet; 15.2 x 72 x 25.5 cm. Accessioned: 1932.

Nineteenth-Century Mumbai Paintings Gallery featuring paintings by J.J. School artists A. Kamadoli (left) and Rao Bahadur M.V. Dhurandhar (right); watercolour on paper, early twentieth century, Dr. Bhau Daji Lad Museum, Mumbai.

EARLY MODERN PAINTING
A New Perspective

THE early twentieth century witnessed the maturing of an art practice in Bombay that can be called Early Modern as it was Western (naturalistic) in technique but Indian in subject matter.[1] It differed significantly from earlier traditional and indigenous painting and sculptural practices, which unfortunately were reviled by the colonial administration and neglected by the new urban elite. Unlike Ravi Varma's mythological and religious paintings that preceded it, the subject matter of these works of art was secular, though religious themes continued to engage artists like M.V. Dhurandhar, who was closely associated with Ravi Varma. The locus of this new art practice was the Sir J.J. School of Art, which over the years had acquired a formidable reputation due to the efforts of its principals John Griffiths, Cecil Burns and Gladstone Solomon. Bombay had suffered a major setback due to the plague which raged intermittently from 1896 till the turn of the century. The V&A Museum, Bombay, and the Sir J.J. School of Art struggled through this period. Many students abandoned their studies. When Cecil Burns took over the School in 1898 after Griffiths retired, he found it in disarray.[2]

Burns, who was a painter, did not seem to have much empathy with his students though he is credited with enforcing strict academic standards according to the tenets of the Royal Academy in London.[3] Trained as a landscape painter, he started informal *plein air* classes at the School, encouraging his students to use watercolours to capture the quality of Indian light. A genre of landscape painting developed in Bombay known as the 'Open Air School' and several well-known artists, like S.L. Haldankar and A.M. Mali (see pp. 324-25), whose works are featured in the Museum's collection, were influenced by this movement. Burns was more concerned with the administration of the School and he established and consolidated a system of Government examinations for art teachers that would make the School the premier teaching institution for the visual arts in the country. He also established the first School of Architecture in Asia, in 1910, as a separate institution under the umbrella of the Sir J.J. School of Art. In 1903, he took over as the curator of the Victoria and Albert Museum, Bombay, and established a close relationship between the School and the Museum, drawing on the resources of the School to supplement those of the Museum.

Not all art connoisseurs, however, were happy with the Bombay style of painting promoted by the School. Ananda Coomaraswamy excoriated the style adopted by the art schools as 'absolute banality and vulgarity' in a text on Modern Indian art for the Empire of India Exhibition in 1911.[4] An acclaimed scholar, Coomaraswamy, along with E.B. Havell, principal of the Calcutta School of Art, and the Tagore family in Calcutta, had spearheaded the rethinking on traditional Indian art, in particular Mughal and Rajput miniature painting and Indian sculpture (see p. 125). Many European critics also claimed that much of the work produced at the art schools did not reflect an

Yog Raj Chitrakar: Memory Drawing X Part II, Nikhil Chopra, 2010, performance at the Museum. Exhibition: *Yog Raj Chitrakar, Memory Drawing X, Part I and II*; West Lawn, 2010.

In the performance, the artist took on the persona of a Victorian lady, apparently a queen, who is imprisoned in the Museum and its garden, and spends her time making a drawing of the building in the conventional nineteenth-century-landscape mode. Yog Raj Chitrakar is a turn-of-the-century Victorian draughtsman based loosely on the artist's grandfather Yog Raj Chopra who was a landscape painter.

'Indian spirit' and the teaching and output of the art schools were frequently criticised at meetings of the various expert societies in London. Havell and Burns had some heated exchanges on the topic at the Royal Society for the Encouragement of Arts, Manufactures and Commerce.[5] Amplifying this chorus was the nationalist movement for Indian independence, which took issue with the rejection of traditional Indian painting by the colonial administrators. Indian writers criticised artists who did not display affinities with earlier forms of Indian art. The newspapers played an important role in expressing public views and Bombay's conservative position during Burns' tenure, and the vocal Bengali nationalist press ensured that Calcutta's non-illusionist oriental style captured the public imagination.

Bombay, however, did not languish for long. The man responsible for the 'revival' of the Bombay style was the new principal of the Sir J.J. School of Art, Gladstone Solomon, who vigorously promoted painting and sculpture and encouraged his students to develop an individual 'Indian' style. Solomon took charge of the School in 1918 after Burns retired. He started a mural painting class in 1919, based on the notion that it was an intrinsically Indian form and that this skill would enable the students to execute public commissions in important state buildings and eventually, in people's homes.[6] Many of the School's students had been earlier engaged in the documentation of the Ajanta paintings and Solomon revived this practice. Ajanta had also been claimed by both the Bengal painters and the nationalists as representing the acme of Indian art and Solomon wanted to show his students' skills.[7]

Solomon was determined to wrest artistic primacy from the Calcutta School and project Bombay as the centre of an 'Indian Art Renaissance', for which he enlisted the support of the Governor, Sir George Lloyd, and other political stalwarts.[8] Unlike Burns, Solomon had an affectionate and paternal relationship with his students, in particular M.V. Dhurandhar, who was headmaster of the School. He entrusted him with important assignments such as leading the teams to paint the pylons that would decorate the streets of Bombay in 1921 during the visit of the Prince of Wales, later King Edward VIII. Solomon also ensured that the School earned distinction at the British Empire Exhibition. The India Room at the exhibition, which was executed by the School, took nine months to put together and engaged all the departments of the School, including 'modellers [as Indian sculptors were called in those days], painters, designers, potters, silversmiths, enamellers, carpet weavers, shape-makers, iron-workers, carpenters, wood-carvers, decorators, and engravers—all having heard the "still small voice" ...'[9]

Solomon, who was a governing member of the Bombay Art Society, encouraged his students to contribute to the Society's annual exhibitions, which were a prominent feature of the cultural life of the city. The exhibitions had gained much fame, and artists across the country vied for the Society's gold medal, which was the most coveted of all art prizes.[10] The openings by the Governor were gala evenings with the cream of Bombay society in attendance. The evening before the opening, there would be a 'conversazione' for the members. S.M. Edwardes, the Police Commissioner (1910–16) and subsequently Municipal Commissioner (1916–18), who described his experience of the city in the delightful book *Byways of Bombay*, always attended the function and often purchased works of art.[11] Solomon notes that in the 1923 Bombay Art Society Exhibition, Indian artists dominated: 'New Art Societies are springing up all over the South West. Of the one hundred and ninety-two artists who exhibited at the Annual Exhibition of the Bombay Art Society in December 1923, one hundred and thirty-six were Indian, of whom thirty-six were ladies. The European Exhibitors were only twenty in all.'[12]

The struggle for a national art style continued as many artists were drawn to the nationalist movement and experimented with different indigenous genres in their search of an 'authentic' Indian voice. Pastoral life and traditions, known as the 'Primitivist' style, informed the work of many artists both in Bengal and Bombay.[13]

Untitled, Cecil L. Burns; watercolour
on paper, 1918, Bombay; 13.7 x 9.7 cm.
Accessioned: 2012.
Cecil Burns was a well-known watercolour
and landscape artist. This untitled
watercolour by Burns is significant as most
of the other works that he painted in India
were damaged in a fire that broke out at
the docks in Southampton, England, after
he returned home. The painting shows a
lotus-filled pond in natural surroundings, and
appears to be inspired by Claude Monet's
series of *Water Lilies*, painted in 1900. The
pond and sky are sharply demarcated by a
yellow and green horizon line. The painting
has a warm afternoon glow and was possibly
copied from a print of Monet's works.

Solomon was determined to ensure that the 'Bombay' style prevailed over what
was called the 'Bengal' style. The denouement in this battle took place during the
competition for the much-coveted Prix de Delhi, which was a public commission
in 1927 to paint murals in the important state buildings being designed by Herbert
Baker for the new capital.[14] Dhurandhar led the Bombay School team in Delhi and
Solomon ensured Bombay won the commission (see pp. 318-19).[15] Several important
citizens of Bombay campaigned for the commission, including the politician and
lawyer M.R. Jayakar. Kanaiyalal Vakil, the art critic of the *Bombay Chronicle*, was a
vocal supporter and Sir George Llyod, the Governor, exerted as much influence as
possible to ensure Bombay won the commission.

Despite this victory Solomon was concerned with the criticism that the Bombay
style was a weak adaptation of the Western academic style and lacked Indian feeling.
He appointed J.N. Ahiwasi (1933–57), an artist from Nathdwara who was familiar with
Rajput miniature painting, to take charge of the Indian design class at the School.
Ahiwasi encouraged his students to adopt bright, flat colours, similar to those of
Rajput miniature paintings, with strong outlines and decorative design schemas.[16]
Ahiwasi's skills were applauded by critics and his adaptation of the Rajput miniature
style to modern subjects would have a resounding impact on his students, as is
evident in the Kekoo Gandhy collection at the Museum (see pp. 328–31). Ahiwasi's
style would continue to influence the School's students even after Independence and
is visible in the student works of painters like S.H. Raza and V.S. Gaitonde, who were
members of the remarkable Progressive Artists' Group in Bombay. The Group was
established in 1947 and changed the course of Indian Modern Art. • TZM

90 NYAYALAYA
by M.V. DHURANDHAR (b. 1867–1944)

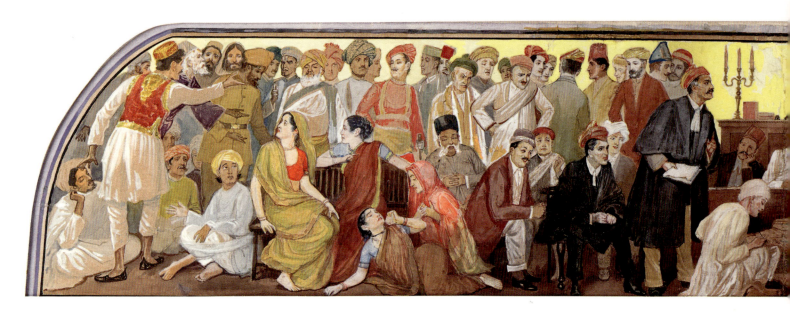

Nyayalaya or Law in Early British Period;
Rao Bahadur M.V. Dhurandhar; watercolour
on paper, 1928, Bombay; 74 x 235 cm.
Accessioned: 1991-92.

MAHADEV Vishwanath Dhurandhar (1867–1944), one of colonial India's most eminent artists, was witness to the accelerated change that was taking place in the country in the early twentieth century. His sharp observational skills and deep-rooted cultural sensibilities produced a humanist and humorous documentation of the era. His works are defined by an indigenous perspective with a visual vocabulary that masters the prevailing colonial naturalist genre and captures the authenticity of both the subject and the context.

Dhurandhar was trained at the Sir J.J. School of Art in Bombay and eventually became its headmaster. His proficiency in European naturalism won him numerous awards. Like most artists of the time, he attempted to negotiate his way through colonial aesthetic standards and pry out new expressive methods.[1] He is known for his ability to represent Indian subjects in a 'historicizing, naturalist still frame' and his 're-indigenized Indian naturalism' in response to Western ideals.[2] In the early twentieth century, the figure of the artist as a romantic outsider challenging orthodoxies was an established convention in the modernist imagination.[3]

Dhurandhar's practice breaks away from this notion. His works, which read as testaments of the time, remain faithful to the academic realist style.

Unlike his contemporaries, Dhurandhar's illustrations reflect a penetrating world view. His works were not merely documentary but reflected a theatrical realism. Bombay had a flourishing Marathi and Parsi theatre practice as well as a thriving studio photography industry in the early twentieth century. Dhurandhar had close associations with Bal Gandharva, one of the most renowned theatre performers of the era, who often visited his studio.[4] The influence of theatre is evident in the striking poses and emotive faces of the figures in his works.

In this painting, *Nyayalaya (Law in Early British Period)*, which depicts a court scene, the artist has captured Bombay's varied communities in their distinct headgear and dress during a crucial moment of the judgement. This work is one of the watercolour sketches Dhurandhar produced during the open Government competition for mural decoration at the Law Members' Chamber of the Imperial Secretariat in New Delhi,

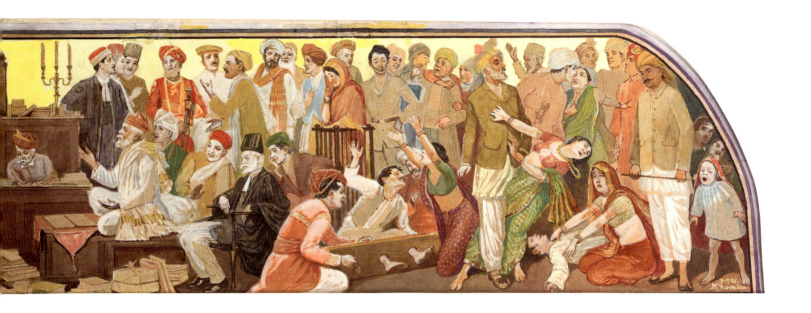

which was designed by Herbert Baker. Dhurandhar won the commission and created four cartoons depicting aspects of the law. Two of these, *Streedhan Lagnasamarambh* (property given to women at the time of wedding) and *Dattavidhan* (adoption), were related to Hindu law; the third was related to Muslim Sharia law (will or testament done by a person for the management of his property after death) and the fourth was *Nyayalaya* (Law in Early British Period).[5]

The themes and finer nuances for the paintings were guided by eminent members of the court. It took one and half months to complete two watercolour paintings, *Streedhan Lagnasamarambh* and *Nyayalaya*, and two pencil drawings of Muslim Sharia law and *Dattavidhan*. The works were finally executed using the marouflage technique of mural painting, where large painted canvases are stuck on the walls as part of decoration instead of painting directly on the wall.[6]

The shape of the painting in the Museum collection indicates its use as a preparatory sketch for a mural work. The work is dramatic and cleverly structured, following the prevailing theatrical fashion. The central panel with the judge, and his judicial officers or clerks, is used to separate the two opposing sides. The lawyer on the right is slumped in his chair in defeat. The lawyers on the other side, younger and more alert, appear to be aggressively making their point in response to what the blushing woman in the witness box, just right of centre, looking embarrassed and frightened, has revealed. You can almost hear the cries of the man in shackles and his loved ones, and sense the arrogance amongst the spectators on the left, with several men smirking, as opposed to the worried concern on the right. Other onlookers in the backdrop are simply enjoying the drama. The judge sits silently in the centre of all the obvious confusion, listening dispassionately.

During the work's progress Dhurandhar received feedback from Gladstone Solomon, the principal of the Sir J.J. School of Art at the time. The size of each panel of the mural is 8 feet by 4 feet at the Law Chamber. Before the installation in Delhi, Dhurandhar organised an informal preview for friends and students which was inaugurated by the renowned barrister M.R. Jayakar. • HK

UNTITLED *by* RUSTOM SIODIA (b. 1881–1946)

Among the painters of the Early Modern, pre-Independence era in Bombay, Rustom Siodia, a Parsi painter, deserves special attention. Siodia's portfolio includes portraits, landscapes and historical works. He was born in 1881 in Bombay and his art education began in 1908 when he enrolled at the Sir J.J. School of Art, Bombay. He went on to study at the Royal Academy of Art, London, until 1913. He is recorded as the first Parsi and the second Indian to train at the prestigious academy, studying under leading artists like John Singer Sargent (1856–1925).[1]

Upon completing his training in London, Siodia set up a studio in the Grant Road area of Bombay around 1915. As an important centre for art in the early decades of the twentieth century, Bombay provided the young artist with substantial opportunities and recognition through the exhibitions held by the Bombay Art Society in which Siodia participated. Siodia was an accomplished portraitist and his style classified him as a 'salon' painter. His artworks were exhibited at annual art exhibitions across India, and won him numerous prizes and medals. A portrait of Erwad Navrojee Bhandari won Siodia a prize at the Fine Art Exhibition in 1913 in Simla, which was one of the most sought-after venues for annual exhibitions in the mid-nineteenth and early twentieth centuries. At the 1916 edition of the Simla exhibition, Siodia won a gold medal for his celebrated portrait of Sir Dinshaw D. Davar Kt., late Justice of the High Court of Bombay.[2] His artistic capability was recognised as early as 1907, when the Madras Fine Arts Society awarded Siodia a silver medal.

The paintings below and on the opposite page, *Untitled* (1925), *Untitled* (1939) and *Untitled* (1922–24) express Siodia's skilful creation of mood and place. His

Untitled, Rustom Siodia; graphite, watercolour heightened with body colour on paper, 1925, Bombay; 50.8 x 37.5 cm. Accessioned: 2021.

Untitled, Rustom Siodia; watercolour heightened with body colour on paper, 1939, Bombay; 27.3 x 19.1 cm. Accessioned: 2021.

bright colour palette was shaped by his Western art education. He created a series of paintings dedicated to the historical sites of Ajanta, Ellora and Elephanta between 1922 and 1925. These paintings demonstrate the influence of quasi-Achaemenid architectural structures, which Siodia had studied deeply in the process of trying to understand his Parsi heritage. The watercolour of the entrance to the Ellora caves (1925) focuses on the architectural impressions of the Kailash temple and the victory pillar. The caves had been a major subject of interest for artists of the Sir J.J. School of Art since their discovery in the 1880s. Siodia successfully realises the cave's intricate carvings through his controlled suggestion of light, shadow and perspective. Ellora's ancient stillness contrasts with the lively nature of the monsoon depicted in *Untitled* (1939). The painting uses a subdued palette to recall

rainy days, with dark swathes of greys and blotches of many green hues to represent the lush wetlands. The painting was made at his studio in Jogeshwari, on the outskirts of Bombay, where he worked from 1929 onwards. In *Untitled* (1922–24), Siodia records what is likely a landscape of the Bombay hinterland. Siodia's extensive work on Indian landscapes expresses his engagement with nature and his deep attachment to the country.

The paintings in the Museum collection are from the artist's peak, when his great skill saw him join a group of acclaimed professional artists in India like M.V. Dhurandhar (1867–1944), A.X. Trindade (1870–1935), A.H. Muller (1878–1952) and Samuel Rahamin (1880–1965). Siodia's artistic career peaked in the 1930s. He travelled to London often to participate in exhibitions, and passed away there in 1946. • IH

Untitled, Rustom Siodia; watercolour heightened with pastel on paper, c. 1922–24, Bombay; 25.4 x 34.9 cm. Accessioned: 2021.

91 SEASCAPES

by P.A. DHOND (b. 1908–2001)

Untitled, P.A. Dhond; watercolour on paper, twentieth century, Bombay; 36 x 53 cm. Accessioned: 1991.

PRESENT-DAY Maharashtra's landscapes and seascapes provided an endless source of inspiration for the Sir J.J. School of Art students, who were taken on annual excursions to hone their skills. Watercolour was the preferred medium as it allowed for swift execution and enabled the young artists to effectively capture the dramatic play of light. Among the most skilled watercolour artists of his generation, Prahlad Anant Dhond (1908–2001) was known for works that stand out for their translucency and affective resonance. Born in Ratnagiri, Dhond was introduced to landscape painting at the Topiwala High School at Malvan. His drawing teacher, Pednekar, had trained at the Sir J.J. School of Art under the guidance of Principal Cecil Burns.[1] Burns' teaching focused primarily on watercolours and his students continued this practice.

The seascape painting above employs the wet-on-wet technique that Dhond adopted, with bold strokes which were a characteristic feature of his work. The contrasting tonal variations of sea and sky, his minimalist brushstrokes and conceptual control set an example of aesthetic and technical proficiency. Dhond was known to fill the sky, land and water in one thick brush stroke each. He worked on completely wet paper for detailing as well. The open composition, the emphasis on accurate depiction of the changing qualities of light, the ordinary subject matter and unusual visual angles signify his particular visual language.

The Konkan coast had a profound impact on his sensibilities during his formative years and he is known to have said, 'Why should I be dependent on a model when the entire panorama of ... nature, beach, waves, ships, coconut grove lay before me?'[2] He was particularly drawn to the scintillating seascapes of British watercolourist William Russell Flint (1880–1969). Dhond was impressed by Flint's vibrant shadow play and controlled application of paint using the wet-on-wet technique. Flint was renowned for his

Untitled, P.A. Dhond; watercolour on paper, twentieth century, Bombay; 36 x 53 cm. Accessioned: 1991.

watercolour oeuvre which was influenced by Realism and Impressionism. He had served as president of the Royal Watercolour Society of Britain (1936–56).[3]

Dhond spent forty years at the Sir J.J. School of Art. He joined the college as a student of fine arts during the tenure of Principal Gladstone Solomon, and worked with M.V. Dhurandhar who was teaching at the School then. His memoir, *Rapan*, published in 1979, gives a detailed analysis and vivid account of the functioning of the School including his training, study tours, teachers and ethos of the time.

In 1932, when Dhond was studying at the School, the Thomas Committee had decided to close the institute due to budgetary restrictions. The students and teachers fought with the authorities against this decision. Solomon made Dhond the students' representative to argue their point of view. After graduating, Dhond was offered a fellowship in the Murals Department under the guidance of G.H. Nagarkar and J.N. Ahiwasi, seminal artists of the Bombay Revivalist Movement. But he chose to enrol for the Art Teachers' Training Programme. He completed his Art Masters in 1937 and joined the Sir J.J. School of Art as the Head of the Art Teachers' Training Programme, a position he held from 1938 to 1958.

During his tenure in the Art Teachers' Department, Dhond worked towards improving teaching methodologies. He studied child psychology and made it a part of his lectures, even though it was not part of the curriculum. He held strong views regarding the eligibility criteria for the Art Teachers' Training Programme. He applied innovative methods of teaching and interpreting visual arts to his students from different age groups. Dhond was appointed the dean of the Sir J.J. School of Art in 1958 and later served as the Director of Art for Maharashtra until 1969. • HK

92 LAKDI BUNDER
by A.M. MALI (active 1905–1921)

ANANT Malhar Mali was born and raised in Kolhapur, a princely state in the Bombay Presidency. In the late nineteenth and early twentieth centuries, Kolhapur emerged as an important artistic and cultural centre under the royal patronage of Chhatrapati Shahu Maharaj, whose progressive ideals nurtured local talent. Mentored by his father, Malhar Mali, and Shahu Maharaj's court painter Abalal Rahiman (1860–1931), Mali developed an interest in art from his early years. He initially worked as an assistant at the Chitrashala Press in Poona, which was known for its lithographs of figurative paintings from Indian mythology. Despite gaining recognition, Mali soon felt dissatisfied in Poona and moved to Bombay in 1911 to further hone his artistic skills and reach a wider market.

In Bombay, he met and befriended Archibald Herman Muller (1878–1960), an Indo-German artist from the Madras School of Art, who had won the gold medal at the 1911 Bombay Art Society's exhibition. The Sir J.J. School of Art was the only institute that taught art in Bombay in the early twentieth century but the syllabus was based on Western art techniques. To break away from the School's rigid teaching, Muller and Mali, like S.L. Haldankar, began conducting private art classes out of a small apartment located on Bombay's Sandhurst Road in the pre-War period.[1]

Mali was skilled in diverse mediums and subjects and won the first prize for 'Best Figure' composition for his painting *Krishna and Arjuna* (1911), 'Best Portrait' in oils and the 'Best Picture' award for his watercolour *Jatayu and Ravana* at the Bombay Art Society's Annual Fine Arts Exhibition (March 1918).[2] At the same time, Marathi magazines *Manoranjan*, *Navyug* and *Karmanuk*, known for their popular literary content, nationalist intent and wide readership, commissioned Mali to contribute illustrations for their covers and for articles penned by Indian writers. The outbreak of World War I resulted in financial hardships for Mali as artistic work was not easily available and in 1916 he had to seek employment at another press in Ghatkopar. He eventually moved to Grant Road and began working at Gurudas Photo Studio on Princess Street, established by his friend Kolbalkar, a photographer who had moved to Bombay from Kolhapur during this period.[3] The emergence of hand-coloured photographs opened up a new avenue for Mali's skill in portraiture.

Mali's body of work includes figure studies, portraits, landscapes, still lifes and lithographs executed in a Western academic realistic style. In the early twentieth century, many artists lived or worked in and around the middle-class housing areas of Girgaum, Grant Road and Byculla, which were close to the seafront in south Bombay as well as Worli. The painting

Lakdi Bunder is probably inspired by Joseph Mallord William Turner's seascapes. Turner (1775–1851) was a master of the seascape genre executed in the Romantic style.

Turner's highly evocative paintings which invoked the sublime had an impact on many Bombay artists. Mali's perspective in *Lakdi Bunder* reflects that of Turner's *Fishermen upon a Lee-Shore in Squally Weather* (1802). *Lakdi Bunder* (the dock where timber was offloaded) was the old name for Bombay's famous *Chowpatty* (seafront) which transformed into the urban landscape of Marine Drive by the 1930s. The timber trade was one of the oldest trades in Bombay as wood was required for various construction purposes and for the earliest mills.

The painting, executed in a wash of turquoise shades, depicts the seafront at sunset, indicated by the contrast of colours, the slight blush and the distinct stroke of crimson near the horizon on the left where the clouds are illuminated. The play of light and shadow was characteristic of the Turner-esque style. In the foreground is an anchored large barge with sails, known as a *machwa*, with people and goods in it. Another smaller canoe with fishing nets that have attracted a crow, is anchored on the shore. A Koli (fisherman) is standing in the water with his fishing net hoisted upon his right shoulder. Two horses, probably used to pull carts loaded with timber or for 'Victorias', as the local horse-pulled carriages were known, are shown walking across the sand. Short, sharp strokes highlight the foam of the sea waves as they crash upon the shore at high tide.

The minimal colour scheme captures the vastness of both the sky and the sea at dusk. The turbulent waves mirror the dark clouds and fuse the sky and the sea into a holistic vision. The comparatively smaller scale of the human figures in the centre emphasises the dominance of nature over the human ideas of progress and commerce.

Mali's ambition to study art in Italy remained unfulfilled due to his untimely death in 1921. However, his artworks are now part of important museums in Aundh, Kolhapur and Bombay. Mali's son, Vasant Anant Mali (1911–2011) went on to become an acclaimed artist as well. • RWB

Lakdi Bunder, A.M. Mali; oil
on canvas, 1920, Bombay;
64.5 x 100 cm. Accessioned: 1990-91.

UNTITLED *by* N.R. SARDESAI (b. 1885–1954)

Untitled,
N.R. Sardesai;
watercolour
on paper, 1922,
Bombay; 9 x 13 cm.
Accessioned: 2015.

One of Bombay Presidency's most distinguished artists, Narayan Ramkrishna Sardesai was born in Ratnagiri in 1886. He studied carpentry and drawing at the Ratnagiri School of Industry, established in 1879 by the British Government. He passed the drawing examination at Kalabhavan, Baroda, in 1905 at the age of twenty. After taking a brief break from his formal education due to financial difficulties, Sardesai joined the Sir J.J. School of Art where he studied alongside S.L. Haldankar, M.K. Parandekar and R.D. Panwalkar. In 1914, Sardesai received the Mayo Medal for painting, which was awarded to outstanding students at the School. After completing his Art Master degree in 1917, he taught painting at the School till 1920.[1]

In the early 1900s, landscape and seascape paintings became a popular genre among artists in Bombay and at other art schools in the Bombay Presidency. It is a genre Sardesai excelled in. The painting in the Museum's collection is rendered in soft earthy washes, in a Post-Impressionist style, and captures the bright afternoon light. The subject matter is a quotidian postcard of Bombay's shoreline. A pop of colour marks the red headwear of the Kolis (fishermen) who are grouped together in the painting's foreground and appear engaged in assessing the day's catch. The shadows of the figures in the foreground indicate a time around late afternoon when fishing activity would have halted.

The influence of Cecil Burns, the principal of the Sir J.J. School of Art, and watercolour artist, is apparent in Sardesai's work. *Untitled* (1922) highlights the backdrop of an urban metropolis and the juxtaposition between different trades and social classes that co-existed. It depicts the Marine Drive stretch that was coming up in the 1920s and 1930s, with figures painted in white, carrying baskets on their heads, on the left of the painting.

Between 1920 and 1930, Sardesai taught art at the Propriety High School in Bombay's Fort area and at the Art Society of India.[2] He won the prestigious gold medal for painting at the Bombay Art Society's annual exhibition in 1929. His works not only serve as excellent examples of a distinct style that prevailed at the time but also portray the life of people in early twentieth-century Bombay.[3] Sardesai's paintings are in the collections of the Chhatrapati Shivaji Maharaj Vastu Sangrahalaya (formerly Prince of Wales Museum), Mumbai, the Sir J.J. School of Art, Mumbai, Nagpur Museum, and Shri Bhavani Museum, Aundh. • **RWB**

UNTITLED *by* AMBIKA DHURANDHAR (b. 1912–2009)

Untitled,
Ambika Dhurandhar;
watercolour on paper,
Bombay, 1954;
20.5 x 32.5 cm.
Accessioned: 1991.

Ambika Dhurandhar inherited her father Rao Bahadur M.V. Dhurandhar's skill and interest in painting. Dhurandhar completed her diploma in painting from the Sir J.J. School of Art in 1931. Landscape painting emerged as an important genre in Bombay in the early 1900s.[1] It was a time when the new interest in painting paralleled development in poetry, moving away from historicism to love for the minutiae of nature.[2] Landscape paintings were primarily done in watercolours with subdued palettes. The emphasis was on highlighting minute details and capturing the play of natural light in compositions. In terms of style, a modified form of Impressionist painting captured the imagination of the young artists at the School. M.V. Dhurandhar remarks in his autobiography, 'As transportation networks grew, students travelled further out of Bombay for these "excursions".'[3] Gladstone Solomon, principal of the Sir J.J. School of Art in the early 1900s, changed the curriculum from its earlier focus on Western academic expression and instead emphasised Indian styles.

The untitled painting portrays a landscape reminiscent of the Konkan region with its coconut trees and traditional Konkani houses. The housing patterns reflect an emerging urban modernity with a mix of traditional designs with thatched roofs and modern RCC housing complexes. The village landscape was changing due to the rapid urbanisation of Bombay and nearby cities. Dhurandhar's extensive travels with her father sharpened her observations of the transition of the urban–rural landscape. Her work recreates the period through attention to detail, and is a fine example of the picturesque tradition depicting the everyday life and landscapes of the hinterland of Bombay.

She completed a diploma (FRCA) in painting from London and won medals at the Bombay Art Society exhibitions. Her works were exhibited in Simla, Delhi, Bangalore, Mysore and Kolhapur. In 1949, she started the Dhurandhar Art School at Khar, Bombay, in memory of her father. • HK

93 UNTITLED
by PRADUMNA TANA (b.1929–2009)

THE collection of forty-three small-format artworks that belonged to the pioneering art collector and gallerist Kekoo Gandhy (1920–2012) (see pp. 329–31) represent work produced at the Sir J.J. School of Art during the Early Modern, formative period from the 1920s to the 1950s, when the students were trying to shake off the shackles of Western art education that had constrained their artistic development and practice. Though we know the names of many of the artists responsible for the works in the collection, with a few exceptions, there is little documented evidence of their going on to become successful artists. The works show the sensuous treatment of the human figure, idyllic pastoral scenes or festival celebrations, and present a lively earthy palette. The students were clearly influenced by Rajput miniature paintings, a practice that would continue to have implications for the Bombay Progressive Group that succeeded them in the 1950s and 1960s. Unlike the earlier focus on landscape, the figure is dominant in these works, and they celebrate a traditional perspective. In many of the paintings, there is a depiction of subjects that typify the emerging understanding of Indian-ness, like the simple villager, who was seen as a poetic ideal. The works capture this sense of innocence and idyll, which is inflected with the nationalist fervour of the 1930s and 1940s.

One of the better-known artists in the collection is Pradumna Tana, who was also a recognised poet in Gujarati. He was closely associated with the folk art revival movement in Gujarat that was pioneered by *Kumar* magazine, an exemplary monthly publication on the arts founded in 1911, that survived for eighty years and became an important forum for showcasing indigenous practice. Tana's work on the opposite page portrays his deep engagement with the folk idiom. Born in Dahanu (Maharashtra), in 1929, he spent his early life in Bombay. In 1954, he graduated in fine arts from the Sir J.J. School of Art. He was deeply influenced by traditional painting and attended a course on mural and fresco techniques at the University of Banasthali Vidyapith, Rajasthan, after graduation.[1] This gave him the opportunity to explore the Rajasthani hinterland, where he became fascinated by the beauty of rural India. His many sketches of village life are testimony to this.

Like many talented artists of his generation, he worked as a designer and research scholar for the Weavers Service Centre in Bombay between 1959 and 1961, and became friends with several of India's pioneering modern artists like K.G. Subramanyan, who headed the Centre at the time. Subramanyan's towering personality had attracted many important artists to the Centre, including Jogen Chowdhury, Manu Parekh and Ambadas. Artists like Haku Shah and Tana were influenced by Subramanyam's ideas about traditional

Portrait of Shivdo, an Old Warli House Help in Dahanu, Pradumna Tana; ink wash on paper, late 1950s, Dahanu; 18.5 x 13.5 cm.
Image courtesy: Antonella Tana.

Opposite:
Untitled, Pradumna Tana; gouache on card, 1956, Bombay; 33.2 x 40.6 cm. Accessioned: 2011.

and folk designs. Tana visited Ahmedabad and Baroda often and became friends with Gulam Sheikh and Bhupen Khakhar, and contributed to their art/literary journal *Vrishchik*.[2]

In 1961, Tana won a scholarship to Italy to deepen his knowledge of European illuminated manuscripts and miniature art. At the Academy of Fine Arts in Naples, he met his future wife, Rosalba, an Italian painter. In 1968, the couple returned to India and both worked as designers for textile firms in Bombay and Delhi. In 1975, the family moved to Como, the 'Silk' city, in Italy, and worked as freelance designers. In 1981, Tana was invited to the US to teach folk art at the School of the Art Institute of Chicago. He went on to teach at several prestigious institutes in Italy, India and the US. He also held several exhibitions of his works which won many awards, and are in national and international collections.[3] • TZM

Left:
Untitled, Subhadra Anandkar;
gouache on card, 1950,
Bombay; 29.2 x 33 cm.
Accessioned: 2011.

•

Left, below:
Untitled, Freny Sarkari;
gouache on card, mid-
twentieth century, Bombay; 17.1
x 23.4 cm. Accessioned: 2011.

•

Opposite, top:
Untitled, R.H. Govindappa,
gouache on card, 1935,
Bombay; 22.8 x 33 cm.
Accessioned: 2011.

•

Opposite, below:
Untitled, unknown artist;
gouache on card,
mid-twentieth century,
Bombay;
27.9 x 40.6 cm.
Accessioned: 2011.

Aquasaurus, Jitish Kallat; resin, paint and steel, 2008;
254 x 688 x 269 cm. Exhibition: *Asymmetrical Objects*;
Industrial Arts Gallery, 2018.

CONTEMPORARY ART
The Artist in Focus

Untitled, Sudarshan Shetty; carved wood, electromagnetic mechanism, steel sword, mild steel, 2010; 355.6 x 279.4 x 106.6 cm. Exhibition: *This Too Shall Pass*; Kamalnayan Bajaj Special Exhibitions Gallery, 2010.

The magnificent, oversized cage that is reminiscent of a palatial entrance is carved on either side with the mythical tree of life. The entrance beckons while a sword swings menacingly in its recesses, like a pendulum slicing time. In the exhibition, Shetty deployed the grandeur of the Museum building to destabilise its authority and symbolism.

AT midnight on August 14, 1947, India's first prime minister, Pandit Jawaharlal Nehru, delivered his historic speech, 'As the world sleeps, India awakens to light and freedom …', sounding the immense hope that underpinned the desire for freedom. But freedom came at a price as the partition of the subcontinent into India and Pakistan would create an unimaginable human tragedy that reverberates even today. On February 28, 1948, the last of the British troops departed from the iconic Gateway of India in Bombay, leaving behind a traumatised and sundered land. This painful birth prompted a search for new paradigms and creative expressions of a fraught and nascent identity that was invested in tradition and at the same time wrestling with it, while seeking to be a part of the global community. The Bombay Progressive Artists' Group epitomised the brave, young, radical energy of the time, and the search for a new aesthetic syntax, as did the Progressive Writers' Association, and the Indian People's Theatre Association, that were nurtured in Bombay.[1] Much of the creative energy of these groups was fuelled by the explosion in films and the sense of freedom that Independence epitomised. Public censure was courted almost like a badge of honour.

The Progressive Artists' Group, whose works comprise much of what is today considered in hallowed terms as 'The Moderns', were a motley, impecunious group. F.N. Souza, the founder and leader, had been expelled from the J.J. School of Art in 1945 for his radical and provocative work. By 1948, the group included S.H. Raza, who was fresh from the J.J. School and whose works rank today with the best in the world; M.F. Hussain, who is India's most celebrated artist, started his career as a film billboard painter; K.H. Ara, who worked as a car cleaner and painted lyrical still lifes in his tiny 10 x 10 ft quarters; S.K. Bakre, an accomplished sculptor; and H.A. Gade, whose powerful plein air compositions verged on the abstract. Over the next few years they were joined by other icons of Indian art like Vasudeo Gaitonde, Krishen Khanna, Mohan Samant and Bal Chabda. Tyeb Mehta and Akbar Padamsee were not formally a part of the group but were close friends of the artists and participated in their discussions. World War II had brought several European emigres to Bombay, many of whom were artists and performers. They invigorated the burgeoning artist community by providing financial and emotional support, as well as critical appraisal of their work.[2] Bombay in the 1950s and 1960s experienced an extraordinary cultural churn as many of the country's icons in art, literature and film debated ideas and grappled with the compelling issues facing the nation.[3]

Through the next few decades Bombay continued to nurture artists of remarkable talent like Nalini Malani (b. 1946) (see pp. 344-45), Gieve Patel (b. 1940) and Sudhir Pathwardhan (b. 1949) who captured the city's many traumas and dilemmas in their works. They responded to the urban angst of labour strikes, disease and poverty defining a narrative and figurative artistic language in defiance of international trends.[4] In 1993, the city that prided itself on its cosmopolitanism experienced bloody communal riots which left it shocked and deeply wounded. Soon after, in 1995, almost half a century after the British left, Bombay's name was changed to Mumbai, divesting the city, at least symbolically, of its painful colonial vestiges and announcing a new period of saffronisation.[5] The turn of the century saw the coming of age of new talent from the J.J. School of Art, including, among others, Atul Dodiya (b. 1959) (see pp. 346–49), Anju Dodiya (b. 1964), Krishnamachari Bose (b. 1963), Sudarshan Shetty (b. 1961) (see p. 334), Jitish Kallat (b. 1974) (see pp. 120, 332-33), Reena Saini Kallat (b. 1973) (see pp. 342-43), Shilpa Gupta (b. 1976) and Riyaz Komu (b. 1971). These artists have had a considerable impact on the contemporary Indian and global art scene, working in multiple mediums such as painting, sculpture, installation, video and photography, and addressing diverse social, political, cultural and gender issues.

This capsule history of the city's modern and contemporary art developments till the turn of the century provides a part of the context for the template that was conceptualised for the contemporary exhibitions programme in 2008, when the Museum opened after the restoration. The effort to decolonise the Museum prompted a new paradigm for contemporary exhibitions that sought to engage audiences in a thought-provoking dialogue about historical and contemporary issues through the Museum's collection and displays. The exhibition strategy invoked the Museum's colonial history by placing the Indian artist, who had been neglected during the colonial period, at the centre, in a gesture of political riposte. Interventions within Museum displays sought to revive artistic agency and produce an exchange between contemporary and historical contexts. Indian artists had been considered unworthy of being displayed in museums during the colonial period and therefore, no collections of modern Indian artists had been acquired then. Most of the Modern paintings at the Museum were acquired post-Independence, though this does not include any of the Progressive Artists' works. In attempting to redeem this neglect and build institutional support for contemporary art, solo artist exhibitions and acquisitions have been an important strategy of the Museum.

The solo artist curated exhibitions was conceived as an artistic and intellectual residency, which invited artists to develop a dialogue with the Museum through a deep investigation of its various conceptual constructs and collections. Artists engaged with the curator and the Museum's staff to unpack little-known histories that reflect pervasive and entrenched attitudes and biases. The curation gave primacy to artists who had graduated from the Sir J.J. School of Art, as the two institutions shared an umbilical relationship. The curatorial strategy, which continues with the hope to involve many more artists, opens up the collection to interrogation and encourages artists to engage with the Museum's complex colonial and ethnographic history. Artists are invited to make interventions throughout the Museum in an effort to destabilise accepted cannons of museal authority, and question notions about the aura and authenticity inscribed in the art object. Artistic processes that invoke artisanal practice as both means and metaphor are foregrounded. The city itself becomes the stage for artistic interpretation and play, refracted through the collection.

Most of the artists invited to present solo exhibitions have had an enduring relationship with the city and the Museum. Sudarshan Shetty, who was one of the first to present his work in the Museum, spoke about his long-time fascination with the Museum, which he has visited regularly since his childhood. His exhibition recorded varied registers of play and seriousness that set the tone for many of the exhibitions that followed. Jitish and Reena Kallat's exhibitions were extraordinary in scale, content and display, encouraging an unprecedented level of discourse with the community on significant issues regarding art practice, the public and the city. Atul Dodiya, who presented his iconic vitrines at the Indian Pavilion, at the 2019

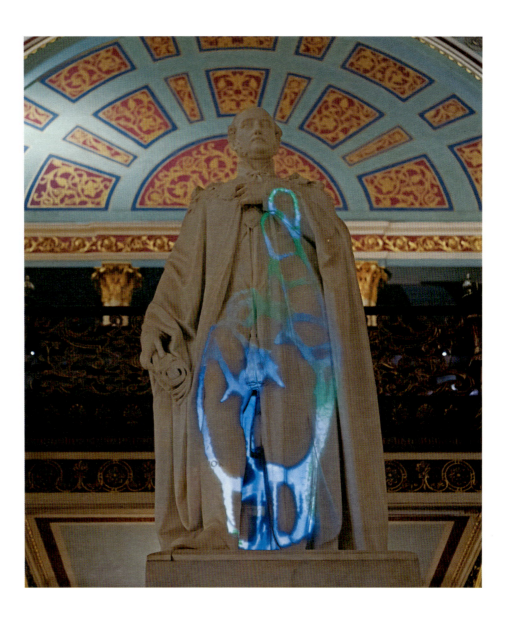

In Search of Vanished Blood, (Variation IV), Nalini Malani; single channel video play, sound design, and performance by Nalini Malani, projection on the marble statue of Prince Albert by Matthew Noble (1864), 2012/2020; 13 minutes. Exhibition: *The Witness*; Industrial Arts Gallery, 2020.

Venice Biennale, captures Mumbai's global scale through a celebration of the quirky and the quotidian in the city, navigating its interstices with wry humour. Nalini Malani, one of India's most celebrated contemporary artists, whose retrospective at the Museum in 2020 presented her practice from early days to her most recent videos, captures the city and the community with a searing honesty and deep empathy. The renowned art critic Geeta Kapur notes about Malani, 'She extracts a language, a hieroglyphic script as it were, from the [city's] street ... putting Bombay on a par with the metropolitan dream/nightmare that haunts the visual imagination of twentieth-century artists, putting it on a par with say Berlin, Paris or New York.'[6]

The Museum's path-breaking shows over the last decade have enabled a recalibration of Indian contemporary art at the local and national level by challenging conventional narratives in an attempt to decolonise the Museum. The exhibitions have enabled a self-reflexive historicity that only such a unique institutional setting provides. • TZM

94 EVOKING THE PAUSE
by SHEBA CHHACHHI

AN exhibition of photo- and video-based objects and installations by the artist Sheba Chhachhi, *Evoking the Pause* was presented at the Museum from October 20, 2011, to December 4, 2011. The artworks referenced Indian tradition in provocative new ways that attempted to recuperate ancient iconography, myth and visual traditions to calibrate an inquiry into our contemporary world. Chhachhi's lens-based images, both still and moving, explore issues of decay and violence, personal and collective memory, the marginal and the forgotten, and the interplay between myth and social sanction. Her photographic work is predicated on building a relationship with her subjects, the photographs emerging from an invitation to perform and reveal the self, excavating dormant histories and latent desires. In the Museum exhibition, Chhachhi configured some of the images using old maps, texts and copies of original artworks from the Museum's archive, to essay a pithy and profound commentary on issues such as social and personal memory; pollution, both in a physical and a metaphorical sense; as well as the potency of language.

Chhachhi connects cultural memory with significant urban issues, such as the abuse of natural resources and the destruction of riverine systems. She explores the relationship between the body and the city through desire, refuse and decay; she underscores the human cost of development through the marginalisation of labour that occurs through every epochal economic churn and harks back to exploitation during colonial times. Women are key protagonists in many of her works, interrogating existing notions of dispossession and displacement within the urban metropolis. The works investigate hierarchies sanctified through rituals and rites of power and dominance.

In *Mistri Ke Haath*, the work in the Museum collection, Chhachhi prints the photograph she has taken of the hands of a labourer who has been laid off work, on a tile which is repeated across the floor of the Museum's entrance atrium, echoing the grid of the floor pattern. The worker holds his obsolete identity card in his hands in a gesture of submission and supplication. This work had a particular resonance in the Museum's space as, despite the colonial interest, promotion and eulogising of Indian craftsmanship, the Indian craftsman was rarely acknowledged and remained anonymous and unrecognised in the Museum.

Mumbai's famous textile mills that built the fortune of the city in the nineteenth century are located nearby. They stand silent and derelict today, shadows of their former grand presence while the city waits anxiously to assert a new identity. In the 1980s, as the city's economy went through turbulent changes and union strikes led to the closure of approximately eighty textile mills in Mumbai, nearly 150,000 labourers were laid off. Many of these labourers lived in the Museum's neighbourhood *chawls* that nurtured the labour movement in the city, as well as the Dalit movement, which is similar to the American Black Panther movement. Workers found themselves disenfranchised, ill-equipped to reinvent their lives in the new globalised economic regime. Itbari Khan is one such worker who holds the last remnant of his life as a factory worker in his hands. Transformed into a repetitive floor tile, the photographic image acts as a reminder, an interruption, a plea, bringing back into the public domain transient and marginalised histories.

The 320 photographs mounted on tiles culminated at the base of Prince Albert's towering statue, in front of which is the statue of David Sassoon, a wealthy opium merchant who commissioned the statue of Prince Albert for the Museum. On the plinth stand photographic portraits of laid-off workers taken by the artist, in a poetic revision of notions and statements of honour and justice. The unknown worker is finally acknowledged and the artist attempts to atone for centuries of exploitation and neglect through this act of recognition and salutation. • TZM

Opposite and below:
Mistri Ke Haath, Sheba Chhachhi; photos on acrylic, wooden tiles and prints, 1999/2011; 30 x 30 cm. Exhibition: *Evoking the Pause*; Industrial Arts Gallery, 2011. Accessioned: 2017.

95 QUINTESSENTIAL
by L.N. TALLUR

THE exhibition *Quintessential* by the artist L.N. Tallur explored an unorthodox approach to forms of representation. Tallur's interest in the metaphysics of objects and the 'aura' of museums defines his sculptural practice. He produces fantastical objects that border on the absurd, unsettling the viewer even as they provoke questions about society's obsessions and delusions. In the exhibition the artist set up a series of hypotheses to substantiate his observations. He used a scientific approach that captured the original intention with which the Museum was established in the nineteenth century. The colonial regime employed scientific tropes to justify elaborate theories of domination and a Darwinian world view. Through a series of revisionist experiments that used the history and objects of the Museum as their premise, Tallur configured installations whose experimental outcomes were to be determined by the viewer, implicating his audience in the object's history. He pushed his audiences to unpack issues that are topical even today (see p. 266).

Tongue firmly in cheek, Tallur used Einstein's theory of relativity as the starting point to explain his universe. Using the basic premise of the tangible and intangible, much as Einstein did, Tallur stated that his objects acquired a '5th dimension' when they are 'museumised'. Einstein's theory, according to Tallur, had a lacuna as it did not account for the fifth dimension. This is the dimension of the 'aura' bestowed by various canonical traditions at both a tangible and intangible level. Museums as art historical institutions that define the canon in terms of an object's value, both monetarily and metaphysically, bestow an aura on the object. Here, Tallur conflated the theories of two great thinkers, Albert Einstein and Walter Benjamin, who defined the theory of the 'aura'. As we become modernised and reject old forms of beliefs, new hegemonies replace the old. Benjamin implies that the sanctum sanctorum has shifted to the museum. Tallur's practice is particularly concerned with how museums and museumised spaces define an object, artist or a movement's trajectory. He seems to imply that curators and experts are the new high priests of our modern world, and sets out to destabilise this perception.

The artist draws on a vocabulary of traditional signifiers that have decayed and reinvents and integrates them into a language of the new world of progress and development. Shiny, shallow surfaces, representing illusory pursuits and lost meanings, compete with the heaviness of old Burma wood and the laconic creaking of obsolete machines to produce a disturbing critique of both the past and the present. He presented a series of 'Hypothesis' that asked the viewer to think through the artwork like an experiment.

Hypothesis: If an object of art is 'Museumised', that creates a fifth dimension; which is a further addition to Einstein's four dimensions (time-space).

General Background: The stone elephant at the entrance to Rajabunder Jetty at Elephanta Island is believed to date to 540 CE. In 1864, the British attempted to carry the elephant, from which the island derives its European name, back to England. During this attempt, the crane crashed and the elephant shattered into several pieces. The fragments were brought to the V&A Museum, Bombay, and were reintegrated by George Birdwood, the then curator of the Museum.

Procedure: An incomplete model of an elephant-like animal body is provided to work on. There are a number of wood blocks that seem to be part of the model elephant. The investigator (viewer) can use these blocks to reconstruct the elephant.

Conclusion and Evaluation: Data gathered during the experiment proves the existence of the power of possession and this in the context of a museum conclusively proves the existence of a 'fifth dimension'.

QED (*quod erat demonstrandum*): The Elephanta elephant (see pp. 30-31) becomes a symbol of history and the many possibilities of recreating and reinterpreting it. A broken elephant shorn of its original grandeur, presented at the Museum, evokes greater reverence today, perhaps, than it did when it was originally created. • TZM

Quintessential, L.N. Tallur; live virtual transmission system, wooden elephant, Daniell print, text, *Account of the Cave-Temple of Elephanta* (1819) in a showcase, model elephant, 2011; 153 x 223 x 123 cm. Exhibition: *Quintessential*; Origins of Mumbai Gallery, 2011-12. Accessioned: 2017.

UNTITLED (COBWEB/CROSSINGS)
by REENA KALLAT

IN a pioneering initiative to engage the public imagination, the Museum partnered with ZegnArt, a project of the Ermenegildo Zegna Group, on a programme titled 'Public'. Seven contemporary artists were invited to engage with the Museum and its immediate environs and create an artwork that reflected on the nature of urban discourse and the tensions embedded in the idea of the 'public'. The exhibition sought to encourage dialogue about the nature of public space and explore the dialectics between art and the urban environment.

Reena Kallat was selected as the winner by an eminent jury, who commended her work for unpacking the fraught relationship between public space and the city's history. The work—a giant web—was exhibited on the main facade of the Museum in an effort to engage the thousands who throng the public square at the entrance in exploring the

colonial and postcolonial identities of the city. As Mumbai's oldest museum, the institution was conceptualised, among other intentions, to articulate a modern identity for its citizens, which over time became frozen and obsolete. The Kamalnayan Bajaj Mumbai Gallery on the upper floor houses a large collection of models and dioramas and other works that present the city and its people through a nineteenth-century lens. Many of the models represent real people whose stories have been lost in the ebb of time. Kallat's work speaks to this sense of shifting identities, and the flow of human capital that creates a constant flux as the city continues to absorb new waves of migrations and recreates itself with changing circumstances. One of the first places these migrants visit is the Museum and the zoo next door. Their reading of the historic city is shaped through these visits to the Museum.

In *Untitled (Cobweb/Crossings)*, Kallat created an oversized cobweb made with hundreds of replica rubber stamps, each bearing a colonial street name that has been replaced by an indigenous one. Together they wove a forgotten history of the city onto the facade of the Museum. The rubber stamp, a mark of bureaucratic authority, has been deployed by Kallat in many of her previous art works as a means of resistance to prescribed identities and as a way of documenting identities that have been vitiated or lost. Similarly, the cobweb, an ephemeral testament of time and decay, is a visual trope the artist deploys cleverly and in different ways, in her artistic oeuvre. It represents the weight of history, the dust of untold stories and of lost archives, that the artist recovers to create a sense of wholeness and to redeem historical fractures.

By recovering the memory of one aspect of the process of decolonisation—the renaming of British street names with Indian or regional ones—the work forms a palimpsest on to which generations may reinscribe their stories. It is a powerful metaphor for the ebb and flow of time, of the victors and the vanquished, and of the delusion of authority. The cobweb, which in nature is a delicate transparent membrane, has become instead a metaphor for heavy bureaucratic processes which seem to have enmeshed the Museum.

The giant cobweb, which is made of 550 resin rubber stamps strung together with a steel cable, weighs over 1 tonne. It had a particular resonance on the façade of the Museum which faces the entrance to the zoo next to which it is situated. It invokes the symbiotic relationship the two institutions shared, as the Museum had a strong natural history focus in its early days. In a first of its kind gesture, ZegnArt Public, who commissioned the project, donated the artwork to the Museum in an effort to nurture cross-cultural relations and expand understanding of cultures through diverse artistic practices. • TZM

Opposite and above:
Untitled (Cobweb/Crossings), Reena Kallat; painted sculptural installation in fibre-reinforced plastic and metal, 2013; 1371.6 x 1828.8 cm. Exhibition: *ZegnArt Public*, Museum's facade, 2013. Accessioned: 2013

NALINI Malani is one of India's most celebrated artists. She received the 2019 Joan Miró prize. The Museum presented a retrospective of her work in January 2020 to much acclaim. In 2013, the Museum had exhibited her work *Listening to the Shades*, in honour of her having received the prestigious Fukuoka Prize for Art and Culture 2013. The exhibition consisted of forty-two facsimile prints on archival paper of the artist's book *Listening to the Shades*, that the artist gifted the Museum.

Malani brings an intense scrutiny of social and political pathologies to her work, which includes a remarkable diversity of mediums, from painting to installation, new media, performance and sound animation. However, in a world where painting as an art form has diminished in significance, Malani continues to be an artist whose painting defines her art form. She has in a sense bridged the lacuna between the new media art of today and the painterly qualities of an earlier generation, and that is one of the many reasons she remains one of the most significant artists working today.

The Fukuoka Prize commended her for 'consistent focus on such daring contemporary and universal themes as religious conflict, war, oppression of women and environmental destruction.'[1]

Malani collaborated with Professor Robert Storr of Yale University to produce the book, based on a modern interpretation of the Cassandra story by Christa Wolf. The book offers a revisualisation of the ancient Greek myth and consists of forty-two reverse paintings that are facsimile printed. The works evoke the traumas of our times, like ghostly characters seeking to redeem the past and rescue the future. In the essay for the book, Professor Storr says, 'Malani's work indicates that she has tapped into fathomless reserves of imagery, reference and metaphor, and from those depths arise painterly effects that invite us to luxuriate in colours, strokes and textures of disorienting but arresting strangeness. Her iconography is equally captivating. Not only does she conjure with difference ... she reaches back to myth, but not in order to re-enchant the world ... but to show us that we can no longer escape a collective awareness that the seeds of our own destruction were not divinely sown but were sown by ourselves.'[2]

Malani sees the artist as a Cassandra of our times. She draws on archetypal images from the Greek myths to represent universal truths. Cassandra, the prophetess who agonisingly sees disaster ahead but is condemned to never be believed, is a metaphor for our common myopia and for the subjugation of the feminine. Cassandra was loved by the god Apollo, who promised her the power of prophecy if she would comply with his desires. Cassandra accepted the proposal, received the gift, and then refused the god her favours. Apollo avenged himself by ordaining that her prophecies would never be believed. She accurately predicted the fall of Troy and the death of Agamemnon, but her warnings went unheeded. • TZM

Opposite:
Listening to the Shades (detail), Nalini Malani; storyboard installation, digital prints on archival Hahnemühle Bamboo Fine Art Paper, 2008/2013; 28.5 x 41.5 cm each. Exhibition: *Listening to the Shades*; Special Projects Space, 2013-14. Accessioned: 2014.
•

Above and below: *Listening to the Shades* (detail), Nalini Malani.

98 7000 MUSEUMS: A PROJECT FOR THE REPUBLIC OF INDIA
by ATUL DODIYA

ATUL Dodiya is one of India's most celebrated and prolific artists. His practice encompasses a vast range of expressions including, painting, printmaking and installations. His exhibition at the Museum, titled *7000 Museums: A Project for the Republic of India* in 2014-15, comprised a comprehensive body of artworks, including oil paintings, watercolours and sculptural assemblages. The works created a layered dialogue with the varied conceptual frameworks of the Museum's collection. They referenced defining moments of history, art history as well as the semantics of museum displays and visitor engagement with art, and the meaning of 'art' itself. Dodiya appropriates the work of his favourite artists, refashioning them as a part of his personal history. He addressed the complexity of various simultaneous happenings in history—in politics, in art and in his own life, through studied yet playful characterisations in his works.

The watercolours series humorously addresses ideas of local cultural representation through a construction of mock museums which represents both a lament and a hope. Dodiya imagines state-of-the-art museums designed by star architects in the small parochial towns of India that have had very little exposure to Modern Art. The incongruity of such interventions and the local reactions performs a contemporary theatrical interpretation of a similar cultural change 200 years ago when the British and other foreign powers arrived in India.

The paintings in oil recreate historical photographs of events from the freedom struggle which recall the magnificent aspirations of the nation's founding fathers. These are ruptured by a strong painterly gesture in colour against the black and white, inspired by Rabindranath Tagore's doodles and from the Museum's archive of the cracks and fissures in the pre-restoration damaged paintings. The gesture sometimes acquires a flourish that recalls the colours and the decorative lines of the building as the artist fuses fact and fantasy into a striking allegory of our times.

In the vitrines Dodiya assembles an encyclopaedic vision of potentialities. Mythical figures take on a contemporary characterisation, invoking the theatrical models and dioramas in the Museum. They nudge painterly references from Tagore, his favourite movies and copies of artworks by great artists Dodiya admires, images from a personal history, or the popular kitsch that abounds in Mumbai's markets. In an inspired binary juxtaposition, Dodiya paints the poems of Arun Kolatkar on the reverse of the vitrines (see p. 20), inscribing a sharp edge into the playfulness, an act that reflects the city itself, built as it is on loss and hope. • TZM

Gallery of Art Expansion Imphal, Atul Dodiya; watercolour on paper, 2014; 76.2 x 55.8 cm. Exhibition: *7000 Museums: A Project for the Republic of India*; 2014-15. Accessioned: 2017.
•
Opposite:
Cabinet III, I, and II, Atul Dodiya; wooden cabinet installation (treated with polyester putty and zinc powder) with photographs, sculptures, paintings and found objects, 2014; 246.3 x 161.2 x 54.6 cm. Exhibition: *7000 Museums: A Project for the Republic of India*; Industrial Arts Gallery, 2014-15.

Looters taking advantage of the Bombay riots, 11 September (left) and *Volunteers at the Congress House – August 1931* (right), Atul Dodiya; oil, acrylic with marble dust and oil-stick on canvas, 2014; 213.3 x 381 cm (left), 182.8 x 182.8 cm (right). Exhibition: *7000 Museums: A Project for the Republic of India*; Kamalnayan Bajaj Special Exhibitions Gallery, 2014-15.

THE artists Shaina Anand and Ashok Sukumaran established CAMP Studio as an artistic practice concerned with the history and politics of technology. In 2015, the Museum presented an exhibition of their work. The centrepiece was the acclaimed and much-travelled film *From Gulf to Gulf to Gulf*.[1] The Indian premiere of the film, which was shown like a movie in a theatre in the heart of the Museum, transformed the historic environment into a cinematic space.

'*As If (I-V)*' was a series of exhibitions across cities in India bringing together CAMP's long term maritime world project in and around the western Indian Ocean. A six-year collaboration with sailors and others who live and work on the edges of this vast landscape from Kuwait to Mombasa, along the Indian, Iranian, East African and Arab coasts, is at the heart of this project that has taken many forms. An unusual map which shares its name with the exhibition title was produced by CAMP in collaboration with young artists from the Clark House Initiative, Mumbai, especially for the Museum exhibition. The work is inspired by a remarkable Gujarati chart of the Gulf of Aden dated around 1810, in which we see a drawing of the Arabian Sea and Somali coasts close together like two bodies almost about to touch. The map, which is remarkable for its scale at 22 x 5 ft, is a poignant reminder of the long ago fracture of the continental drift, which is now bridged by the ubiquitous sea trade manned by Gujarati sailors since the seventeenth century. In the map, *Country of the Sea*, the coastlines come

Country of the Sea, CAMP; single exposure solar cyanotype print on cotton fabric, 2015; 670.5 x 152.4 cm.
Exhibition: *As If – III Country of the Sea*; Kamalnayan Bajaj Special Exhibitions Gallery, 2015. Accessioned: 2015.

closer together and evoke the cultural proximities and divides produced by these seas, so important to the city of Mumbai, which also features prominently at one of its edges. The map reverses the colonial gaze 'from the boat' and the sea becomes the territory to be mapped and explored.

The map was produced as a single exposure solar cyanotype print. More than 100 cities and small ports from Khor al Zubair/Basra to the Mozambique corridor, and from Mumbai to Berbera, are marked on the map. But the shape of the map disorients an easy reading of this territory as typical physical geography. It provokes an image of the sea as its own 'country', with frontier towns at its edges reversing the land-sea paradigm. The work establishes the materiality of the sea that we (some of us) see out of our windows in Mumbai, but whose other faraway edges we have lost awareness of. It brings these edges back into geological and cultural circuits, as if the pre-historic 'breakaway' of the Indian landmass from Africa in, what has been called Gondwanaland, was never a complete success.

The map was a pivotal work of CAMP's solo exhibition, *As If -III 'Country of the Sea'* that took place at the Dr. Bhau Daji Lad Museum in March 2015. It was a companion piece to a suite of works from the Wharfage project that included the film *From Gulf to Gulf to Gulf* (2013), the photographic installation *The Annotated Gujarat and the Sea*, (2011) and constellation of cruciforms *Boat-Modes* (2012).

CAMP's work over several years has mapped, through film, text and systemic interventions, the living histories of sailors and port labourers and workers on the edges of the trade agendas of countries and corporations. These communities have been living on the sea and are almost forgotten by the state and the trading houses. They come together in a moving spirit of fraternity, gathering into their fold disparate cultures brought together by the sea and the exigencies of their livelihood. A series of works narrate their lives, capturing their struggles and their defiant humour. • TZM

by ROHINI DEVASHER

'The deep-time sciences (astronomy, geology) demand a double feat of imagination on the part of their practitioners: to compass the gargantuan time scales in which life evolves or stars form; and to project their own discipline far enough back into the past and forward into the future so that the patterns that emerge only after eons can be recorded and detected. They are the guardians of the far past in the service of the far future.'
—Lorraine Daston

The exhibition in 2016, *Speculations from the Field*, presented at the Museum, showcased recent work by the artist Rohini Devasher, whose practice explores art, science and fiction through fieldwork and research in botany, geology and astronomy.

The artist's 'field' explores terrestrial sites, as well as deep space and deep time, as the locus of both the human imagination and its extraordinary ambition. In the artist's rendering in different media, an inert object takes on a disturbingly sensual form. Her interest in recording and mapping the skies, sea forts, observatories and other such scientific centres and surveillance systems, recalls the early history of the Museum which was a similar site for such mappings. She has worked with the Museum's natural history collection to unpack its implications as a site of collection and a form of instituted collective perception (see p. 96). Devasher has referenced the Museum's rarely seen reserve collection of natural history artefacts, a remnant of the times when it was the erstwhile Government Central Museum, with the emphasis on science, biology and geology.

Using the familiar systems employed by scientists to document and understand the world, systems that were used to record and assess the new worlds that were being conquered by the West in the nineteenth century, Devasher examines and records the residues and remnants of past eras in her video *Shivering Sands*, capturing lost years in slow motion. She directs our gaze to future worlds through planetary configurations in *Meridian: Experiments in Time Travel*, making us stop for a moment to recall the transience of all things. She engages in these explorations much as an archaeologist or astrophysicist might do. She destabilises our perception of what might seem immutable and permanent. Like the Museum that is a record of past worlds or a prediction of emerging futures, but is also the space where perceptions are debated and challenged, Devasher's work provokes us to question foundational notions and reorient our gaze.

In *Meridian*, the artist worked with the Philips Planisphere (showing the principal stars visible for every hour in the year) from the Museum collection to create stellar charts based on the Museum's location and given hour. Planispheres are instruments of time travel. They enable us to project backwards or forwards in deep time. Contemporary interactive planispheres allow us to plot the night sky backwards and forwards through millennia. *Meridian* is part archaeological record and part engineered fiction. It presents pages from a timeline of the far future, a series of maps, both temporal and spatial. Each map charts the sky above the Dr. Bhau Daji Lad Museum on August 20, the date of the opening of the exhibition, at 6.30 p.m. and 10 p.m. across 20,000 years, beginning in 416 CE through this year, 2016, 5016, 9016 etc. until 21016 CE. • **TZM**

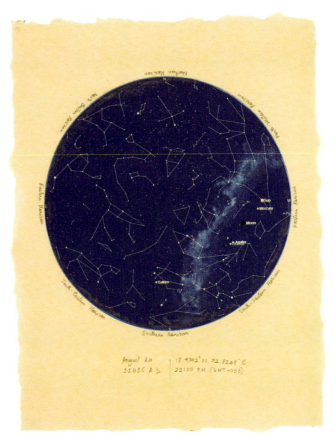

Above:
MERIDIAN: Experiments in Time Travel (detail), Rohini Devasher
•
Opposite:
MERIDIAN: Experiments in Time Travel, Rohini Devasher; archival print on Hahnemühle paper, pencil, 2016; 30.4 x 39.3 cm each. Exhibition: *Speculations from the Field*; Industrial Arts Gallery, 2016. Accessioned: 2016.

101 NOTES ON LABOUR
by PRANEET SOI

PRANEET Soi is an artist who has been deeply engaged in exploring the process of creation that goes beyond the conceptual to encompass the corporeal. His work explores the lives of those involved with the actual production of an object or artwork—the labourers and craftsmen, who are frequently unacknowledged. He is deeply interested in issues surrounding the politics of labour and his work and process of creation reflect this concern. In Kolkata, Kashmir and China, he has immersed himself over extended periods of time in workshops that have privileged the creativity of the artisans involved as much as his own artistic vision. These collaborations have resulted in unique works that profoundly change the equations between the artist and the artisan, between what is recognised as fine art or seen as mere skill or craftsmanship. It addresses questions that are at the heart of the Museum's invitation to artists to interrogate its history, which effaced records of the many artisans who produced the extraordinary works in the Museum.

The Industrial Arts Gallery on the ground floor of the Museum presented a newly commissioned work (opposite).

Opposite:
Notes on Labour, Praneet Soi; mural, aluminium, plywood, acrylic paint, A4 drawings and prints, 2017; 487.6 x 243.8 cm. Exhibition: *Notes on Labour*; Industrial Arts Gallery, 2017. Accessioned: 2017.
•
Below:
Notes on Labour (detail), Praneet Soi.

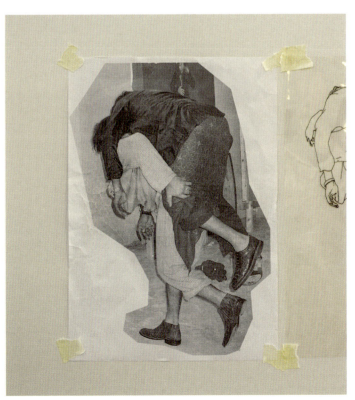

A specially designed curvilinear wall echoed the curvature of the tympanum, a defining feature of the Museum. It presented the painted concave surface to viewers as they entered the Museum, becoming a canvas, which pays homage to the craftsman. The convex surface behind becomes the studio wall which showcases the collaborative method used by the artist with working-notes and sketches taped informally to its surface (below, left).

The Kamalnayan Bajaj Mumbai Gallery on the upper floor contains historical vitrines that represent Mumbai's culture and its south face houses the Kamalnayan Bajaj Special Exhibitions Gallery, so that the entire Museum becomes an envelope within which artists perform a dialogue. Soi dedicated the first room of the gallery to Kumartuli, a workshop in north Kolkata where craftsmen specialised in making religious clay effigies had abandoned their skills in search of employment, and where Soi began his ongoing series *Notes on Labour (Part 1)*. The central room in the gallery was dedicated to Soi's continuing engagement with the atelier of the craftsman Fayaz Jan in Srinagar. Titled *Tile as Archive*, a hundred handmade and painted papier-mâché tiles are arranged in a square measuring 300 x 300 cm (see p. 200). The work is an archive of the traditional Kashmiri patterns, borders and floral tropes used within this atelier's compositions for several generations. The surrounding walls that were painted black contained diagrams sketched out in chalk. An illustration from Da Vinci's *Codex Atlanticus*, explaining the optical phenomena of anamorphosis, which reveals optically hidden images to the knowledgeable viewer, was the central image on the wall. Anamorphosis is a metaphor the artist engages in describing the political turmoil that blights the state of Kashmir.

The third room of the gallery was dedicated to an installation Soi created with a porcelain craftsman in Guangzhou (Old Canton) in China. The installation explored the creative influences and links between Kashmir and China.

The adjacent Origins of Mumbai Gallery transformed into an interactive environment housing Soi's *Astatic Machines*. Designed to communicate the artist's studio methodology to a larger audience, these are drawing machines inspired by Paul Klee's *Pedagogical Sketchbook*. Images from Lockwood Kipling's Journal, which are housed in the Museum, were interspersed with imagery from Klee's manual and Soi's archive. Printed on acetate sheets and placed upon the over-head projectors that sit atop the carts they were projected upon a partially painted black chalkboard wall. Viewers were encouraged to place the acetates upon the projectors and trace them out with chalk, layering the images to make their own compositions, modifying and remaking the colonial aesthetic legacy. • TZM

ACKNOWLEDGEMENTS

This book has been a long time in the making as I was researching the subject of colonial art institutions in Mumbai for a PhD thesis, for which I was registered at Jawaharlal Nehru University, New Delhi, before I joined the Museum full time in 2008. But the idea of reading the Museum's development through the history of the city came up in discussion with Bonita Shimray, the editor at HarperCollins who is managing the project. She was keen that the book be a lens on the city. It was an exciting challenge, though it meant going back to the editing table to review the material from a different perspective. My friend and long-time collaborator on several exhibitions and projects, Rahaab Allana, introduced me to HarperCollins, which has made working on this book a pleasurable and exciting experience. I am grateful for the cooperation and diligence of Shatarupa Ghoshal, the copy editor, and Sanjeev Kumar, the designer, of the HC team.

I am most grateful to our designer Ruchita Madhok, with whom I have worked closely to achieve our objective of a book that would do justice to both the enormous research and the extraordinary visuals. She has been patient and understanding about all the changes and revisions. Her experience working at the V&A, London, in exhibitions research has given her a sound perspective on how to handle such a complex project. Anil Rane, our photographer, has done a terrific job and has always been ready to walk the extra mile. Jyotsna Nambiar our copy editor has been most cooperative in complying with tight deadlines.

The Museum staff has worked diligently, often beyond the call of duty, to make this book happen. I want to acknowledge the dedicated contribution of our former lead curator, Himanshu Kadam, who recently took up a new assignment in Dubai. Ruta Waghmare-Baptista, who has succeeded him, has been a huge support and her eye for detail is excellent. Gargi Mashruwala, who has been with the Museum since the agreement to refurbish it was signed in 2003, is always there to help us through times of crisis, and provide a calm, reassuring perspective. Our curatorial assistant, Shiruy Billimoria, has assisted everyone with their research and painstakingly compiled the information in our archives and Vijay Nakti has diligently organised it. Several curatorial assistants and docents have helped with research over the years enriching our archives with their efforts.

Conservation architect Vikas Dilawari, who worked closely with me during the restoration of the Museum building, has continued to advise and guide us in the challenging task of maintaining the stability and appearance of the building. We have shared a long and meaningful partnership working on the conservation of heritage sites in Mumbai. I would like to thank Monisha Ahmed and Anjani Khanna who worked with me on the restoration and revitalisation plan for the Museum in 2000, and have remained devoted to the Museum. Monisha helped me understand the intricacies of publishing and Anjani helped me think through difficult editorial choices. Radhika Desai worked with me on the display design during the restoration and I continue to value her inputs. Abhay Sardesai, editor of *Art India*, has been an advisor for the Museum's pioneering course in Modern and Contemporary Art History. I am grateful for his editorial inputs for parts of the book.

Peter Hoffenberg, whose magisterial work, An Empire on Display, has been an important resource for our research, shared information and details regarding international exhibitions, which were most helpful. Julius Bryant, Christopher Marsden and Anna Jackson at the V&A, London, were most kind in trying to find images for us despite Covid restrictions. I am grateful to Tessa Blackstone, former chairman of the British Library and a family friend, for her help in accessing

Admiralty Chart of the Port of Bombay, Surveyed by the Officers of Royal Indian Marine under the direction of Commander E. H. Dauglish, R.I.M, 1920-21, with additions from Surveys by the Chief Engineer, Bombay Port Trust to 1950 and correction from Surveys by the Royal Indian Navy to 1947; July 20, 1894, London: Admiralty; 104 x 71 cm. Accessioned: 2021.

information at the library. Anne Buddle, former curator at the National Galleries of Scotland and Advisor to the President of the NGS, has been most helpful with finding rare books. Kavita Singh, former Dean, School of Arts and Aesthetics, who is an expert on miniature painting was most helpful in our research on our miniature collection. I would like to thank Rupika Chawla for her assistance in procuring the Ravi Varma images. Her iconic book on Ravi Varma was a most valuable resource. I am also thankful to the eminent scholar Dr Pratapaditya Pal for his help with the Tibetan manuscript.

Our trustees have been a great inspiration and have helped steer the Museum to achieve the best. The Municipal Corporation of Greater Mumbai, which owns the Museum, has taken a keen interest in the project. I have had the privilege of working with several outstanding municipal commissioners and civic leaders and I am grateful for their guidance. Mr Sitaram Kunte, the present chief secretary of the state, was the additional municipal commissioner in charge of the restoration project. Later, he became municipal commissioner in 2012 and ex-officio co-chairman of the Museum Trust. Under his guidance, we prepared the Museum's path-breaking expansion plan.

Pheroza Godrej, Shyam Benegal and Pradip Shah, our expert trustees are eminent citizens of not just Mumbai but India, and their counsel has been of great benefit to the Museum and I deeply value their friendship. Jyotindra Jain has been my guru, someone I have looked up to and whose work and accomplishments I greatly admire, and I am grateful for his help and advice. Rajan Jayakar took over from me as INTACH Mumbai Convenor in April 2018, and his support and legal advice have been most valuable.

Our donor trustees, Minal and Niraj Bajaj in particular, have been an enormous source of strength and support for me personally and for the Museum. They are the ideal donors, never interfering and always there to hold your hand in times of crisis. Rahul Bajaj's great enthusiasm for this project has encouraged us to achieve our dreams, and I am most grateful for his generosity and words of wisdom.

This book would not have been possible without the contribution of Mukesh Ambani, who for the last six years has provided generous support to the Museum, routed through the Bank of America's Charitable Foundation. I am grateful to both Mukesh and Nita for their support.

My three brothers, Mansoor, Arshad and Fareed, have urged me to get the book written and not dwell too much on making it perfect. My husband, Vikram, and my two daughters, Malika and Ahilya, have always been my anchor. Vikram has read parts of the book, suggesting changes and providing a thoughtful and insightful perspective. My daughters have been most generous and allowed me the time required for such an ambitious project to materialise.

I would like to remember my parents—Dr Rafiq and Fatima Zakaria, who instilled in my brothers and myself a love of history, culture and literature. Their deep devotion and love for their country and this city set an extraordinary example for us.

Lastly, I want to thank all the Museum staff for their dedication, and the many friends and supporters of the Museum whose interest and participation have made restoring and revitalising the Museum, as well as writing and editing this book, a most memorable journey.

TASNEEM ZAKARIA MEHTA   22 October 2021

Headwears of the Bombay Presidency, plaster of Paris and pigments, 1930. On view in the Kamalnayan Bajaj Mumbai Gallery, Dr. Bhau Daji Lad Museum, Mumbai.

CONTRIBUTORS

ARTIST BIOGRAPHIES

CAMP, Mumbai-based collaborative studio; co-founded by Shaina Anand (b. 1975), Sanjay Bhangar (b. 1985) and Ashok Sukumaran (b. 1974) in 2007; other Artists: Simpreet Singh, Zinnia Ambapardiwala, Zulekha Sayyed; based in Chuim Village. *Select Solo Exhibitions:* Nam June Paik Art Center Prize Exhibition, Seoul, South Korea, 2021; Brunei Gallery, SOAS, London, UK, 2020; Argos Center for Art and Media, Brussels, Belgium, 2019; De Appel, Amsterdam, Netherlands, 2019; Dr. Bhau Daji Lad Museum, Mumbai, 2015. *Select Group Exhibitions:* Tate Modern, London, UK, 2019–2021; Chicago Architecture Biennale, Chicago, USA, 2019; Chennai Photo Biennale, Chennai, 2019.

SHEBA CHHACHHI, b. 1958; lives in New Delhi. *Select Solo Exhibitions:* Volte Gallery, Mumbai, 2016; Dr. Bhau Daji Lad Museum, Mumbai, 2011; Khoj Studios, New Delhi, 2010; Galleria Paolo Curti / Annamaria Gambuzzi & Co, Milan, Italy, 2009; Walsh Gallery, Chicago, USA, 2006. *Select Group Exhibitions:* Aicon Contemporary, New York, USA, 2021; Tate Modern, London, UK, 2019; Chennai Photo Biennale, Chennai, 2019.

NIKHIL CHOPRA, b. 1974; lives in Goa. *Select Solo Exhibitions/ Performances:* Metropolitan Museum of Art, New York, USA, 2019; Chatterjee & Lal, Mumbai, 2018; Galleria Continua, San Gimignano, 2012; Dr. Bhau Daji Lad Museum, Mumbai, 2010; Kitab Mahal, Mumbai, 2005. *Select Group Exhibition:* San Francisco Museum of Modern Art, San Francisco, USA, 2019.

ROHINI DEVASHER, b. 1978; lives in New Delhi. *Select Solo Exhibitions:* Project 88, Mumbai, 2019; Dr. Bhau Daji Lad Museum, Mumbai, 2016. *Select Group Exhibitions:* Sharjah Biennial, Sharjah, UAE, 2019; Kaserne Basel, Switzerland, 2019.

ATUL DODIYA, b. 1959; lives in Mumbai. *Select Solo Exhibitions:* Vadehra Art Gallery, New Delhi, 2020; Galerie Templon, Paris, France, 2018; Dr. Bhau Daji Lad Museum, Mumbai, 2014-15; National Gallery of Modern Art, New Delhi. *Select Group Exhibitions:* Venice Biennale, 2019, Venice, Italy; Art Museum at the University of Toronto, 2019.

JITISH KALLAT, b. 1974; lives in Mumbai. *Select Solo Exhibitions:* Norrtälje Konsthall, Sweden, 2021; Frist Art Museum, Nashville, USA, 2020; National Gallery of Modern Art, New Delhi, 2017; Philadelphia Museum of Art, Philadelphia, USA, 2016; Art Gallery of New South Wales, Sydney, Australia, 2015. *Select Group Exhibitions:* Foundation Thalie, Brussels, Belgium, 2021; Columbia Museum of Art, Columbia, USA, 2020; Venice Biennale, 2019, Venice, Italy.

REENA SAINI KALLAT, b. 1973; lives in Mumbai. *Select Solo Exhibitions:* Norrtalje Konsthall, Sweden, 2021; Musée National des Arts Asiatiques Guimet, Paris, France, 2020; Manchester Museum, Manchester, UK, 2017. *Select Group Exhibitions:* Migros Museum of Contemporary Art, Zurich, Switzerland, 2020; The

National Museum of Modern and Contemporary Art, Gwacheon, South Korea, 2020; Bangkok Art Biennale, Bangkok, Thailand, 2020; Institute of Contemporary Art, Boston, USA, 2019; Havana Biennale, Havana, Cuba, 2019.

NALINI MALANI, b. 1946; lives in Mumbai. *Select Solo Exhibitions:* Kunstmuseum, The Hague, Netherlands, 2021; Serralves Museum of Contemporary Art, Porto, Portugal, 2020; Whitechapel Gallery, London, UK, 2020; Fundació Joan Miró, Barcelona, Spain, 2020; Dr. Bhau Daji Lad Museum, Mumbai, 2020; Castello di Rivoli – Contemporary Art Museum, Turin, Italy, 2018; Centre Pompidou, Paris, France, 2017. *Select Group Exhibitions:* Museum of Modern Art, New York, USA, 2021; São Paulo Art Biennial, Brazil, 2021; Venice Bienniale, Italy, 2019; Moderna Museet, Stockholm, Sweden, 2019.

SUDARSHAN SHETTY, b. 1961; lives in Mumbai. *Select Solo Exhibitions:* AKbank Sanat, Istanbul, Turkey, 2019; Dr. Bhau Daji Lad Museum, Mumbai, 2017; National Gallery of Modern Art, New Delhi, 2016; Staatliches Museum Schwerin, Germany, 2015; Galerie Kringinger, Vienna, Austria, 2012.

PRANEET SOI, b. 1971; lives in Amsterdam and Kolkata. *Select Solo Exhibitions:* Van Abbe Museum, Eindhoven, Netherlands, 2020-21; The Mosaic Rooms, London, UK, 2019; Calouste Gulbenkian Museum, Lisbon, Portugal, 2018; Centre for Contemporary Art Derry, Londonderry, UK, 2017; Dr. Bhau Daji Lad Museum, Mumbai, 2017; Experimenter, Kolkata, 2017. *Select Group Exhibitions:* MAIIAM Contemporary Art Museum, Chiang Mai, Thailand; Marres, Huis voor Cultuur, Maastricht, Netherlands, 2021; IFFR, Rotterdam, Netherlands, 2019.

L.N. TALLUR, b. 1971; lives in Bengaluru and Seoul. *Select Solo Exhibitions:* Grounds for Sculpture, New Jersey, USA, 2019-20; Arario Gallery, Seoul, South Korea, 2015; SCAD Museum of Art, Georgia, USA, 2013; Dr. Bhau Daji Lad Museum, Mumbai, 2011.

THUKRAL AND TAGRA, Jiten Thukral (b. 1976) and Sumir Tagra (b. 1979); live in Gurgaon. *Select Solo Exhibitions:* Nature Morte, New Delhi, 2021; Kunstverein Ludwigsburg, Stuttgart, Germany, 2020; Yorkshire Sculpture Park, Wakefield, UK, 2019; Dr. Bhau Daji Lad Museum, Mumbai, 2015. *Select Group Exhibitions:* Asian Art Museum, San Francisco, USA, 2021; MMAG Foundation for Art & Culture, Amman, Jordan 2020; Le Tripostal, Lille, France, 2019; Art Gallery of Alberta, Canada, 2019.

BIBLIOGRAPHY

Abraham, C.C. 'Health, Physical Education and Recreation for India.' *The Indian Journal of Social Work*, Vol. 6. Mumbai: Tata Institute of Social Sciences, 1946.

Adams, J., and R.C. West. 'Money, Prices, and Economic Development in India, 1861–1895.' *Journal of Economic History*, Vol. 39, No. 1, pp. 55–68, 1979.

Adarkar, N., ed. *The Chawls of Mumbai: Galleries of Life*. Mumbai: ImprintOne, 2011.

Ahuja, N.P., and L. Belfrage. *A Mediated Magic: The Indian Presence in Modernism 1880–1930*. Mumbai: The Marg Foundation & Axel and Margaret Ax:son Johnson Foundation, 2019.

Aitken, E.H. *The Agricultural Ledger* 1897–No. 10. Calcutta: Office of the Superintendent, Government Printing, 1897.

Aitken, E.H., and R.A. Sterndale, eds. *Journal of the Bombay Natural History Society*, Vol. 1. 1886.

———. *The Agricultural Ledger 1897—No. 10*. Calcutta: Office of the Superintendent, Government Printing, 1897.

All India Swadeshi Directory 1933. Allahabad: Allahabad Law Journal Press, 1933.

Allana, R. 'The Art of Realism: Painted Photographs from India.' *The Newsletter*, No. 51. Leiden: International Institute for Asian Studies, 2009.

Allsen, T.T. *The Royal Hunt in Eurasian History*. Pennsylvania: University of Pennsylvania Press, 2006.

American Association for the Advancement of Science. 'The International Fisheries Exhibition. Second Paper.' *Science*, Vol. I, No. 20, 1883.

Anderson, J.D. 'Sir Herbert Risley, K.C.I.E., C.S.I.' *Man*, Vol. 12, pp. 1–4. Royal Anthropological Institute of Great Britain and Ireland, 1912. American Association for the Advancement of Science.

Ansari, S.F.D. *Sufi Saints and State Power: The Pirs of Sind, 1843–1947*. Delhi: Cambridge University Press, 1992.

Annual report of the Board of Regents of the Smithsonian Institution, showing the operations, expenditures, and condition of the institution for the year 1883, Washington: Government Printing Office, 1885.

Appasamy, J. *Tanjavur Painting of the Maratha Period*. Vol. 1. Delhi: Abhinav Publications, 1980.

Archer, M. *Patna Painting*. London: David Marlowe Ltd. for The Royal Society of India, 1948.

Archer, M., and W.G. Archer. 'Natural History Paintings'. *Indian Painting for the British 1770–1880*, pp. 91–98. Oxford: Oxford University Press, 1955.

Archer, M., and T. Falk. *India Revealed: The Art and Adventures of James and William Fraser 1801–35*. London: Cassell & Co, 1989.

Archer, M., and G. Parlett. *Company Paintings: Indian Paintings of the British Period*. London and Ahmedabad: Victoria & Albert Museum and Mapin Publishing, 1992.

Archer, M., C. Rowell, and R. Skelton. *Treasures from India: The Clive Collection at Powis Castle*, London: Herbert Press, 1987.

Archer, W.G. *Indian Paintings from the Punjab Hills: A Survey and History of Pahari Miniature Painting*, Vol. 1. London & New York: Sotheby Parke Bernet, 1973.

———. W.G. *The Loves of Krishna: In Indian Painting and Poetry*. London: George Allen & Unwin Ltd., 1957.

Armitage, G. 'The Schlagintweit Collections.' *The Indian Journal of History of Science*, Vol. 24, No. 1, pp. 67–83. New Delhi, 1989.

Arnold, C.E. 'The Bombay Improvement Trust, Bombay Millowners And The Debate Over Housing Bombay's Millworkers, 1896–1918.' *Essays in Economic & Business History*, Vol. XXX, No. 1, 2012.

Bahulkar, S. *M.V. Dhurandhar: The Romantic Realist*. New Delhi: National Gallery of Modern Art in collaboration with DAG, 2018.

Bahulkar, S., and D. Ghare. *Dhrishyakala*, Vol. 1. Mumbai: Popular Prakashan, 2013.

Baker, H.D. *Special Consular Reports No. 72: British India with Notes on Ceylon, Afghanistan, and Tibet*. Washington: US Govt. Printing Office, 1915.

Baker, M., and B. Richardson. *A Grand Design: The Art of the Victoria and Albert Museum*, London: V&A Publication, 1999.

Balasubramanyam, K. *Handicraft Survey Monographs, Part VII-A, Census of India* 1961, Vol. XI, Delhi: Manager of Publications, 1965.

Banerjea, J.N. *The Development of Hindu Iconography*. Calcutta: Calcutta University Press, 1956.

Barringer, T., and T. Flynn. *Colonialism and the Object: Empire, Material Culture and the Museum*. London/New York: Routledge, 1998.

Bartlett, J.A. *British Ceramic Art: 1870–1940*. Atglen, Pennsylvania: Schiffer Publishing Ltd, 1997.

Bayly, C.A. *The Raj: India and the British, 1600–1947*. London: National Portrait Gallery, 1990.

———. *Rulers, Townsmen and Bazaars: North Indian Society in the Age of British Expansion 1770–1870*. Cambridge: Cambridge University Press, 1983.

Beach, M.C. *The New Cambridge History of India: Mughal and Rajput Painting*. Cambridge: Cambridge University Press, 2008.

Bengal Government. *Official Report of the Calcutta International Exhibition, 1883–84*, Vol. 2. Calcutta: Bengal Secretariat Press, 1885.

Benson, J. 'The Art of Abri: Marbled Album Leaves, Drawings, and Paintings of the Deccan.' *Sultans of Deccan India, 1500–1700: Opulence and Fantasy,* eds N. Haider and M. Sardar. New York: The Metropolitan Museum of Art, 2015.

Betta, C. 'Marginal Westerners in Shanghai: The Baghdadi Jewish community, 1845–1931.' *New Frontiers*. Manchester: University Press, 2000.

Bhagwat, N. *Development of Contemporary Art in Western India (1850 to 1964)*. Unpublished PhD Thesis, Baroda: The Maharaja Sayajirao University, 1983.

Bhatia, U. 'Chaitu at Tehri Garhwal.' *Marg: A Magazine of the Arts*, Vol. 50, No. 1. Mumbai: Marg Publications, 1998.

Bhattacharya, S. *The East India Company and the Economy of Bengal from 1704 to 1740*. 2nd edition. Calcutta: Firma K.L. Mukhopadhyay, 1969.

Birdwood, C.G.M. 'APPENDIX I.—Sir George Birdwood on the Indian Village Potter.' *The Indian Craftsman*, Probsthain's Oriental Series. London: Probsthain & Co., 1909.

———. 'Illustrations From The Records And Relics Of The Late Honourable East India Company.' *Journal of Indian Art*, Vol. 3, Nos. 25–32, 1890.

———. *The Industrial Arts of India,* Vols I and II. London: Chapman and Hall, 1880.

——— to Mr C.D. Mahaluxmival. Letter in the *Journal of the Bombay Branch of the Royal Asiatic Society*, Vol. 24, Nos. 71–73. Byculla, Bombay: Education Society's Press, 1922.

———. *Paris Universal Exhibition of 1878: Handbook to the British Indian Section*. Royal Commission, 1878.

———. *Report of the Agri-Horticultural Society, for the Year 1865*. Bombay, 1866.

———. G.C.M. *Report on the Government Central Museum and on the Agricultural and Horticultural Society of Western India for 1863: With Appendices, Being the History of the Establishment of the Victoria and Albert Museum and of the Victoria Gardens*. Bombay: Byculla Press, 1864.

Blair, S., and J.M. Bloom, eds. *Rivers of paradise: Water in Islamic art and culture*. Yale: University Press, 2009.

Blakston, W.A., W. Swaysland, and A.F. Wiener. *The Illustrated Book Of Canaries and Cage-Birds, British and Foreign*. London: Cassell & Co, 1878.

Bliss D.C. The Bombay Bullion Market. US Government Printing Office; 1927.

Blunt, A. 'Imperial Geographies of Home: British Domesticity in India, 1886–1925.' *Transactions of the Institute of British Geographers*, Vol. 24, No. 4, 1999.

Boesi, A. 'Paper Plants in the *Tibetan World: A Preliminary Study*'. *Tibetan Printing: Comparison, Continuities, and Change*, eds. H. Diemberger, K. Ehrhard, and P.F. Kornicki. Brill, 2016.

Bogle, J.M.L. *Town Planning in India*. London: Oxford University Press, 1929.

Bombay (Presidency). *Gazetteer of the Bombay Presidency*, Vol. 18, No. 2. Bombay: Government Central Press, 1885.

Bombay Cooperatives Industries Report. 1947.

'Bombay Pottery.' *Journal of Indian Art*, Vol. II, No. 17. London: W. Griggs, 1887.

Borthakur, A., and P. Singh. 'History of Agricultural Research in India.' *Current Science*. Bangalore: Current Science Association, 2013.

Bose, D.M, S.N. Sen, and B.V. Subbarayappa. 'Western Science in India up to the End of the Nineteenth Century.' *A Concise History of Science in India*. New Delhi: Indian National Science Academy, 1971.

Brayne, F.L. *Better Villages*. London: Oxford University Press, 1937.

Breckenridge, C. 'The Aesthetics and Politics of Colonial Collecting: India at World Fairs.' *Comparative Studies in Society and History*, Vol. 31, No. 2, 1989.

Breeks, J.W. *An Account of Primitive Tribes and Monuments of the Nilagiris*. London: India Office, 1873.

Briggs, A. *Victorian Cities*, Vol. 2. California: University of California Press, 1993.

Bryan, M. *Dictionary of Painters and Engravers: Biographical and Critical*, Vol. 1, London: G. Bell and Sons, 1886.

Bryant, J., and S. Weber, eds. *John Lockwood Kipling: Arts & Crafts in the Punjab and London*. New York and New Haven: Bard Graduate Center Gallery and Yale University Press, 2017.

Bulley, A. *The Bombay Country Ships 1790–1833*. London and New York: Routledge, 2013.

Burgess, J. *The Rock Temples of Elephanta or Gharapuri, Described and Illustrated by James Burgess*. Bombay: D.H. Skyes & Co., Vining & Co., 1871.

Burney, S. 'Orientalism: The Making of the Other.' *Counterpoints*, Vol. 417, New York: Peter Lang AG 2012.

Burns, C.L. *Catalogue of the Collection of Maps, Prints and Photographs Illustrating the History of the Island of Bombay*. Bombay: Times Press, 1918.

———. 'The Functions of Schools of Art in India.' *Journal of the Royal Society of Arts*, Vol. 57, No. 2952. London: RSA, 1909.

———. 'A Monograph on Ivory Carving.' *Journal of Indian Art and Industry*, Vol. 9, No. 75. London: W. Griggs & Sons, 1900.

———. *A Monograph on the Gold and Silver Work in the Bombay Presidency*, Government Central Press, 1904.

Bury, S. 'Christopher Dresser, at the Camden Arts Centre.' *The Burlington Magazine*, Vol. 121, No. 921. 1979.

Campbell, J.M. *Gazetteer of the Bombay Presidency (Ratnagiri and Savantwadi Districts), Vol. X*. Bombay: Government Central Press, 1880.

———. *Gazetteer of the Bombay Presidency, Vol. XIII, Part I: Thana*. Bombay: Government Central Press, 1882.

———. *Gazetteer of the Bombay Presidency, Vol. XVIII, Part II. Poona*. Bombay: Government Central Press, 1885.

Cave, H. *The Book of Ceylon*. London: Cassell & Co., 1908.

Chaiklin, M. 'Surat and Bombay Ivory and Commercial Networks in Western India.' *The Dutch and English East India Companies*, eds A. Clulow and T. Mostert. Amsterdam: Amsterdam University Press, 2018.

Chandra, M. *A Handbook to the Indian Art Collection in The Prince of Wales Museum of Western India, Bombay*. Bombay: Order of the Trustees, 1938.

Chandavarkar, R. 'Plague panic and epidemic politics in India, 1896 -1914', *Epidemics and Ideas: Essays on the Historical Perception of Pestilence*, eds. T. Ranger, and P. Slack. Cambridge: Cambridge University Press, 1995.

Chatterjee, K. 'Card and Culture: Cultural Cosmopolitan in Mughal India.' *On Modern Indian Sensibilities: Culture, Politics, History,* eds I. Banerjee-Dube and S. Gooptu. London and New York: Routledge, 2018.

Chatterjee, S. 'People of Clay: Portrait Objects in the Peabody Essex Museum'. *Museum History Journal*, 6:2, 203–21, 2013.

Chavan, K. 'Maratha Painting.' *Bulletin of the Deccan College Research Institute*, Vol. 58. Pune: Deccan College Post-Graduate and Research Institute, 1998.

Chawla, R. *Raja Ravi Varma: Painter of Colonial India*. Ahmedabad: Mapin Publishing, 2010.

Chisholm, H., ed. 'Nathubhoy, Sir Mangaldas.' *Encyclopædia Britannica,* Vol. 19 (11th ed.). Cambridge: Cambridge University Press, 1911.

———, ed. 'Shankarsett, Jagannath.' *Encyclopædia Britannica*, Vol. 24 (11th ed.). Cambridge: Cambridge University Press, 1911.

———. 'Refiguring the Colonial City: Recovering the Role of Local Inhabitants in the Construction of Colonial Bombay, 1854–1918.' *Buildings & Landscapes: Journal of the Vernacular Architecture Forum*, Vol. 14. Minneapolis: University of Minnesota Press, 2007.

Chopra, P. *A Joint Enterprise: Indian Elites and the Making of British Bombay*. Minneapolis: University of Minnesota Press, 2011.

Chung, T. 'The Britain–China–India Trade Triangle (1771–1840).' *Proceedings of the Indian History Congress 34*, 1973.

Codrington, K. de B. 'Birdwood and the Study of the Arts of India.' *Journal of the Royal Society of Arts*, Vol. 118, No. 5163. London: RSA1970.

Cohn, B.S. 'The British in Benares.' *An Anthropologist Among the Historians and Other Essays*, eds B.S. Cohn and R. Guha. Delhi: Oxford University Press, 1990.

———. *Colonialism and its Forms of Knowledge: The British in India*. Princeton: Princeton University Press, 1996.

Cole, H.H., and W. Tayler. *Catalogue of the Objects of Indian Art Exhibited in the South Kensington Museum*. London: G.E. Eyre and W. Spottiswoode, 1874.

Coleman, F.M. *Typical Pictures of Indian Natives (Reproductions from Specially Prepared Hand-Coloured Photographs)*, 4th edition. Bombay: Times of India Press, 1899.

Conze, E. *The Perfection of Wisdom in Eight Thousand Lines and its Verse Summary*. Bolinas: Four Seasons Foundation, 1975.

Church, A.H. 'Some Points of Contact Between the Scientific and Artistic Aspects of Pottery and Porcelain.' *Journal of the Society of Arts*, Vol. 29, No. 1466. London, 1880.

Coomaraswamy, A.K. T*he Arts and Crafts of India & Ceylon*. London and Edinburgh: TN Foulis, 1913.

———. *The Dance of Siva: Fourteen Indian Essays,* New York: The Sunwise Turn, Inc., 1918.

———. *The Indian Craftsman*. London: Probsthain & Co., 1909.

———. *Mediaeval Sinhalese Art*. Essex: Normal Chapel, 1908.

———. 'The Modern School Of Indian Painting.' *Journal of Indian Art and Industry*, Vol. 15, No. 120. London: W. Griggs & Sons, 1912.

———. *Rajput Paintings*. London: H. Milford, Oxford University, 1916.

———. 'Rajput Paintings.' *The Burlington Magazine for Connoisseurs*, Vol. 20, No. 108. London: The Burlington Magazine Ltd, 1912.

———. *Transformation of Nature in Art*. Massachusetts: Harvard University Press, 1934.

Croil, J. *Steam Navigation and its Relation to the Commerce of Canada and the United States*. Toronto: W. Briggs, 1898.

Crowe, J. *Report of the Director of Public Instruction (Bombay 1857–1858)*. Byculla, Bombay: Education Society Press, 1859.

Culin, S. *Chess and Playing Cards*. Washington: Government Printing Office, 1898.

Culture and Leisure Committee. 'Relocating the Statue of Earl Haig.' *EDINBURGH, The City of Edinburgh Council Report*, No. 9, June 23, 2009.

Curio. 'Ceramics: Artistic Decorative Pottery.' *The Art Amateur*, Vol. 2, No. 1. New York, December 1879.

Da Cunha, J.G. *The Origin of Bombay*. Bombay: Royal Asiatic Society, 1900.

Daboo, J., and J. Sinthupan. *Mapping Migration: Culture and Identity in the Indian Diasporas of Southeast Asia and the UK*, United Kingdom: Cambridge Scholars Publishing, 2018.

Dabashi, H. *The Shahnameh: The Persian Epic*. New York: Columbia University Press, 2019.

Dalmia, Y. *The Making of Modern Art: The Progressives*. Oxford: Oxford University Press, 2001.

Dani, A.H., and V.M. Masson, eds. *History of Civilizations of Central Asia: Development in Contrast: From the Sixteenth to the Mid-Nineteenth Century*, Vol. 5. Paris: UNESCO, 2003.

Dalvi, M. '"This New Architecture": Contemporary Voices on Bombay's Architecture Before the Nation State.' *Tekton: A Journal of Architecture, Urban Design, and Planning*, Vol. 5, Issue 1, pp. 56–73, 2018.

Daly, S. 'Kashmir Shawls in Mid-Victorian Novels', *Victorian Literature and Culture*, Vol. 30, No. 1, 2002.

Das, S. *Jadughar: 200 Years of the Indian Museum 1814–2014*. Kolkata: Indian Museum, 2014.

David, M.D. *Bombay: The City of Dreams (A History of the First City in India)*. Bombay: Himalaya Publishing House, 1995.

———. *History of Bombay, 1661–1708*. Bombay: University of Bombay, 1973.

Davidson, Olga M., and M.S. Simpson, eds. *Ferdowsi's Shahnama Millennial Perspectives*. Boston: Ilex Foundation, 2013.

Dehejia, V. *Impossible Picturesqueness: Edward Lear's Indian Watercolours, 1873-1875*. New York: Columbia University Press, 1989.

Dehejia, V., R.H. Davis, R. Nagaswamy, and K.P. Prentiss. *The Sensuous and the Sacred: Chola Bronzes from South India*. New York: American Federation of Arts, 2002.

Dehejia, V., Y. Sharma, and D. Khera. *Delight in Design: Indian Silver for the Raj*. Ahmedabad: Mapin Publishing, 2008.

Dentu, E., and P. Petit, eds. *L'Exposition Universelle de 1867 Illustree Vol. 1*. Publication Internationale Autorisee par le Commission Imperale. Paris: Bureaux d'abonnements, 1867.

Deodhar, B.R. *Pillars of Hindustani Music*, trans. R. Deshmukh. Bombay: Popular Prakashan, 1993.

Desai, K. *Jewels on the Crescent: Masterpieces of Chhatrapati Shivaji Maharaj Vastu Sangrahalaya*. Ahmedabad: Mapin Publishing and Chhatrapati Shivaji Maharaj Vastu Sangrahalaya, 2003.

Deshpande, B.S., and G.K. Rao. *Deliverance or the Escape of Shivaji the Great from Agra*. Poona: Vishramdham DG Post, 1929.

Desmond, R. 'Photography in Victorian India.' *Journal of the Royal Society of Arts*. Vol. 134, No. 5353. London: RSA, 1985.

Despatch Relating to Education–East India. *Extracts from the Report of the Director of Public Instruction in the Central Province, 1866–67*. Bombay, 1867.

Dhond, P.A. *Rapan*. Mumbai: Mauj Publications, 1979.

Dhurandhar, A.M. *Majhi Smaranchitray*. Mumbai: Majestic Publishing House, 2015.

Dhurandhar, M.V. *Kalamandiratil Ekkechalis Varshe (Forty-One Years in the Temple of Art), 1819–1931*. Bombay: Majestic Publishing House, 1940.

Diemberger, H. 'The Younghusband-Waddell Collection and its People: The Social Life of Tibetan Books Gathered in a Late-Colonial Enterprise.' *Inner Asia*, Vol. 14, No. 1, 2012.

Dossal, M. 'Conflicting Interests and "Harmonious Planning": Bombay, c. 1898–1928.'

Proceedings of the Indian History Congress, Vol. 60. Indian History Congress, 1999.

——— *Theatre of Conflict, City of Hope: Mumbai 1660 to Present Times*. Oxford: Oxford University Press, 2010.

Douglas, J. *Bombay and Western India*, Vol. 1. London: Sampson Low, Marston & Company, 1893.

Driver, F. 'Face to Face with Nain Singh: The Schlagintweit Collections and Their Uses.' *Naturalists in the Field: Collecting, Recording and Preserving the Natural World from the Fifteenth to the Twenty-First Century*, ed. A. MacGregor. Leiden/Boston: Brill, 2018.

Driver, F., and S. Ashmore. 'The Mobile Museum: Collecting and Circulating Indian Textiles in Victorian Britain.' *Victorian Studies*, Vol. 52, No. 3: 353–85, 2010.

Driver, J.E.S. *A Descriptive Catalogue of the Tibetan Manuscripts Held at the Bodleian Library, Oxford, c. 1970*, revised by D. Barrett. Oxford: Bodleian Libraries, 1993.

Drewitt, F.D. *Bombay in the Days of George IV: Memoirs of Sir Edward West, Chief Justice of the King's Court During Its Conflict With the East India Company, With Hitherto Unpublished Documents*. New York, Bombay and Calcutta: Longmans, Green, and Company, 1907.

D'Souza, F. 'From Manor House to Marine Base: The Story of the Naval Establishment in Mumbai.' *Zero Point Bombay: In & Around Horniman Circle*, eds K. Ganesh, U. Thakkar and G. Chadha. New Delhi: Lotus Collection, Roli Books, 2008.

Duran, J. 'The Nagaraja: Symbol and Symbolism in Hindu Art and Iconography.' *Journal of Aesthetic Education*, 24 (2), 37–47, 1990.

Dutta, A. *The Bureaucracy of Beauty: Design in the Age of its Global Reproducibility*. New York, London: Routledge, 2007.

Dwivedi, S., and R. Mehrotra. *Bombay: The Cities Within*. Mumbai: Eminence Designs Pvt Ltd, 2001.

Dyson, K.K. *A Various Universe, A Study of the Journals and Memoirs of British Men and Women in the Indian Subcontinent, 1765–1856*. Delhi: Oxford University Press, 1978.

Dziamski, P., N. Weismann, and D. Chand. *Fatah Al Khair: Oman's Last Ghanja*. Al Roya Press & Publishing House, 2010. Article received through the kind offices of Mick De Rutyer from Flinders University, Australia.

Eaton, N. 'The Art of Colonial Despotism: Portraits, Politics, and Empire in South India, 1750–1795.' *Cultural Critique* (70), pp. 63–93, 2008.

Edney, M.H. 'Defining a Unique City: Surveying and Mapping Bombay after 1800.' *Bombay to Mumbai: Changing Perspectives*, eds P. Rohatgi, P. Godrej and R. Mehrotra. Mumbai: Marg Publications, 1997.

———. *The Bombay City Police: A Historical Sketch, 1672–1916*. London: Oxford University Press, 1923.

———. *By-ways of Bombay*. Bombay: D.B. Taraporevala Sons & Company, 1912.

———. *The Gazetteer of Bombay City and Island, Vols. 1, 2, 3*. Bombay: The Times Press, 1909.

———. *The Rise of Bombay: A Retrospect*. Bombay: The Times Press, 1902.

Egerton, W *A Description of Indian and Oriental Armour*. London: W.H. Allen & Co., 1896.

———. *An Illustrated Handbook of Indian Arms*. London: W.H. Allen, 1880.

Ellis, T.P. *Monograph on Ivory Carving in the Punjab*. Lahore: Government Press, 1900.

Falconer, J. *India: Pioneering Photographers: 1850–1900*. London: The British Library and The Howard and Jane Ricketts Collection, 2001.

Falzon, M.A. *Cosmopolitan Connections: The Sindhi Diaspora 1860–2000*. Leiden: Brill, 2004.

Fern, E.R. *Victoria and Albert Museum: Catalogue of the Industrial Arts Section*. Bombay: Byculla Press, 1926.

Fernandes, G.P. *Report on the Arts and Crafts of the Bombay Presidency*. Bombay: Government Central Press, 1932.

Ferris, G.T. *Gems of the Centennial Exhibition: Consisting of Illustrated Descriptions of Objects of an Artistic Character, in the Exhibits of The United States, Great Britain, France, Spain, Italy, Germany, Belgium, Norway, Sweden, Denmark, Hungary, Russia,*

Japan, China, Egypt, Turkey, India, Etc., At the Philadelphia International Exhibition of 1876. New York: Appleton, 1877.

Finkel, I.L., and C. Mackenzie. *Asian Games: The Art of Contest.* New York: Asia Society, 2004.

Finkelstein, G. '"Conquerors of The Künlün"? The Schlagintweit Mission to High Asia, 1854–57.' *History of Science*, Vol. 38, No. 2, June 2000.

Firouzeh, P. 'Convention and Reinvention: The British Library Shahnama of 1438 (Or. 1403).' *Iran*, Vol. 57, No. 1, pp. 49–70, 2019.

Floor, W. 'The Woodworking Craft and Its Products in Iran.' *Muqarnas*, Vol. 23, 2006.

Forbes, J. *Oriental Memoirs: A Narrative of Seventeen Years' Residence in India.* London: White, Cochrane, and Co., 1813.

Foster, W., and S.T. Sheppard, eds. *Bombay in the Days of Queen Anne Being an Account of the Settlement by John Burnell.* London: Printed for Hakluyt Society, 1933.

Franz, M. 'From Dinner Parties to Galleries: The Langhammer-Leyden-Schlesinger Circle in Bombay – 1940s through the 1950s.' *Arrival Cities: Migrating Artists and New Metropolitan Topographies in the 20th Century*, eds B. Dogramaci, M. Hetschold, L.K. Lugo, R. Lee and H. Roth. Germany: Leuven University Press, pp. 73-90, 2020.

French, J.C. *Himalayan Art.* Oxford: Oxford University Press, 1931.

Fryer, G. 'John Fryer, F.R.S. and His Scientific Observations, Made Chiefly in India and Persia between 1672 and 1682.' *Notes and Records of the Royal Society of London*, Vol. 33, No. 2, pp. 175–206. London: RSA, 1979.

Fryer, J. *A New Account of East-India and Persia in Eight Letters Being Nine Years Travels, Begun 1672 and Finished 1681.* London: Printed by R.R. for Ri. Chiswell, 1698.

Gandhi, J. *A Tale of Native Towns of Mumbai: Bhuleshwar, Girgaum, Malabar Hill.* Jagdish Gandhi, 2010.

Godrej, P.J., Mistree, F.P. (eds.) *Across the Oceans and Flowing Silks* and *No Parsi is an Island* (Hoskote R. Adajania, N. and Godrej, P.J. eds.). Mumbai: Spenta Multimedia, 2013.

Gogate, P.P., and B. Arunachalam. 'Area Maps in Maratha Cartography: A Study in Native Maps of Western India.' *Imago Mundi*, Vol. 50, No. 1, 1998.

Goldstein, J., ed. *The Jews of China*, Vol. 1. New York, London: ME Sharpe, 1998.

Gole, S. 'Elephanta and Salsette Illustrated: Early Archaeological Studies in Western India.' *India: A Pagent of Prints*, eds P. Rohatgi and P. Godrej. Bombay: Marg Publications, 1989.

Gonyo, D. *Envisioning India: South Asians, Exhibitions and the Development of Nation in the Late Nineteenth and Early Twentieth Centuries.* PhD dissertation, University of Brighton, 2015.

Goswami, M. *Producing India: From Colonial Economy to National Space.* Chicago and London: University of Chicago Press, 2004.

Goswamy, B.N., and E. Fischer. *Pahari Masters: Court Painters of Northern India* (Series: Artibus Asiae Supplementum 38). Zurich: Artibus Asiae, 1992.

Goswamy, K. *Kashmiri Painting.* New Delhi: Aryan Books, 1998.

Government, India Bombay. *List of art manufactures, exclusive of textiles, of the Bombay Presidency.* Bombay: Government Central Press, 1885.

Government of Bombay. *Annual Report of the Sir J. J. School of Art Bombay, for the year 1938-39.*

Government of Bombay. *Sir George Clarke Technical Laboratories and Studios: Pottery Department – Prospectus.* MSA: ED Bombay, 1915.

Gray, B. 'Moor's "Hindu Pantheon."' *The British Museum Quarterly*, Vol. XIV, no. 4, 1940.

Great Britain. Parliament. House of Commons. "Fourteenth Annual Report of the Deputy Master of the Mint, 1883", *Twenty-Seventh Report of the Commissioners of Her Majesty's Customs on The Customs (for 1883), Parliamentary Papers*, Vol 23, London: Eyre and Spottiswoode, 1884.

Great Exhibition of the Works of Industry of all Nations. 'Official Descriptive and Illustrated Catalogue,' Vol. 2. London: W. Clowes and Sons for Spicer Brothers, 1851.

Griffiths, J. 'Brass and Copper Wares of the Bombay Presidency.' *Journal of Indian Art and Industry*, Vol. 7, No. 55. London: W. Griggs & Sons, 1896.

Guha, A. 'Parsi Seths as Entrepreneurs, 1750–1850.' *Economic and Political Weekly*, Vol. 5, No. 35, pp. M107–115, 1970.

Guha, S. '"Nineveh" in Bombay and Histories of Indian Archaeology.' *Journal of the Asiatic Society of Bangladesh* (Hum.), Vol. 62, No. 1, 2017.

Guha-Thakurta, T. *The Making of New 'Indian' Art: Artists, Aesthetics and Nationalism in Bengal, c. 1850–1920.* Cambridge: Cambridge University Press, 1992.

———. *Monuments, Objects, Histories: Institutions of Art in Colonial and Postcolonial India.* New York: Columbia University Press, 2004.

———. 'Westernization and Tradition in South Indian Painting in the 19th Century: The Case of Raja Ravi Varma.' *Studies in History 2*, No. 2, 1986.

———. 'Women as 'Calendar Art' Icons.' *Economic and Political Weekly*, Vol. 26, No, 43, 1991.

Gupchup, V. 'Paeans in Stone and Oils: Statuary and Portraiture in the Asiatic Society.' *Zero Point Bombay: In & Around Horniman Circle*, eds K. Ganesh, U. Thakkar and G. Chadha. New Delhi: Lotus Collection, Roli Books. 2008.

———. *Sir George Birdwood: The Promoter of Goodwill between East and West.* Mumbai: Popular Prakashan, 2014.

Gupte, B.A. *Craniological Data from the Indian Museum (Ethnographic Survey).* Calcutta: Government Printing Press, 1909.

———. 'Embroidery.' *Journal of Indian Art and Industry*, Vol 2. No. 18. London: W. Griggs & Sons, 1887.

———. *Hindu Holidays and Ceremonials: With Dissertations on Origin, Folklore and Symbols.* Calcutta: Thacker, Spink & Co, 1916.

———. 'Madras, Tanjore & Mysore.' *Journal of Indian Art and Industry*, Vol. 1, No. 14. London: W. Griggs & Sons, 1885.

———. 'Thana Silks.' *Journal of Indian Art and Industry*, Vol. 1, No. 5. London: W. Griggs & Sons, 1885.

Gupta, D.C. *Annual Report of the Department of Industries, Bombay Province, for the year 1938-39.*

Guy, J. 'A Boat Model and State Ritual in Eastern India.' *Bulletin De L'École Française D'Extrême-Orient*, Vol. 86, pp. 105–26, 1999.

———. 'Roaming the Land: Narasimha's Journey from Mythic Hero to Bhakti Devotion: The Lion Avatar in South Indian Temple Drama.' *Orientations*, Vol. 47, No. 3, pp. 32–43, April 2016.

Guy, J., and D. Swallow, eds. *Arts of India, 1550-1900*, London: Victoria & Albert Museum, 1990.

Haider, N. 'International Trade In Precious Metals And Monetary Systems Of Medieval India: 1200–1500 A.D.' *Proceedings of the Indian History Congress*, Vol. 59, 1998.

Hapgood, S. *Early Bombay Photography.* Ahmedabad: Mapin Publishing, 2015.

Harris, J., ed. *A Companion to Textile Culture.* New York: Wiley-Blackwell, 2020.

Havell, E.B. 'Art Administration in India.' *Journal of the Royal Society of Arts*, Vol. 58, No. 2985. London: RSA, 1910.

Hazareesingh, S. 'Colonial Modernism and the Flawed Paradigms of Urban Renewal: Uneven Development in Bombay, 1900–25.' *Urban History*, Vol. 28, No. 2, Cambridge University Press, 2001.

Head, Raymond. 'Indian Crafts and Western Design from the Seventeenth Century to the Present.' *RSA Journal*, Vol. 136, No. 5378, pp. 116–31, 1988.

Hendley T.H. *Handbook to the Jeypore Museum.* Calcutta: Calcutta Central Press Company, 1895.

———. 'Illustrations and General Notes: Portraits by Indian Artists; Symbolism; Mythology.' *Journal of Indian Art and Industry*, Vol. 15, No. 120. London: W. Griggs & Sons, 1912.

———. 'Indian Museums.' *Journal of Indian Art and Industry*, Vol. 16, Issue 35. London: W. Griggs & Sons, 1914.

———. 'Metal Work.' *Journal of Indian Art*, Vol. IV, No. 35. London: W. Griggs & Sons, 1891.

Hendley, T.H., W.B. Dawkins, and J.D. Crace. 'Indian Museums: a Centenary Retrospect.' *Journal of the Royal Society of Arts*, Vol. 62, no. 3193, pp. 207–21. London: RSA, 1914.

Hill, C.V. 'Colonial Gardens and the Validation of Empire in Imperial India.' *Journal of South Asian Studies*, Vol. 1, No. 2, 2013.

Hobhouse, H., ed. *The Crystal Palace and the Great Exhibition: Science, Art and Productive Industry: The History of the Royal Commission for the Exhibition of 1851.* London: A&C Black, 2002.

Hoffenberg, P. *An Empire on Display: English, Indian, and Australian Exhibitions from the Crystal Palace to the Great War.* Berkeley: University of California Press, 2001.

Hornell, J. *The Origins and Ethnological Significance of Indian Boat Designs.* Calcutta: Asiatic Society, 1920.

Houston, J. *Representative Men of the Bombay Presidency: A Collection of Biographical Sketches, with Portraits of the Princes, Chiefs, Philanthropists, Statesmen and Other Leading Residents of the Presidency.* Bombay: C.B. Burrows Care William Watson & Co., 1897.

Hunter W.W. *Report of the Indian Education Commission.* Calcutta: Superintendent of Government Printing, 1883.

Imarte, M. 'Sardesai, Narayan Ramakrishna.' *Dhrishyakala*, eds S. Bahulkar and D. Ghare. Mumbai: Popular Prakashan, 2013.

'India at the Antwerp Exhibition.' *Journal of Indian Art*, Vol. I, No. 7. London: W. Griggs & Sons, 1885.

Indian Pictorial Education, Vol. 1, No. 3. Bombay: Times Press, 1930.

Inglis, S. 'Suitable for Framing: The Work of a Modern Master.' *Media and the Transformation of Religion in South Asia*, eds L.A. Babb and S.S. Wadley. Philadelphia: University of Pennsylvania Press, 1995.

INTACH. 'Report on the Afghan Church Restoration.' *Indian National Trust for Arts and Cultural Heritage* (Mumbai Chapter), 2005.

Jaffer, A. *Furniture from British India and Ceylon: A Catalogue of the Collections in the Victoria & Albert Museum and the Peabody Essex Museum.* London: Victoria and Albert Museum, 2001.

Jain, J. *Bombay/Mumbai: Visual Histories of a City.* New Delhi: Centre for Indian Visual Culture, 2013.

———. *Indian Popular Culture: 'The Conquest of the World as Picture.'* Kolkata: Ajeepay Press, 2004.

———. 'The Visual Culture of the Indo-British Cotton Trade.' *A Story of Early Indian Advertising*, Vol. 68, No. 3. Mumbai: The Marg Foundation, 2016.

Jain, J., and J. Jain-Neubauer. *Company School: Indo-British Painting in Colonial India from the Swaraj.* Noida: Swaraj Art Archive, 2016.

Jain, K. *Gods in the Bazaar: The Economies of Indian Calendar Art.* Durham (North Carolina) and London: Duke University Press, 2007.

Jain-Neubauer, J. 'Curiosity and its Aesthetics: Alexander von Humboldt, Prince Waldemar of Prussia, the Schlagintweit Brothers and India.' *Indo-Asiatische Zeitschrift*, Vol. 17. Berlin, 2013.

Jaipur Albert Hall Museum and C. Singh. *Treasures of the Albert Hall Museum, Jaipur.* Department of Archaeology and Museums, Government of Rajasthan: Jaipur, 2010.

Jhaveri, K.M. *The Present State of Gujarati Literature.* Bombay: University of Bombay, 1934.

Jones, O. *The Grammar of Ornament.* London: Day and Son, 1856.

Joshi, N.M. *Urban Handicrafts of the Bombay Deccan.* Poona: D.R. Gadgil, 1936.

Kale, P. 'Goan Intellectuals and Goan Identity: An Unresolved Conflict.' *Economic and Political Weekly*, Vol. 29, Nos. 16/17, 1994.

Kantawala, A. 'Art Education in Colonial India: Implementation and Imposition.' *Studies in Art Education*, Vol. 53, No. 3. Alexandria, VA: National Art Education Association, 2012.

Kapur, G. *When Was Modernism: Essays on Contemporary Cultural Practice in India.* New Delhi: Tulika Books, 2000.

Karl, B. *Embroidered Histories: Indian Textiles for the Portuguese Market During the Sixteenth and Seventeenth Centuries.* Vienna: Böhlau Verlag Wien, 2016.

Karpinski, C. 'Kashmir to Paisley.' *The Metropolitan Museum of Art Bulletin*, Vol. 22, No. 3, pp. 116–23, November 1963.

Keer, D. 'Dr. Bhau Daji Lad, G.G.M.C.' *Journal of the Royal Asiatic Society*, Vol. 38. Bombay, 1963.

Kelkar, N.M. *Story of Sir J.J. School of Art: 1857–1957.* Bombay: Government Central Press, (date non precisée/ 1969).

Khan, O. *Paper Jewels: Postcards from the Raj.* Ahmedabad: Mapin Publishing, 2018.

Khandalavala, K., and M. Chandra. *New Documents of Indian Painting—A Reappraisal.* Bombay: The Board of Trustees of The Prince of Wales Museum of Western India, 1969.

Kidambi, P. *The Making of an Indian Metropolis: Colonial Governance and Public Culture in Bombay, 1890–1920.* London: Routledge, 2016.

Kidambi, P., M. Kamat and R. Dwyer, eds. *Bombay before Mumbai: Essays in Honour of Jim Masselos.* New York: Oxford University Press, 2019.

Kinsley, D. *Hindu Goddesses: Visions of the Divine Feminine in the Hindu Religious Tradition.* New Delhi: Motilal Banarsidass, 1988.

Kipling, J.L. 'Indian Ivory Carving.' *Journal of Indian Art and Industry*, Vol. 1, No. 7. London: W. Griggs & Sons, 1885.

———. 'The Industries of the Punjab.' *Journal of Indian Art and Industry*, Vol. 2, No. 23. London: W. Griggs & Sons, 1888.

Kiralfy, I. *Official Catalogue of the Empire of India Exhibition: Earl's Court, London, S.W., 1895.* London: J.J. Keliher & Co., 1895.

Kistler, L.H., C.P. Carter, and B. Hinchey. 'Planning and Control in the 19th-Century Ice Trade.' *The Accounting Historians Journal*, Vol. 11, No. 1, pp. 19–30, 1984.

Khullar, S. *Worldly Affiliations: Artistic Practice, National Identity, and Modernism in India, 1930–1990.* California: University of California Press, 2015.

Kochhar, R.K. 'Ardaseer Cursetjee (1808–1877), the First Indian Fellow of the Royal Society of London.' *Notes and Records of the Royal Society of London*, Vol. 47, No. 1. London, 1993.

Kooiman, D. 'The Political Geography of Communal Conflict: British versus Indian Modes of Governance.' *Conflict in a Globalizing World: Studies in Honour of Peter Kloos.* eds A. Koster, P. Smets and B. Venema. Netherlands: Royal Van Gorcum, 2002.

Kossak, S. *Indian Court Painting: 16th–19th Century.* New York: Metropolitan Museum of Art, 1997.

Kumar, A. 'Keigwin's Bombay (1683–84) and the Maratha-Siddi Naval Conflict.' *Proceedings of the Indian History Congress*, Vol. 75. New Delhi: Indian History Congress, 2014.

Lawrence, W.L. *The Valley of Kashmir.* London: Oxford University Press, 1895.

Lear, E., and R. Murphy. *Edward Lear's Indian Journal: Watercolours and Extracts from the Diary of Edward Lear (1873–1875).* London: Jarrolds, 1953.

Lectures on the Results of the Great Exhibition of 1851: Delivered Before the Society of Arts, Manufactures, and Commerce. London: D. Bogue, 1852.

Lenman, B.P. 'The Transition to European Military Ascendancy in India, 1600–1800.' *Tools of War: Instruments, Ideas and Institutions of Warfare, 1445–1871*, ed. J.A. Lynn. Urbana and Chicago: University of Illinois Press, 1990.

Levy, T.E, A.M. Levy, D.R. Sthapathy, D.S. Sthapathy, and D.S. Sthapathy. *Masters of Fire: Hereditary Bronze Casters of South India.* Bochum: Deutsches Bergbau-Museum, 2008.

Lin, C.L. 'Japanese Shipping in India and the British Resistance, 1891–1918.' *The International History Review*, Vol. 32, No. 2. Taylor & Francis, 2010.

Llewellyn-Jones, R. *A Fatal Friendship: The Nawabs, the British, and the City of Lucknow.* New York: Oxford University Press, 1985.

———. "Painting in Lucknow, 1775 - 1800". *Forgotten Masters: Indian Painting for the East India Company*, ed. William Dalrymple. London: Philip Wilson Publishers, 2020.

London, C.W. *Bombay Gothic.* Mumbai: India Book House, 2002.

Lydekker, R., H.N. Hutchinson, and J.W. Gregory. *The Living Races of Mankind.* London: Hutchinson & Co., 1902.

MacDonald, D. *Journal of the Bombay Natural History Society*, No.1, Vol. II, 1887.

MacKenzie, J. *Orientalism: History, Theory and the Arts.* Manchester: Manchester University Press, 1995.

Maclean, J.M. *A Guide to Bombay, Historical, Statistical and Descriptive.* Bombay: Bombay Gazette Steam Press, 1892.

Mahaluxmivala, P.D. *History of Bombay Electric Supply and Tramway Company, Ltd.* Bombay: B.E.S.T. Company, 1936.

Maholay-Jaradi, P. 'Courting Craft, Design, and Industry'. *Fashioning a National Art. Baroda's Royal Collection and Art Institutions (1875–1924).* New Delhi: Oxford University Press, 2016.

Markham, S.F., and H. Hargreaves. *The Museums of India.* London: Museums Association, 1936.

Markley, R. '"A Putridness In The Air": Monsoons and Mortality in Seventeenth-Century Bombay.' *Journal for Early Modern Cultural Studies*, Vol. 10, No. 2, pp. 105–25. University of Pennsylvania Press, 2010.

Markovits, C. 'Bombay as a Business Centre in the Colonial Period.' *Merchants, Traders, Entrepreneurs: Indian Business in the Colonial Era.* London: Palgrave Macmillan, 2008.

———. *The Global World of Indian Merchants, 1750–1947: Traders of Sindh from Bukhara to Panama.* Cambridge: Cambridge University Press, 2000.

Martin, E.B., and L. Vigne. `The Decline and Fall of India's Ivory Industry.' *Pachyderm*, No. 12, 1989.

Martineau, J. *Life and Correspondence of Sir Bartle Frere*, Vol. II. London: John Murray, 1892.

Maskiell, M. 'Consuming Kashmir: Shawls and Empires, 1500–2000.' *Journal of World History.* Hawaii: University of Hawai'i Press, 2002.

Masselos, J., and P. Kapoor. *Bombay Then, Mumbai Now*, New Delhi: Lustre Press, Roli Books, 2009.

Masteller, K., and J.B. Spurr. *Silver & Shawls: India, Europe and the Colonial Art Market: August 27, 2005–January 25, 2006.* Cambridge, MA: Harvard University Art Museums, 2005.

Mathur, A. 'Setting the Stage: India and Japan in History'. *India–Japan Relations: Drivers, Trends And Prospects.* S. Rajaratnam School of International Studies, pp. 1–15, 2012.

Mathur, S. *India by Design: Colonial History and Cultural Display,* California and London: University of California Press, 2007.

———. 'Living Ethnological Exhibits: The Case of 1886.' *Cultural Anthropology*, Vol. 15, No. 4, pp. 492–524, November 1, 2000.

Mathur, S., and K. Singh. *No Touching, No Spitting, No Praying: The Museum in South Asia.* New Delhi: Routledge, Taylor and Francis Group, 2015.

Matthee, R. 'Iran's Relations with Europe in the Safavid Period. Diplomats, Missionaries, Merchants, and Travel.' *The Fascination of Persia: The Persian-European Dialogue in Seventeenth-Century Art & Contemporary Art of Tehran*, ed. A. Langer. Chicago: University of Chicago Press, 2013.

Maxwell, T.S. 'The Visvarupa Iconographic Tradition: North Indian Images of Visvarupa Visnu 5th–13th Centuries CE.' *The Archaeological Report of Professor T.S. Maxwell*, Vol. I, 1990.

Mayer, R.A. *Lockwood De Forest: Furnishing the Gilded Age with a Passion for India.* Newark: Associated University Presses, 2008.

McGowan, A. '"All that is Rare, Characteristic or Beautiful": Design and the Defense of Tradition in Colonial India, 1851–1903'. *Journal of Material Culture*, 10 (3), 2005.

———. 'Convict Carpets: Jails and the Revival of Historic Carpet Design in Colonial India.' *Journal of Asian Studies*, Vol. 72, No. 2, Cambridge: Cambridge University Press, 2013.

———. *Crafting the Nation in Colonial India.* New York: Palgrave Macmillan, 2009.

McMunn, G.F., and E. Lovett. *The Armies of India.* London: Adam and Charles Black, 1911.

Mehta, T.Z. *Restoration and Revitalisation of the Dr. Bhau Daji Lad Mumbai City Museum.* Mumbai: Dr. Bhau Daji Lad Museum Trust, 2009.

Melbourne International Exhibition. *Official Record: Containing Introduction, History of Exhibition, Description of Exhibition and Exhibits, Official Awards of Commissioners, and Catalogue of Exhibits.* Melbourne: Mason, Firth & M'Cutcheon, 1882.

'Memorial Fountain, Bombay.' *The Art Journal* (1875–1887), New Series, Vol. 1. New York: D'Appleton & Co, 1875.

Menon, A.S. *Kerala District Gazetteers, Trivandrum.* Trivandrum: Superintendent of Government Press, 1962.

Metcalf, T. *An Imperial Vision: Indian Architecture and Britain's Raj.* London: Faber & Faber, 1989.

———. 'Ideologies of the Raj.' *The New Cambridge History of India.* Cambridge: Cambridge University Press, 1995.

Michell, G. *Deccan Heritage Foundation Guidebook Series: Elephanta.* Mumbai: Jaico Publishing House, 2002.

———. *Islamic Heritage of the Deccan.* Mumbai: Marg Publications, 1986.

———, ed. *Living Woods: Sculptural Traditions of South India.* Bombay: South Asia Books, 1992.

Milani, M. *Sufism in the Secret History of Persia.* London: Routledge, 2014.

Mills, J.H., and S. Sen, eds. *Confronting the Body: The Politics of Physicality in Colonial and Post-Colonial India.* London: Anthem Press, 2004.

Misra, B.B. *India: The Indian Middle Classes: Their Growth in Modern Times.* Bombay: Oxford University Press, 1961.

Mitra, S.C. 'Art. IX: A Plea For The Formation Of A Linnaean Society In Calcutta.' *Calcutta Review*, Vol. 92, No. 183. Calcutta University Press, pp. 196–203, 1891.

Mitter, P. *Art and Nationalism in Colonial India, 1850–1922: Occidental Orientations.* Cambridge: Cambridge University Press, 1994.

———. 'The Formative Period (Circa 1856–1900) Sir JJ School of Art and the Raj.' *Architectural Styles in British India: 1837–1910.* Bombay: Marg Publications, 1994.

———, 'Indian Artists in the Colonial Period: The Case of Bombay.' *Art and Visual Culture in India 1857–2007*, ed. Gayatri Sinha. Mumbai: Marg Publications, 2009.

———. *Much Maligned Monsters: A History of European Reactions to Indian Art.* Chicago: University of Chicago Press, 1992.

———. *The Triumph of Modernism: India's Artists and the Avant-garde, 1922–47.* London: Reaktion Books, 2007.

Moor, E. *The Hindu Pantheon.* London: J. Johnson, 1810.

Moses, H. *Sketches of India: With Notes on the Seasons, Scenery, and Society of Bombay, Elephanta, and Salsette.* London: Simpkin, Marshall & Company, 1850.

Montauban, M.E. *A Year and a Day in the East, Or, Wanderings Over Land and Sea.* London: Longman, Brown, Green and Longmans, 1846.

Mukharji, T.N. *Art-Manufactures of India.* Calcutta: Superintendent of Government Printing, 1888.

———. 'Bidriware.' *Journal of Indian Art*, Vol 1, No. 6. London: W. Griggs & Sons, 1885.

———. 'Carved Stone Work, Agra.' *Journal of Indian Art and Industry*, Vol. 1, No. 13. London: W. Griggs & Sons, 1886.

Mukhopādhyā, T. *Art-Manufactures of India Specially Compiled for the Glasgow International Exhibition, 1888.* Calcutta: Superintendent of Government Printing, 1889.

Nagaswami, R. *Art and Culture of Tamil Nadu.* New Delhi: Sundeep Prakashan, 1980.

Nathan, R. *Plague in India, 1896, 1897,* Vol. I. Simla: Government Central Printing Office, 1898.

Nathubhai, T.M. *Hindu caste, law & custom*, Bombay: Times of India Press, 1903.

Nayar, P.K. *Colonial Voices: The Discourses of Empire.* Chichester, West Sussex: John Wiley & Sons, 2012.

Neela, N., and G. Ambrosia. 'Contribution of Marathas of Tanjore to Art and Architecture.' *Shanlax International Journal of Arts, Science & Humanities*, Vol. 3, No. 3, January 2016.

Neumayer, E., and C. Schelberger. 'Raja Ravi Varma: Portrait of an Artist.' *The Diary of C. Raja Raja Varma*. New Delhi: Oxford University Press, 2005.

Nightingale, F., B. Nergaard, and M. Vicinus. *Ever Yours, Florence Nightingale: Selected Letters*. Cambridge, MA: Harvard University Press, 1990.

Niranjana, T. *Musicophilia in Mumbai*. Durham: Duke University Press, 2020.

Nizamuddin, A.M. *The Sikandar Nama, e Bara, or Book of Alexander the Great*, trans. Capt. H.W. Clarke. London: W.H. Allen, 1881.

Ohri, V.C. *The Technique of Pahadi Painting: An Inquiry into Aspects of Materials, Methods, and History Based upon Observation and Field-Work*. Shimla: IIAS, 2001.

Olin, M. 'Self-Representation: Resemblance and Convention in Two Nineteenth-Century Theories of Architecture and the Decorative Arts.' *Zeitschrift Für Kunstgeschichte*, Vol. 49, No. 3, 1986.

Oshinsky, S.J. 'Christopher Dresser (1834–1904).' *Heilbrunn Timeline of Art History*. New York: The Metropolitan Museum of Art, 2000.

Ovington, J., and H.G. Rawlinson, eds. *A Voyage to Surat in the Year 1869*. London: Oxford UP, 1929.

Pai, D.A. *Monograph on the Religious Sects of India Among the Hindus*. Bombay: The Times Press, 1928.

Pal, D. *The Painter*. New Delhi: Random House India, 2011.

Pal, P. *Art of Tibet, A Catalogue of the Los Angeles County Museum of Art Collection*, expanded edition. California: Los Angeles County Museum of Art, 1990.

———. ed. *East Meets West: A Selection of Asian and European Art from the Tata Collection in the Chhatrapati Shivaji Maharaj Vastu Sangrahalaya, formerly Prince of Wales Museum of Western India*. Mumbai: Marg Publications and Chhatrapati Shivaji Maharaj Vastu Sangrahalaya, 2010.

Pal, P., and V. Dehejia. *From Merchants to Emperors: British Artists and India, 1757–1930*, New York: Cornell University Press, 1986.

Palsetia, J. *The Parsis of India: Preservation of Identity in Bombay City*. Vol. 17. Brill, 2001.

Paniker, K.A. *Medieval Indian Literature: An Anthology, Vol. 3*. New Delhi: Sahitya Akademi, 1959.

Panikkar, S.K. 'Indigenism: An Inquiry into the Quest for "Indianness" in Contemporary Indian Art'. *Indian Art, an Overview*, ed. Gayatri Sinha. New Delhi: Rupa & Co., 2003.

Papas, A. 'Bombay Mystical City: Muslim Shrines and Saints in the Urban Fabric from 1800 to Present.' *Saintly Spheres and Islamic Landscapes*, eds D. Ephrat, E.S. Wolper, and P.G. Pinto. Brill, 2020.

Parasnis, D.B. *Poona in the Bygone Days*. Bombay: Times Press, 1921.

Parpia, S. 'The Imperial Mughal Hunt: A Pursuit of Knowledge.' *Ilm: Science, Religion and Art in Islam*, ed. S. Akkach. Adelaide: University of Adelaide Press, 2019.

Pedram, B., M. Hosseini, and G. Rahmani. 'The Importance of Painting in Qajar Dynasty Based on the Sociology Point of View.' *Journal of History Culture and Art Research*, Vol. 6, No. 3, pp. 985–98, 2017.

Pendsay, S.N. *The B.E.S.T. Story*. Bombay: Bombay Electric Supply & Transport Undertaking, 1972.

Perkins, P. *Edward Harrison Barwell: 19th-Century Northampton Ironfounder*. Northampton: NIAG, 2019.

Philip, K. *Civilising Natures: Race, Resources and Modernity in Colonial South India*. New Jersey: Rutgers University Press, 2003.

Pinney, C. *Camera Indica: The Social Life of Indian Photographs*. Chicago: Chicago University Press, 1997.

———. 'Colonial Anthropology in the "Laboratory" of Mankind.' *The Raj: India and the British, 1600–1947*, ed. C.A. Bayly and Brian A. London: National Portrait Gallery, 1990.

———. *The Coming of Photography in India*. London: British Library, 2008.

———. *Photos of the Gods*. London: Reaktion Books Ltd, 2004.

Playne, H.F. 'The District and Civil Military Stations in India.' *Thacker's Indian Directory*. Calcutta: Spink & Co., 1917–20.

Polu, S.L., 'Plague and Cholera—The Epidemic versus the Endemic.' *Infectious Disease in India, 1892–1940*. London: Palgrave Macmillan, 2012.

Powell, B.H.B. *Handbook of the Manufactures and Arts of the Punjab*. Lahore: Punjab Printing Company, 1872.

———. 'On Some Of The Difficulties Of Art Manufactures.' *Journal of Indian Art*, Vol I, No. 5, London: W. Griggs, 1885.

Prakash, G. *Another Reason: Science and the Imagination of Modern India*. New Jersey: Princeton University Press, 1999.

———. *Mumbai Fables*. New Jersey: Princeton University Press, 2010.

Prakash, P. 'Women and Sports: Extending Limits to Physical Expression.' *Economic and Political Weekly*, Vol. 25, No. 17, April 1990.

Preeti. 'Colonial Codification of Education in India until 1920.' *Journal of Indian Education*, Vol. 42, No. 2, pp. 29–44, 2016.

Price, L. 'Animals, Governance and Ecology: Managing the Menace of Venomous Snakes in Colonial India.' Cultural and Social History, Vol. 14, No. 2, 2017.

Procida, M.A. 'Servants of Empire.' *Married to the Empire: Gender, Politics and Imperialism in India, 1883–1947*. Manchester and New York: Manchester University Press, 2002.

Proceedings of the Art Conference Held in the Technical Institute at Lahore on the 1st, 2nd, 3rd, and 4th January 1894. Calcutta: Government Central Printing Office

Qazvini, N.H., and M.H. Kermani. 'An Analysis of the Evolution of Kashkul through the Lens of Hans Robert Jauss.' *The Scientific Journal of Bagh-e-Nazar*, Vol. 15, No. 62, pp. 57–68, August 2018.

Raeside, I.M.P. 'Dattātreya.' *Bulletin of the School of Oriental and African Studies*. University of London, Vol. 45, No. 3, 1982.

Raghunathji, K. 'Bombay Dancing Girls.' *The Indian Antiquary, a Journal of Oriental Research*, Vol. XIII, pp. 165–78, June 1884.

Rajadhyaksha, A. 'The Phalke Era: Conflict of Traditional Form and Modern Technology.' *Interrogating Modernity: Culture and Colonialism in India*, eds T. Niranjana, P. Sudhir, V. Dhareshwar. Calcutta: Seagull Books, 1993.

Ramanna, M. 'Florence Nightingale and Bombay Presidency.' *Social Scientist*, Vol. 30, Nos. 9/10, pp. 31–46, 2002.

———. *Western Medicine and Public Health in Colonial Bombay, 1845–1895*, Vol. 4. New Delhi: Orient Blackswan, 2002.

Ranade, R. *Sir Bartle Frere and His Times: A Study of His Bombay Years, 1862–1867*. Bombay: Mittal Publications, 1990.

Randhawa, M.S. 'Kangra Valley Painting.' *The Krishna Legend in Pahari Painting*. New Delhi: Lalit Kala Akademi, 1956.

Ranganathan, M., ed. *Govind Narayan's Mumbai: An Urban Biography from 1863*. London: Anthem Press, 2008.

Reeves, R. *Cire Perdue Casting in India*. New Delhi: Kanak Publications, 1962.

Rekha, N. 'The Patna School of Painting: A Brief History (1760–1880).' *Proceedings of the Indian History Congress*, Vol. 72, pp. 997–1007, 2011.

Report of the Bombay Chamber of Commerce for the Year 1889–90. 'Letter From D. MacDonald, M.D., Secretary and Curator, V&A Museum, Bombay, to the Chief Secretary to Government, Bombay, No. 1016 of 1888–89, Bombay, 14th March 1889.' Bombay: Gazette Steam Press, 1890.

Report of the Director of Public Instruction, Bombay, for the year 1855-56. Byculla, Bombay: Education Society Press, 1857.

Report of the Director of Public Instruction, Bombay, for the year 1856-57. Byculla, Bombay: Education Society Press, 1858.

Report for the United States National Museum under the direction of the Smithsonian Institution for the year 1884. Washington: US Government Printing Office, 1885.

Riddick, J.F. *The History of British India: A Chronology*. USA: Greenwood Publishing Group, 2006.

Ringer, M.M. *Pious Citizens: Reforming Zoroastrianism in India and Iran*. New York: Syracuse University Press, 2011.

Risley, H.H. *The Tribes and Castes of Bengal: Ethnographic Glossary, Vol. I*. Calcutta: Bengal Secretariat Press, 1891.

Rossi, B. *From the Ocean of Painting: India's Popular Paintings, 1589 to the present*. New York : Oxford University Press, 1998.

Rousselet, L. *India and its Native Princes: Travels in Central India and in the Presidencies of Bombay and Bengal*. London: Chapman & Hall, 1875.

Roy, T. 'Economic History and Modern India: Redefining the Link.' *Journal of Economic Perspectives*, Vol. 16, No. 3, 2002.

———. 'Home Market and the Artisans in Colonial India: A Study of Brass-Ware.' *Modern Asian Studies*, Vol. 30, No. 2, 1996.

———. *Traditional Industry in the Economy of Colonial India*. Cambridge: Cambridge University Press, 1999.

———. 'Were Indian Famines "Natural" Or "Manmade"?' *LSE Economic History Working Paper*, No. 243, 2016.

Royle J.F. 'Lecture XI – The Arts and Manufactures of India.' *Lectures on the Results of the Great Exhibition of 1851*, ed. H. Cole. London: David Bogue, 1852.

Rungta, R.S. *The Rise of Business Corporations in India, 1851–1900*, No. 8. Cambridge: Cambridge University Press, 1970.

Russell, W.H. *The Prince of Wales' Tour: A Diary in India, with Some Account of the Visits of His Royal Highness to the Courts of Greece, Egypt, Spain and Portugal*. London: Rivers & Company, 1877.

Rustom Siodia, Artist, c. 1918–1920. (Courtesy of Chatterjee & Lal, Mumbai).

Sadwelkar, B. *The Bombay Art Society, 1888-1988, Story of Hundred Years: Research for a Brief History of the Bombay Art Society with a Collection of Old Records and Rare Works of Art of Old Masters*. Bombay: The Society, 1989.

Sahgal, B., M. Dossal, V. Dilawari, M.R. Almeida, and K.Bagli. *Rani Bagh 150 Years: Veermata Jijabai Bhosale Udyan & Zoo*. New Delhi: Oxford University Press, 2013.

Sahu, K.B. 'A Peep into Dhanu Yatra.' *Odisha Review*, Vol. 71, No. 6, Odisha, 2015.

Said, E. *Orientalism: Western Concepts of the Orient*. New York: Pantheon, 1978.

Sangari, K. *Arc Silt Dive: The Works of Sheba Chhachhi*. New Delhi: Tulika Books, 2016.

Saraf, D.N. *Arts and Crafts, Jammu and Kashmir: Land, People, Culture*. New Delhi: Abhinav Publications, 1987.

Sarkar, O. 'Science, Surveying and Scientific Authority: The Brothers Schlagintweit in "India and High Asia", 1854–57', *South Asia: Journal of South Asian Studies*, 2017.

Sawant, S. *Imaging Land, Imagining Landscape: Painting in Colonial India (1793–1947)*. Unpublished PhD, Delhi: Jawaharlal Nehru University, 2014.

Schaller Penwell, E., and G.N. Kulles. *The Morton D. Barker Paperweight Collection*. Illinois: Illinois State Museum, 1985.

Schmitz, B. *Lahore: Paintings, Murals, and Calligraphy*. Mumbai: Marg Publications, 2010.

Schoen, B. *The Fragile Fabric of Union: Cotton, Federal Politics, and the Global Origins of the Civil War*. Baltimore: Johns Hopkins University Press, 2009.

Schwartzberg, J.E. 'Geographical Mapping.' *The History of Cartography*, Vol. 2, No. 1. Chicago: University of Chicago Press, 1992.

Scriver, P., and V. Prakash, eds. *Colonial Modernities: Building, Dwelling and Architecture in British India and Ceylon*. London: Routledge, 2007.

Sen, A. *The Structure and Organisation of the Bengal Native Infantry with Special Reference to Problems of Discipline (1796–1852)*. London: SOAS University of London, 1961.

Sengoopta, C. *Imprint of the Raj: How Fingerprinting was Born in Colonial India*. London: Macmillan, 2003.

Shaffer, H. *Adapting the Eye: An Archive of the British in India, 1770–1830*. New Haven: Yale Center for British Studies, 2011.

Shah, A.M. 'Anthropology in Bombay, 1886-1936', *Sociological Bulletin*, 63 (3), 2014.

Shah, C.P. *Report on the Possibility of Pottery Manufacture in the Province of Bombay*. Bombay: Government Central Press, 1941.

Sharma, B.S. 'Typical Pictures of Indian Natives.' *History of Photography*, Vol. xii, No. 1, pp: 77–82, 1988.

Sharpe, W.R.S. *Bombay: The Gateway of India*. Bombay: Bombay Port Trust, 1930.

Shastri, A. 'James Prinsep and the Study of Early Indian History.' *Annals of the Bhandarkar Oriental Research Institute*, Vol. 80, Nos. 1/4, 1999.

Sheppard, S.T. *Bombay Place-Names and Street-Names: An Excursion Into the By-ways of the History of Bombay City*. Bombay: The Times Press, 1917.

———. *The Byculla Club, 1833–1916: A History*. Bombay: Bennett, Coleman & Co. Ltd., 1916.

Shirgaonkar, S.B. *Artist A. H. Muller and His Art*, Michigan: Michigan University Press, 1975.

'Silver Work and Enamel Competition.' *Journal of Indian Art*, Vol. I, No.3. London: W. Griggs, 1884.

Simpson, W. *India Ancient and Modern: A Series of Illustrations of the Country and People of India and Adjacent Territories, Vol. 1*. London: Day and Son, 1867.

Simpson, W., and G. Eyre-Todd, eds. *The Autobiography of William Simpson*. London: T. Fisher Unwin, 1903.

Sims, E. 'The Illustrated Manuscripts of Firdausī's "Shāhnāma" Commissioned by Princes of the House of Tīmūr.' *Ars Orientalis*, Vol. 22, pp. 43–68, 1992.

Singh, K. 'The Museum Is National'. *India International Centre Quarterly*, 29 (3/4), 2002.

Singh, V. *Interpreting Medieval India: Early Medieval, Delhi Sultanate, and Regions (circa 750-1550)*, Vol. 1, Delhi: Macmillan, 2009.

'Sir George C.M. Birdwood, K.C.I.E., C.S.I, M.D., L.L.D.: His Life and Work.' *Journal of Indian Art and Industry*, Vol. 8, No. 65. London: W. Griggs & Sons, 1899.

Sloan, K., and A. Burnett, eds. *Enlightenment: Discovering the World in the Eighteenth Century*, London: British Museum Press, 2003.

Smith, A., D.B. Brown and C. Jacobi, eds. *Artist and Empire: Facing Britain's Imperial Past*. London: Tate Publishing, 2016.

Smith, C.H.F., and M. Stevenson. 'Modeling Cultures: 19th-Century Indian Clay Figures.' *Museum Anthropology*, Vol. 33, Issue 1, 2010.

Smith, K. 'The Afterlife of Objects: Anglo-Indian Ivory Furniture in Britain.' *World History*, Vol. 23, No. 1, 2012.

Smith, V.A. *A History of Fine Art in India and Ceylon*. Oxford: Clarendon Press, 1911.

———. 'Remarks On Mogul (Indo-Persian) Paintings And Drawings.' *Journal of Indian Art and Industry*, Vol. 15, No. 120. London: W. Griggs & Sons, 1912.

Solomon, W.E.G. *The Bombay Revival of Indian Art—A Descriptive Account of the Indian Room Constructed and Decorated By the Staff and Students of the School of Art*. Bombay: Sir J.J. School of Art, 1924.

———. *Introductions in Mural Paintings of the Bombay School*. (With Illustrations.) Bombay: Times of India Press, 1930.

Solvyns, B. *Les Hindoûs*. Paris: L'auteur, 1808–1812.

Spencer, A., ed. *Memoirs of William Hickey (Volume II 1775–1782)*. London: Hurst & Blackett, 1918.

Srinivas, N.M., and A.M. Shah. 'The Myth of Self Sufficiency of the Indian Village.' *Economic Weekly*, September 10, 1960.

Srinivasan S. 'Carving a global icon: The Nataraja bronze and Commaraswamy's legacy'. *Asian art and culture: A research volume in honour of Ananda Commaraswamy's*, Colombo: Department of Information, Government of Sri Lanka, 2012.

Stampari, T.H.G., Consultant Surveyor to the Government of India. *A Short Pamphlet on the Principles of Housing, Planning, etc. as Applied to Villages*. Bombay, 1935.

Steggles, M.A. *Statues of the Raj.* London: BACSA, 2000.

Stone, G.C. *A Glossary of the Construction, Decoration and Use of Arms and Armour in All Countries and in All Times.* Portland: Southworth Press, 1934.

Storr, R. *Nalini Malani Listening to the Shades.* Milano: Edizioni Charta, 2008.

Strip, P., and O. Strip. *The Peoples of Bombay. Bombay:* Thacker & Co. Ltd., 1944.

Stronge, S. *Decorative Art of India: The Studio Library of Decorative Art.* London: Studio Editions, 1990.

Swallow, D. 'The India Museum and the British-Indian Textile Trade in the Late Nineteenth Century.' *Textile History,* Jan 1; 30(1): 29-45, 1999.

Tarapor, M. 'John Lockwood Kipling and British Art Education in India.' *Victorian Studies,* Vol. 24, No. 1. Indiana: University Press, 1980.

Tallur, L.N. *Chromatophobia: The Fear of Money,* Seoul: Arario Gallery, 2011.

Taylor, M. *Empress: Queen Victoria and India,* Yale: Yale University Press, 2018

Temple, R. *Oriental Experience: A Selection of Essays and Addresses Delivered on Various Occasions.* London: J. Murray, 1883.

Thampi, M., and S. Saksena. *China and the Making of Bombay,* Bombay: KR Cama Oriental Institute, 2009.

Thackston, W.M., tr., ed., and annotated. *The Jahangirnama: Memoirs of Jahangir, Emperor of India.* New York: Oxford University Press, 1999.

The Bhagavad Gita: With an English Translation and Explanatory, and an examination of its Doctrines Notes. London and Madras: Christian Literature Society, 1899.

The Fisheries Exhibition Literature, Vol. XII. London: William Clowes and Sons, Limited, 1884.

The Historical record of the imperial visit to India 1911, compiled from the official records under the orders of the Viceroy and Governor-General of India. London: J. Murray, 1914.

Thirunavukarasu, D. 'Dr. Ananda K. Coomaraswamy – An Interpreter of the Language of Art.' *Journal of the Sri Lanka Branch of the Royal Asiatic Society,* vol. 23, Royal Asiatic Society of Sri Lanka (RASSL), 1977.

'The Report Of The Indian Plague Commission.' *The British Medical Journal,* Vol. 1, no. 2157. BMJ, 1902.

Thomas Cook (Firm). *India, Burma and Ceylon. Information For Travellers and Residents. With Four Maps.* London: Thomas Cook & Son, 1897.

Thurston, E. *Castes and Tribes of Southern India,* Vols. I, A and B. Madras: Government Press, 1909.

———. *The Madras Presidency with Mysore, Coorg and the Associated States.* Cambridge: Cambridge University Press, 1913.

———. *Monograph on the Ivory Industry of Southern India, with Seven Plates.* Madras: Government Press, 1901.

———. *Monograph on Wood-Carving in Southern India with Twenty-Two Plates.* Madras: Superintendent of Government Press, 1903.

———. 'Wood-Carving in Southern India.' *Journal of Indian Art and Industry,* Vol. 10, No. 86. London: W. Griggs & Sons, 1904.

Tikekar, A. *Founders and Guardians of the Asiatic Society of Mumbai: George Buist.* Bombay: Indus Source Books, 2016.

Tillotson, G. 'The Jaipur Exhibition of 1883.' *Journal of the Royal Asiatic Society,* Vol. 14, No. 2. Cambridge: Cambridge University Press, 2004.

Tindall, G. *City of Gold: The Biography of Bombay.* New Delhi: Penguin Books, 1992.

Tripati, S. *Traditional Boats and Navigation in Odisha.* New Delhi: Indus-Infinity Foundation, Pentagon Press, 2015.

Trivedi, P., and D. Bartholomeusz (eds.). *India's Shakespeare: Translation, Interpretation, and Performance.* Newark: University of Delaware Press, 2005.

Tweedie, W. *The Arabian Horse, His Country and People: With Portraits of Typical or Famous Arabians and Other Illustrations.* Edinburgh and London: William Blackwood & Sons, 1894.

Upadhyay, S.B. 'Cotton Mill Workers in Bombay, 1875 to 1918: Conditions of Work and Life.' *Economic and Political Weekly,* Vol. 25, No. 30, 1990.

Untracht, O. *Traditional Jewelry of India.* London: Thames & Hudson, 1997.

Varner, G. *The Mythic Forest, the Green Man and the Spirit of Nature.* New York: Algora Publishing, 2006.

Venniyoor, E.M.J. *Raja Ravi Varma.* Government of Kerala, 1981. pp. 29–30.

Verma, S.P. 'Material Culture As Discerned From Mughal Paintings.' *Proceedings of the Indian History Congress,* Vol. 37, pp. 563–69, 1976.

Vicinus, M., and B. Nergaard, eds. *Yours, Florence Nightingale, Selected Letters.* Virago Press, 1989, Letter, 19 Sept. 1863.

Victoria & Albert Museum Bombay. *Annual Administration Reports; 1872-73; 1875-76; 1876-77; 1885-86; 1886-87; 1887-88; 1888-89; 1890-91; 1898-99; 1903-04; 1904-05; 1905-06; 1908-09; 1909-10; 1910-11; 1911-12; 1912-13; 1913-14; 1914-15; 1915-16; 1916-17; 1919-20; 1922-23; 1925-26; 1926-27; 1927-28; 1928-29; 1929-30; 1932-33; 1933-34; 1934-35; 1935-36; 1938-39, 1940-41; 1941-42; 1942-43; 1944-45; 1945-46; 1946-47; 1948-49, 1951-52; 1955-56.* Bombay: Government Central Press.

Vicziany, M., and J. Bapat. 'Mumbādevī and the Other Mother Goddesses in Mumbai.' *Modern Asian Studies.* Cambridge: Cambridge University Press, 2009.

Voelcker, J.A. *Report on the Improvement of Indian Agriculture.* London: Eyre and Spottiswoode, 1893.

Von Brescius, M. *German Science in the Age of Empire.* Cambridge: Cambridge University Press, 2019.

Von Schlagintweit, H. 'Notes on Some Ethnographic Casts.' *Journal of Anthropological Society of London,* Vol. 2. Royal Anthropological Institute of Great Britain and Ireland, 1864.

Wacha, D.E. *Shells from the Sands of Bombay: Being My Recollections and Reminiscences, 1860-1875.* Bombay: KT Anklesaria, 1920.

Wales, J.A.G. *A Monograph on Wood-Carving in the Bombay Presidency.* Bombay: Government Central Press, 1902.

Walker, D. *Flowers Underfoot: Indian Carpets of the Mughal Era.* New York: The Metropolitan Museum of Art, 1997.

Walker, M. 'Courtesans and Choreographers: The (Re)Placement of Women in the History of Kathak Dance.' *Dance Matters: Performing India,* eds P. Chakravorty and N. Gupta. New Delhi: Routledge, 2010.

Wardle, T. *Colonial and Indian Exhibition, 1886, Empire of India—Special Catalogue of Exhibits by the Government of India and Private Exhibitors.* London: William Clowes, 1886.

Watson, J.F. *India: A Classified and Descriptive Catalogue of the Collections Selected from the India Museum and Exhibited in the Indian Department of the Philadelphia Centennial Exhibition of 1876.* London: India Museum, 1876.

———. *The Textile Manufactures of India and the Costumes of the People of India.* London: India Office, 1866.

Watt, G. *Indian Art at Delhi 1903: Being the Official Catalogue of the Delhi Exhibition, 1902–1903,* Calcutta: Superintendent of Government Printing, 1903.

Welch, S.C. *India: Art and Culture 1300–1900.* New York: The Metropolitan Museum of Art, 1985.

Westrip, J. *Fire and Spice.* London: Serif Books, 2014.

Wilkinson, W.R.T. *Indian Silver, 1858–1947: Silver from the Indian Sub-continent and Burma Made by Local Craftsmen in Western Forms.* London: Wynyard Wilkinson, 1997.

Windover, M. 'Exchanging Looks: "Art Dekho" Movie Theatres in Bombay.' *Architectural History,* Vol. 52, Wales: SAHGB Publications Ltd., 2009.

Wise, R. *A Fragile Eden: Portraits of the Endemic Flowering Plants of the Granitic Seychelles.* Princeton, New Jersey: Princeton University Press, 1998.

Woodfield, I. 'The Hindostannie Air: English Attempts to Understand Indian Music in the Late Eighteenth Century.' *Journal of the Royal Musical Association,* Vol. 119, No. 2, pp. 189–211, 1994.

Woods, M. 'The Other and the Other modernism: Art Deco Picture Palaces of Bombay.' *Proceedings of XIXth International DOCOMOMO,* 2010.

Wright, D. 'James Baillie Fraser: Traveller, Writer and Artist 1783–1856.' *Iran*, Vol. 32, pp. 125–34, 1994.

Yule, H., and A.C. Burnell. *Hobson-Jobson: A Glossary of Colloquial Anglo-Indian Words and Phrases, and Kindred Terms, Etymological, Historical, Geographical and Discursive.* London: J. Murray, 1903.

Zebrowski, M. *Deccani Painting.* New Delhi: Roli Books International, 1983.

Zubrzycki, J. *The Mysterious Mr Jacob: Diamond Merchant, Magician and Spy.* Delhi: Random House India, 2012.

Zutshi, C. '"Designed for Eternity": Kashmiri Shawls, Empire, and Cultures of Production and Consumption in Mid-Victorian Britain.' *Journal of British Studies*, Vol. 48, No. 2, pp. 420–40, 2009.

Newspaper Archives:

The Bombay Gazette: February 24, 1862; March 11, 1864; February 29, 1868; July 24, 1868; February 14, 1873; February 15, 1873; February 24, 1873; March 24,1873; May 8, 1886; November 6, 1889; November 22, 1889; March 24, 1890; February 13, 1891; February 7, 1893; December 10, 1904; December 12, 1904; accessed via Granth Sanjeevani.

Illustrated London Weekly. March 1, 1873. Accessed on July 17, 2020; accessed via Granth Sanjeevani.

The Times of India: March 11, 1864; March 10, 1873; March 26, 1890; February 7, 1905; September 24, 1912; March 16, 1918; May 7, 1918; accessed via Granth Sanjeevani.

The Bombay Chronicle: February 23, 1916; September 7, 1918; April 25, 1925; August 9, 1930; January 16, 1934; June 6, 1935; November 15, 1935; December 8, 1936; February 12, 1938; March 30, 1940; December 5, 1945; December 7, 1945; December 10, 1945; December 25, 1945; July 14, 1957; accessed via Granth Sanjeevani.

The Age, Melbourne: October 27, 1934; accessed via NLA Trove Newspaper.

The Lancet: January 13, 1855.

The Pioneer: March 31, 1911.

Online:

Ahmed, M. 'Zoroastrian Woman's Shalwar Sections And Chador-Shab', *Woven Treasures: Textiles From The Jasleen Dhamija Collection*, SaffronArt Catalogue, October 19--20, 2016, https://www.saffronart.com/customauctions/PostWork.aspx?l=22537, accessed March 01, 2019.

Bhagavad Gita, 4.6–8, prabhupadabooks.com/classes/bg/4/6-8/new_york/july/20/1966, accessed on December 26, 2020.

CAMP. 'From Gulf to Gulf to Gulf, 2013', https://studio.camp/works/g2g2g/, accessed on October 15, 2020.

Darwin Correspondence Project. 'Letter No. 9534', https://www.darwinproject.ac.uk/letter/DCP-LETT-9534.xml, accessed on July 12, 2020.

Guha, A. 'Krishnalila in Terracotta Temples of Bengal', *Temples of Bengal*, 2012. http://www.chitrolekha.com/V2/n1/03_Krishnalila_in_Terracotta_Temples_of_Bengal.pdf, accessed on December 14, 2020.

Handicrafts Development Corporation of Kerala Ltd Online, https://www.keralahandicrafts.in/, accessed on December 28, 2020.

Hoffenberg, P.H. '1871–1874: The South Kensington International Exhibitions.' *BRANCH: Britain, Representation and Nineteenth-Century History*, ed. D.F. Felluga. Extension of *Romanticism and Victorianism on the Net*, https://www.branchcollective.org/?ps_articles=peter-h-hoffenberg-1871-1874-the-south-kensington-international-exhibitions, accessed on July 9, 2020.

Isaac, S. 'Venomous Snakes and the Indian Medical Service: Sir Joseph Fayrer's Thanatophidia of India 1872', September 6, 2019, https://www.rcseng.ac.uk/library-and-publications/library/blog/venomous-snakes-and-the-indian-medical-service/, accessed on March 5, 2020.

Kitagawa, J. M., D.L. Snellgrove, F.E. Reynolds, et al. *Buddhism. Encyclopedia Britannica*, 2020, https://www.britannica.com/topic/Buddhism, accessed August 10, 2019.

Losty, J.P. 'An Album of Maratha and Deccani Paintings - Part 2', Asian and African Studies Blog, June 07, 2014, https://blogs.bl.uk/asian-and-african/2014/06/an-album-of-maratha-and-deccani-paintings-add21475-part-2.html, accessed September 01, 2020.

———. '"A very ingenious person": The Maratha artist Gangaram Cintaman Tambat.' *Asian and African Studies Blog*, August 28, 2014, https://blogs.bl.uk/asian-and-african/2014/08/the-maratha-artist-gangaram-cintaman-tambat.html, accessed October 04, 2021.

National Army Museum online collection. https://collection.nam.ac.uk/detail.php?acc=1953-02-5-1, accessed on December 28, 2020

Pattanaik, D. 'Marks on the Forehead', https://devdutt.com/articles/marks-on-the-forehead/, April 16, 2013, accessed on December 14, 2020.

P&O Heritage, online archives. https://www.poheritage.com/our-archive, accessed on December 5, 2020.

Prasad, P.K. 'Bombay's Transition to Modernity: The Dawn of Art Deco in Bombay', *Art Deco Mumbai*, 2017, https://www.artdecomumbai.com/research/bombays-transition-to-modernity-the-dawn-of-art-deco-in-bombay/, accessed on February 20, 2021.

Rajeev, S.S. 'Carving a Niche for Artists', *The Hindu*, September 30, 2016, https://www.thehindu.com/society/history-and-culture/Carving-a-niche-for-artists/article14928376.ece, accessed on August 24, 2020.

Rajeev, S.S. 'Carving a Niche for Arts', *The Hindu*, October 27, 2017, https://www.thehindu.com/society/history-and-culture/rich-heritage-of-the-exquisite-ivory-artefacts-of-thiruvananthapuram/article19931690.ece, accessed on August 24, 2020.

Ray, M. Candlestick, *Encyclopædia Britannica*, 2016. https://www.britannica.com/art/candlestick, accessed May 10, 2019.

Reynolds-Finley Historical Library Online Archive. 'Florence Nightingale, The Letters: Sanitation in India.' https://library.uab.edu/locations/reynolds/collections/florence-nightingale/letters-sanitation-in-india, accessed on December 06, 2020.

Robert Lehman Collection, 1975; 1975.1.2458, 'Carpet with vine scroll and palmette pattern; Wool pile on cotton foundation, c. late 19th century' (THE MET, New York).

Royal Mint Museum, London. 'William Wyon'. https://www.royalmintmuseum.org.uk/journal/people/william-wyon/, accessed on December 5, 2020.

Russell Flint. *Sir William Russel Flint*, https://www.russellflint.com, accessed on January 7, 2021.

SaffronArt, 'P.A. Dhond (1908–2001): An Obituary.' https://www.saffronart.com/sitepages/ArticleDetails.aspx?ArticleId=72, accessed on January 07, 2021.

Sarce, J.M. 'Art and Architecture of the Qajar Period', *Encyclopaedia Iranica*, 1986, https://iranicaonline.org/articles/art-in-iran-v-qajar-1-general, accessed on October 2, 2020.

Sharma, M.S. 'What Statue-Topplers Around the World can Learn from India.' *The Times of India*, September 3, 2017, accessed on August 27, 2019.

Stache-Rosen, V. 'Story-Telling in Pinguli Paintings', *Artibus Asiae*, Vol. 45, No. 4, 1984, pp. 253–286, https://www.jstor.org/stable/3249740, accessed on 24 Aug 2020..

Sudarshan Art & Craft. 'About', http://sudarshancrafts.com/about/, accessed on July 2020.

Tattoli, C. 'The Surprising History (and Future) of Paperweights.' *The Paris Review*, September 20, 2017, https://www.theparisreview.org/blog/2017/09/20/the-surprising-history-of-paperweights/, accessed on 30 September 2021.

Maharashtra State Archives (MSA):

General Dept. and Education Dept. Files: GD 1848, Vol. 43; GD 1854, Vol. 31; GD 1856, Vol. 73; GD 1857, Vol. 55; GD 1858, Vol. 65; GD 1859, Vol. 37; ED 1859, Vol. 15; GD 1862, Vol. 21; GD File, 1873, Vol. 56.

V&A Museum, Bombay, Archives:

Victoria & Albert Museum, Bombay, Museum Archives: File 44; File 45; File 48; File 49; File 51; File 52; File 54; File 59; *Parsi Punchayat Album; Specimens Register.*

NOTES

INTRODUCTION

1. MSA, GD 1854, Vol. 31, 125.
2. Tikekar, 2016, p. 10; MSA, GD 1857, Vol. 55, 95–139.
3. Sadwelkar, 1989, p. x.
4. Tindall, 1992, pp. 23–25.
5. Maclean, 1892, pp. 86, 111.
6. Sharpe, 1930, p. 17.
7. Tindall, pp. 22–23.
8. *Report of the Director of Public Instruction*, 1857, pp. 134–35; *Report of the Director of Public Instruction*, 1858, p. 99.
9. *Report of the Director of Public Instruction*, 1857, pp. 134-35; MSA, GD 1857, Vol. 55, 175–202.
10. MSA, ED 1859, Vol. 15, 215–18.
11. Kelkar, 1969, pp. 135–44.
12. Edwardes, 1923, p. 49.
13. Tikekar, pp. 49-50; MSA, ED 1859, Vol. 15, 215–18.
14. Birdwood, 1864, p. 11.
15. Ibid., p. 50.
16. Ibid., p. 65.
17. MSA, GD 1862, Vol. 21, 323-26; Fern, 1926, p. 5
18. *Report of the Bombay Chamber of Commerce*, 1890, pp. 589–91.
19. Ibid.

BOMBAY/MUMBAI
The Making of a City

1. Solomon, 1924, pp. 2-3
2. See Wacha, 1920. Dinshaw Wacha describes the relentless growth in his delightful book on the city.
3. Chopra, 2011, pp. 161-162.
4. Prakash, 2010, pp. 60–64.
5. MSA, GD 1862, Vol. 21, 335–39.
6. Tindall, 1992, p. 203; Prakash notes that by 1872 [when the Museum opened] reclamations had added 4 million sq yards to the city, increasing it from 18 to 22 sq miles (see Prakash, 2010, p. 44).
7. Khotachiwadi and Matharpakadi presently preserve just a semblance of their former architectural identity—a load-bearing timber style derivative of Portuguese Colonial blended with regional sensibilities featuring sprawling verandas, projected balconies and Mangalore roof tiles.
8. Gandhi, 2010, p. 42.
9. Personal observation on heritage walks.
10. Chopra, 2007, pp. 116–18.
11. See Wacha, pp. 341–52. He describes in detail the city's engagement with theatre both in English and in local languages. Jugganath Sunkersett set up a theatre in his house.
12. Dwivedi and Mehrotra, 2001, p. 157.
13. Masselos and Kapoor, 2009, p. 14.
14. Maclean, 1892, p. 186.
15. See London, 2002. Governor Bartle Frere knocked down the Fort walls. He chose the grand Gothic style, that was the high fashion of the time, for the important institutional buildings of Bombay. The style took on a lively indigenous character with the city's architects and craftsmen employing elaborate Indian designs, animals and plants to embellish the buildings.
16. Chopra, 2007, pp. 110–15; Prakash, 2010, p. 51. Prakash says '... the physical space was treated as an abstract object that could be manipulated and reshaped at will. This involved the repression of existing meanings of particular cultural significance that people attached to specific places.'

17. Dalvi, 2018, pp. 56–73. Dalvi explains how various Civic Trust schemes provided for the bulk of middle-class housing in the city and created precincts that are mainly Art Deco in character, giving the city a new modern look that was different from the earlier monumental Neo-Gothic government buildings.

1. Mumbadevi

1. Da Cunha, 1900, p. 36.
2. Vicziany and Bapat, 2009, p. 512.
3. David, 1973, p. 6.

1A. Lord Ganesha

1. Edwardes, 1923, p. 105.

2. The Elephanta Elephant

1. Michell, 2002, p. 97.
2. Russell, 1877, pp. 151–55.
3. Burgess, 1871, p. 1; Yule and Burnell, 1903, pp. 341–42.
4. Birdwood, 1922, pp. 201–03.
5. Foster and Sheppard, 1933, p. 86.

3. Heptanesia Relief Maps

1. Da Cunha, 1900, p. 23
2. *The Historical record of the imperial visit to India 1911*, 1914, p. 49.
3. Sheppard, 1917, pp. 46, 119.
4. Quoted in Burns, 1918, p. 2. This was a popular English proverb in the seventeenth century, used also by Rev. Ovington (see Ovington and Rawlinson, 1929, p. 87)

4. Fryer's Map

1. Fryer, 1979, p. 175.
2. Markley, 2010, p. 112.
3. Fryer, 1689, p. 66.
4. Fryer, 1979, p. 177.
5. Douglas, 1893, p. 145.

5. Bombay Castle

1. Dossal, 2010, p. 9.
2. D'Souza, 2008, pp. 75-76.
3. Dwivedi and Mehrotra, 2001, p. 19.
4. Ibid., p. 46; D'Souza, p. 78. Govind Narayan says that the Bombay Fort was called 'Kala Killa' or black fort by the locals. Flags of ships arriving from different countries were hosted on the Fort ramparts to announce the arrival of the ship to the residents. (See Ranganathan, 2008, pp. 127-28)
5. Edwardes, 1923, p. 9.

6. Chhatrapati Shivaji Maharaj's Escape

1. Kumar, 2014, p. 320.
2. Deshpande, 1929, pp. 32–47.

7. Peshwa Map

1. Gogate and Arunachalam, 1998, p. 139.
2. Ibid., p. 129.
3. Schwartzberg, 1992, p. 423.

8. Boats in Bombay Harbour

1. Hornell, 1920, pp. 13–15.
2. Sharpe, 1930, pp. 5, 11.
3. Ibid., p. 13.
4. Ibid., p. 29.
5. Fern, 1926, pp. 16–18.
6. Hornell, pp. 10–11.
7. V&A Museum Bombay, 1908–09, pp. 158–59.

9. Thomas Dickinson's Map

1. Edney, 1997, p. 43.
2. Dossal, 2010, p. 74.
3. Burns, 1918, p. 8.
4. Edney, p. 46.

9A. Limits of the Town of Bombay

1. Dwivedi and Mehrotra, 2001, p. 34.
2. Edwardes, 1909, Vol. I, p. 31.

10. Queen Victoria

1. Steggles, 2000, p. 5.
2. Kelkar, 1969, p. 121.
3. Sharma, *The Times of India*, September 3, 2017.

11. Prince Albert

1. Steggles, 2000, p. 32.
2. Baker and Richardson, 1999, p. x.
3. Fern, 1926, p. 5.
4. Hobhouse, 2002, p. 9.
5. Taylor, 2018, pp. 51-52

12. Dr. Bhau Daji Lad

1. *The Lancet*, January 13, 1855, p. 48.
2. Speech reproduced in Birdwood, 1864, p. 16.
3. Guha-Thakurta, 2004, p. 95.
4. Trivedi and Bartholomeusz (eds.), 2005, p. 14.
5. Hapgood, 2015, p. 25.

13. George Birdwood

1. 'Sir George C.M. Birdwood: His Life and Work', *JIAI*, Vol. VIII, 1899, p. 45.
2. MSA, GD 1856, Vol. 73, 25–28, 135–40.
3. McGowan, 2009, p. 48.
4. Havell, 1910, p. 286.
5. *Ibid.*

14. Juggannath Sunkersett

1. Chisholm, 1911, p. 801.
2. Fern, 1926, pp. 4–5.
3. *The Times of India*, March 11 1864, p. 3; *The Bombay Gazette*, April 18 1864, p. 3.

15. David Sassoon

1. Quoted in Tindall, 1992, p. 164.
2. Betta, 2000, pp. 38–41.
3. Goldstein, 1998, p. 145.
4. Steggles, 2000, p. 172.

16. Jamsetjee Jeejeebhoy

1. Kidambi, Kamat and Dwyer, 2019, p. 21; Prakash, 2010, p. 37.
2. Prakash, 2010, p. 37.
3. Bulley, 2013, pp. 197-98.
4. Mayer and De Forest, 2008, p. 47.
5. Godrej and Mistree, 2013, p. 98, 253.
6. Moses, 1850, pp. 255–58.

17. Street Scene of Old Bombay by Eduard Hildebrandt

1. Bryan, 1886, pp. 655-56. *Berliner Montagspost* (Berlin Monday Mail) was one of the main weekly German newspapers in the 19th century. Hildebrandt's book was titled *Reise um die Erde* (Journey around the World).

18. City Views

1. Pinney, 2008, pp. 11-12.
2. Hapgood, 2015, pp. 24-25; Pinney, 2008, p. 10.
3. Pinney, 2008, p. 12.
4. Quoted in Falconer, 2001, p. 8, 14
5. V&A Museum Bombay, 1910-11.

19. B.E.S.T Tram

1. David, 1995, pp. 199–202. On May 7, 1886, E.C.K. Ollivant, the Municipal Commissioner, rode in the first tram on the route from the old terminal near Byculla Station to Victoria Gardens (see, *The Bombay Gazette*, May 8, 1886, p. 5).
2. Mahaluxmivala, 1936, p. xix.

20. Fitzgerald Gas Lamp

1. Kochhar, 1993, p. 39.
2. Edwardes, 1909, Vol. III, p. 51.
3. Perkins, 2019, pp. 28-29.
4. MSA, GD 1873, Vol. 56, 269-70.

20A. Khada Parsi Gas Lamp

1. 'Memorial Fountain', 1875, pp. 207–08.
2. V&A Museum Archives, *Parsi Punchayat Album*, Vol. 3.

21. The Ice House
1. Drewitt, 1907, p. 4.
2. Kistler, 1984, pp. 19-20. When ice was first introduced in Bombay, it was sold for four annas a pound (see, Wacha, 1920, p. 307).
3. Edwardes, 1909, Vol. III, p. 301.

21A. The Byculla Club
1. Sheppard, 1916, pp. 155–58.

22. Bombay Silver Rupee
1. Birdwood, 1890, Vol. III, p. 43.
2. Bhattacharya, 1969, pp. 103-04.
3. Adams and West, 1979, pp. 55–57.

23. Worli Estates
1. Upadhyay, 1990, p. 87.
2. Arnold, 2012, p. 115.
3. Dossal, 1999, p. 732.

24. The Bombay Plague
1. *Report Of The Indian Plague Commission*, 1902, p. 1093.
2. Chandavarkar, 1995, p. 207.
3. Dossal, 1999, p. 729.
4. Ibid., p. 730.
5. Nathan, 1898, p. 59.

25. Bellasis Road Chawls
1. Sheppard, 1917, pp. 30-31.
2. Hazareesingh, 2001, p. 240.
3. Upadhyay, 1990, p. 87.
4. Adarkar, 2011, p. 2.

25A. Lord Sandhurst Statue and Trowel
1. Dwivedi and Mehrotra, 2001, p. 109.
2. Culture and Leisure Committee, 2009, p. 17.

26. Drainage Map of Bombay
1. Markovits, 2008, p. 131.
2. Briggs, 1993, pp. 16-17.
3. Martineau, 1892, pp. 38-39; Ramanna, 2002, pp. 110-135.

27. Relief Map of Greater Bombay
1. V&A Museum Bombay, 1934-35, pp. 265-66.
2. Dwivedi and Mehrotra, 2001, p. 127. The Museum's geological collection includes stone and mineral specimens from Bhor Ghat that was blasted to lay railroad tracks, connecting Bombay to the rest of the country.
3. Ibid., p. 289.

28. Eros Cinema
1. Tindall, 1992, p. 14
2. Prasad, *Art Deco Mumbai*, 2017.
3. Windover, 2009, p. 204.
4. *The Bombay Chronicle*, February 12, 1938, p. 10.
5. Woods, 2010, pp. 359–65.
6. Dalvi, 2018, p. 69; Windover, 2009, p. 222.

NATURAL HISTORY
Documenting the Exotic
1. Sloan and Burnett (eds.), 2003, pp. 13–23.
2. Birdwood, 1864, p. 54.
3. Hill, 2013, p. 141.
4. Maclean, 1892, p. 245. In the late nineteenth and early twentieth centuries, Victoria Gardens was a popular destination for Europeans and locals alike, hosting a variety of open-air fetes, band concerts, flower exhibitions, and balloon rides. On November 29, 1867, Anna Bishop, the renowned English operatic soprano singer, performed at the fete in the garden, which was organised by the Agri-Horticultural Society of Western India. She was the most travelled vocalist of the nineteenth century.
5. Birdwood, 1866, pp. 25-26.
6. Birdwood, 1864, p. 64.
7. Ibid., p. 65.
8. MSA, GD 1856, Vol. 73, 377–83.

9. Despatch Relating to Education–East India, 1867, p. 160.
10. V&A Museum Bombay, 1908-09; 1910-11; 1911-12; 1922-23.
11. MSA, GD 1857, Vol. 55, 172–202.
12. Despatch Relating to Education, p. 160.
13. *The Bombay Gazette*, July 24, 1868, p. 2. The Framjee Cowasjee Institute's committee, led by Juggannath Sunkersett, donated a collection of minerals, rocks, and fossils to the Museum when it was housed in the Town Hall in February 1862 on the condition that they will be displayed in a gallery that would be named 'Framjee Cowasjee Museum of Natural History' at the current Museum premises. However, no action was taken, and an enquiry into the matter was undertaken in the 1930s (see *The Bombay Gazette*, February 24, 1862, p. 187; *The Bombay Chronicle*, November 15, 1935, p. 12).
14. *The Bombay Gazette*, March 24, 1890, p. 6.
15. Birdwood, 1864, p. 9.
16. MSA, GD 1862, Vol. 21, 337-38.
17. V&A Museum Archives, File 47.
18. Mitra, 1891, p. 200; Shah, 2014, p. 355.
19. Thurston, 1909, p. xviii.
20. Gupte, 1909, pp. 2–4.
21. V&A Museum Bombay, 1888-89.
22. V&A Museum Bombay, 1875-76, p. 4.

29. Gold Medal, 1883 International Fisheries Exhibition
1. *Annual report of the Board of Regents of the Smithsonian Institution for the year 1883*, 1885, p. 84.
2. *Report for the United States National Museum under the direction of the Smithsonian Institution for the year 1884*, 1885, pp. 87–89.
3. *The Fisheries Exhibition Literature*, Vol XII, pp. 455, 461.
4. *Great Britain. Parliament. House of Commons*, 1884, p. 16.

29A. Hors Concours Medal, 1867 Exposition Universelle
1. Dentu and Petit (eds.), 1867, pp. 365-66. Dr George Birdwood, the Curator of the Museum, was appointed as the Special Agent for the Government of Bombay to secure local products for the 1867 Paris Universal Exposition.
2. Jain, 2016, pp. 34–49.
3. Ibid., p. 36.

30. The Thanatophidia of India by Joseph Fayrer
1. Isaac, 2019.
2. Price, 2017, pp. 201–17.
3. Darwin Correspondence Project.
4. Mukharji, 1888, p. 72.
5. V&A Museum Bombay, 1887-88, p. 238; MacDonald, 1887, p. 70.

30A. Parakeet
1. Aitken and Sterndale (eds.), 1886, pp. 1–3.
2. V&A Museum Bombay, 1916-17, p. 212.
3. Blakston et al., 1878, pp. 431-32.

31. Oriental Memoirs by James Forbes
1. Dyson, 1978, p. 182.
2. Forbes, 1813, Vol. I, p. 85.
3. Ibid., p. 100.
4. Forbes, 1813, Vol. III, pp. 274-75.
5. Ibid., p. 314.
6. Dyson, pp. 183, 189.
7. Forbes, Vol. IV, pp. 277, 284, 299-300.
8. Ibid., p. 288.
9. Dyson, p. 186.

31A. Views in the Himala Mountains by James Fraser
1. Wright, 1994, p. 126.
2. Archer and Falk, 1989, p. 35.

32. Schlagintweit Casts
1. Jain-Neubauer, 2013, p. 71.
2. Finkelstein, 2000, p. 181. 'Humboldtian model' was a learning model conceptualised by Alexander von Humboldt's elder brother, Wilhelm von Humboldt, in the nineteenth century that encouraged the integration of arts and sciences with research to achieve both comprehensive scientific and cultural knowledge.
3. von Brescius, 2019, p. 144. The Schlagintweit brothers acknowledged the importance of Buist's work on meteorological and ethnographic studies in shaping their own observations.
4. Jain-Neubauer, p. 83.
5. Armitage, 1989, p. 71.
6. von Brescius, p. 142.
7. Driver, 2018, pp. 464-65.
8. MSA, GD 1859, Vol. 37, 17–41.
9. Jain-Neubauer, p. 82.

32A. An Account of the Primitive Tribes and Monuments of the Nilagiris by James W. Breeks
1. Philip, 2003, p. 146.
2. Ibid., pp. 166-67.
3. Ibid., p. 167. The exhibition was open to visitors for just over two weeks from February 24 to March 14, 1868, but was visited by over 12,000 people.

33. The People of India by John F. Watson and John W. Kaye
1. Pinney, 1997, pp. 24–28.
2. Desmond, 1985, pp. 55–57. Vol VI highlights 'Mahratta Pundits' (359) from western India. The areas in and around the Bombay Presidency (except Karachi and the Sindh) have not been included in the volumes. Watson and Kaye focus on including people from those regions that actively participated in the 1857 Uprising or lesser-known aboriginal areas in order to collect 'information'.
3. List of photographers credited: J.C.A. Dannenberg, R.H. DeMontmorency, E. Godfrey, W.W. Hooper, Major Houghton, H.C. McDonald, J. Mulheran, Capt. Oakes, G. Richter, Shepherd & Robertson, B. Simpson, B.W. Switzer, H.C.B. Tanner, C.C. Taylor, and J. Waterhouse.
4. Pinney, pp. 28-29.
5. Ibid.

33A. The Oriental Races and Tribes by William Johnson
1. Ranganathan, 2008, pp. 343-44.
2. Ibid., p. 363. Narayan Daji, along with several other notable photographers of the period, owned a studio on Rampart Row in Bombay from 1855 to 1862.
3. Pinney, 1997, pp. 29-30.
4. Falconer, 2001, p. 22.

INDUSTRIAL ARTS
A New Taste for Design
1. *Lectures on the Results of the Great Exhibition of 1851*, 1852, p. 398.
2. *Great Exhibition of the Works of Industry*, 1851, p. 917.
3. Jaffer, 2001, pp. 313–15.
4. Birdwood, 1880, Vol. I, pp. 131–37.
5. Ibid., p. 125.
6. Ibid., pp. 131, 134-35.
7. Ibid., pp. 131; Mitter, 1994, pp. 34-35; McGowan, 2009, pp. 132-33. B.H. Baden-Powell mentioned that 'A traveller in India, who did us the honour to visit our Punjab Exhibition in 1882 remarked jokingly that it seemed as if the only way to get native workmen to do anything was to shut them up in jail!' (See Powell, 1885, p. 37.)
8. Birdwood, pp. 132, 134–37.

9. Mitter, pp. 34–43.
10. Havell, 1910, p. 278.
11. McGowan, pp. 107-08.
12. Ibid., p. 109.
13. Kelkar, 1969, p. 26.
14. Burns, 1909, pp. 635–66.
15. McGowan, p. 11. One of the most important initiatives of the colonial government to stimulate trade and an understanding of Indian crafts was the publication of the *Journal of Indian Art and Industry*, published quarterly from 1884 to 1917. It presented detailed histories, particularly of designs and forms, to shape producers' and consumers' tastes. These articles were typically accompanied by colour chromo-lithographic illustrations. Among the *Journal*'s eminent contributors were John Lockwood Kipling, the editor of the *JIAI* for several years, and George Birdwood, the former Curator of the Museum. W. Griggs printed the volumes in London.
16. 'India at the Antwerp Exhibition', *JOIA*, Vol. I, 1885, p. 54. The Bombay Committee presented the Museum garments worn by the Koli community in Gujarat which had been sent for the exhibition by the princely state of Idar.
17. *The Bombay Gazette*, November 22, 1889, p. 4; *The Times of India*, March 26, 1890, p. 5.
18. Quoted in Gonyo, 2015, p. 131.
19. *The Times of India*, February 7, 1905, p. 8.
20. Ibid., p. 8; Kelkar, p. 153.
21. V&A Museum Bombay, 1904-05, p. 147.
22. *The Bombay Gazette*, December 12, 1904, p. 6.
23. *The Bombay Gazette*, December 10, 1904, p. 6.
24. *Report of the Bombay Chamber of Commerce for the Year 1893*, 1894, p. 736.
25. Jhaveri, 1934, pp. 95-96.
26. Mathur, 2007, p. 29. By the 1880s, Liberty & Co. had become a household name in England due to their fabrics and prints, with outlets in London and Paris. With the rise in demand for oriental artefacts, several firms, such as Procter and Co. and Howard and Co., sold at international exhibitions and established stores in London.
27. Mitter, p. 229.
28. Coomaraswamy, 1909, p. 73.
29. Ibid., Appendix V - E.B. Havell, p. 111; Havell, 1910, pp. 289-90.
30. McGowan, pp. 189-90.
31. Sawant, 2014, pp. 103-04.
32. Smith, 1912, pp. 66-67.

34. George Terry & the 1873 Bombay Exhibition
1. MSA, GD 1873, Vol. 56, 176-77. Other members of the Committee included Mr J.A. Forbes, Mr Narayan Wasoodeo, Mr Frank Souter, Col. H.F. Hancock, Mr Byramjee Jeejeebhoy, the Rev. Dr J. Wilson, and Hormusjee Bomanjee Wadia.
2. Ibid.; *The Bombay Gazette*, February 15, 1873, p. 2.
3. Ibid.
4. *The Bombay Gazette*, February 14, 1873, p. 2.
5. *The Times of India*, March 10, 1873, p. 3.
6. *The Bombay Gazette*, March 24, 1873, p. 2.
7. V&A Museum Bombay, 1872-73, p. 2.
8. MSA, GD 1873, 176.

34A. Watcombe Pottery
1. V&A Museum Bombay, 1872-73.
2. Church, 1880, p. 87.
3. Bury, 1979, pp. 814–16.

35. Wonderland Art Pottery
1. McGowan, 2009, p. 183.
2. Burns, 1909, p. 630.
3. McGowan, pp. 15-16, 48-49; Temple, 1883, pp. 485-86.
4. 'Bombay Pottery', *JOIA*, Vol II, 1887, p. 2.
5. Cole and Tayler, 1874, pp. 200–06.
6. 'Bombay Pottery', p. 2.
7. Bryant and Weber (eds.), 2017, pp. 227–28; 'Bombay Pottery', pp. 2–3.

8. 'Bombay Pottery', p. 3.
9. Hoffenberg, 2001, pp. 46-47, 159.
10. 'Bombay Pottery', p. 3.
11. Kelkar, 1969, p. 156; McGowan, p. 183.
12. Kelkar, p. 191.

35A. George Clarke Pottery
1. Kelkar, 1969, pp. 155–57.
2. Burns, 1909, p. 634.
3. Burns, p. 634; Kelkar, p. 159.

36. Bombay Blackwood Screen
1. McGowan, 2009, p. 31.
2. Jaffer, 2001, p. 330; Birdwood, 1880, Vol. II, pp. 35–37.
3. Jaffer, p. 330.
4. Mayer and De Forest, 2008, p. 59.
5. Ibid., p. 36.
6. Ferris, 1877, pp. 56–59. 'The art of India was largely represented at the Centennial Exhibition in shawls, carpets, earthenware, and arms. But its most characteristic and suggestive expression was in a set of furniture from Bombay. This contribution of furniture was manufactured by Messrs. Watson and Co. of Bombay. The material used in the construction is called blackwood.'
7. Head, 1988, p. 124.
8. Mayer and De Forest, pp. 167-68.
9. McGowan, pp. 132–38.
10. A request for the blackwood screen for an exhibition in London (February 1930) was turned down by the family of Mungaldas Nathubhoy, who stated 'it must remain in the country.'

36A. Mungaldas Nathubhoy (1832–1890)
1. In 1862, he founded a fellowship at Bombay University which allowed graduates to spend some time in Europe. A bequest in his will enabled the University to establish seven similar scholarships.
2. Nathubhai, 1903, p. 9.
3. Masselos and Kapoor, 2009, p. 13.

37. Bombay Boxwork
1. Chaiklin, 2018, p. 117.
2. Jaffer, 2001, p. 314.
3. Birdwood, 1880, Vol. II, pp. 40–41.
4. MSA, GD 1858, Vol. 65, 329-30.
5. Chaiklin, p. 103.
6. Coomaraswamy, 1913, p. 182.
7. Watt, 1903, pp. 156-57.
8. Floor, 2006, p. 172.
9. Birdwood, p. 40.
10. Jaffer, p. 313.
11. Ibid.
12. Montauban, 1846, p. 50.

38. Carved Ivory Box
1. Martin and Vigne, 1989, p. 6.
2. Ellis, 1900, p. 16.
3. Ibid., pp. 6–16.
4. Mukharji, 1888, p. 235.

39. Soapstone Dish
1. Fern, 1926, p. 30.
2. Varner, 2006, pp. 149-50.
3. Bengal Government, 1885, p. 293; McGowan, 2009, pp. 54-55. The dish in the Museum's collection was acquired in 1884. John Griffiths, Superintendent of the Sir J.J. School of Art, made purchases of artware, including the soapstone collection, from the 1883 Calcutta Exhibition on behalf of the Museum.
4. Tillotson, 2004, p. 118. Nathu Ram had showcased his works in various exhibitions, including the Jaipur Art and Industrial Exhibition of 1883 and the Delhi exhibition of 1903-04. It is likely that Griffiths purchased the Museum dish from him as the similarities are striking.

5. Birdwood, 1864, p. 8.

40. Horn Candelabra
1. Ray, *Encyclopedia Britannica*, 2016.
2. Watt, 1903, p. 196.
3. Duran, 1990, p. 40.
4. The collection further comprises horn objects from Ratnagiri that were crafted to reflect the interest in natural history documentation of the nineteenth century. A beetle, blackbuck, black scorpion, buffalo, bull, cockroach, crane, elephant, lizard, peacock and stag are beautifully articulated in buffalo horn. The exhibit also includes a tiger made from dark-coloured buffalo horn and inlaid with ivory from Trivandrum.
5. Bengal Government, 1885, pp. 71-72.
6. Watt, p. 197.
7. Aitken, 1897, p. 4.

41. Sandalwood Panel
1. Thurston, 1903, p. 3. 'Gudi' means 'temple' in Kannada. Gudigars were a community of artisans engaged in carving on temples.
2. Wales, 1902, pp. 4-5.
3. Watt, 1903, p. 152; Thurston, p. 6.
4. Thurston, 1904, p. 49.
5. Wales, pp. 4-5.
6. Ibid.
7. The Museum's sandalwood objects acquired between 1892 and 1941 included carved blotting cases, caskets, boxes, panels, watch stands, sculptures and fly whisks.
8. Simpson and G. Eyre-Todd, 1903, pp. 164-65.

41A. Sandalwood Casket
1. Thurston, 1903, p. 7.
2. Watt, 1903, p. 150.
3. Thurston, p. 6.

42. Battle Axe
1. Bengal Government, Vol 2, 1885, p. 65.
2. Egerton, 1880, p. 20.
3. Ibid., p. 21.
4. Ibid., p. 104.
5. V&A Museum Bombay, 1914-15; 1929-30, p. 218.

42A. Koftgari Shield
1. Pal (ed.), 2010, p. 50.
2. Egerton, 1896, p. 47.

43. Koftgari Paper Weight
1. Hendley, 1891, p. 21.
2. Kiralfy, 1895, p. 214.
3. Mukharji, 1888, pp. 178-79; Egerton, 1896, p. 69.
4. Schaller Penwell and Kulles, 1985, p. 4; Tattoli, C. *The Paris Review* (online), September 20, 2017. Paper weights became fashionable throughout Europe in the mid-nineteenth century with the advent of inexpensive paper and a reliable mail service.

44. Bidri Tushta & Surahi Set
1. Mukharji, 1885, Vol 1, pp. 40–44.
2. Blair and Bloom (eds.), 2009, pp. 35–38. The subject of water and purity figures prominently in Islamic texts. In contrast to stagnant water, flowing water is considered pure as it washes away impurities.
3. Jones, 1856, 'Plate XLIX - Indian No. 1'.
4. Michell, 1986, p. 117.

45. Silver Trophy Cup
1. Hoffenberg, 2001, p. 161.
2. Dehejia et al, 2008, p. 127.
3. Birdwood, 1878, p. 60; 1880, Vol. I, p. 151. Dutch silverwork employed scrolling and floral patterns. Birdwood attributes the designs executed on Raj silver produced in Kutch, Lucknow and Dacca to the influence of Dutch silverware.
4. The Whiting Manufacturing firm used a

combination of geometric patterns inspired by Persian designs, and floral scrollwork designs and forms inspired by Kutch silverware on tea service sets (see Dallas Museum of Art website).
5. Dehejia et al, p. 10.
6. Mukharji, 1888, pp. 168-69.
7. Birdwood, 1880, Vol. I, p. 151.

45A. Silver Tea Cup & Saucer
1. Dehejia et al, 2008, p. 154.
2. Ibid.

46. Silver Fruit Bowl
1. Dehejia et al, 2008, p. 22–24; Bliss, 1927, p. 8.
2. Dehejia et al, p. 20.
3. Birdwood, 1878, p. 60.
4. Dehejia et al., p. 102.
5. Ibid.
6. Ibid., pp. 21-22.
7. Ibid., p. 213.

46A. Silver Pitcher
1. V&A Museum Archives, Specimen Register, p. 48.
2. Kiralfy, 1895, pp. 277-78; Watt, 1903, pp. 33-34.

47. Silver Enamel Hukkah
1. Rousselet, 1875, p. 290.
2. Spencer, 1918, p. 136.
3. V&A Museum Bombay, 1910-11.
4. Birdwood, 1880, Vol. I, pp. 165–67; Fern, 1926, p. 130.
5. Birdwood, p. 167.
6. Ibid.
7. Fern, p. 130; Mukharji, 1888, pp. 175.
8. Birdwood, p. 167. In 1886, to encourage the craftsmen to send articles to exhibitions, the Bombay School of Art offered two awards of Rs 180 each for the best specimens on enamel on silver (see *JOIA*, Vol I, 1884, p. 5).

48. Brass Thaal
1. Fern, 1926, p. 129.
2. Hendley, 1891, 'Plate – 40'. Hendley states that a craftsman's approach to representing the zodiacs and lunar mansions was more decorative than scientific, hence signs and stars of some mansions may appear as out of order.
3. Ibid., p. 11; Mukharji, 1888, pp. 186–209.
4. Solomon, 1924, p. 12.
5. Hendley, p. 17.
6. Roy, 1996, p. 366.
7. Ibid., pp. 359-64.

49. Lacquered Leather Ganjifa Suite
1. Chatterjee, 2018, pp. 39–44.
2. Ibid., pp. 44-45.
3. Culin, 1898, p. 928.
4. Chatterjee, p. 42.
5. Chavan, 1998, p. 183.
6. Birdwood, 1880, Vol. II, p. 61; Stache-Rosen, 1984, p. 254. Artistic standards set by the Mughal-styled Ganjifa were adapted across India during this period and gave rise to many regional variations.

50. Papier-Mâché Box
1. Lawrence, 1895, pp. 383-84; *All India Swadeshi Directory 1933*, pp. xix, xxxiv.
2. V&A Museum Bombay, 1932-33, 1938-39.
3. Saraf, 1987, pp. 125–29.
4. Ibid.
5. Zutshi, 2009, p. 422.

50A. Papier-Mâché Panel
1. Maskiell, 2002, p. 29.
2. Ibid.; Birdwood, 1880, Vol. II, p. 157.
3. Fern, 1926, p. 23. In 1897, in accordance with the Bombay High Court, all affairs related to the management of the mosque were vested in a board of eleven directors, triennially elected by

the Kokni Muslim Jamat of Bombay. A 'nazir' is appointed by the board and manages all executive functions.
4. Powell, 1872, pp. 39-40. See *kaddar* and *butha* shawl patterns; the embroidery consists of a single or a group of flowers in the shape of a pinecone.

51. Lacquer Fruit Tray
1. Fern, 1926, pp. 21-22.
2. Ansari, 1992, p. 29.
3. Ibid., p. 20.
4. Fern, pp. 21-22. Indian patterns of scrolling foliage on Hala pottery appeared widely in picture books including Owen Jones' *The Grammar of Ornament*.
5. Watt, 1903, p. 214.
6. Ibid., pp. 211-12.
7. Fern, p. 18.
8. Markovits, 2000, pp. 116-17.
9. Falzon, 2004, p. 132.

52. Yerawada Jail Carpet
1. McGowan, 2013, pp. 391-92.
2. Mukharji, 1888, pp. 388-98.
3. Watt, 1903, p. 432.
4. Robert Lehman Collection, 1975; 1975.1.2458, '*Carpet with vine scroll and palmette pattern; Wool pile on cotton foundation, c. late 19th century*' (see The Metropolitan Museum of Art, New York website).
5. Walker, 1997, p. 8.
6. McGowan, p. 392.
7. Ibid.
8. Campbell, 1882, pp. 401-02; McGowan, pp. 395-406.
9. McGowan, p. 404.
10. Robert Lehman Collection, 1975.

53. Bridal Salwar
1. Schoen, 2009, pp. 26-31.
2. Birdwood, 1880, Vol. II, pp. 234-35.
3. Jain, 2016, p. 36.
4. Ringer, 2011, p. 18.
5. Palsetia, 2001, p. 3. The *Qisseh-i Sanjan* or Story of Sanjan, written in 1599 by the Parsi priest Behman Kaikobad Sanjana, and the *Qisseh-i Zanushtian-i Hendustan*, written by the Parsi Shapurji Maneckji Sanjana in Navsari between 1765 and 1805, estimate the arrival of Parsis in India around 716 CE.
6. Although Aurangabad was the main centre for production of *Himroo* sarees, *Himroo* silks were sent to Surat, where Arab merchants purchased them. This particular saree in the Museum's collection was probably purchased from Surat.

53A. Kinkhab
1. Mukharji, 1888, pp. 364-65.
2. Birdwood, 1880, Vol. II, pp. 94–96; Fern, 1926, p. 61, 133.
3. Bayly, 1983, p. 208.
4. Mukharji, p. 367.
5. King, 2005, pp. 19–55.

54. Coco de Mer Dervish's Bowl
1. Qazvini and Kermani, 2018, p. 62.
2. Ibid., pp. 64-65.
3. Thurston, 1904, p. 48.
4. Wise, 1998, p. 24.
5. Papas, 2020, pp. 335–65. The publication was issued in 1816 and is regarded as the earliest known Persian text on the metropolis' cosmopolitan nature and multi-faith society. The birth and death years of the Sufi saints remain indefinite, however, the years they were actively preaching in the region are recorded.

55. Stone Foo Dogs
1. Thampi and Saksena, 2009, pp. 20-21. Until 1860, one-third of India's export of cotton was shipped

to China, mostly from Bombay.
2. Ibid., p. 22.
3. Chung, 1973, p. 87.
4. Mathur, 2012, p. 5.

56. Steam Ship Siam
1. Croil, 1898, p. 146.
2. V&A Museum Archives, Specimen Register, p. 187
3. Melbourne International Exhibition, 1882, p. 616.
4. P&O Heritage website. The Port of Bombay handled at its various docks and bunders between six and seven million tons of cargo and the total number of overseas passengers embarking and disembarking at Bombay exceeded a quarter of a million annually.
5. Thomas Cook (Firm), 1897, p. 10.

PEOPLE OF INDIA
Interrogating Identity
1. Lear and Murphy, 1953, p. 37; Dehejia, 1989, p. 6.
2. Mathur and Singh, 2015, p. 47.
3. Royle, 1852, p. 388.
4. MSA, GD 1857, Vol. 55, 46–65.
5. Shaffer, 2011, pp. 3–7, 16; Parasnis, 1921, p. 53.
6. Parasnis, pp. 8, 53, 130; Losty, August 28, 2014; Shaffer, p. 7. The School closed in 1795 when James Wales passed away.
7. Campbell, 1885, p. 202.
8. Fern, 1926, p. 9.
9. Campbell, p. 204.
10. See Jain and Jain-Neubauer, 2016.
11. Metcalf, 1995, pp. 113–59.
12. Ibid., pp. 66–112.
13. Ibid., pp. 123–26. *The People of Bombay* describes the various communities through a typically colonial perspective (see Strip, P. and O. Strip, 1944).
14. Prakash, 1999, pp. 3–14, 17–48.
15. Risley, 1891, pp. xxxii–xxxiv.
16. Khan, 2018, pp. 75–129.
17. V&A Museum Archives, File 51, Letter from Fern to Deputy Municipal Commissioner, May 5, 1926.
18. Watt, 1903, p. 450.
19. Birdwood, 1878, pp. 84-85; Mukharji, 1888, pp. 62–69, 73. T.N. Mukharji defends the Krishnanagar clay models while noting that Mr Locke, Superintendent of the School of Art at Calcutta, thought of the models as mere 'toys', as opposed to sculptures, due to the usage of real fabric, hair and wool.
20. V&A Museum Bombay, 1903-04; 1909-10; 1911-12; 1915-16; 1916-17.
21. Anderson, 1912, pp. 1–4.
22. V&A Museum Archives, File 59.
23. *The Times*, May 22 1886, p. 5, quoted in Metcalf, 1989, p. 146.
24. Hoffenberg, 2001, pp. 159-60.
25. Kiralfy, 1895, p. 13.
26. Mathur, 2000, pp. 497-98. Mathur details the controversial strategy employed by the international exhibitions and merchants like Liberty to create living human zoos (see Mathur, 2007, pp. 33–42, 67–79). Breckenridge outlines the evolution of the panorama which informed these displays and writes a scathing criticism of the colonial policy of display and collecting (see Breckenridge, 1989, pp. 197–99).
27. *The Bombay Chronicle*, September 7, 1918, p. 11.
28. Ibid.; V&A Museum Bombay, 1916-17, pp. 212-13, 1929-30, p. 218.
29. V&A Museum Bombay, 1915-16, p. 226.

57. Sewak Ram
1. Archer, 1948, pp. 11-14.
2. Llewellyn-Jones, 2020, pp. 26–33.
3. Archer, p. 18.
4. Rekha, 2011, p. 999.
5. Archer, p. 17.
6. Rekha, p. 1002.

57A. Mica Painting
1. V&A Museum Bombay, 1932-33, p. 217.
2. Archer and Parlett, 1992, pp. 203-04.
3. Archer, 1948, p. 38.

58. Deccani Brahmin
1. Pinney, 1997, p. 56.
2. Coleman, 1899, p. 9.

58A. Parsi Couple
1. Guha, 1970, p. M107.
2. Daboo and Sinthupan, 2018, p. 29.

59. Sinhalese
1. Cave, 1908, p. 85.
2. Edwardes, 1909, Vol. I, p. 410; Coleman, 1899, p. 48.
3. Ranganathan, 2008, p. 121.
4. Dwivedi and Mehrotra, 2001, p. 57.

59A. Arab
1. Tweedie, 1894, p. 300.
2. Edwardes, 1909, Vol. I, p. 201.
3. Ibid., p. 264.

60. The Collection of Textile Manufactures of India by John Forbes Watson
1. Driver and Ashmore, 2010, p. 353. See Swallow, 1999, pp. 30–35 for a detailed history of the preparation of these volumes by Watson.
2. Driver and Ashmore, 2010, p. 371.
3. Watson, 1866, pp. 6-7.
4. Ibid., p. 1; *Report of the Bombay Chamber of Commerce for 1867-68*, 1869, p. 180.
5. Watson, p. 1; Armitage, 1989, p. 77.

60A. Embroiderer
1. Gupte, 1887, p. 15.
2. Ibid., pp. 16-17.
3. *The Bombay Gazette*, February 29, 1868, p. 2.

61. Repousse Craftsmen
1. McGowan, 2009, pp. 61-62.
2. Griffiths, 1896, p. 15.
3. Ibid.
4. Watt, 1903, p. 61.

61A. Bombay Servants
1. Blunt, 1999, p. 422, 429.
2. Kale, 1994, p. 911.
3. Procida, 2002, p. 88, 100.

62. A Dancer
1. Niranjana, 2020, p. 20, 25.
2. Woodfield, 1994, p. 202.
3. Raghunathji, 1884, pp. 165-66.
4. Ibid., p. 167.
5. Woodfield, p. 202.
6. Niranjana, p. 16, 25.
7. Walker, 2010, pp. 290-91.

62A. Taus
1. Deodhar, 1993, p. 261.

63. Vasudev
1. Pai, 1928, pp. v-vi.
2. V&A Museum Bombay, 1909-10, p. 210.

63A. Fakirs
1. Edwardes, 1923, p. 15. After the Fakir–Sannyasi revolt of c.1764–1850 in Bengal, the British viewed fakirs as rebellious, and by the early twentieth century, they became anxious about the fakirs' presence and influence. The surge in diseases was another factor for restricting their movement. Fakirs, who were once a popular postcard subject among British travellers, now became the focus of criminal investigations.

63B. Sect Marks
1. Pai, 1928, p. 40.

2. Untracht, 1997, p. 25.
3. Pattanaik, 2013.

64. Surya
1. Fern, 1926, pp. 36-37.
2. Moor, 1810, p. ix.
3. Hendley, 1912, p. 81; Gray, 1940, pp. 102-03.
4. Llewellyn-Jones, 1985, p. 5.
5. Smith and Stevenson, 2010, pp. 40–43.
6. Watt, 1903, p. 89.
7. Mukharji, 1888, pp. 69-70.

65. The Mahratta Regiment
1. Lenman, 1990, p. 120.
2. National Army Museum online.
3. McMunn and Lovett, 1911, p. 167.

65A. Kelat-I-Ghilzie
1. Fern, 1926, pp. 131-32.
2. Royal Mint Museum online.
3. INTACH Report, 2005.

65B. Indigenous Soldiers
1. Forbes, Vol. I, 1813, p. 377.
2. Sen, 1961, pp. 7-8.

66. Traditional Games
1. Finkel and Mackenzie, 2004, pp. 59–63.
2. Nayar, 2012, pp. 161–200.
3. Preeti, 2016, p. 32.
4. Hunter, 1883, pp. 1–7.
5. Abraham, 1946, pp. 253–63. Gymkhanas were established in Bombay as clubs for outdoor recreation. In the 1890s, the British Government granted grounds on the Kennedy sea-face (Marine Drive) to the Parsi, Hindu, and Islam Gymkhanas to encourage sports among the local population.
6. Fern, 1926, pp. 96-99.
7. Prakash, 1990, p. 21.

67. Emperor Jahangir on Shikar
1. V&A Museum Bombay, 1909-10, p. 210; 1929-30, p. 218.
2. Thackston, 1999, p. 167.
3. Ibid., p. 174.
4. Allsen, 2006, p. 136, 175.

68. Agricultural Improvements
1. V&A Museum Bombay, 1913-14, p. 216.
2. V&A Museum Bombay, 1927-28, p. 221.
3. Bose, Sen and Subbarayappa, 1971, pp. 484–567.
4. Voelcker, 1893, pp. 1–9.
5. Riddick, 2006, p. 68.
6. Roy, 2016, pp. 1–24.
7. Roy, 2002, p. 113.

69. Village Water Sanitation Improvement
1. Brayne, 1937, pp. 195-96, 301.
2. Nightingale, Nergaard and Vicinus, 1990, p. 244; Ramanna, 2002, pp. 31–46.
3. Reynolds-Finley Historical Library Online Archive.
4. Polu, 2012, p. 50.
5. Brayne, pp. 21–69.

69A. An Ideal Indian Village
1. Stampari, 1935, p. 1.
2. Brayne, 1937, pp. 210-11, 296; Letter from Dr SC Upadhyaya (no. 2694, 9 April 1930).

RAJA RAVI VARMA
The Influence of a Master
1. Jain, 2013, pp. 9–12.
2. See Chawla, 2010, and Pal, 2011.
3. Dehejia, et al., 2008, p. 34; Fernandes, 1932, p. 60. Chawla records the ubiquitous visual presence of Ravi Varma's oleographs in the household temples and residences of the Nattukotai Chettiars and the reproductions of his work on

tiles used in their homes, ceramic sculptures imported from Japan as decorative objects, silver repousse, Tanjore paintings and even temple sculpture (see Chawla, 2010, p. 253).
4. Mitter, 1994, pp. 179–80.
5. Guha-Thakurta, 1991, pp. 94-95.
6. Raja Ravi Varma spent a month in Bombay in 1891 at Grant Road and nearly a year in 1892 while renting a studio in Khotachiwadi, Girgaum. From 1894 to 1904, Raja Ravi Varma and his brother spent long periods in Bombay each year. (See Neumayer and Schelberger, 2005).
7. Mitter, p. 207.
8. The Sri Chitra Art Gallery was established in 1935 by Sri Chithira Thirunal, the Maharaja of Travancore. Chawla, pp. 144–51.
9. Mathur and Singh, 2015, p. 152; Neumayer and Schelberger, pp. 209-10.
10. Neumayer and Schelberger, p. 29.
11. Chawla, p. 143.
12. Guha-Thakurta, 1986, p. 193.
13. Venniyoor, 1981, pp. 29–30; Neumayer and Schelberger, pp. 304-05; *Bombay Gazette*, February 13, 1891, p. 5.
14. *Bombay Gazette*, February 7, 1893, p. 2.
15. Chawla, p. 220.
16. Ibid., p. 281.
17. Ibid., pp. 285–91.
18. Smith, 1911, p. 347.
19. Mitter, p. 242.
20. Jain, pp. 19–33.
21. Dehejia et al., pp. 45–47.
22. V&A Museum Archives, File 54; V&A Museum Bombay, 1919-20, p. 220.
23. Chawla, pp. 303–05; Pinney, 2004, p. 61.
24. See Rajadhyaksha, 1993, for his analysis of the impact of Raja Ravi Varma.

70. Narasimha
1. Guy, 2016, pp. 32–43.
2. *Bhagavad Gita*, 4.6–8.

70A. Dattatreya
1. Raeside, 1982, p. 498.
2. Chawla, 2010, p. 97.
3. Gupte, 1916, plate 4.

71. Embassy of Shri Krishna
1. The Kurukshetra war, also known as the Mahabharata war.
2. Mitter, 1994, p. 207.
3. Chawla, 2010, p. 243.
4. Ibid., p. 200.

71A. Sita in Ashokvan
1. Chawla, 2010, pp. 158–60.

72. Rama's Coronation
1. Guha-Thakurta, 1986, p. 194.
2. Bahulkar, 2018, pp. 38-39.
3. Chawla, 2010, p. 262.

72A. Vishnu on Garuda
1. Jain, 2004, pp. 50–57, 71–73.
2. Jain, 2013, p. 30.
3. Maholay-Jaradi, 2016, p. 5–7.

73. Saraswati
1. Baker, 1915, pp. 302-03; Mitter, 1994, p. 215. By the turn of the twentieth century, Chinese, Japanese and European decorative porcelain wares/collectibles frequently circulated in Bombay through auction houses like Sorabjee Cowasjee located in the Fort area.
2. Pinney, 2004, pp. 26-27.
3. Guha-Thakurta, 1992, pp. 95-96, 106.
4. Mitter, p. 202.

74. Parvati and Ganesha
1. Chawla, 2010, p. 168. Raphael (1483–1520), the renowned Italian Renaissance artist, painted

multiple versions of the 'Madonna'. Ravi Varma's painting may have been inspired by 'The Sistine Madonna', painted c. 1512–14.

74A. Jewellery Box
1. Fernandes, 1932, p. 60.
2. Chawla, 2010, pp. 128-29.

CLASSICAL ARTS
Commodifying Culture
1. Codrington, 1970, p. 138.
2. Jain, 2007, pp. 91-92.
3. V&A Museum Archives, File 48, No. 23, April 24, 1924, E.R. Fern to Bombay Municipal Corporation.
4. Ibid, V&A Bombay, 1923-34, p. ix.
5. V&A Museum Bombay, 1885-86. Cole was later appointed the Archaeological Superintendent of the North Western provinces and eventually made the Curator of Ancient Monuments for India from 1880 to 1885.
6. Guha-Thakurta, 2004, pp. 56, 59-60.
7. Guha, 2017, p. 72; MSA, GD 1848, Vol. 43, 61–65. There were three shipments of Assyrian artefacts between 1846 and 1848, excavated by Austen Henry Layard, intended for the British Museum that arrived in Bombay on their way to London. There was great consternation when some of the artefacts were exhibited in Bombay, with Layard accusing the authorities of 'vandalism'. However, the artefacts were displayed on the explicit orders of the Governor of Bombay.
8. V&A Museum Archives, File 49, Letter no. 6642, October 15, 1923.
9. Kelkar, 1969, pp. 50.
10. Jain, 2013, p. 7.
11. McGowan, 2009, pp. 6, 16. Thurston, who was principal of the School of Art in Madras, notes that the School was using temple designs as templates for the students' production of artwares. He says, 'A collection of designs from different pagodas [temples] in the state has been made, and proves very useful.' (See Thurston, 1901, p. 6.)
12. Guha-Thakurta, p. 45.
13. McGowan, pp. 60–127.
14. Gonyo, 2015, pp. 188–220.
15. Jain, 2007, pp. 115–21.
16. Mitter, 1994, pp. 246–54; Burns, 1909, pp. 629–50; Havell, 1910, pp. 274–98. Havell sparred vigorously in various public fora with the V&A Museum Bombay's first curator, George Birdwood. He contested Birdwood's more conservative and prejudiced views about Indian 'fine' arts. He also disagreed with Burns' more conservative approach.
17. Coomaraswamy, *JIAI*, Vol. XV, 1912, pp. 67–69.
18. V&A Museum Archives, File 45, June 25, 1929, E.R. Fern to Deputy Municipal Commissioner.
19. V&A Museum Bombay, 1927-28, p. 223. E.R. Fern notes that he put together an 'Old Indian Historical Picture room' that displayed half tone and colour photographs and prints of old miniatures as originals were rare and expensive. This room demonstrated a European historiography of India, beginning with the Buddhist period up to the Mughals. The display showcased a range of regional miniature schools. Mughal and Maratha (probably Deccani) formed the most prominent display. Guzerat miniatures from Jaina manuscripts were also included.
20. *The Age*, October 27, 1934, p. 23.
21. V&A Museum, Bombay, 1932-33, pp. 218-19; V&A Museum Archives, File 54.
22. Goswami, 2004, p. 244; Kidambi, 2016, pp. 195–97.
23. *The Bombay Chronicle*, August 9, 1930, p. 4. The paper was founded by Sir Pherozeshah Mehta in 1910 with the help of J.B. Petit.
24. V&A Museum Bombay, 1945-46, p. 210; *The Bombay Chronicle*, December 5, 1945, p. 4; December 7, 1945, p. 2; December 10, 1945, p. 7; December 25, 1945, p. 3.
25. *The Bombay Chronicle*, January 16, 1934, p. 3; June 6, 1935, p. 5; March 30, 1940, p. 2.
26. *The Bombay Chronicle*, December 8, 1936, p. 13.

75. Radha–Krishna
1. Thurston, 1901, p. 3.
2. *The Hindu*, October 27, 2017; Thurston, p. 5. The department produced carved ivory objects for sixteen years and even jail convicts were taught to carve.
3. *The Hindu*, September 30, 2016.
4. Fern, 1926, p. 14.
5. Thurston, p 6.
6. Kipling, Vol. 1, 1885, p. 49.
7. Watt, 1903, p. 185.
8. V&A Museum Bombay, 1941-42, p. 303; 1948-49, p. 251; 1951-52, p. 273; 1955-56, p. 281.

75A. Maharaja Khanderao Gaekwad II of Baroda (1828–1870)
1. Birdwood, 1864, p. 70.
2. *The Bombay Gazette*, November 6, 1889, p. 5.

76. Lakshmi–Narayana
1. Balasubryamanyam, 1965, p. 27.
2. Thurston, 1903, p. 10.
3. McGowan, 2009, p. 11.
4. Solomon, 1924, pp. 27–29, 37.
5. Thurston, p. 5.
6. Menon, 1962, p. 373.
7. See Handicraft Development Corporation of Kerala Ltd. online

77. Parvati
1. V&A Museum Archives, File 45, SRCM/926, January 13, 1961, Dr S.C. Upadhyaya to Deputy Municipal Commissioner. The sculpture was acquired by curator Dr S.C. Upadhyaya (1939–64) from Khadi Village Industries Emporium. He stated that they were 'excellent specimens of South Indian craftsmanship'.
2. Coomaraswamy, 1934, pp. 166-67.
3. Thirunavukarasu, 1977, p. 29.
4. Srinivasan, 2012, p. 246.
5. Reeves, 1962, pp. 105-06.
6. Levy et al., 2008, p. 49.
7. Coomaraswamy, 1908, p. 154; Thurston states that sculptures made for artistic purposes, though treated as sacred, were never worshiped unless they were of stone or metal (See Thurston, 1903, p. 5).
8. Dehejia et al., 2002, pp. 54-55.
9. Kinsley, 1988, p. 35.
10. Singh, 2002, pp. 176–96.

78. Nabakeli
1. Sudarshan Art & Craft online.
2. Ibid.
3. Guha, 2012, pp. 35-36.
4. Guy, 1999, pp. 105-26.
5. Tripati, 2015, pp. 3-4.
6. Sahu, 2015, p. 68.
7. Paniker, 1959, pp. 817-24.
8. Singh, 2009, pp. 356-57.

79. Kashi Vishwanath Temple
1. Tarapor, 1980, pp. 68–81.
2. Shastri, 1999, p. 191.
3. V&A Museum Bombay, 1932-33, p. 217.
4. Mukharji, 1888, p. 193.
5. *Indian Pictorial Education*, 1930, p. 3.
6. *Illustrated London Weekly*, March 1, 1873, p. 211.

79A. Meenakshi Temple
1. Gupte, JOIA, Vol. I, No. 14, 1885, p. 108.
2. Cole, 1874, p. 104.
3. V&A Museum Archive, File 44. Curator Dr S.C. Upadhyaya (1939–64) had seen a similar model of the temple at the office of the Regional Tourist Officer (Bombay Central Railway Station), from whom he procured the modeller's address.

80. Flower Study
1. Haider, 1998, p. 238.
2. Khandalavala and Chandra, 1969, pp. 4–6.
3. Firouzeh, 2019, p. 50.
4. Dani and Masson (eds), 2003, p. 564.
5. Matthee, 2013, p. 23. Artists began experimenting with foreshortening and employing perspective in their representations of flower and bird paintings.
6. Sarce, 1986.
7. Pedram et al., 2017, p. 987.
8. Nizamuddin, 1881, p. 686. Inspired by Ferdowsi's *Shah Nameh*, Nizami chose Alexander the Great as the subject for his heroic tale. His poetry expressed strong values through Alexander's valour, challenges and victories. The *Khamseh* was written in the last quarter of the twelfth century, a period of political unrest in Persia. It reflects a culture that valued fantasy and artistic expression in literature, even during turbulent times.

81. Mughal Courtier
1. Walker, 1997, p. 129. The Deccan was an important carpet-weaving region during the late seventeenth and the eighteenth centuries, well-known for its prayer carpets, brocades, and chintzes.

81A. Shahjada
1. Verma, 1976, p. 564.
2. Beach, 2008, p. 81; Welch, 1985, p. 173.

82. Ascetic
1. Zebrowski, 1983, p. 10.
2. Beach, 2008, pp. 110–15.
3. Zebrowski, pp. 9-10.
4. Beach, p. 114.
5. Benson, 2015, p. 157.
6. Niranjana, 2020, p. 20, 25; *The Bombay Chronicle*, April 25, 1925, p. 7.

83. Ragamala
1. Kossak, 1997, pp. 3–23.
2. Zebrowski, 1983, pp. 244–82.
3. Losty, June 7, 2014.

84. Vishwarupa Darshana
1. *The Bhagavad Gita*, 1899, pp. 37-38.
2. Ibid., p. 38.
3. Maxwell, 1990.
4. Archer, 1957, p. 93.
5. Ibid.

85. Krishna's Life
1. Randhawa, 1956, pp. 5–10.
2. Ohri, 2001, p. 102.
3. Coomaraswamy, 1912, pp. 315–25.
4. Goswamy and Fischer, 1992, pp. 7–12.
5. The *Bhagavata Purana*, composed between the sixth and the tenth centuries CE, is a sacred text in the Vaishnav tradition.
6. Bhatia, 1998, p. 59.
7. Goswamy and Fischer, p. 371.
8. Kipling, 1887, pp. 40-41.
9. Coomaraswamy, 1916, p. 21. It was Coomaraswamy who acquired a set of Kangra miniatures for the Museum of Fine Arts in Boston and sold them to Denman Waldo Ross, the benefactor of the MFA.

86. Jodhabai
1. Losty, April 11 2016.
2. Archer and Parlett, 1992, p. 216.
3. Schmitz, 2010, p. 114.
4. George Birdwood praises the work of Zulfikar

Ali Khan, one of the first and most popular miniature artists in Bombay from Delhi, famous for miniature paintings on ivory that were sent to the South Kensington exhibitions in 1871–74 (see Birdwood, 1880, Vol. II, pp. 62-63).

86A. Jacob (1849–1921)
1. The Great Game was a period of intense political rivalry during the nineteenth century between the British Empire and Czarist Russia to exert control over Central Asia, the north-western frontier of India, and Afghanistan.
2. Zubrzycki, 2012, pp. 283, 320. Jacob exemplified the typical British dealer in Bombay who made money by buying and selling Indian antiquities.
3. *The Age*, October 27, 1934, p. 23.

87. Navagrahas & Ashtadikpalas
1. Chavan, 1998, p. 190.
2. Neela and Ambrosia, 2016, p. 74.
3. Appasamy, 1980, p. 39.
4. Rossi, 1998, pp. 166–68.
5. Ibid.
6. Inglis, 1995, p. 57.
7. Jain, 2007, p. 83.
8. Archer and Parlett, 1992, pp. 21–23.

88. Shah Nameh
1. Dabashi, 2019, pp. 13-14.
2. Davidson and Simpson (eds), 2013, p. 87.
3. Ibid., pp. 86–101.
4. Goswamy, 1998, pp. 1–11.
5. V&A Museum Bombay, 1932-33, p. 219.

89. Ashtasahasrika Prajnaparamita
1. Diemberger, 2012, pp. 132–38.
2. Conze, 1975, p. ix.
3. Kitagawa et al., *Encyclopedia Britannica*, 2020.
4. Boesi, 2016, pp. 511, 514
5. V&A Museum Bombay, 1932-33, p. 219.

EARLY MODERN PAINTING
A New Perspective
1. Mitter, 2007, p. 10.
2. Burns, 1909, p. 629; *The Times of India*, May 7, 1918, p. 8.
3. Dhurandhar, 1940, pp. 44-45; Burns, pp. 629–41.
4. Coomaraswamy, *JIAI*, Vol. XV, 1912, p. 68.
5. Smith, 1911, pp. 348–50; Burns, pp. 629–50; Havell, 1910, pp. 274–98.
6. Solomon, 1924, pp. 61–71.
7. Mitter, pp. 186-87.
8. Ibid., pp. 194–202.
9. Solomon, p. 6. Yashodra Dalmia and other scholars have criticised Soloman's 'paternalism', as despite his support for Indian Art he refused to see it on par with Western Art (see Dalmia, 2001, pp. 27-28). However, Partha Mitter states 'we cannot but be impressed with Solomon's

achievement in establishing Bombay as one of the two major artistic centres of India, an achievement that contributed much to the later phase of the Progressive Artists of postcolonial India.' (See Mitter, 2009, p. 38.)
10. Bhagwat, 1983, p. 40.
11. Ibid., pp. 40–44.
12. Solomon, p. 101.
13. Mitter, p. 29.
14. Ibid., pp. 202-10.
15. Several important citizens of Bombay campaigned for the commission including the lawyer Mukund Ramrao Jayakar and Kanaiyalal H. Vakil, the Art and Dramatic Critic of the *Bombay Chronicle*. Vakil was a champion of Indian artists and was a dominating and influential position in the art world of India generally and Bombay particularly. He vigorously promoted the students of the Bombay School of Art, especially to secure the work of mural paintings in some of the public buildings in New Delhi. He was also instrumental in formulating the Prize of Delhi Scheme to encourage promising Indian artists. (See Mitter, 2007, pp. 177–225.)
16. Kelkar, 1969, p. 103; *The Bombay Chronicle*, July 14, 1957, p. 9.

90. Nyayalaya by M.V. Dhurandhar (b. 1867–1944)
1. Jain, 2007, pp. 145-46.
2. Ibid., pp. 121, 145.
3. Sawant, 2014, p. 104.
4. Dalmia, 2001, p. 14.
5. Mitter, 2007, p. 204.
6. Ibid. p. 205.

90A. Untitled by Rustom Siodia (b. 1881–1946)
1. Mitter, 1994, p. 99.
2. *Rustom Siodia, Artist*, (n.d), pp. 18, 25–26.

91. Seascapes by P.A. Dhond (b. 1908–2001)
1. Sawant, 2014, pp. 164–67.
2. Dhond, 1979, pp. 20–30.
3. Russell Flint, *Sir William Russell Flint*.

92. Lakdi Bunder by A.M. Mali (act. 1905–1921)
1. Bahulkar and Ghare, 2013, pp. 407–09.
2. *The Pioneer*, March 31, 1911, p. 6; *The Times of India*, September 24, 1912, p. 5; *The Bombay Chronicle*, February 23, 1916, p. 5; *The Times of India*, March 16, 1918, p. 17.
3. Bahulkar and Ghare, pp. 407–09.

92A. Untitled by N.R. Sardesai (b. 1885–1954)
1. Imarte, 2013, p. 522.
2. Ibid.
3. Rao Bahadur M.V. Dhurandhar had praised Sardesai as an excellent teacher and painter who could also execute figure composition flawlessly.

92B. Untitled by Ambika Dhurandhar (b. 1912–2009)
1. Mitter, 2007, p. 149.
2. Bhagwat, 1983, p. 98.
3. Dhurandhar, 1940, p. 57.

93. Untitled by Pradumna Tana (b. 1929–2009)
1. Conversation between Antonella Tana, daughter of Pradumna Tana, and Tasneem Zakaria Mehta, 2019.
2. Conversation between Gulam Mohammed Sheikh and Tasneem Zakaria Mehta, 2019.
3. Conversation between Antonella Tana, daughter of Pradumna Tana, and Tasneem Zakaria Mehta, 2019.

CONTEMPORARY ART
The Artist in Focus
1. Prakash, 2010, pp. 128–36.
2. Dalmia, 2001, gives a vivid and wonderful account of this period.
3. Panikkar, 2003, p. 114.
4. Khullar, 2015, pp. 1–40. A group of Bombay artists from the 1960s onwards engaged with more abstract themes. One of the finest, Prabhakar Barwe, worked between abstraction and semi-abstraction, informed by his experience of working at Weavers' Service Centres across India. Nasreen Mohamedi moved from Bombay to Baroda in order to take up a position as a faculty member in the 1970s, and would become an important influence on a new generation of artists. Nepali-born (but Bombay resident) Laxman Shreshtha experimented with the formal qualities of painting. Jehangir Sabavala, a maverick whose early education in France was to have a profound impact on his style, veered towards a figurative practice that sought a sense of the numinous.
5. The Shiv Sena, one of the Indian saffron parties, has been running the Municipal Corporation of Greater Mumbai, which is responsible for the city's development, since 1985.
6. Kapur, 2000, p. 31.

97. Listening to the Shades by Nalini Malani
1. See Nalini Malani, Arts and Culture Prize 2013 on Fukuoka Prize website.
2. See Storr, 2008.

99. As If – III: Country of The Sea by CAMP
1. CAMP, *From Gulf to Gulf to Gulf, 2013*. The film *From Gulf to Gulf to Gulf* (83 mins), produced by CAMP in 2013, was a result of four years of dialogue, friendship and exchange between CAMP and a group of sailors from Kutch, who come to Sharjah often.

Opposite:
Muse of Science, Matthew Noble, marble, 1869, London.
Presented to the Museum by David Sassoon.

•

Front endpaper image:
Admiralty Chart of Bombay Harbour, Chiefly from Surveys by Commander L. S. Dawson, R. N; the Port of Bombay and Eastern portion of the Harbour; 14 January 1885, with corrections up to 1951; London: 111 x 71 cm. Accessioned: 2021.

•

Back endpaper image:
Map of Island of Bombay; plate 51, *The Imperial Gazetteer of India, Atlas, Vol. XXVI*, Oxford: Clarendon Press, 1909; 26 x 21.5 cm. Accessioned: 1945-46.

Museum interior after restoration in 2007.
**View of the Industrial Arts Gallery,
Dr. Bhau Daji Lad Museum, Mumbai.**

Warli
Nawa Pada
Mhatar Pachari
Tank
Elphinstone
Mudli Pakhadi
Sumbhu Mhadeo Pakhadi
Tulsi Pipe Rd.
Railway Works
Fergusson Rd.
Parel Sta.
Haines Road
Love Grove Sluices
Mama Hajani
Road
Race Course
Tank
Haji Haya
Tulsi Pipe Road
Mahalakshmi Sta.
Jacob Circle
Hindoo Burial Ground
Clerk Rd.
Mahalakshmi Temples
Arthur Road
Byculla Sta.
Hosp.
Ripon Road
Swimming Bath
Beach Candy
Battery
Byculla Club
Hotel
Mills
Cumbala Hill
Hotel
The Bee Hive
Grant Rd. Sta.
Gowali Tank
Grant Road
Frere Brt.
Ch.
Theatre
Parsi Towers of Silence
Kennedy Brt.
French Brt.
Wilson College
Reservoir
Police
Level